Popular Film Culture in Fascist Italy

Popular Film Culture in Fascist Italy

THE PASSING OF THE REX

James Hay

INDIANA UNIVERSITY PRESS
BLOOMINGTON AND INDIANAPOLIS

Manufactured in the United States of America.

Library of Congress Cataloging-in-Publication Data

Hay, James, 1952–
    Popular film culture in Fascist Italy.

    Bibliography: p.
    Includes index.
        1. Moving-pictures—Italy—History.   2. Fascism
and motion pictures—Italy.   I. Title.
PN1993.5.I88H39   1987   791.43'0945   86-45476
ISBN 0-253-36107-9

1   2   3   4   5   91   90   89   88   87

CONTENTS

Appendixes   249

For my parents,
James and Janet Elizabeth Hay,
and for Paul Benjamin

Acknowledgments

I would like to acknowledge briefly some people whose timely advice and assistance for this book cover at least six years and two continents.

First, I would like to mention in this regard my early friends in Umbria (Jo Mcintire, Sali Amaru, Giovanni Carnevali, and Fiorella Lombardi) for their gentle nurturing of my ideas in the 1970s about Italian culture and political history—ideas which were shaping me in more ways than I understood at that time.

I am particularly indebted to my mentors at the University of Texas–Austin during those same years (Tom Schatz, Horace Newcomb, Emile McAnany, Jim Kaufmann, Millicent Marcus, Gian-Paolo Biasin, Archie Green, and Gayatri Spivak) for their support and their guidance in helping me focus my dissertation and the early draft of this manuscript. I should also mention here too my fellow graduate student and friend Guido DeVita for his ofttimes sobering criticism during the initial stages and his reminders that there is always more to be done.

Others in the United States that I would like gratefully to acknowledge for their helpful suggestions and interested responses include Peter Bondanella, David Thorburn, and Phil Wander. I would like to thank Jesse Delia and my colleagues at the University of Illinois for being so supportive during my completion of the manuscript in Champaign–Urbana. And I feel especially obliged to mention the exchange of ideas after I arrived here with Larry Grossberg and, generally speaking, with the members of the Unit for Critical and Interpretive Theory.

My gratitude extends likewise to Joan Catapano at Indiana University Press for her tireless commitment to my project, to Charles Silver and Stephen Harvey at the Museum of Modern Art in New York, and to Tom Sheehan, Emily Seiger, and Barbara Harris at the Motion Picture Division of the Library of Congress for their having made the task of researching this book more fruitful and enjoyable.

In Italy, my work was greatly facilitated by the help of Guido Cincotti and his staff at the Cineteca Nazionale in Rome and of Walter Alberti at the Cineteca Italiana in Milan. Guido Fink and Franco Minganti unselfishly offered their time in helping me polish this manuscript; to them and to my other friends and colleagues at the Università di Bologna I will always be grateful for having helped me to open and build my ideas about this book.

Finally, I would like to thank Laura Reneau; her sacrifice, patience, and faith in my work have made this entire task easier and more rewarding.

JAMES HAY
Champaign, Illinois 1986

Preface
Grandfather Fascism and *Amarcord*

In a 1980 interview, Federico Fellini somewhat sardonically admits that he was pleased by those critics who claimed that *Amarcord* was one of the most accurate representations of the essence of Italian Fascism.[1] His pleasure, he explains, results from his belief that he did not attempt an exposé on Fascist Italy; he sees the film instead as "*un esame di coscienza*," a study of the "closed ethos of a boy who knew nothing of the world outside of his small Italian coastside village during the 1930s." For this boy, the political reality of Fascism was nothing more than his immediate relationships with family, schoolfriends, and neighbors. Like his father, mother, priest, or schoolteachers, it was simply another "imposition."

Perhaps the irony of Fellini's vision of Fascist Italy is that it may *seem* to lack the overtly political explanation that most historians offer. Fellini obviously recognizes and satirizes the rituals which imparted to young Titta's world an otherwise comfortable sense of order; and the youthful aspirations and restless impetuosity of Titta and his adolescent companions repeatedly underscore the untenable nature of this order. Yet Fellini allows for the boy's perceptions of the world—restricted as they are to his village and immediate countryside—to become a central (but richly variegated) perspective in the film. Much of the tension created in the narrative results from the play between signs of change and stasis and from the adolescent Titta's struggle to discover an identity in this period of flux and of family/communal crisis. Fellini remarks in another interview that he had even considered entitling *Amarcord*, *Il borgo*—"in the sense of a medieval enclosure, a lack of information, a lack of contact with the unheard of, the new."[2] But the dramatic conflict and humor continually result from the *seepage* of outside forces that impinge upon the customs of this provincial community and contribute to Titta's "maturation."

As its actual title suggests, the film is a fond remembrance; but, as Fellini explains in the interview, it is not pure nostalgia. Rather, it attests to his inability to examine critically a part of history that is "part of him," that constitutes him. The frequently ironic mood of the film results from a dialectical tension between two types of time. Though Fellini's subject concerns a particular historical period that is perceived in a hypothetical present by Fellini, the narrative is basically circular—beginning and ending with local rituals and natural occurrences which signal to the boy the advent of spring. To amplify this irony, Fellini includes a town chronicler, whose efforts to relate to the audience the historical significance of certain landmarks in the town are continually thwarted by an unseen heckler. Through its historical and mythic time, Fellini's film is at once a documentation of the boy's mythical world as well as a fable about the boy's sense of the way things are. This temporal dialectic also reveals much about Fellini's interpretation of Fascism. Though the action is confined to the seemingly remote seaside village, it is paradigmatic of social interaction in Italy during this period. And here lies the reason for which many contemporary critics have described *Amarcord* as one of the most accurate examinations of Italian Fascism: the film explores the cultural mythology that mediated political consciousness, and at a level where it was and is most vital—a local (personal, intimate, and communal) level.

In a personal or psychological sense, Fellini's *Amarcord* is an adult director's conscious attempt to give cinematic presence to a *coscienza* or ideology through various childhood or subconscious images. His audience is invited to confront these images through the centralized perspective of young Titta. In structuralist terms, *Amarcord* demonstrates the manner in which social, political, and economic realities are explored, questioned, and shaped through a cultural mythology in the midst of crisis. The audience reconstructs the political realities of Italian Fascism through their temporary bond with Titta's mythical world. So, rather than demystify Fascism by exposing it merely as repressive ideology, Fellini demythologizes and deconstructs Titta's limited domain. The boy's myths have a positive function in his life; they enable him to make sense of his world and to realize a transcendent and often comic value in routine occurrences and mundane images. Fellini "remembers" his childhood as a *text*, i.e., as a series of epiphanies or symbolically charged moments that are related and meaningful because they are inextricable from a constellation of ever-present "second-order sign systems" or myths (whose meaning also changes with respect to successive events that effect Titta's maturation). *Amarcord*, in this sense, is best understood by reviewing the iconography or fetishes which comprise Titta's world: the Grand Hotel, the church, the Rex, Gradisca's derrière, and so on. These emblems are complexly imbricated into the nexus of his familial and communal relationships; they all loosely interweave to form what can be described as the town's fabric of consensus. As Fellini indicates in the aforementioned interview, nothing existed outside this *coscienza:*

> America, democracy for me were Fred Astaire who danced on highly polished terraces or Greta Garbo who looked at us with that melancholy air, like a headmistress. It really wasn't possible to imagine anything else, that Nenni was in exile or that Gramsci was in prison. Above the podium at school there was on one side a photo of that baboon with that kind of casserole pot on his head, on the other side there was one of the king with his impressive plumed hat, in the middle the pope, and above them, barely visible, was a tiny crucifix. This was the social, political and metaphysical reality. So familiar as to become vague and ineffable.[3]

Perhaps it is most significant, for purposes of considering the social, political, and cultural transformations in Italy during this period, that Fellini remembers understanding Fascism, his town, and that which lay beyond it in terms of photographic or cinematic images—images which, by their mimetic, ubiquitous, and (in the case of movies) epic presence, seemed to validate the nature of things.

In *Amarcord*, the town cinema, whose proprietor is known as Ronald Colman, appears regularly amidst the film's primary action; and one scene, wherein Titta vicariously gratifies his desire for Gradisca while watching a Gary Cooper movie, actually occurs in the cinema. The cinema is part of the community's stability—one of its "institutions"—but it also participates in its changes, regularly bringing new images from outside. By continually situating the town cinema amidst the affairs of family and community, Fellini calls attention to the function of cinema (a relatively new and "marginal" form at that time in the Italian provinces) in maintaining the town's fabric of consensus and, in Titta's case, in managing personal tensions. But he also calls attention to ways that the exotic images and "roles" of the cinema are appropriated and mimicked or acted out in a variety of ways by various citizens in the community; in this way, the cinema creates subtle yet profound strains in the town's fabric of consensus, making its traditional communal frameworks of interpretation appear contrived and absurd even to those who employ them. Thus, while cinema appears deeply embedded in the culture of this town, it also contributes to its rather "leaky" consensus.

Fellini's ironic and self-reflexive references to the cinema also speak to the *life* of cinema as a cultural form; they open the early codes of cinema to pastiche and parody—especially with respect to the cult of *divi* and *dive* that grew around the traditional cinema and that is very much part of the ethos of this provincial town. The characters in *Amarcord* are not, for that matter, widely recognized movie personalities (with the possible exception of Magali Noel, who appears in Fellini's *La dolce vita* and *Satyricon*). Because Fellini deconstructs the ways that images and movie roles mediate social and political roles and realities in this town, his own cinematic style in some ways seems deliberately to invoke and to resonate with those of this era. Though his predilection for filming at the studios of Cinecittà distinguishes his films from those of many of his contemporaries in Italy, his highly stylized use of make-up, set design, special effects, and hyperbole acquires a particularly distinct significance in *Amarcord*, conjuring the *mise-en-scène* or ambience of cinematic production in the 1920s and 1930s (a style which in many ways still accommodated the artifice of theatrical forms but which now, through its artificiality, conjures the less advanced technology of the day). The one scene filmed in the countryside has less to do with a postwar tradition of cinematic realism in Italy (as does the outdoor shooting in his previous two films, *Clowns* and *Roma*, which are both about the documentation of spectacle through cinema) than it has to do with a tradition of Naturalism—used here to give the audience a sense of the cultural sea upon which this island of a town seems to float. One could also cite other ways in which Fellini has eclectically constructed a diegesis comprised of *traces* from prewar film styles. This occurs most notably through a narrative mode that is unique among his later films in its continuity (unfolding, in a mythic sequence of events, through seasonal changes) and one that is rooted in and parodies early Italian film comedies, family melodramas, and newsreels (e.g., the Fascist rally). It is also evident in his appropriation of common popular cinematic icons (e.g., the Grand Hotel and the Rex) and of musical styles and refrains (e.g., "Stormy Weather") from this period.[4]

This deconstructive strategy achieves a much clearer expression in the first five minutes of Fellini's *E la nave va (The Ship Sails)*, wherein Fellini reproduces and parodies early film's still awkward but central role in mediating reality (sensitizing the viewer to a variety of codes in filmic diegesis) and in documenting modern history. In *Amarcord*, on the other hand, there is the ever-present photographer who is ready to document every ritual and spectacle in the town—the school picture, the Fascist rally, the celebration of St. Joseph's Day, the arrival of the caliph and his harem, the passing of the Rex, and Gradisca's wedding banquet. And on several occasions, once at the beginning in the school photo and at the end in the wedding photo, the actors look directly into the camera (the photographic and cinematic one) and seem to pose momentarily for us. These instances, more vividly than at any other point in the movie, remind us that *Amarcord* is very much about viewing (and *reviewing*) images, about image and spectator. In fact, the movie itself, as a *storia* (in the Italian sense, a fable/ narration and history), is comprised of what could be described as a series of significant images or traces—bridged in the Spectator's mind by the circularity of the seasonal/historical changes. Understood in this way, *Amarcord* offers an imaginative model of historical excavation and documentation but also a self-reflexive model of cinematic spectacle itself (of the way historical realities are constructed through changing techniques/technologies for imaging and narrating). The initial series of still shots in the movie, with the circulating fluff, achieves a similar effect to that of an Impressionist's dots, of objects in atmosphere, of an image that the Spectator cannot quite yet discern clearly. At the same time, they are a kind of code—i.e., grainy "stuff" which catches the light, brings the image into focus, and then holds it by disappearing.

There is, as Roland Barthes has noted, a significant difference between cinema and the photographic image, between something that "has posed" before the lens and something that "has passed" before it. Again, *Amarcord* repeatedly combines and juxtaposes these effects. We view these characters' fears and aspirations through the images which for them have become charged with meaning, but from a perspective that makes them comic, grotesque, and (above all) astonishing. Throughout this film, Fellini tests our impulse to fix meaning through photographic—here tintype—images (of a faith that images do fix meaning and time), and he attempts to come to terms with forces that change and prevent that kind of fixity or fixation.

Of course, some critics can argue that Fellini fails to expose the material avenues for organizing the socioeconomic foundations of communal lifestyles, or that Fascism was a sleep that descended upon an unsuspecting and passive populace. After all, the story is more the boy's (and his sense of play) than his father's. But by exploring the dominant myths of this community from within and without, Fellini portrays Fascism not simply as a political or economic reality but as mediated by a variety of codes—equally important of which are the cultural codes (particularly cinematic, photographic, and musical ones). And, though Fascism (as a codified system) is diffused in this film, it is also seen as part of an inevitable and even necessary meta-language, i.e., as part of other discourses which intersect and overlap with it. Therefore, if *Amarcord* can be said to be about Italian Fascism, it is in that it goes outside of Fascism as political phenomenon or system to explore the *meanings of its messages* through an array of "dramatic interpretations" by citizens in the town—characters whose personal fantasies and role-playing constantly intrude upon our perception of the town's "sacred" rites (e.g., the heavyset boy who imagines the effigy of Il Duce—vaguely reminiscent here of the "great and powerful Wizard of Oz"—sanctifying his union with the girl of his dreams at a Fascist rally). In this sense, Fellini demonstrates a sensitivity both to the syntagmatic aspects of his subject (by treating Fascism in historical, local contexts) and to the paradigmatic or metaphorical aspects (by treating this "popular culture" as a model of Modern social and political change and consciousness).

This last point also helps elucidate the film's title ("I remember" in the local dialect of Fellini's youth) and his statements about the relevancy in 1974 of his vision of Fascism:

> I don't wish to say that we Italians have not yet grown beyond adolescence and fascism. . . . [And yet] I have the impression that fascism and adolescence continue to be, in a certain measure, permanent historical seasons of our lives: adolescence of our individual lives, the Fascism of our national life.[5]

While the film's title might easily be applied to almost any of his movies (most easily the later ones), it seems to attest to a need to respond to questions latent in cinematic and in a variety of other cultural discourses in Italy during the 1970s.

Amarcord is not, for that matter, the only Italian film of the seventies whose action occurs during the years of the Fascist regime. Film production from this period in Italy now seems replete with movies set in that time. One need only consider, besides *Amarcord*, De Sica's *Giardino dei Finzi-Contini*, Passolini's *Salò e le centoventi giornate di Sodoma*, Wertmuller's *Film d'amore e d'anarchia*, *Pasqulino settebellezze*, and *Fatto di sangue fra due uomini per causa di una vedova (si sospettano moventi politici)*, Bertolucci's *Strategia del ragno*, *1900*, and *Il conformista*, Scola's *Una giornata particolare*, and even Visconti's *La caduta degli dei* or Cavani's *Il portiere di notte* (both of which deal with Nazism). Though their portrayals of Fascism and of this period in Italian history are not uniform, they all make manifest a desire among Italian directors and their audiences to readdress a subject that had been conspicuously absent in Italian film production since the postwar years. These films have contributed to the release of what Lino Miccichè has described as "*un cadavere nell'armadio.*"

Some of these films do seem to perpetuate traditional postwar images and tropes, e.g., the Fascist as the quintessential agent of social and political repression. Passolini's *Salò*, for instance, has been described by many critics as an overly excessive portrayal of physical and sexual atrocities committed by the Fascists. Much the same criticism has been directed at Donald Sutherland's role as Attila in Bertolucci's *1900*; and one finds similarly traditional representations in Wertmuller's *Amore e anarchia* and *Fatto di sangue*. One might just as easily assume from *Giardino dei Finzi-Contini* (another film about this peroid which uses the walled garden as one of its central metaphors) that Fascism was a lethal anesthesia which lulled an entire country into passive conformity.

But, while I by no means wish to ignore the individual craftsmanship of these films, it seems evident that Italian cinema in part became a forum for the ventilation of attitudes about Fascism and for the renegotiation of profound cultural and social values and of political reorientations. Movies such as Scola's *C'eravamo tanto amati* and Fellini's *E la nave va* are graphic examples of a desire among Italian filmmakers not only to reassess cultural traditions, codes, and stereotypes, but also to explore their cinema's function in that culture and its history. It would be grossly erroneous to say that these comtemporary films do not differ from the traditional Hollywood "anti-Fascist" film or one such as Luciano Salce's *Il Federale* (*The Fascist*, 1965), both of which depict Germans as congenital brutes and those who joined the Italian Fascists as misguided but good-hearted buffoons. The recent ones are less involved with apologetics than with an examination of the social codes of Fascism, its psychological origins, and the myths that produced its political realities. Film critic Joan Mellen has argued that

> the entire period of radical upsurge to which the younger directors now dealing more seriously with fascism belong can be dated usefully with the death of Stalin in 1953 and the Hungarian revolution of 1959 on the other. The reassessment of the Soviet Union meant an intellectual liberation of Marxists . . . and a new appetite for analysis of capitalism in disintegration, or what it often results in, fascism. Free from having to apologize for the atrocities of Stalin's Russia, young intellectuals could finally look at the fascist period from a socialist point of view.[6]

While Mellen's article examines films from a variety of Western countries, it seems (at least in part) to account for the preoccupation among Italian film-makers during the 1970s with this period in their country's political history. (I would question, however, her observation that the renewed interest in Fascism was limited only to younger intellectuals and directors or that they dealt with the subject more "seriously" than did their older counterparts). In 1970s Italy, a tradition of Marxist realism gives way to attempts to demystify the authority of the Fascist by deconstructing the "anti-heroic" nature of resistance movements in *Amore e anarchia* and *Una giornata particolare*, by examining its myths in *Strategia del ragno* and *Amarcord*, or by exploring the "sexual politics" of social consciousness as in *Un fatto di sangue*, *Il conformista*, or *Portiere di notte*. The contemporary films which examime the psychological undercurrents that may have sustained Fascism also lend support to the notion that it was not a histor-ically specific phenomenon.

In other respects (and this is a point I develop in my introduction), Italian filmmakers' preoccupation with Fascism was part of a more extensive dialogue among film critics and historians about the social and political function of cultural forms and about the traditional "prerogative" of Neorealism and of aesthetic criticism in general. Despite their superficial representational affinities with postwar characterizations, these more recent films call into question the codes of film realism, whether in narration, characterization, or *mise-en-scène*. The renegotiation of cultural, political, and aesthetic values is actually made possible by the refinement of visual and narrative styles which are able to give dramatic presence to the "deep structures" of social and political action. The revived interest in Fascism is, then, bound up with cultural as well as with stylistic changes that enable Italian filmmakers to reassess and redefine its place in modern Italian culture and political consciousness. It is useful here to consider Tullio Kezich's observation that the renegotiation of attitudes about Fascism resulted from a reinterest in popular cinema, as opposed to auteuristic cinema which younger filmmakers and critics considered "aristocratic and authoritative."[7] Kezich explains that "Oedipus is the true protagonist" in the current reinterest in Fascism. Whereas Neorealists rejected Father Fascism—i.e., they only saw it as repressive—younger filmmakers have adopted a more ambivalent (not entirely conciliatory) position by coming to new terms with the subjects most frequently associated with cultural production in Fascist Italy, particularly genre films and American cinema, while in critical circles, or in some of the films of Bertolucci or Scola, attempting either to exorcise the spectre of auteurism and realist styles or principles or to acknowledge the inadequacy of these impulses.

But one should turn as well to Fellini's *Amarcord*, where the audience perceives "Fascist culture" through self-conscious adaptations of "ways of seeing" in the 1930s. Unlike the younger Bertolucci, Fellini "grew up" watching prewar films. Perhaps even as a response to his critically acclaimed status as *auteur*, Fellini's *Amarcord* (like the finale of his *La città delle donne*) is a self-reflexive return to a role as spectator of popular movies—of movies and images that constituted his childhood.[8] While others have attempted to demystify Fascism through psychological or social exposé, his film incisively affirms that myths are an inescapable and even a necessary aspect of social interaction and discourse; still, *Amarcord*, like the Taviani brothers' *La notte di San Lorenzo* (*Night of the Shooting Stars*), also reminds us that those myths may not lead to the *salvation* of a community. Fascism here is seen as much in terms of a young boy's fantasies as the product of a collective imagination; as much in terms of an isolated historical period as of a community (or *communitas*) in the throes of profound cultural change.

Popular Film Culture in Fascist Italy

Introduction

The Production of Popular Film Culture in Fascist Italy

In 1974, the same season which saw the release of *Amarcord, Il portiere di notte, Mussolini ultimo atto, Il delitto Matteotti, La Villeggiatura, 1900,* and *Missione nell'Italia fascista,* the Mostra Internazionale del Nuovo Cinema convened in Pesaro with the purpose of reexamining the Neorealist tradition of filmmaking. Here journalists and cineastes such as Miccichè expressed a need to qualify Cesare Zavattini's statement in 1945 that Italian filmmakers of the 1930s "did not produce one real film," or Carlo Lizzani's remark in 1953 that the "vacuousness" of thirties Italian films typified an entire generation, or Mario Gromo's observation in 1945 that Italian thirties films were too "artificial" and "mediocre."[1] One of the more immediate problems for participants at this conference was to agree upon an appropriate point of departure for a discussion of Neorealism. Why, for instance, should Neorealism be said to begin in 1945 with Rossellini's *Roma, città aperta,* or even in 1943 with Visconti's *Ossessione?* Was it necessary to reach further back and to consider films not part of the almost sacred Rossellini–Visconti–De Sica trinity, to reach into what had come to be considered in Italian film scholarship as the "black hole" of Italian film history? And even if one were to begin with this nucleus of Neorealist film production, e.g., Rossellini, Visconti, and De Sica, was it not also necessary to recognize that they themselves had learned their craft through film programs in Fascist Italy—Rossellini (along with Antonioni, Lattuada, and Barbaro) in the GUF (Gruppo Universitario Fascista) and De Sica as an actor? A "verist" style or impulse (as I intend to demonstrate later) had already been evident in narrative films such as Mario Camerini's *Gli uomini, che mascalzoni!* (1932) or Raffaello Matarazzo's *Treno popolare* (1933), not to mention documentary film production or projects such as *Camicia nera* (1933) which combined documentary and narrative film styles; and, as Aprà and Pistagnesi have correctly noted, Blasetti's *Vecchia guardia* (1935) is an example of realism in the Rossellinian sense—anti-escapist cinema tied to political themes of the day (Fascist themes in Blasetti's case).

In order to understand why these shifts in attitude among film critics occurred when they did and as they did, it is necessary to consider briefly Neorealism's relationship to critical methods both in the 1930s and in the 1970s. Neorealism developed as the Italian film industry in the postwar years was attempting to discover a new economic, technological, and social foundation upon which to reorganize. Unlike the postwar theoreticians, Italian film critics during the late 1920s and early 1930s usually addressed two concerns: the aesthetic or stylistic

I

qualities of a film (generally its theatrical qualities, e.g., acting style, set design, etc.) and the audience's response.[2] This attitude is indicative of the role of intellectuals in Italy during the regime, which, as Anna Panicali has observed, was to bridge art and culture and to level any differences between themselves and their audience.[3] Unlike the Neorealist theoreticians after the war, Italian critics during the twenties and thirties paid little attention to the relationship between filmmaker and his film. Organizational directors and theorists such as Luigi Freddi in "Arte per il popolo" and Luigi Chiarini in *Il cinematografo* discuss during the 1930s the merits of arts which address the sensibilities of the public. A central problem for these same critics, however, was how to reconcile an aesthetic bias against a seemingly apolitical cinema, i.e., "escapist" films, with a populist ethic. Because this type of criticism captured the spirit of Italy's emerging film culture, it manifested the ideological tensions between a tradition of Italian criticism steeped in aesthetics and a more modern need to address and to legitimize popular spectacle.

Also during the 1930s, programs sponsored by the Cine–GUF and later by the Centro Sperimentale produced a new generation of cineastes—"children" of the cinema who were inspired with a sense of Italy's film culture. By the later 1930s, the younger wave of critics and filmmakers had become involved with, if not responsible for, some of the first film digests in Italy, e.g., *Bianco e nero* and *Cinema*. However, their increasing involvement in these film circles and their enthusiasm for cinema as an art form (or at least as its own discipline) seem to have diminished their interest in film as a "popular" form.

There is no doubt that the questions sparked by the 1974 Pesaro conference also resulted from the need among a young generation of film critics (a genera-tion much more conciliatory to popular Hollywood movies and once again interested in the success of Italian cinema as an industry) to weigh the durability of its own country's classical film styles. If Neorealist codes were learned by a generation whose sense of film Culture (with a capital "C") privileged the filmic text and the relationship between a filmmaker and his films, this younger genera-tion was nurtured by a different sense of film culture—one with a little "c," wherein one was more eager to discuss the cinematic *text* in terms of its *context*.

The ideological rift between these two generations of Italian film scholarship was not easily redressed. Largely as a result of the aforementioned questions and methodological concerns, a decision was made after the 1974 conference to review, the following year, films produced in Italy between 1929 and 1943. The 1975 conference, however, was largely devoted to three of the more familiar directors of the period; realizing the impossibility of exploring the complexity of this field, participants at the 1975 conference decided to screen and to review, the next year, films by less frequently discussed filmmakers.

Naturally, these colloquia were not without some controversy; debates con-tinued even after the conferences in 1976 and into the pages of the Italian newspaper *La Repubblica*. In this editorial dialogue, Carlo Lizzani, one whose ideas about film were most ostensibly aligned with a Neorealist practice, re-affirms his skepticism about the historical importance of such films and admonishes those who seek to legitimate their study. Lizzani's observations are in turn questioned or derided by critics such as Miccichè or Alberto Farassino, Beniamino Placido, et al., who adamantly condemned the penchant of traditional critics such as Lizzani to reduce or dismiss all Italian cinema in the thirties as "escapist" or as a "mythological reformulation of the real."

While the works of more recent Italian critics and film historians have certainly been inspired by contemporary European Marxist theory, by feminist studies, or by psychological theory, particularly that of Reich, it seems that semiotics and structuralism have done most to highlight the hermeneutic complexity of analyzing film culture in Fascist Italy. For one, semiotics offers the potential for exposing the connotative and ideological richness and complexity of highly conventionalized and formulaic cultural forms, even though some have employed it to distinguish reactionary, authoritarian, or "closed" forms from those which question and problematize the experience of reading and seeing through codified systems. One could point here to semiotic approaches to cinema (especially those of Barthes or Eco) which are largely concerned more with classical cinematic styles. What is important in the work of those who have used semiotics and structuralism to discuss film and/or ideology is their appreciation for the complexity of relationships among codes, texts, and signifying systems in a culture. It is precisely this perspective which discourages the sort of reductivism common in more traditional discussion of cinema as "mass" entertainment (with all of the pejorative overtones that that term has come to convey). A "textualist" analysis has the potential for opening to discussion the broadly heterogeneous field of the filmic text, to explore it as a nexus of political, social, aesthetic, and cultural threads. And it is from this view that culture itself has come to be described as a codified field of *production* and as a network of *signifying systems*.

If, as structuralist theories seem to acknowledge, movies can be said to exalt the themes, myths, and interpretive frameworks of their audiences, how do later critics or historians best understand these films through the lens of their own value system or range of signifying practices? These problems, of course, complicate the work of foreign film critics as well, and seem to account in part for the unwillingness or simply the inability of American critics and film historians to work through or around a semiotic or structuralist approach to popular Italian cinema. While it may be difficult for contemporary and especially younger Italian critics to avoid reading films produced in their own country through the cultural and political codes of the day, it appears even more difficult for American critics in some cases to get past formalistic discussions of films to see how they are constituted through many national discourses. American scholars of Italian cinema have, in fact, done much to maintain a Neorealist critical monopoly. I am referring here not only to the work of formalistic criticism and film histories, but also to auteuristic analyses such as those by Andrew Sarris, or the aesthetic criticism of John Simon—all modes of criticism which, like that of Carlo Lizzani, would be disposed to ignore film production in Italy between the two World Wars or to dismiss it as propagandistic or as "white telephones."

This methodology does little to encourage an increased sensitivity to the complexity and contraditions of *popular* films (or other cultural forms) in foreign countries and, in particular, Italian films from the twenties and thirties.

Admittedly, part of the difficulty for American (and even Italian) film scholars in rediscovering what Savio, Arbasino, Aprà, and Pistagnesi have described as the "unknown Italian cinema" lies in the limited availability of these films. Though the count varies somewhat, it is believed that of the approximately seven hundred feature films produced in Italy between 1929 and 1943, less than half still exist (and in some cases only the negatives or fragments of these films remain). In this country, fewer than fifty such feature films exist in various archives.[4] Moreover, nearly all of these films are presently unavailable for public circulation. Between October 5 and December 21, 1978, the Museum of Modern Art in New York sponsored a film retrospective entitled "Before Neorealism: Italian Cinema 1929–1944." This exhibition, which presented forty-four films from this period, marked the first showing of such a large collection of these films in this country; and it was the first time since 1941 that most of them had been shown publicly in America.

Beyond the relative inaccessibility of these films, however, one is still faced with the fact that scholarship in English on Italian cinema from this period has never really developed a "non-essentialist" and interdisciplinary methodology for discussing pre–Neorealist cinema as but one material and signifying process in the production of a larger cultural, political, and industrial fabric—a fabric which, while making discussions of "essences" very problematic, is a rich site for exploring the practices and strategies necessary to construct collective realities. Here the work of British sociologist and culturalist Raymond Williams offers some invaluable guidelines both for general sociological research or social histories and for film and media scholarship. Some of his recent work in *The Sociology of Culture* is representative of recent attempts in Britain to develop a methodological agenda which works past traditional materialist and Marxist notions of ideology and hegemony, and past traditional idealist or anthropological notions of culture as an "informing spirit," to a new sociology of culture that, unlike these traditional approaches, does not ignore the complex processes by which a culture or an ideology is produced. This kind of "process analysis" is important in a discussion of cinematic or other forms of cultural production in Fascist Italy because it affords a much richer understanding of the collaborative, competitive, and multi-discursive nature of cinematic productions and of the ways that film production and reception worked and reworked cultural ideology than has been provided by traditional film critics and historians such as Armes, Leprohon, or Lizzani. Yet Williams's ideas about cultural production and social process also differ from traditional Marxist and materialist notions of cultural production, in which cinema is understood *as* ideology or as being directed by ideology and in which ideology suggests cultural homogeneity; this traditional approach tends to overemphasize cinema's conservative function and presupposes that cinema simply reaffirms the status quo and that ideology is self-perpetuating. For Williams, culture is an amalgam of signifying systems and a constant reworking of values; and it is his rejection of traditional materialist approaches to culture that impels him to call for a new sociology. While it is necessary to recognize vivid distinctions among industrial systems, political systems, generational (kinship and family) systems, and even cinema as yet another signifying system, it is also important to recognize that all these systems are elements of a wider and more general signifying system: what Williams calls "a social system."

First, Williams's approach would encourage both film and social historians to revamp the traditional notion of 1930s films in Fascist Italy as propaganda. Here I am referring to the Marxist "domination theories" about film and media production proposed by Adorno and Horkheimer or, more specifically, to those who discuss Fascism in purely political and economic terms. The image of Fascism promoted in this type of analysis is typically that of an "incubus"[5] which descended upon an unsuspecting and passive public or that of the undoing of a previously "civilized" people by a "cunning corrupter of men."[6] By concentrating on the political and economic structures of Italian Fascism, these historians often ignore the confluence of cultural codes and symbology in the affairs of state. They fail to examine the popular images or iconography through which culture and ideology were transmitted and perceived in Fascist Italy. Or, if they do examine them, as social historians Philip Cannistraro, Victoria de Grazia, A. James Gregor, or Edward Tannenbaum do in their more recent studies, they discuss them as vehicles for a purely political ideology and policy, i.e., as *political* propaganda, and direct their attention largely to examples of censorship or to the activities of the Ministry of Popular Culture and of the Dopolavoro— avoiding any rigorous discussion of the cultural codes by which audiences *read* these images, i.e., the movie public's role in constructing social reality, their felt need for the cinema's clear signs of a moral universe and its models for living.

For social historians and theoreticians, myths are "developed" by political bodies to legitimize their own rule; "symbols," as sociologist and political scientist Robert P. Clark suggests, "have their greatest value in politics as media to bestow the psychic benefit of a given policy on those sectors or individuals who do not receive any material benefit from this policy, and who do not have the opportunity to participate in this information."[7] If one were to apply these notions about myth and symbols in an analysis of Italian Fascism, it might appear as though Fascism were a monolithic and clearly delineated ideology, and that *it* created a homogeneous society, that *it* produced consensual forms. From this perspective, popular forms of entertainment are viewed as agents for normalizing society; more emphasis is attached to their ability to resolve crises or to conceal conflict and never to their ability to amplify the contradictions at the base of society which necessitate models of permanence and change.

It is certainly true that 1920s and 1930s Italian society, in the throes of modernization, experienced a great deal of instability and uncertainty about its past and its future; modernization, as sociologist Cyril Black notes, tends to atomize a society and to deprive its members of the sense of community and belonging without which individual fulfillment cannot be satisfactorily achieved. Here, however, I do not intend to examine simply how political policy responds to and often exploits the social pressures engendered by these changes. (This is a field of sociological inquiry which is more effectively treated in an already ample body of social and political history—especially with regard to Italian Fascism, since it and other "totalitarian" polities have traditionally offered sociologists attractive examples by which to demonstrate that social action is only an unending effort to maintain dominance.) I intend instead to investigate a cultural form which at that historical moment most vividly highlighted these tensions and enabled those in Italy most affected by modernization to cope with the highly unstable nature of their cultural foundation. Although I do not wish to ignore the regime's attempts to mobilize or to organize a popular culture, I prefer to examine the complex field of cultural codes and techniques through which political and other varieties of social action and performance occurred and through which they could be envisioned.

In this respect, my own theoretical position about social formations and ideology can be aligned in part with that of Clifford Geertz, who argues that

> the battlefield image of society as a clash of interests thinly disguised as a clash of principles turns attention away from the role that ideologies play in defining (or obscuring) social categories, stabilizing (or upsetting) social expectations, maintaining (or undermining) social norms, strengthening (or weakening) social consensus, relieving (or exaggerating) social tensions.[8]

Geertz also correctly observes that ideology cannot be grounded easily in stable social and psychological structures but that it is an amalgam of contradictory impulses:

> [A]s a metaphor extends language by broadcasting its semantic range, enabling it to express meanings it cannot or at least cannot yet express literally, so the head-on clash of literal meanings in ideology—the irony, the hyperbole, the overdrawn antithesis—provides novel symbolic frames against which to match the myriad "unfamiliar somethings" that, like a journey to a strange country, are produced by a transformation in political life.[9]

It would be grossly simplistic to assume (as I attempt to explain at more length in the last two chapters of this book) that Italian films in the 1930s were overtly propagandistic; the only feature films which deal directly with Fascism are *Camicia nera*, *Vecchia guardia*, some of the colonial films, and parts of *Piccoli naufraghi*. One could, however, by adopting Althusser's notion of an Ideological State Apparatus or Jacque Ellul's notion of "horizontal" or "sociological" propaganda, discuss the classical film styles in Italy as reaffirming their audiences' sense of order, which is certainly a more transparent form of propaganda. But Williams's approach, in offering a much more heterogeneous model of culture and of the role which cultural forms such as film play in mediating reality, makes this view of propaganda problematic. By underscoring the diverse and resistant impulses among the signifying practices that comprise cultural production, it calls into question the sort of cultural consensus produced by propaganda. If, for instance, one examines films in Fascist Italy as but one means of "organizing" public realities, to what extent was a Fascist ideology imposed? To what extent did Italian movie audiences (that socioeconomic group which most acutely experienced the pressures of modernization) desire and need a sense, i.e., images and models, of solidarity and community offered by movies? How did cinema (as almost a new religious spectacle) gratify this desire for a sense of transcendence? And, finally, how does one account for the kinds of paradoxes and ambivalences that are inscribed in the narrative structures and characterizations of these movies and in the discourses surrounding these movies?

These same questions should induce both film and social historians to rethink more traditional approaches to "mass" arts—approaches which usually offer the most monolithic representations of popular culture and are characteristic of the sociological approaches to Italian Fascism (what A. James Gregor describes as a "mass mobilizing regime"). Denis Mack Smith, for instance, in his comprehensive history of modern Italy, offers a rather cynical appraisal of Fascist culture, occasionally relating in a sardonic fashion the eccentric measures exerted by the regime to "standardize culture." Traditionally, mass art criticism is adopted in order to discuss the public arts in presumably nondemocratic societies, to expose or demystify the insidious nature of what might otherwise seem to be innocuous entertainment, and, as in the case of Dwight McDonald, to equivocate mass culture or "homogeneous" culture with totalitarianism. The term "popular culture" is seldom applied to Fascism or to other totalitarian regimes, since Fascism itself is usually conceived as a purely political ideology around which grew a political consensus. One discusses Fascism in terms of its leaders, its policy, and its propaganda and not as an expression of an emerging and heterogeneous popular culture.

Williams's call for a sociology of culture, on the other hand, attempts to demonstrate not only the inevitability of the social organization of culture but the complex, changing, and often resistant processes of cultural and ideological production (even in "totalitarian" states). I would add to this that the "languages" of popular culture are not uniform nor necessarily stable but that they are competitive and contradictory and are, because of these contradictions, given to an endless process of negotiation. I would also point to Russian semiotician Jurij Lotman, who notes that *every* culture manifests tendencies to both a noncontradictory and unified meta-language and a system of cultural expression whereby the semiotic mechanism multiplies and diversifies. For Lotman, communication in any culture would be impossible without this meta-language and unnecessary without a constantly shifting field of contradictory imperatives. My own approach to popular film culture in Fascist Italy attempts to examine ways in which the cinema was inscribed with the tensions set up by this fluctuating field of contradictory models and "imperatives" and how, in amplifying and channeling these tensions, cinematic production developed a national–popular rhetoric (systems of codes and techniques) that, while in some ways derivative, were instrumental in constituting for many Italians the means to a cultural Voice. As I intend to demonstrate through analysis of Italian film production from this period, the presence of these tensions is evidence of a profound cultural ambivalence which is itself a dynamic agent of cultural change.

In an approach to a popular film culture in Fascist Italy which focuses on the interplay of cultural, social, and political processes, it becomes necessary to recognize several important historical changes which affected the nature of cultural organization and representations in Italy between the two World Wars. One cannot, for instance, ignore the "new" middle classes and the working classes created by rapid industrialization in the 1920s—a phenomenon which occurred somewhat later and much more quickly in Italy than in other European countries. And, while this socioeconomic group did comprise much of Italy's movie audience, it is equally necessary to distinguish between the types of films screened at the first-run movie houses and those at second- and third-run theaters and to avoid reducing Italy's popular film culture to a class concern. In this respect, it is important to consider how the "new order," as it was frequently referred to by party spokesmen, was not without certain historically specific fears and desires, and how popular films in Italy (as social rituals) gave dramatic presence to those fears and desires in a manner which traditional techniques and modes of production were unable to offer. As social rituals, popular Italian films enabled their audiences to renegotiate or clarify their changing cultural, material, and political environments, to discover meaning in a world where the traditional authority of Church and State had significantly eroded. Audiences could observe characters forge communities in an impersonal urban milieu, amidst a hostile African wilderness, or admist the decadence, transience, and cosmopolitanism of life in the Grand Hotels. The narrative resolutions of these films frequently promised a "new order"—one often inspired by rural traditions yet capable of facing the challenges of an urban, industrial society.

Again, this is not to say that these films did not accommodate contradictory readings or that they were not part of a pervasive ambivalence about this new order. One of the central cultural conflicts for Italian movie audiences in the twenties and thirties occurred as, in Geertz's terms, "epochalist" and "essentialist" impulses, i.e., as an identification with modern, cosmopolitan images as well as an identification with more traditional, rural values which seemed threatened by the very influx of foreign cultural forms. The "aesthetics" of *Stracittà* and *Strapaese* in Italy are perhaps the most ostensible manifestations of this conflict. Much of this cultural ambivalence is related to expanding distribution networks—networks which fairly rapidly had cut across regional boundaries in Italy and which had facilitated the dissemination of foreign (especially Hollywood) movie images or models. Because Fascist Italy's new order, its *cultura popolare*, was contingent on a variety of cinematic images and narrative formulas, it too must be discussed as multi-accentual and at times contradictory. Here one cannot ignore the role that the cinema, as a "public" technology of the times, assumed in providing an undoubtedly more grandiose, epic, and heroic image of the world and of the the nation than did other contemporary or previous media and cultural forms. It would also be safe to argue that the bigger-than-life image afforded by cinema screens did much to instill in movie audiences, that group most acutely affected by the anxieties of rapid modernization, a sense of belonging to a larger national family or tribe.

The sense of community—of a national–popular culture—cannot, however, be easily dissociated from Italy's political unification; in this sense (and here I would point to the seminal work of Walter Benjamin in the 1930s), cultural forms such as film are grounded in politics only insofar as politics itself has come to assume the function in society of religious ritual. While contributing to the formation of Italy's popular culture, cinema (as a culture industry) and the expanding network of film distribution also modified Italy's sense of "cultural domain" and hence hastened intercultural discord. The demise of the Italian film industry after World War I, according to Italian film historian Gian-Piero Brunetta, can be attributed in large part to Italian producers' unwillingness to abandon film styles and subjects which had brought the prewar films international acclaim and profit. This unwillingness to address the demands of a national audience in the twenties no doubt accelerated the expansion of American distribution networks. It seems no coincidence, therefore, that the collapse of Italy's film industry occurred at exactly the same time as the rise to power of Italian Fascism. But I see the policies developed along various stages of the rebuilding of Italy's film industry as being directed only in part by the Fascist government. It seems that the interests of Fascist ideologues and leaders had come to overlap with the interests of those interested in producing and making better, more competitive films in Italy; just as Italy's political figures had to discover their constituency, i.e., their broadest base of support, so did Italian filmmakers attempt to reclaim their audiences from American cinema by rediscovering and addressing the tastes of national audiences.

The plight of Italy's film industry in the twenties and thirties offers some intriguing examples of cultural politics (i.e., the conflicts and alliances among various signifying practices in the production of a popular culture) and of the dynamic relationships among a country's cultural policy, its culture industries, and its popular culture. All of these concerns are historically the result of modernization: the technology, the industrialization, and the class of consumers for which these forces made way. Although one can still apply structuralism's Nature/Culture paradigm to the formations of Italy's popular culture in the twenties and thirties, one cannot neglect how this sense of culture pervaded various social, economic, and political activities through cultural practices. For this reason, Williams's call for a new sociology of culture—one which examines the processes of encoding and decoding and which examines culture as a "signifying system through which social order is communicated, reproduced, experienced, and explored"—offers some indispensable guidelines for discussing Italian cinema in terms of a popular film culture.

To discuss cinema in Fascist Italy in terms of a popular film culture is to emphasize the increasing *centrality* of cinema in routing and managing cultural, political, and social tensions. My examination of Fascist Italy's popular film culture attempts to account for commercial and governmental efforts to develop centralized institutions as well as for the culture's felt need for a common center, one to which these cinematic messages always refer and through which Italy's burgeoning *cultura popolare* could create for itself a new image. When I speak of the "production" of a popular film culture, I am not intending to weight either the role of those who encode (those who own and direct the material means of production) or the role of those who decode films (the audience or consumer). I am, however, more committed to acknowledging the audience's role in this process, since it has largely been ignored in traditional scholarship. To view cinema as cultural production, as a complex dialogic process of mediation (i.e., of provisional balances and negotiation in the chain of signification), reminds one that those who "direct" this production do not simply initiate messages but are themselves responding to certain perceived obstacles and tensions. Neither, however, do I want to call them both producers, as "reception theories" are prone to do. It is important to understand and to maintain their differences in order to keep sight of the generative and mediated nature of this process. It is precisely this difference, this sense of diversity, that enables one to recognize how the need for a meta-language in this culture resulted from a perceived crisis and how this process is predicated upon continual balancing and negotiation.

As I attempt to explain in the succeeding chapters, Fascist Italy's "new order" resulted from a national desire to acquire a modern and slightly cosmopolitan image as well as to recuperate traditional, "rural" values. The cinema made these images more accessible than did perhaps any other medium at that time. Centralization, however, does not in this case refer to a homogeneous social structure but rather to the need felt by the producers of culture (and here I would include audiences as well as film producers or parastate agencies) to discover a common language in order to maintain a vital link with their cultural heritage while asserting themselves (culturally, economically, and politically) on an increasingly international stage. A discussion of popular film culture in Italy should not ignore cinema's relationship with other cultural forms in the twenties and thirties. It is important, however, to recognize that the cinema was the culture industry at the center of Italy's desire to assert and to defend through cultural policy, especially with respect to foreign culture industries, Italian ideals of the day. Luigi Freddi, the director from 1934 to 1940 of the Direzione Generale per la Cinematografia in the Ministry of Popular Culture, articulates these goals in 1937 when he writes:

> The Nation that is able to avoid the harsher realities that involve all the world will be one where all the citizens (even the so-called "private" citizens) know how to think and act not merely out of self-interest but also and moreover out of regard for the collective group—the Nation. . . .
>
> The most powerful force in the last three years that has hastened this attitude has been filmmaking. . . .
>
> It is also for this reason that the new national film production, precisely because it is a sign of a time in our history that is truly Italian and Fascist, is acquiring an international reputation and meaning.[10]

Film Culture and "Film Literacy"

The emergence of cinema in Italy as a popular form and as a means of formulating a national–popular culture resulted in part from a felt need by Italian filmmakers in this period to distance their work from other national cinemas and from what was frequently referred to as "filmed theater." In 1930, Italian critic Corrado Pavolini remarks on the necessity for a type of cinematic expression in Italy that conveys a uniquely national character: "If one looks closely at what constitutes the success of film production in America, Germany, or Russia, one recognizes immediately that their success results from their being the kind of cinema that, in those countries, is rooted in a national psychology or feeling which manifests itself through/as cinematographic formations."[11] Pavolini goes on to explain in the same essay that Italian cinema needs to distinguish itself not only from the cinema of other nations but also from its early ties to theater: "Cinema is not a transposition onto the screen of a bour-geois theater that is equally shared among every civilized country; instead it is the only modern expression of a national collectivity, and therefore profoundly different from one people to another."[12]

It is true that Italian films before World War I were influenced by theatrical codes. The illusion of a stage-proscenium, the drawing-room sets of films such as *Lydia* (1910), *Ma l'amore mio non muore* (1913), and *La donna nuda* (1914), the currency of stage actors and actresses such as Duse and Bertini, the continuous musical scores, and scripts adapted from stage plays are but a few of the more conspicuous similarities between early Italian film and nineteenth-century the-atrical melodrama and opera. One could also point to the scarcity of movie theaters in prewar Italy or to the widespread screening of films in conjunction with theatrical performances. (Some of the first movie palaces begin to appear in Italian cities just before World War I, but construction of new cinema theaters during and immediately after the war was very slow.) The late 'teens and 1920s' most popular and relatively successful films were the strongman and acrobatic spectacles that featured such male superheroes as Bartolomeo Pagano, Alfredo Boccolini, Giovanni Raicevich, Domenico Gambino, Luciano Albertini, and Carlo Aldini, to name a few. And while the trends in early Italian film produc-tion demand a much more complex and rigorous analysis than I am prepared to offer here,[13] suffice it to say that these films evolve more from a tradition of the circus and the variety show than they do from traditional nineteenth-century theater. The very late 1920s and the 1930s, the so-called renaissance of the Italian cinema which I discuss at greater length in chapter 2, was a period when Italian cinema began to cultivate its own actors and actresses. Although throughout the 1930s some actors and actresses in Italian cinema (Vittorio De Sica, Fosco Giachetti, Germana Paolieri, et al.) had come from theater backgrounds, the late 1930s saw an industry that had already developed its own stable of actors and actresses—a somewhat younger generation whose careers had begun in the cinema. In Italy in the 1920s and 1930s, however, the desire to purge cinema of these theatrical qualities began to assume ideological resonances, especially for those like Pavolini who saw theater as an expression of the older, Liberal, upper-bourgeois order. This rhetoric is apparent, for example, in the evolution of film criticism during the late 1920s and the 1930s when film criticism took two directions: one which continued, as Casetti has noted, to appropriate the terminology of theater criticism and another which sought to develop new categories and a new critical vocabulary. The appearance of film sections in newspapers as early as the late 1920s and the publication of film journals and magazines primarily in the 1930s provided other institutional avenues for disseminating ideas about cinema.[14]

During the 1920s and 1930s, cinema was becoming an apparatus, a *techne*, a "Voice" for amplifying realities that were in many ways unprecedented. It is in this way that cinema can be said to have contributed significantly in these years to a redefinition of public experience and of communal life in Italy. Unlike theatrical melodrama and opera in Italy during the nineteenth century, early cinema was not *exclusive* (nor was it as steeped in local culture as was traditional folkloristic spectacle). Although there were different categories of movie houses, cinema itself was available to audiences of any socioeconomic status. Moreover, advanced systems of distribution facilitated an increased variety of shows in any locality, while on a national and international scale these networks allowed a larger number of people from more diverse backgrounds to view the same films. Whereas nineteenth-century theater and opera focused on upper-bourgeois and occasionally aristocratic characters and social experience, cinema challenged these characterizations through a language that had a potential for dismantling the codes of theater culture. This is not to say that cinema in Italy at this time supplanted the theater altogether. In fact, theater itself moved in two directions: (a) from the "closed" confines of the traditional theaters to open-air arenas, piazzas, and hillside settings which could more easily accommodate larger audiences and further conceal the "theatricality" of public spectacle by presenting drama amidst nature, while transforming the environs into a stage for spectacle;[15] and (b) from the more genteel and reserved traditional houses to cabarets etc., where the "fourth wall" of nineteenth-century stage production was completely obliterated and where performers established a more intimate (though sometimes militant and aggressive) bond with their audiences. But cinema did offer its audiences something which neither theater nor radio could offer: bigger-than-life images whose mere presence suggested transcendence and inspired awe while at the same time entertaining. In this respect, cinema in Italy shared both outdoor theater's sense of grandeur and limitlessness and the cabaret's sense of relaxed intimacy and sensuousness. As a kind of hybrid mode of performance, it seemed more adapted to reaching broader social strata while, in the same sense, entertaining by addressing the conflicts and tensions between high and low social/cultural experience.

To speak of an emerging film culture is not to refer here simply to the obvious fact that cinema, unlike radio, brought its audiences out of their homes and was therefore a more "public" experience. Movies did, however, redefine their audiences (and they enabled those audiences to redefine themselves as a public) through their new signs, their new techniques, and their increasing "centrality" in Italian society. As Italian author and playwright Massimo Bontempelli notes in the pages of the Fascist newspaper *Il Tevere* as early as 1926: "The art of cinematography has now found the most favorable conditions possible for dominating the largest, the most varied, the most complete public and for being able to place itself as the most central art of the age."[16] Changing modes of address (i.e., the technology, as I mean it here, and the literacy of these techniques and codes), in changing the direct discursive relationship between text and audience, inevitably reshape the traffic of cultural symbols; this process also reconstitutes social and political realities and reshapes a nation's sense of cultural domain or territory—its international identity. In so doing, changing modes of address, as mediators of culture and ideology, meet a collective need for a sense of new possibilities and new modes of enquiry. (This is somewhat the same point that Elizabeth Eisenstein makes about the printing press when she discusses it as a technology that, while not in itself deterministic, enables a new set of possibilities.) As I intend to demonstrate in the succeeding chapters, these transitions, and the gradual experimentation with and realization of the possibilities afforded by the cinema, were in Italy bound up with a hegemonic crisis, with a breakdown in traditional modes of ordering collective experience. By "hegemonic" I am not referring simply to a body of "practical" solutions that might have imparted a fixed structure or framework for symbolic exchange, but more to the relative preference for and (more precisely) the emergence of certain discursive conventions and techniques that facilitated at this time strategic alliances among groups most affected by social and cultural changes. Cinema, as a social language and a collective Voice, gradually began to be adopted by a growing number of Italians who might otherwise have been alienated when material conditions, as a result of rapid industrialization and modernization, changed much more rapidly than did cultural symbolism. In this sense, the 1920s and 1930s are a period when the facilities or technology for this increasingly popular form of expression began to be institutionalized—both in terms of their increasingly direct relationships with other social and political institutions and in terms of the relatively specific functions attached to certain filmic signs. Still, it is necessary to keep in mind that institutionalization, especially in this case, does not mean that the messages of Italian cinema were understood and applied in a uniform fashion or that cinema was merely an instrument for control, for conformity. Cinematic performance underscored and at times celebrated social change, it highlighted the frictions and tensions resulting from this change, and it demonstrated the inadequacies in previously proven customs and attitudes. Moreover, because cinema continued to be viewed as a form deeply tied to less socially acceptable cultural arenas, such as cabarets, nightclubs, etc., it never became entirely centralized in Italian social life in the same sense in which one might think of other social institutions. In the next few paragraphs I will attempt to summarize briefly some of the ramifications in Italy of cinema's emergence as a national–popular form that was never entirely institutionalized or marginalized.

First, by directing attention to the codification of certain film signs, I intend to gauge the extent to which the social significance of a "film culture" is bound up with the emergence of film in Italy as a social language and the literacy of this language. By examining film as a social language, I am not attempting to ignore its potential as an artistic form; but, as Italian critic Corrado Pavolini pointed out in 1930, "We affirm that, because of the state of things, even the best Italian [film] production, which is the most pressing problem, cannot occur unless one recognizes the contingent problem: that of creating a national cinematographic consciousness/standard."[17] In one sense, this Italian film culture was constituted by a *filmic dialogue* among those agents (at all levels of the production chain) who could be said to have produced this culture. Two points need to be made here, however. My reference to film as an emerging social language should not be confused with traditional linguistic discussions of language as a closed system. Nor is it necessarily an attempt to recall the efforts by Raymond J. Spottiswoode in the 1930s to chart a "film grammar" (an attempt which is nonetheless worth noting here, since it was translated into Italian and appeared in an early volume of the Italian film journal *Bianco e nero*)[18] or to recall the early effort of Christian Metz to define a *grande syntagmatique* of filmic discourse. Instead, what I have in mind here is a definition of language that emphasizes its social practice or performance and that directs attention to its historically indispensable role in *mediating* or producing the realities and ideologies of the moment. My view corresponds with that of media culture theorists John Fiske and John Hartley, who, taking a cue from anthropologist Edmund Leach, note that "there is no pristine experience which social man can apprehend without the culturally determined structures, rituals and concepts supplied to him via his language. Language is the means by which men enter into society to *produce* reality (one part of which is the fact of their living together in linguistic society)."[19] My discussion of the cinematic image and the diegesis of Italian movies from the twenties and thirties are continuations of this view about film's role in constructing social reality through a rhetoric of accessible and popular communicative techniques and codes. To say, however, that filmic reality (the "authority" of its messages) is provisional because it is shaped by available technology and a public literacy of those techniques/technology is to underscore the necessity of charting significant patterns and shifts in these processes and also to recognize how the historical moment came to be captured in these films. In order better to understand the processes and the generative features of cinema as an emerging social language, it is therefore necessary to note the "polyphonous" and multi-vocal nature of this language (to borrow a key term from the work of M. M. Bakhtin). An awareness of this multi-vocality helps elucidate how, for instance, the transition from silent to sound films in Italy was connected with a crisis concerning the Italian written language, as a national language; and it helps explain some of the tensions that occurred as Italian cinema began to distance itself from a more traditional theater culture. Cinema, as new technology or facility, made traditional discursive practices problematic and attempted to invent new signs which surmounted the inadequacies of established discursive modes and of ordinary literary language. But moreover, by developing new, "clearer" signs, cinematic production rejected traditional assumptions about its audience and, in so doing, redefined them. For this reason, Italian films' social role as an emerging language enables us to understand better its role in producing "the nation" and a *cultura popolare* (an end which Antonio Gramsci sees all *languages* achieving). The emergence of film's social role as language occurred as the cinema developed conventions and codes through which audiences learned to see the world around them and to imagine one outside their own. By the late 1930s, not only the impressive numbers of cinema theaters and movie audiences, but precisely the increased familiarity with these codes and conventions, enabled, for Italians at all levels of society, a vital and complex culture.

The emergence of a popular film culture in Italy took place through a filmic dialogue. It is, therefore, necessary to review the sort of codes used to conduct (to centralize and to expand) this dialogue. The units in the *encyclopedia* of Italy's popular film culture that I have adopted in the succeeding chapters is one way to get at the dialogic and multi-vocal nature of cinematic production in Fascist Italy. (And, at the same time, I have used the term "encyclopedia" to avoid the kind of fixity implied by terms such as "lexicon" and "dictionary.")[20] It is not intended to suggest, however, that these units were not engaged in a formulaic way (although not as a traditional formalist or Proppian position might try to show) or that these codes necessarily guaranteed a film's success.

But, if the increasing institutionalization of cinema as social practice and language can be seen in the emergence of what can be called a rhetoric of popular film, it is also evident in cinema's increasingly direct relationships with other social and political institutions. One cannot, for instance, ignore the efforts of the OND (Opera Nazionale Dopolavoro), a semiautonomous state agency that supervised the efforts of local groups interested in organizing leisure activities, in facilitating greater nationwide access to the cinema. The OND, co-opted by the Fascists in 1927 (before film production in Italy began its recovery), had, by 1938, 767 permanent cinemas under its supervision.[21] These theaters were second- or third-class cinemas which charged reduced or no admission. Another enterprise of the OND during the 1930s was a fleet of traveling "cinema wagons" that in 1937 numbered 42 and claimed to have reached approximately 9,900,000 spectators in 28,641 showings.[22] The circuit of these mobile cinemas was a way of disseminating some of the same films (commercial as well as government newsreels and documentaries) across different regions in Italy. These screenings also generally occurred outdoors, making the experience itself an emblem of direct access and communality. The frequency of newsreels and government-sponsored documentaries, however, was not so much the result of state directives as of pressure by private theater owners against what they saw as unfair competition. And it is this kind of friction that, as I explain in chapter 7, is just one of the difficulties in institutionalizing popular film culture.

A more overtly political measure that brought cinema in Italy into more direct relations with governmental activities was the organization of the Istituto

LUCE (L'unione cinematografica educativa). This film agency, which I also discuss in more detail in chapter 7 officially became a state agency in 1924 and became increasingly responsible for producing and distributing newsreels and documentaries. Both in terms of the content and style of its films and in terms of its structural changes and continuities, the film production and the policy of LUCE were most involved in the politicization of Italy's emerging film culture. (As Gian Piero Brunetta notes, its own history parallels—is the "litmus test" for—internal transformations in Fascist politics during the 1920s and 1930s.)[23] Another significant, though largely emblematic, manifestation of the politicization of Italian film culture occurred with the initiation of the Mostra cinematografica di Venezia in 1932. This yearly exhibition served to bring to Italy films from all over the world and, through their "competition" with Italian films, to enhance attitudes at home and abroad about Italian cinema. But this sort of national pageant, devoted to promoting cinema as a cultural form and intended as an apolitical event, gradually began to serve political ends, as in 1935 when awards were presented in Mussolini's name and in the name of the Propaganda Minister for best Italian films.

In 1935, under the direction of Luigi Freddi (the director of the Direzione Generale per la Cinematografia from 1934 to 1940), plans were made for the construction of a centralized production studio, Cinecittà, and for the Centro Sperimentale to serve as a centralized educational institute for the preparation of professionals to work in all aspects of cinematic production (directing, acting, set designing, etc.).[24] Already, by the early 1930s, the state had become involved in organizing a network of cinematic studies for Italian youth through the GUF. The Cine–GUF, as they were generally known, were also a means of cultivating film professionals through a variety of more local programs on film production, although some historians also relate their activities to the formation of cinema clubs and cinema journals.[25] And, as Brunetta observes, the activities of the Cine–GUF offered some young men an opportunity for "escaping their provincial culture, for creating networks that were really very anti-conventional and less conditioned by specific standards of competency."[26] It is also important to recognize here, however, that, although the GUF was responsible for the promotion and extension of a national dialogue through film and about film (specifically about the study of cinema and about the political and cultural basis for cinema), it simultaneously fostered regional interests in alternative forms of film production—ones outside of the more prevalent commerical cinema. As I noted earlier, some of the prominent figures of Italian postwar cinema worked through these groups.

These attempts to organize educational facilities to enable a greater understanding about the techniques of filmmaking and for encouraging a certain amount of creativity or experimentation with these skills may for some be the most obvious example of a film literacy in Fascist Italy. I would contend, however, that the gradual institutionalization of cinematic technology in these decades—both in terms of the emerging rhetorical codes, techniques, and models and in terms of the increasingly direct relationship with social and political institutions that I have briefly enumerated here—attests to a more pervasive, transparent, and (for this reason) more powerful engagement of film literacy at this time. What seems often overlooked in a discussion about access to the facilities for cultural production is the way that the codes (as facilities) become so diffused as to *appear* to convey meanings that were not codified. The entire discussion of film literacy will undoubtedly seem spurious to those who see film (especially the classic, popular, commerical variety) as but a window to or a mirror of the real world. This assumption neglects the signifying processes through which a public *learns* to read films and, in so doing, learns to see and interact (in a period increasingly made up by cinematic production). The assumption also ignores how, being learned, these techniques and models become (in an institutional or in a less arbitrary fashion) part of a culture's larger "educational" forces and processes, i.e., its ways of structuring or disseminating (or teaching) cultural knowledge and ideology. The questions and concerns about a national cinema could not have occurred before Italians developed a vocabulary of filmic codes and conventions (though the degree and sophistication of this vocabulary varied) and thus became sensitive to the adequacies and inadequacies of available movies. It was also only by directors' and audiences' shared literacy of signs and sign-systems of cinema that Italy could begin to develop and extend its own cinematic production. Cinema, in other words, developed as an ideological or cultural form *through* the institutionalization and literacy of its codes and practices. And, by acknowledging the importance of literacy in all varieties of social and cultural performance, one is led to emphasize the generative qualities of cinematic production, actively seeking differences and historical modifications that are inevitable in these processes of signification.

My use of the term "film literacy" should not be confused here with more traditional "functionalist" studies on literacy, although it is significant (in understanding the role of film as a social language) that, as late as 1931, 21 percent of Italians were functionally illiterate and that the number of Italians viewing newsreels far outnumbered those reading newspapers.[27] It is precisely cinema's role in extending or in making more problematic or extraordinary the messages conveyed by spoken or written language that is part of the cinema's ideological character. The inadequacy of traditional literacy theory is exposed when it is forced to deal with these contemporary discursive activities, and it is this treatment of texts that raises some problematic questions which more traditional historical discussions of literacy seem unwilling to broach because of their restricted or single, holistic concept of language and, to a certain extent, of cultural production. By literacy I mean the ability to use a technology or a set of techniques for communicating and decoding symbolic action. By examining film in Italy as an emerging social language, and by considering film culture through the national access to cinema and a film literacy in Italy, we are taken back to Williams's call for a sociology of culture that focuses squarely on the amalgam of signifying systems (the processes of encoding and decoding) that produce culture and ideology.

I will return, therefore, to a point I made at the beginning of this section: that cinema, as an emerging national language, enabled its public to model all manners of action and consciousness and, through these models, to engage in a historical, national, and international dialogue on changing social concerns and on concerns characterized more than ever as "popular" (i.e., of and for the *popolo*). This process-oriented and dialogic approach to cultural production emphasizes the changing vocabularies and techniques for producing and reproducing meaning and for mediating change and continuity in a collective consciousness. It also acknowledges that a culture or historical period is produced through a variety of literacies, some more preferred, some emerging and thus reshaping the traffic of symbols and the audiences' sense of cultural domain. (This idea is not unlike that of Gramsci when he discusses the "complex molecular processes" that make up a nation's *language* system.)

While I am not trying to avoid discussing the cultural policy that attempted both to change and to stabilize the film industry, or to avoid discussing film as a commodity whose symbolic value may have been related to its material value in an economic system of exchange, or to avoid discussing it as an instrument for maintaining political stability, it is first necessary to acknowledge that all of these subjects are part of (and can be better understood through) the growing body of cinematic conventions, techniques, and signs that were becoming a force in Italian society.

As early as 1929, Italian film theorist and director Raffaello Matarazzo writes that:

> Cinema is a discovery of the people. It has been the inevitable and potent intuition of the nebulous and variegated masses who possess, without actually realizing it, the power to consecrate the success of an emerging form/industry. . . . Its potential (if not its actual) importance in our day seems increasingly more profound. Today's generation is educated not with the signs and drawings on a blackboard, but, one could say, with the screen projection of popular movies [*films culturali*].[28]

And a year later he continues: "Cinema is already part of the cultural life of a nation. The various literary periods of history will even be articulated through movies and our descendants will possess movie houses that they will consider their own form of library."[29] Matarazzo's comments should not be gauged merely as they pertain to cinema as an industry, a commodity, or a political tool but in the way they underscore cinema's role as a communicative technology and as an agent for mediating cultural change and continuity. The more these facilities became institutionalized, the more they began to serve as conduits for comparative exchange, as a matrix for asserting and testing the body of assumptions or myths that were felt to distinguish Italy from other cultures (both contemporary and previous ones). And it is these outward-and inward-looking impulses that are inscribed in Italian cinematic production—both at a textual level (with the exchange of images and meanings) and at an economic level (with a policy concerning distribution of movies and public access to them).

Ideology and Image

In deciding on the best methodology for analyzing Italian films from Fascist Italy and/or addressing the relationship of political consensus, ideology, and cultural codification, I am struck by the manner in which Fellini's *Amarcord* examines this period in terms of the *coscienza* of its young protagonist, Titta, and of the provincial community in which he lives. In presenting this constellation of images, which maintains the town's sense of community and its fabric of consensus, Fellini never privileges any one agent as being more influential than another. Fascism is, for the town's inhabitants and especially for the boy, one code among many—inextricable from the others. The boundaries of this community seem to be delineated not so much by precise or clear geographical coordinates or material markers as by symbolic signs which recur and are revaluated throughout the movie. Examples would be the cinema, the Grand Hotel, the boy's house, the school, the church, etc., though one could even include less static emblems such as Gradisca's hats or, in the boys' eyes, her derrière. On the one hand, these images help establish for the film's audience a sense of topography and a fixed dramatic space. But they also constitute a network of myths (both for the inhabitants and for Fellini) that serve as "carnivalized" zones for the town's tireless play and wonder (though, in their diversity, they are responsible for tensions in the community and signal changes occurring in the cultural environment). The fact that Fellini's characters are generally caricatures with predictable idiosyncrasies requires that they too be read as myths whose identities are bound up with their gravitation to any one of these places in the town (Ronald Colman and the movie house, Lalo and his group at the bar, etc.). All these images do impart to this spatio-temporal domain a sense of order, for the characters as well as for the audience, although Fellini repeatedly reminds us that this order is provisional. In one respect, these images are "indexical"; they help differentiate the internal zones of this world and, in so doing, identify its restrictive limits. On the other hand, they are "symbolic" (or conceptual) and impart to the characters' actions and events around them a special, transcendent significance.

At times, however, there are even more transient images which enable the community to get in touch with what lies beyond the town; the coming of the Rex, the fluff in the air, the quiet but glorious unfolding of the count's peacock in the snow, and the cardboard effigy of Mussolini at the Fascist rally would be examples. The snow and fluff seem to be especially powerful in this regard, relating to history, cultural change or Time (the seasonal fluff), and to geographical–social expansion; it redefines every other element for a while and, in the scene with Gradisca in the "maze," expresses in a wonderful fashion Titta's sense of searching. These latter images are more clearly symbolic, eliciting as they do a wonder from the townspeople and charging them with an almost sacred sense of belonging to something larger than they find in their own community.

Fellini's *Amarcord* presupposes that images (whether those we fabricate ourselves, perceptually, or those fabricated for us, artistically or commercially) are an essential component of social interaction and knowledge. They constitute the parameters of our perceptual field, our moral and political ethos; and they allow us to negotiate what lies beyond this vista or what is absent. The omnipresent photographer in *Amarcord* or the narrator/cinematographer in *E la nave va* also call attention to the way that the technology for imaging has played a key role in documenting modern experience and mediating our perceptual understandings of actions around us. By calling attention to photo/cine strategies in such a self-reflexive manner, however, Fellini underscores the exoticism or clumsiness of these earlier apparatuses and, in so doing, reminds us that the reality they have produced is only provisional.

Images are *produced* (i.e. projected or conceived) through systems or codes of representation and exchange; image production is therefore a signifying activity. As Roland Barthes explains in his essays on the rhetoric of images, the modern "technology" for producing these images contributes to obscuring or masking the signifying processes involved in image production. He notes that we perceive photographic images, for example, in a paradoxical fashion; photography conveys connoted or coded messages that seem to address us on the basis of messages without a code. Because we tend to read the messages of photographic and cinematic images through signs which are codified into sets of connotations or systems of meaning, the reality of the image is provisional.[30] Barthes maintains, however, that these images do not *seem* discursive or provisional, only conciliatory or even "authoritative " since they serve to *validate* in a tautological way the natural order and value of things. The commercial image offers a unified Nature without calling attention to the chain of procedures and the motives which constitute and direct its messages and the values of these messages.

Much effort has been devoted to explaining how this kind of "masking" in images serves an ideology. Bill Nichols, for instance, proposes that "ideology *uses* the fabrication of images and the processes of representation to persuade us that how things are is how they ought to be and that the place provided for us is the place we ought to have" (italics mine).[31] For Nichols, as for Barthes, images gratify audiences' desires to recognize an order or consistency in their lives and their place in that order.

While this view of images and ideology helps explain the necessary and inevitable role of images in stabilizing a social order and its value, it tends to ignore (as Nichols admits) the generative and historical qualities of both ideology and modern cultural forms, such as cinema, through which images are produced. Ideology cannot be said to "inform" outside a culture's signifying practices and the availability of techniques that make possible certain modes or conventions of communication and exchange. Imaging (as a signifying activity) *re*-constitutes and transforms the individuals and groups involved in this process of signification by framing, organizing, and thus *changing* the way we view ourselves, each other, and our place in this interaction. To acknowledge that images transform and reconstitute our perceptions implies that they do not merely *affirm* an order or that that order is not itself transformed through the production of images (at all points in the chain of signification). Moreover, photographic and cinematic images, as codified reality, are learned and taught, and it is just as necessary to consider how historical and cultural processes for transmitting images—public access to and familiarity with these techniques—shape and reshape audiences and their ideologies.

This last point should remind us that there are historical and cultural differences in imaging. Fellini's *Amarcord* helps reveal the inevitable ways that a group structures its visual, concrete environment—its cultural space—by distinguishing and even celebrating the significant features or zones of this shared environment. The images in popular, commercial cinema in many ways also are constituted by or inscribed with those signs and structural features that the "film community" holds most vital and, hence, that are most easily recognized or read. Jurij Lotman, in his theory of cultural texts, offers an equally useful adjunct to this conceptualization of cultural orientation through topological or "spatial" models:

> One of the universal peculiarities of human culture, possibly connected with the anthropological features of human consciousness, is the fact that world view invariably acquires features of spatial characteristics. The very construction of a world order is invariably conceived on the basis of some spatial structure which organizes all its other levels.[32]

This is not to say that a culture's world view is based on a single spatial model or that spatial modeling occurs in a unilateral fashion. The "construction" of a world view suggests a polyphony of spatial models and the complex interaction of these models, just as the term "spatial modeling" calls attention to the materials and techniques that were necessary or available for organizing and framing both visual and aural information. This sense of cultural domain is, therefore, learned through an audience's visual literacy or familiarity with these forms and through their participation in (their access to) the processes of spatial modeling.

If, as Nichols suggests, ideology is a collective self-image, "the image society gives of itself in order to perpetuate itself," this image is visualized only through a series or field of spatial structures or, again, through the complex processes of what Lotman describes as spatial modeling. My own approach is devoted to exploring the range and differences among the spatial models that cinema offered in Italy. By the late 1920s and the 1930s, film production in Italy was (for a variety of reasons) in the process of discovering and assimilating a vocabulary of competing spatial models; through these competing models, the movie public was able to form attitudes about changing social relationships and values. My categorization of these films attempts, in part, to elucidate these kinds of spatial distinctions or differences, since the differences (as in Fellini's *Amarcord*) are themselves signs of a changing cultural landscape. In discussing movie-making as a mode of spatial modeling, I devote substantial attention not only to the *mise-en-scène* and architectonics of the cinematic image but also to its rhetorical significance as an arena or stage for addressing (in a highly accessible fashion) certain problems, questions, or tensions produced by shifting avenues for social interaction and by the new possibilities afforded by cinema itself. No one of these models can easily be described as "dominant" since each offered a kind of rhetorical response to propositions, questions, and alternatives posed by any and all of the other models. The competition among these spatial models encouraged different attitudes or an ambivalence about the changing social and cultural environment—an insight that is crucial to understanding and recuperating the vitality of a culture's world view and cinema's emerging role in shaping that view.

By examining competing spatial models, I am not attempting to refute points raised by Barthes or Nichols, i.e., that "classical" or popular cinema reshapes the world to make it more intelligible but masks the processes of this transformation, or that audiences develop perceptual habits from the conventions or codes for structuring space. Neither am I attempting to ignore the specifically filmic strategies or cues for organizing the space within the frame or on the screen. What seems just as important (and often lacking) in ideological critiques, however, is how filmic realism or spectacle is part of a historical and cultural process of refining filmic techniques, of gaining access to these techniques or of making them accessible, and is part of audiences' growing familiarity and pleasure in these strategies. Here, for instance, it is important to consider how the larger-than-life size of the movie screen offered audiences a spatial frame that was unprecedented in its ability to convey epic and heroic gesture or characterization and the grandeur or exoticism of visual landscapes and architecture (especially in an age when these qualities also figured prominently in Italy's political rhetoric). In this same respect, however, it is necessary to recognize that techniques for structuring space or framing action continued to borrow from theatrical codes, though editing facilitated and encouraged a more sustained centrality of action and focus of visual lines of tension than could be achieved on the stage. And though parts of a substantial number of films were shot outdoors, most continued to use the more structured and manageable (for purposes of lighting, etc.) sound stages.

The 1920s and 1930s was a period that did encourage, as a result of the film industry's need for development and economic stabilization, innovation of techniques for imaging. Here one could cite director Mario Camerini's relative commercial success with a more mobile camera that signaled a significant departure from the more photographic tendencies of earlier Italian films and that set a precedent for a more realistic field of perception. Yet these innovations, because they resulted from a need to get in touch with a larger Italian audience and to compete with more successful film styles (particularly those from Hollywood), were often attempts to interpret or translate proven or more successful codes—whether those were earlier theatrical ones or filmic ones more recently popularized in Italy through foreign movies.

Film Narrative as Social Ritual

The strategies for imaging through film cannot entirely be explained in terms of spatial modeling—a term that tends to gloss over the dynamic flow/disruption of images that constitute movie making and watching. While the realism of a photographic image may depend in part upon a viewer's sense that the "event" *did* occur, cinematic realism results more from a viewer's feeling that the event *is* occurring. The difference, of course, is based in a very general sense on cinema's kinetic or transitive properties, i.e., montage, synchronous sound, etc., which can contribute to a viewer's sense of spatial continuity. Because this sense of spatial continuity depends upon a coherence of action, it is a film's narrative and particularly its *logic* of action that offers audiences a unified and meaningful view of a Nature. As Stephen Heath has noted, "it is narrative significance that at any moment sets the space of the frame to be followed and 'read,' and that determines the development of the filmic cues in their contributions to the definition of space in frame (focus pull, for example, or back lighting). . . . The vision of the image is its narrative clarity and that clarity hangs on the negation of space for place, the constant realization of centre in function of narrative purpose, narrative movement."[33] The realism or intelligibility (readability) of narrative film does not result merely from events that unfold diachronically but rather from the sense that the succession of tightly interlocking mediate and intermediate events, the causes and effects, seems logical or natural.

This brings us then to the "rules" for making and reading narratives in movies. In order to address broad and variegated (regional) audiences, a commercial or state-subsidized cinema (since both involve cinematic production whose general economy is highly systematized) is compelled to draw upon and continually refine narrative conventions or formulas. These formulas provide necessary referential systems and a framework for understanding a film's action and for seeing the succession of events as logical. It is for this reason that Barthes (expanding earlier narrative theories by Propp and Russian formalists) suggests that "to read is to name; to listen is not only to perceive a language, it is also to construct it."[34] The social and cultural force of a film, then, can depend upon the filmmaker's, actors, and audience's relative familiarity with or shared literacy of these formulas. Popular narrative formulas are a kind of discursive shorthand in popular culture; they are what John Cawelti has called the "basic patterns" of cultural representation and orientation. It is, however, precisely because these formulas are so accessible that the narrative seems to unfold "naturally" and without codes. An audience is not, in other words, inclined (nor or they encouraged) to view the narrative as being *narrated*. In a period when narrative codes and techniques are just beginning to become systematized, and as long as they remain a dynamic social force, a narrative will generally not be thought of as having an authorial or narratorial agent. (As I will explain later, movie advertisements in Italy during the 1920s and 1930s seldom bore the names of film directors; usually only the names of stars and, in the case of American films, of production companies—a sign that they were American. Later, the postwar disenchantment with the narrative codes of the 1920s and 1930s was bound up with a reorientation toward a more auteuristic aesthetic.)

In a popular film's attempt to reach the broadest audience, its narrative is inscribed with a variety of social and ideological discourses and is endowed with a potential for accommodating a broad range of meaning. Consequently, the arrangement of events and choices in a narrative reveal a great deal about the *dominant* concerns of audiences and ways in which they are disposed to relate and manage the tensions that accompany these concerns. Because the narrative of a popular film addresses dominant concerns, its conflicts and their resolutions are ideal and value-laden. Another way of putting this is to say that the economy of popular film and its systemization of narrative forms condense social conflict and cultural change to the interaction of a more limited and generally intimate group (couple, family, or "tribe") who themselves are ideal representatives or figurations of the larger community; this is why film stars are culturally processed models of collective values. A movie narrative, however (unlike those in theater or television), involves a sequence of actions that fill a larger-than-life-sized screen, where the conflicts that disrupt the equilibrium of characters' intimate and interpersonal relationships are amplified into frequently epic proportions.

In addressing the concerns of a variety of audiences, a popular film narrative exposes the inadequacies or changes that have produced these concerns and the film's narrative conflicts. The film's messages about these inadequacies and changes, however, often tend to be paradoxical. Depression-era Hollywood comedy such as La Cava's My Man Godfrey, for example, or a musical such as Gold Diggers of 1933 affirm both the egalitarian attributes and the self-interests of those with money and power; both movies also demonstrate the inadequacies of traditional myths while demonstrating the importance of traditional values in addressing modern problems. Attempts by the film's narrative to manage or redress these conflicts necessitate a model capable of channeling the conflicting and contradictory interests or desires, and frequently at the center of this model is a character who mediates these paradoxical impulses. (In classical Hollywood genres, there is even a ritualized figure such as the Gangster, the Music Man, the Westerner, etc.) In some narrative systems, the figure who mediates the film's conflicting values serves as an agent of narrative resolution; in other formulas, he is torn and destroyed by his role as mediator.

The "authority" or force of narrative closure results from the film's ability to bring these opposing or contradictory impulses into an ideal or mythical equilibrium that, through balance, affords pleasure or admiration. To say, however, that conventional film narratives attempting to achieve this balance merely affirm the status quo and regulate deviant or progressive views of social order and interaction ignores the ideal and provisional nature of this balance or the historical force of the contradictions the narrative raises. The narrative conventions also conjure a set of codes that make any variation from these codes or any changes in social attitudes (both of which are part of the narrative conflict) clearer and more meaningful to an audience familiar with the narrative conventions. Moreover, they enable exploration and testing of the social order through a framework whose matrix is both ideological and material. Both the movie audiences and the filmmakers, therefore, not only construct this framework, but in constructing it they redirect it—the contradictions generating a desire in the spectators that the ideal resolution can only partly or momentarily gratify.

Often lost by later audiences is a sense of the force (the interest, the drama, the humor) of the narrative's conflicts and the characters' dilemmas, or of how these narrative formulas were shaping and shaped by the material organization or systemization of production techniques. Rather than seeing the historical nature of the processes and even the struggles by a film to achieve a balance among contradictory impulses, and between encoders and decoders, later audiences frequently observe only the imbalances (i.e., the clichés) created by historically different codes. Cinema emerged in Italy during the 1920s and 1930s as a technology (a set of techniques or codes) which, through audiences' and filmmakers' literacy of these techniques, transformed traditional narrative formulas and demanded new ones. The cinema addressed itself in material, political, and formal ways to the inadequacies of older orders and systems (and the tropes, situations, actions, and actors that gave them their force and vitality). And, in so doing, it encouraged audiences and filmmakers to begin looking for new experiences and new ways of representing experience.

Silent cinema in Italy before World War I and immediately thereafter largely adapted its subjects and narrative codes from nineteenth-century theatrical melodrama and historical or French and Italian Realist literature (though, even in this period, cinema offered audiences realism and spectacle that theater audiences were demanding but that theater seemed increasingly incapable of satisfying.)[35] Stories generally concerned the same kind of upper-crust characters and other drawing-room or classical settings characteristic of these more traditional forms. Few literary authors or playwrights, however, contributed directly to the cinema, finding it difficult—as did D'Annunzio—to bring their lengthy and sometimes florid descriptions into the discursive economy of silent film. Many of the actors and actresses from the Italian stage were recruited for these early films, and the more famous ones were mostly known as *divi* and *dive* of the stage (e.g., Duse, Bertini, Borelli).

A succession of events in the following decades—the unsuccessful merger of eleven major Italian production companies (the Unione cinematografica italiana) in the years immediately following World War I, the subsequent "collapse" of the Italian film industry during the mid-1920s, the so-called renaissance of film production through the organizing skills of Stefano Pittaluga and his Cines studios in the late 1920s and early 1930s, and the inauguration of the LUCE–Cinecittà complex under Luigi Freddi by the mid-1930s—not only reshaped the industrial structure of Italian filmmaking but also contributed to gradual though always tenuous re-formularization and systemization of Italian film narratives and genres. By the late 1930s, for instance, the Italian film industry had cultivated a stable of actors and actresses; and, while some of them came from popular theatrical and radio backgrounds, they became recognized as *dive* and *divi* of the screen. While as many as half of the film narratives in the 1930s (especially in the late 1930s) were still based on theatrical or literary models—particularly historical models[36]—screenplays were increasingly original collaborative efforts or adaptations from already successful movies. Many of the scriptwriters and story writers for the Italian cinema in the 1930s had worked in both cinema and theater during the 1920s,[37] but their contributions as literary or theatrical artists were not publicized or directly responsible for distinguishing the film itself.[38] Screenwriters Aldo De Benedetti and Alberto De Stefani, however, contributed more directly to the cinema in the 1930s—their efforts accounting for around 20 percent of Italian screenplays and imparting a narrative consistency to Italian film production throughout this decade.[39] These trends again affirm that narrative formulas, in their emerging and most dynamic stages, lack a sense of an individual author or a clear narrative voice or the kind of self-reflexivity characteristic of avant-garde or less "systematized" (i.e., institutionalized) forms. (One notable exception to this last observation is Max Ophuls's *La signora di tutti* in 1934, a film wherein there is a certain amount of narrative framing and internal narration).[40] Italian films by the 1930s inevitably continued to rely on the "proven" formulas of theater and popular romance; but, as cinema in Italy became a more popular cultural form, these formulas were redirected and reshaped through their competition with an emerging body of equally powerful *cinematic* conventions. And, since most of the more successful movies in Italy during the 1920s were foreign (mostly American), Italian film attempted in some ways to emulate or adapt these foreign models. Yet, for these narratives to seem realistic, to convey clear messages and to address audience concerns, they could not appear to be translations; instead they had to underscore the genuinely Italian patterns or logic of experience. Both of these impulses are inscribed in the narrative situations and conflicts of Italian films, and they account for the development of narrative patterns and film genres. My categorization of popular films in Italy should underscore these larger patterns or trends, but it is equally important to realize that the conflicts of films in any of these chapters may address concerns or tensions resulting from these historic changes and the increasingly international flow of films as a cultural form. In its attempts to stabilize production, the Italian film industry was compelled not only to reorganize its material base but also to develop films that could address audience concerns; and, through these collective concerns, a body of spatial models and narrative systems began to emerge that, while conflicting and contradictory, provided a necessary field of reference against which to assimilate social change and ideology.

The Nature of Consensus through Popular Film

Traditional approaches to twentieth-century culture studies, Dwight McDonald's cynical and reductive discussions of "mass culture," or the Frankfurt school's treatment of culture industries, generally attend to the regulative and authoritative function of popular forms such as film.[41] Citing what they see as the uniform obedience of the "masses" who consume and are "captivated" by these products, they argue that the sensibilities of middle-class society have changed little in the last two centuries. This kind of essentialist approach to popular cultural forms fails to acknowledge any of the complex processes of signification, of encoding and decoding messages, that occur through popular cinema; because cinema is not seen as a process of signification made possible only through the availability of techniques and a rhetoric, they gloss over the historical difference in cultural production through cinema. While Bill Nichols's approach to cinema and ideology (an approach that follows theories of perception and recognition advanced by Jacque Lacan and Louis Althusser) examines ways in which a viewer is "recruited" into a *dominant* ideology or way of seeing, it does not explore how individual films communicate through a referential field of cultural production, nor does it explore how a body of films produces the codes necessary for perception and understanding. While many of the more recent psychoanalytic and ideological critiques devote more attention than traditional approaches to the interaction of film text and viewer, they tend to see in "classical" cinema the clearest examples of films that "preconstruct" their "subjects" by providing inducements and leading them through an itinerary intended to instill in them a sense of a free, unified self and a stable ego.

What all of these approaches often lack is, first, a sense of the "play" and negotiation of cinematic experience, how the viewer's pleasure results in part from ways that films break wih the world of social manners and customs. These approaches frequently lack a sincere willingness to acknowledge that movie experience is never entirely inside or outside the realm of social experience, i.e., that the viewer is "determined" only by the text or by social experience. Those who insist that film merely constitutes the viewer as subject ignore ways that films, as sites for the construction of models of cultural change, lead viewers to possibilities of action and perception that are prohibited by, incompatible with, or difficult to see in the existing social order and custom. A narrative film is, in some very important ways, a "carnivalization" of social experience; and society, viewed through the film's diegesis, may itself appear provisional and arbitrary. While the range of conflict and contestation in an older or foreign narrative film may appear narrow, the film's appeal and power must be weighed in terms of its ability to address audience concerns and to make their experience more intelligible by amplifying the inadequacies of traditional or established modes of social interaction and discourse, or by invoking partially forgotten ones that seem appropriate under the circumstances of filmic production. As I intend to demonstrate in the succeeding chapters, popular movies appeal by simultaneously demonstrating the inadequacies and adequacies of established models, by eliciting from viewers an ambivalence about the movies' messages—but always through a diegesis that carnivalizes social experience and whose temporal economy repeatedly affirms the flexibility and mobility among established social categories. The sense of closure that may result from a film narrative's redressive action does not neutralize conflict but only marginalizes the viewer's ambivalence, positioning it where it continues to exert tension and to pull at this balance or the meaning he may draw from the contradiction. One could even go so far as to say that a film's ending may not gratify, since closure signals the end of the sense of play and contradiction which provides viewers pleasure. It is the sense of closure that signals the powerlessness of the text; an ending is inevitable, beyond the control of the film. To focus on this ambivalence does not elucidate how viewers are controlled or persuaded through a popular medium such as cinema; and in this sense it makes a study of audience effects problematic by opening a theoretical space between text and viewer. But it does help us recognize the felt gaps in control—a perceived crisis—and how filmic diegesis and film literacy become means (a set of techniques) for rearranging the social order and the cultural formations that seem to produce these gaps.

Because viewers learn, reinvent, and assimilate the codes necessary to understand a film's messages, it is difficult to accept the efficacy of the notion of an ideal spectator—one preconstructed by the film itself. Discussing cinema as the production of meaning, and as a complex process of encoding and decoding, reminds us that the codes necessary to understand a film are continually negotiated and operate through other discourses or other roles in this social milieu which are themselves part of the process of making and watching a film. The viewer is, in this sense, constituted by a variety of discourses, some congruent with and affirming some of the film's messages and some competing with them.[42] As Teresa de Lauretis notes, in response to a similar observation by Claire Johnston, "spectators are not, as it were, in the film text or simply outside the film text; rather . . . they intersect the film as they are intersected by cinema."[43] An emphasis on cinematic *production* does not discount the inevitable referential framework of codes necessary for making and viewing films. But, by examining how this framework is structured, it acknowledges its diverse and provisional nature, and it acknowledges ways that individual forms gradually reshape this framework. The spectator's role in this process, then, is not determined by the conventions (the "*langue*," in Saussure's dichotomy) or by a social totality or a "dominant" ideology which these conventions might seem to uphold. Rather the subject/object relationship is caught up in history and the "dialogic" processes of cultural production. This is a formulation of the "subject" that can be aligned with Antonio Gramsci's observations on language, popular culture and hegemony—observations which have frequently become the centerpiece of ideological critiques and cultural studies in England and Italy. For Gramsci, or for more recent theorists working past early Marxist or early structuralist and semiotic models, the viewer/reader is not easily explained in terms of individuality or subjectivism since the "subject" is seen as a series of active relationships and constituted by an "infinity of traces."[44] Gramsci's views offer a more dynamic and generative view of hegemony and a view of popular culture as a continual process of recombination and appropriation.

Popular films, examined in this way, are forces in a hegemonic process that constitute and reconstitute the historical and cultural fields of perception and myth. The hegemonic values that viewers learn from and bring to watching films are learned only by translating them and applying them to specific historical challenges and situations. This point, however, brings us back to the discussion of literacy, as it pertains to cinema as signifying activity and to culture as a nexus of signifying systems.

By discussing cultural production as a discursive and appropriative activity, one allows for a distinction between text and spectator. My emphasis on the literacy of cultural forms is an extension of this line of reasoning about the text-viewer and text-producer relationships. Media messages conjure (even though they attempt to distance themselves from) historically contiguous frameworks of knowledge and practice; otherwise, there would be no basis for communication. But the production and reception of these messages is not identical; as Stuart Hall and others have noted, the "correspondence" between encoding and decoding "moments" is not given but constructed.[45]

The notion of cultural production and a processual approach to cinema raise questions about the permanence of social consensus. To understand the fabrication of social consensus, it is again necessary to examine the rhetorical practices, the techniques and models, through which viewers visualize possibilities of continuity and change. Cultural reproduction does not occur in a unilinear fashion; discursive practices do not (as traditional "mass culture" theorist suggest) replicate traditional beliefs or attitudes in a mechanical fashion. Formal change and diversity are part of cultural production, even in a state-controlled or so-called totalitarian society; though from a perspective outside that culture, the range of change and diversity may easily appear more restricted or narrow than in one's own social millieu. As Raymond Williams has noted:

> Even when we have given full weight to all that can be reasonably described as replication, in cultural as in more general social activities, and when we have acknowledged the systematic reproduction of certain deep forms, we have still to insist that social orders and cultural orders must be seen as being actively made: actively and continuously, or they may quite quickly break down. That some of this making is reproduction, in its narrowest as well as in its broadest sense, is not in doubt. But unless there is also production and innovation, most orders are at risk, and in the case of certain orders (most evidently that of the bourgeois epoch, centred on the drives of capitalist accumulation) at total risk.[46]

Williams's point could be taken one step further by adding that, while cultural production is both progressive and conservative, and that, while consensus depends upon continual innovation, the social fabric is commensurate with the relative literacy of a cultural form, i.e., with the public's ability to read and represent the spatial models and narrative codes necessary to visualize or imagine continuity and change. And in a period when a communicative form is just emerging, significantly if not radically new challenges to cultural tradition are posed by its new perceptual field. The struggle to systematize this form is, in this sense, a search for new interpretive possibilities and models of social action.

Cinema became a social and cultural force through a growing public literacy of its formal conventions—both as a discursive mode and as an emerging body of film genres and styles. This is not to say that much of the public possessed a representational or "instrumental" literacy of cinematic techniques; filmmaking and photography were in the 1920s and 1930s still seen more as a skill for professionals or as a hobby for those able to afford the costly material technology or the leisure for making one's own movies. The public did, however, gradually acquire what can be called a *cultural* or *encyclopedic literacy* of these conventions and techniques; a literacy which was necessary for cultural production and reproduction. The term "literacy" is crucial here to remind us that social transformations and ideologies are mediated through these models and conventions. But, again, film literacy at this time must be viewed as an ability to decode a discursive system that is not socially privileged. Popular cinema in Italy at this time, while not the "official" social language, is a "mythical" language. In fact it is born from an impulse to overturn the standards and elitism of literary language in order to serve as a *popular* language—one in which the signs are *immediately* intelligible and recognizable and are organized through structures in which the *popolo* is most literate. But in the process of distancing itself from traditional or socially restrictive codes, and in producing a "language"/culture through which to measure these codes, cinematic production began to develop its own systems and referential frameworks—ones which in prewar Italy were tentative and contradictory.

One final point should be made here about literacy and cultural production. Cultural or reproductive literacy is not necessarily conceptual or critical, as Paulo Friere has noted. A "critical literacy" enables audiences to see how reality is constructed or messages are mediated or to see these cinematic codes as part of more pervasive ideological currents; for this reason, Friere has seen critical literacy as having a subversive and revolutionary potential. The rationale of "mass culture" theorists presumes that the social environment created by culture industries discourages critical literacy precisely because of this potential to recognize the ideology that informs the more conventionalized, popular forms. Certainly, the Italian cinema, as an emerging language of national–popular culture, was generally unable to accommodate the more modernist and self-reflexive qualities of, say, Pirandello's, Bontempelli's, or Brecht's style of theater.[47] On the other hand, the 1930s were a period in Italy when cinema, particularly because of its cross-cultural appeal, became more frequently conceptualized as a conventional medium which was inseparable from a flourishing national spirit. And to better understand the generative nature of this sense of social, cultural, and political domain, it is important to recognize the progressive, conservative, and even revolutionary impulses in the policy and organization of the industry as well as in the film texts themselves.

Consensus is a figurative trope in social analysis. Seen amidst historical flux or in terms of cultural production, it is difficult to fix. This is not to say that there is not a continual drive, especially by political bodies and those agents who attempt to orchestrate consensus, to tap cultural myths and symbols in order to give a sense of an order that is fixed. In attempting to reach consensus, however, new meanings are continually added to the culture's traditions—a process that produces tensions and conflicts among figures of group representation and shared meanings. Consensus, therefore, makes up a variegated field of cultural experience. The feeling of consensus is, in other words, always the realization of the vitality and rich diversity of the "community"; it is the inability and unwillingness by members of a group to see themselves as myriad replications of one another or as replications of another culture/nation.

In her discussion of the organization of leisure time in Fascist Italy, de Grazia examines how public policy transformed the militancy of the *popolo* after World War I into a "culture of consent." To understand how this militancy was rechanneled, it is also necessary to realize that this *popolo* was addressed, defined, and constituted by a variety of discourses and models accessible to this group not only by political measures but *through* their codified forms of representation where they became a rhetorical trope. The models produced through cinematic production enabled this public to visualize itself as a community and as a political/social force. But this community, in the process of emerging, was fraught with contradictions (much more so than the use of the term *popolo* in political rhetoric might lead us to believe).

Methodology: Charting a National–Popular Film Culture

My approach to Italian cinema in the 1920s and 1930s is not intended to be a historical analysis of Fascism, in the traditional sense of social-historical exegesis as documentation of a social order and consciousness or of a political agenda. Instead, I only propose another way of reviewing this period in hopes that these materials and their organization may raise questions about or make more problematic some longstanding assumptions inherent in or perpetuated by traditional analysis of popular forms, of propaganda, and of social consensus. The more one attempts to understand a "culture industry," cultural policy, and popular culture in terms of their production by individuals with historically specific goals and motives and with techniques and facilities whose relative availability enabled or encouraged both conservation as well as experimentation, the more difficult becomes the task of substantiating a "governing" reality of the time or an essential level of national truth or common knowledge shared across a broad spectrum. By focusing squarely on the procedures of signification and cultural exchange, social change no longer appears unilinear, since the meaning of any framework on which this change may be gauged is continually mediated and renegotiated. Clifford Geertz offers a particularly relevant metaphor in this regard when he notes that

> The appropriate image, if one must have images, of cultural organization, is neither the spider web nor the pile of sand. It is rather more the octopus, whose tentacles are in large part separately integrated, neurally quite poorly connected with one another and with what in the octopus passes for a brain, and yet who nonetheless manages both to get around and to preserve himself, for a while

anyway, as a viable if somewhat ungainly entity. . . . Culture moves rather like an octopus too—not all at once in a smoothly coordinated synergy of parts, a massive coaction of the whole, but by disjointed movements of this part, then that, and now the other which somehow cumulate to directional change.[48]

It is not, then, that this approach is concerned only with discontinuity and diversity by ignoring social and political consensus. But by examining Italy's *cultura popolare* in the 1920s and 1930s as it has been mediated through cinematic production, one is compelled to acknowledge the provisional nature of consensus, meaning, and equilibrium, and the constant search for new ways of achieving consensus, integration, and class alliances. This kind of approach to cultural production can clearly be aligned with Gramsci's ideas about hegemony, which, unlike Althusser's notion of a "dominant" ideology, describes consensus more as a historical *tendency* or "balance" among competing codes.

In emphasizing audiences' cultural or "reproductive" literacy of films at this time, I have directed attention to ways that popular discourses occur through cultural *texts*, i.e., those processes of constructing significance out of interrelated sensory units (primarily visual and aural ones) comprising a collective experience. The very discussion of an emerging literacy, however, presumes a public's relative familiarity with a variety of techniques or codification procedures necessary to convey a film's messages. On the other hand, various attempts to institutionalize cinematic forms and popular literacy of these forms make it difficult (if not impossible) to adopt an approach that ignores the material organization of these forms, modes of distribution, and policy that developed around all of these concerns. Semiotic analysis (particularly that of Barthes, Eco, or Lotman) offers useful guidelines for discussing ways in which movies produce visual signs that mediate reality and ways in which a movie's action mediates public values and meaning—in short, our understanding of our social and cultural environment. These signs are intelligible, however, only because of the public's familiarity with specific codes, whose vitality depends upon a continual conservation and invention of new signs. In the *process* of signification, codes are never activated in a uniform way; and it is, therefore, difficult to speak of a "dominant" code that is solely responsible for film's realism or the *inevitability* of its action. What occurs instead is a momentary convergence or overlapping of codes, whose very convergence creates both provisionally shared meanings *and* ambiguity. Historicizing the text in this way means, as Tony Bennett has noted, that there is no "pure text, no fixed and final form of the text which conceals a hidden truth which has but to be penetrated for criticism to retire, its task completed."[49] The text, he explains, always and only exists amidst a variety of historically concrete and changing forms. Thus, while it is important to develop an approach that can examine ways that the codes by which films are made and read organize cinematic production (at all its levels), it is just as necessary to understand that these codes never quite constitute a stable, "closed" system of production or give rise to homogeneous consensus about the meaning of the films produced.

My approach to Italy's emerging popular film culture is in part inspired by the seminal work of Siegfried Kracauer, whose analysis of the "psychological dis-position" of German movie audiences between 1918 and 1933 offers an invaluable methodological paradigm. As he acknowledges in his preface, his aim is not to discuss films from this period "for their own sake" but to increase our knowl-edge of pre-Hitler Germany. Despite his intentions to concentrate largely on this period, his efforts reveal a great deal about Nazism—but Nazism as a man-ifestation of cultural undercurrents rather than simply as the culmination of political and legislative events. One of Kracauer's contributions to film criticism is his sensitivity, on the one hand, to the collective character of film produc-tion—to its organizational power—and, on the other hand, to audiences' active roles in determining the agenda of their country's film production. Here he questions the notion that films directly manipulate their audiences, and he high-lights film production's ability to coordinate individual energies and desires through its own teamwork and its images of collective action.

But, while Kracauer attempts to avoid discussion of a *fixed* national character, i.e., "a national character pattern elevated above history," he does tend to ignore the variegated nature of Germany's psychological profile. His treatment of Nazi propaganda films effectively demonstrates the regime's ability to project ideol-ogy which facilitated, in his mind, the homogenization of culture. It is abso-lutely necessary to recognize that in pre-Hitler German culture, Germany's culture industry and its cultural politics were significantly different from those in other countries at the same time—even those in Fascist Italy. (Perhaps the most significant difference between these two culture industries resides in Germany's more longstanding and successful UFA and the considerably closer monitoring by the Nazis of this organization—and of cultural production in general—and in Italy's willingness simply to "protect" and subsidize an industry oriented more to a supply-and-demand ethic.) Thus, whereas I accept Kracauer's notion that movies, especially those between the two World Wars, hastened political mobilization (a process that occurred in a number of nations), I must also agree with his assumption that movies are products of a particular cultural milieu, whose ideological imperatives and cultural traditions differ significantly from those in other countries.

I have concerned myself with cinematic production in Italy during the late 1920s and 1930s because this period offers some of the clearest examples of attempts to institutionalize an increasingly popular medium in response to cultural and hegemonic crises. And, while many historians have seen in this period a kind of social stagnation, it is just as important to acknowledge signs of cultural vitality and the generative nature of cultural forms which were actively attempting to discover or invent a national–popular language. Cultural produc-tion involves impulses to systematize modes of self-description, of naming and defining those properties that are most widely valued and celebrated. Those within the culture may have a sense of diversity and vitality about their cultural and social environment that is unapparent to succeeding generations or to those outside that culture and its literacy of cultural forms. On the other hand, in attempting to systematize their cultural production, those within the culture marginalize some information or elements, and it is this "extra-systematic" information that may indeed seem to later generations or to those outside the culture a wellspring of that culture's vitality. Describing cinematic production in Italy during the 1920s and 1930s, as a stage in an evolutionary process, is made difficult by the fact that any historical or cultural description is always more organized than its object—especially when one attempts to develop one's own *system*, which necessarily excludes some elements as being irrelevant.

Because, as German literary theorist Hans Robert Jauss has noted, history is a *process* of cultural reception and production which occurs through a variety of cultural forms, the project of a historian (like that of an ethnographer) should be devoted to continually collecting, mapping, and deciphering the *traces* or left-over data from this process. A historian does not, however, simply *record* this information; in deciphering the "story"—his object—a historian redefines it and thus couches it in a style that itself connotes an order. David Chaney, remarking on a similar observation by Geertz, suggests that "the connotative order of style is part of the logic of situations, but it is an order that the ethnographer, as well as the historian, participates in not observes."[50] Others, including the distinguished British historian Edward Hallet Carr, have under-scored the dialogic nature of historical discourse and exposition by observing that history itself is not factual but processed—its validity resulting largely from a consensus reached by readers about the historian's organization of information and by the ability of the historian to process his information in a way that is accessible to his audience. The historian's perspective should not, therefore, be construed as entirely privileged or objective, since his perception and rendering of his object of study is always mediated and codified—his "facts" never arbitrary.

My own project is not intended to offer a final, definitive statement about Italian Fascism or Italian prewar cinema. Rather, it is an attempt to revive and reintroduce these neglected texts into the discourses of film history. In this sense, my subject is as much about Fellini's *Amarcord* and a contemporary dialogue on film, history, and cultural politics as it is an attempt to reconstitute the dialogic nature of cinematic production in the 1920s and 1930s. It is also an attempt to understand *differences* in the definition and representation of Fascism, popular culture, history, and film's place in the construction and reconstruction of these subjects. I must also admit that I do not attempt to draw absolute conclusions about the structures of thought during this period as they are revealed in film images and narratives. Certainly, my list of films is fragmented and incomplete.[51] On the other hand, I am not intending to present the social and political milieu as a coherent body of events, only to articulate the var-iegated and often conflicting implementation of ideological codes. As long as one is immersed in imaging and myths as evidence, one is trapped in a play of mirrors wherein one moves from reflection to reflection. Levi-Strauss poses the problem most succinctly when he states that "myth analysis does not have and cannot have as its object to show how men think. . . . Thus we do not aim to show how men think in myths, but how myths think themselves in men, and

without their knowing it."[52] My own approach to the codes of cinematic production is not a traditional structualist or myth-ritual analysis of this period; I
am very much interested in examining the material organization of cinematic
production and the policy that emerged concurrent with this effort to organize
production. Levi-Strauss's comment, however, makes problematic some of the
central assumptions that have guided numerous traditional social histories and
sociological studies of mass media, namely that one's theoretical/analytical
model somehow neutralizes ambiguity and contradiction in the study of effects
and that the events or actions which can be discussed empirically are not continually mediated and somehow occur within a stable and unified system.

Many of these concerns have entered into my decision about how best to
organize my materials. In order to examine cinematic production in Fascist Italy
and the emergence of cinema as a *popular* form, I am not only interested in
explaining efforts to systematize cinematic production but also in charting the
large zones of ambivalence that are part of cultural change, cultural production.
By working primarily through a textualist approach, i.e., one that begins with
and builds on models of feeling and "root metaphors" (in order to reconstruct
their various groupings and then to consider connections and tensions among
these groupings), I am better able to underscore the "octopoid" systemization of
cultural production. Because a film produced in this period took on meaning
and significance amidst a variety of historically concrete and changing forms,
each film is discussed (or placed) amidst a field of competing forms; each interpretation acknowledges or is intended to bring into play the tensions exerted by
the other models. By discussing a film in terms of its production amidst a field of
contradictory models and ideological imperatives, one is better able to recognize
the film as process, i.e., as responses to a changing cultural environment and as
an increasingly powerful voice in a dialogue about these changes.

During the 1920s and 1930s, cinematic expression constituted a modern language best able to represent the tensions, fears, and desires of Italy's rapidly
changing social and cultural environment. Film distribution facilitated a broader
discourse, making the social "marginality" of cinematic expression an increasingly preferred mode of addressing these concerns. As cinematic production emerges as a national–popular language, it is inscribed by material, social,
and cultural pressures from within and without (much as was the "*borgo*" in
Amarcord). Out of necessity, it drew from and translated foreign cultural models
(particularly cinematic ones) that had become by the late 1920s a force in the
national consciousness and vocabulary. At the same time, however, it attempted
to rework or conserve qualities of traditional Italian models or of forms previously enjoyed by a more elite social group.

In the following chapters, I have charted a "tropological" catalogue or *encyclopedia* of Italian film culture in the 1930s—a transcription, if you will, of some of
the key rhetorical figures in this popular language. Through these discursive
categories, I examine the structured "ways of seeing" and the values attached to
those ways. As social theorist C. Wright Mills has noted (drawing from similar
notions by Kenneth Burke): "Back of a vocabulary lies a set of collective ac-

tion. . . . In studying vocabularies, we detect implicit evaluations and the collective patterns behind them—'cues' for social behavior."[53] Again, however, my intention is not to examine Italy's Fascist ideology, but Italian cinematic production, which (like all acts of signification) is in part an ideological practice. I focus squarely on the techniques and forms of cinematic expression that, in their diversity, both necessitated and enabled what Gramsci described as the national–popular culture. This analysis of film's form (as historical, rhetorical, ideological process) leads me to consider the "codes" of cinematic production and exchange, and the mythology of the popular film culture. And, while each tropological field can be said to have its own history and its own mediators, these fields constitute a historical milieu—a Nature. To mobilize these myths should, if little else, remind us that worlds are *made* (and *remade*).

I *Castelli in aria*: The Myth of the Grand Hotel

> The Grand Hotel. People come. People go.
> And nothing ever happens.
>
> —Dr. Ollernschlaz, *Grand Hotel* (1932)

The Grand Hotel as Revolving Door to the "Bel Mondo"

Federico Fellini's use of the town's Grand Hotel in *Amarcord* is by no means gratuitous. For the young Titta, the hotel is an almost sacred shrine whose façade conceals exotic characters (a Prince or a Caliph) and erotic mysteries (his uncle dancing till dawn with a voluptuous Nordic vacationer). The Grand Hotel is, for the provincial community, its touchstone with a more cosmopolitan set—with that which comes from Beyond. It is the locus in the town for romance and sentimental affectation. Moreover, in Fellini's attempt to represent the "*coscienza*" of this period through certain cinematic conventions of the day, the Grand Hotel belongs to yet another code—being one of the most prominent icons or stages in films of the 1930s.

The European *hôtel de luxe* was an ideal cinematic space for the dramatic action of the films in the 1920s. It bears a marginal similarity to German Expressionism's carnivalization of cinematic space, though it is more accessible to middle-class sensibilities and much less dark and insidious in its evocation of the shadows and illusions of social existence.[1] The *mise-en-scène* of the cabaret that the lovers discover in Murnau's *Sunrise* (1928) (and less so in his *The Last Laugh*, 1924) would be an example of this setting. Essentially, however, it enabled filmmakers to appropriate theatrical set design from late nineteenth- and early twentieth-century bourgeois comedies and Naturalist dramas, which occurred indoors in boudoirs or drawing rooms and involved characters from an aristocratic or upper middle-class milieu. Even uses of the hotel in later popular forms resonate with these early stylizations. But the films in the twenties whose events transpired in a luxury hotel, at a resort, or on a transatlantic liner offered a relatively shallow dialectical conflict between socioeconomic factions; the characters in these films were generally of the same upper-bourgeois status as in the earlier Naturalist theater. Perhaps the director who most frequently adopted the Grand Hotel as dramatic space was Erich von Stroheim; films such as *Blind Husbands* (1919) and *Foolish Wives* (1921) both concern an American couple on vacation in Europe whose marriage is nearly wrecked by a beguiling foreigner (usually von Stroheim). These romantic melodramas, and others such as Mauritz Stiller's *Hotel Imperial* (1926) and Herbert Brenon's *Dancing Mothers* (1926), did much to disseminate a myth of the Grand Hotel. For 1920s American and European audiences, a Monte Carlo hotel was paradigmatic of an urbane yet slightly jaded and decadent lifestyle—tainted as it was by values that were outside the (then burgeoning) petit-bourgeois ethos and sense of order, yet fascinating for the same reason. For American audiences, the mystique of Europe, images of leisure and of passion, were all a part of the cluster of associations evoked by a Grand Hotel. For the middle-class European audiences, however, these images seemed less indexical signs of Europeanness than portrayals of what the wild, raw new people of the Western world, the Americans, were doing in characteristically American ways. Mario Baffico, an Italian director who returned to Italy from making pictures abroad, stated in 1933 that:

> The enormous fortune that has befallen the American cinema in the last few years should not be attributed solely to its early financial organization but also to the widespread acceptance of the product itself which has piqued the interest of the world because it reveals the passions, the feelings, the character and the customs of American men and women in all those manifestations of their way of life that no book, play, or journalistic report could document with such exactness.[2]

And as Robert Sklar points out: "It would be fair to say that Europeans did not go to American movies to see themselves, nor did they consider Gloria Swanson or John Gilbert 'Europeans' no matter what nationality they were presumably portraying."[3] In an age of rapid technological enterprise, the Grand Hotel was, unequivocally, an international sign, and a sign of the film industry's increasingly international character. One could even argue that, after the First World War, such visual signs as the luxury hotels, trains, and "transatlantics" greatly facilitated film's transcultural appeal. Certainly in Italy these modern film settings were bound up with an "epochalist" impulse that manifested itself through cinema both culturally and economically. For the young Titta in *Amarcord*, the Grand Hotel is emblematic of cosmopolitan leisure and the romance which that lifestyle affords. It is off limits to him but alluring to him for the same reason. It is very much at the center of his own perception of the world, since the leisure, playfulness, and spectacle that it embodies pervade his own adolescent world.

The Grand Hotel, as a "spatial model" in popular film culture, becomes in the 1930s a frequent vehicle for exercising the modern, art-deco sensibility. It is through this styling of set design that these films also depart from the codes of Naturalist sets (i.e., the drawing room) in nineteenth-century theatrical productions. And in Italy, it is through this styling that the film industry found a model more congruous with the modern tastes of their audiences. While art-deco may have informed the designs of furniture, architecture, etc., it was more a vision that (as William Everson has mentioned) was most vividly realized through popular film. Laura Nucci, an Italian actress of the period, has also affirmed that the art-deco set designs corresponded less to actual interior designs of homes in Italy than to a popular view of modernity.[4]

Besides being the result of changing sensibilities in spatial modeling, the Grand Hotel was also a product of the advent of sound. Due to technological necessities and ideological imperatives, the silent comedies, the adventure and "strongman" spectacles, and the Westerns of the 1920s dealt primarily with individual action—with "heightened essences, archetypes of certain kinds of human behavior."[5] The use of sound, however, enabled filmmakers to foreground human communication (as opposed to mime or gesture) and social intercourse—conversation, eye contact, "vibrations" between two or more people. While action in films from the 1920s may be set in a Grand Hotel, the hotel assumed a different role in the 1930s when it became an ideal space for conversational melodramas and comedies whose narratives involved more complex and multiple interactions among characters. In this way, sound enabled cinema to transpose to the screen some of the complexity of interrelationships in literary narrative; and thus, the twenties' *hôtel de luxe* also became a convenient diegetic model for exploring themes through the plurality of voices one finds in novels. Already Thomas Mann had exploited the rhetorical possibilities of luxury hotels and resorts in *Death in Venice* (1911) and even in *The Magic Mountain* (1924). In Mann's novels, the hotel displaces twentieth-century urban problems to a domain characterized by death and disease.

But, in Italian films discussed in this chapter (as in their American counterparts), the Grand Hotel instead serves as both a carnivalized space and an arena for contestation between upper-crust and petit-bourgeois values. The hotel, both an iconic reminder of traditional Naturalist theater and a visual affirmation of the outmodedness of those codes, offered a powerful *mythos* for amplifying the ideological conflict generated by social and cultural change. It is with Vicki Baum's extremely popular *Grand Hotel*, and Edmund Goulding's adaptation of her novel, that the modern *hôtel de luxe* was canonized and celebrated as its own myth. In Goulding's film, the hotel's "grandeur" manifests itself as a metaphorical hall of mirrors that magnifies and redoubles characters' fears and desires, and it is a diegetic arena for presenting a veritable Mount Olympus of *divi* and *dive*. The success of Goulding's *Grand Hotel* can be attributed in part to its adroit structuring of meta-information about the film's characters/stars; nor could such a complex narrative have been possible without the advent of sound, which helps accentuate the personality differences among this large cast of stars. The quasi-Olympian nature of the hotel results in part from the off-camera personae of the film's central characters, i.e., the fact that Beery, Garbo, and John Barrymore were established stars and myths in their own right. But the hotel itself, as symbolic sign, imparts to the characters' actions a transcendent significance.

For a national audience, for whom images of family offer indispensable models of collective identity, and for the petit-bourgeois sensibility that stresses conservative and "family" values, the Grand Hotel represents a realm in which family ties and, hence, values are no longer arbitrary and are often suspended. On vacation (staying at a hotel), one is not obliged to conduct oneself in a manner determined by the social and familial identity from which one has come. Presumably, the inhabitants of a hotel are strangers, with whom one can form a more transient and existential bond. Therefore one can do things that one could not realize at home; this is undoubtedly the situation of Otto Kringelein (Lionel Barrymore) in *Grand Hotel*. But, for those who are wealthier and more cosmopolitan, the hotel is simply "a way of life"; their quasi-divine status results from their dwelling in a domain that is in some ways divorced from the accepted social order. Baron Felix von Gargern (John Barrymore) and Grusinkaya (Greta Garbo) would be examples of characters who seem to abide eternally in the *bel mondo* of the Grand Hotel; here too one need only consider the other films in which Barrymore or Garbo live in hotels.

As an arena for social ritual, the Grand Hotel can be said to bring into heightened emotional conflict recognizable social types: e.g., the industrialist, his anonymous clerk, a bankrupt aristocrat, a stenographer, and a prima ballerina. This intimate network of easily identifiable types reduces broader, more complex social and ideological conflicts and contradictions, and, in so doing, it magnifies them. Yet by magnifying them through full, rounded signs, it masks their ambiguities; hence they are more readily managed. The "carnivalesque" nature of a Grand Hotel (as cultural model) results from its dialogic and "multivocal" expression of a social order that is highly mobile and unstable (the hotel is intended, after all, for those in transit). Its paradox is that it is both a hierarchical and a democratic realm—one that makes the alignment of disparate social types seem more plausible and more exhilarating. Though the hotel is privileged, i.e., for those more economically well off, it enhances mobility more than the boudoirs of traditional bourgeois comedy. It appears "open" to anyone who can pay for a room there and hence serves as a promise and a lure to petit-bourgeois audiences: it is recognizably out of reach and yet attainable (the regular inhabitants of the Grand Hotel simply seem to have more leisure time). In Goulding's film, the possibility of value, meaning, and status seem to materialize as Otto Kringelein and Fräulein Flämmchen depart—dazed by the emotional intensity of their experience yet spiritually (and economically) charged by it.

Rotaie: Romance along the Highway

In Italian cinema during the 1930s, the Grand Hotel is a visual leitmotif of the art-deco decor and baroque opulence characteristic of what traditional film critics and historians have described as "white telephones." One of the goals of this chapter, however, is to reevaluate this pseudogenre by considering the Grand Hotel as narrative and rhetorical strategy and as a highly ritualized, interpretive model of social experience. It is easy perhaps to understand why traditional critics often dismiss this period as an enormous repository for "white telephones," since one of the very first Italian sound films, Mario Camerini's *Rotaie* (*The Rails*, 1929), draws heavily upon the aura of the Grand Hotel and the modern myths of travel. It is somewhat more difficult, however, to ignore how this film examines the allure of the myth itself. Particularly important in this respect is the way the protagonists' experience in the film's Grand Hotel is bracketed by the futility of their existence outside it, in much the same way that Murnau and Carl Mayer introduce their lovers to the City in *Sunrise* (a film that resembles *Rotaie* in many ways).

Rotaie (conceived by Corrado D'Errico) can be examined in three stages—each one relatively autonomous. The first part of the film concerns a young, unmarried, petit-bourgeois couple's attempt to commit suicide in a third-rate hotel on the outskirts of a city. (The young man is played by Maurizio D'Ancora, one of the now famous Gucci brothers.) *Rotaie* was initially conceived, shot, and edited as a silent film, and, as Camerini explains, the decision to add music was made after completing the project. But, in the film's opening act, which uses only one title, the lack of sound seems entirely congruous with the dazed condition of the lovers, especially since narrative, photography, and editing combine to encourage an immediate bond between the audience and this couple. For instance, checking into the hotel for their last embrace, the couple seem so oblivious to the chattering of the hotel clerk and so withdrawn into their own plans that the audience's inability to hear the clerk's words only intensifies their *angst* and the audience's recognition of it. The audience is never provided with an exact motivation for their self-destructive feelings, other than some point-of-view shots of the girl reading a letter from her mother about the inability of the girl's boyfriend to ever amount to anything. Instead, the couple's environment itself is made to appear as the primary catalyst. The first scenes in front of and within the cheap hotel are shot in very dim lighting since it is night and raining. The only light in the street where we first encounter them emanates from an electric sign that reads HOTEL, and the shadowy hotel interiors seem anything but a sanctuary. And, just after the young man drops the lethal potion into a glass of water in their room, the audience views them, sitting quietly apart but for touching hands, *through* the glass's fizzing contents.

The audience is not really made aware of the lover's plans until this moment. Thus, through the black and tawdry environment, the audience is gradually led into the couple's sense of guilt (an unmarrieds' rendezvous in a hotel) and desperation. Just before they reach for the poison, however, the vibrations created by a train rumbling and whistling loudly just under their window overturn the glass. From this point, the train becomes a recurring and almost cosmic sign for the lovers and the audience. When the young man runs to the window to look after it, the sky is suddenly filled with light; the musical score changes from solemn chords to a much more gay jazz rhythm. Here the brightness gives way to a phantasmagoria of electric lights and signs that are superimposed as a collage; and the epiphanic moment climaxes with the word LUNA (moon) spelled out in the midst of electric lights that are made to resemble stars

A train station is a refuge for the young lovers in *Rotaie* (d. Camerini, 1930)—The Museum of Modern Art/Film Stills Archives

in the urban night sky. The couple then steal out of the hotel, inspired by their own bond and obliquely by their new vision of their environment, and seek shelter from the rain in a train station.

Both the couple's and the audience's perspective in this station is filtered, as it is in the 1933 Cines documentary *Ritmi di stazione* (see chapter 7), through the popular iconography of modern travel. The couple marvel at an array of posters advertising exotic hotels, vacations in Capri, and transatlantic voyages. On screen, the collage of posters is captured through fade-in and fade-out shooting; and then a close-up of one poster, an art-deco rendition of train rails, fills the screen to form an enormous, Expressionist sign. Emotionally drained by their exhilaration and having just spent their last cents for a drink to console the weak girl, the couple want to leave but lack the money to do so. In the bustle of the station, however, a well-dressed and portly man rushing to catch a train drops a wallet stuffed with money. The young man retrieves it and unsuccessfully attempts to hail the man. So, after ogling a shiny train and its fashionable passengers about to depart, they quickly board and find seats in a first-class compartment. "Where are we going?" the young girl asks her lover. "Where the others go," he replies.

Their experience in the luxurious first-class accommodations begin the second part of the narrative—a transition made clearer by the dawn of a new day. An effort is made here to convey a sense of the train's power (through whistles and other sound effects) and its speed (through shots of the rails and of the wires and cables above that are superimposed to create the image of a metal web). They arrive at a Grand Hotel in Stresa, the setting for the entire middle part of the movie. Besides appearing to be architecturally a replica of *Amarcord's* Grand Hotel, the hotel is an art-deco spectacle of modern leisure and sport: speed boats, fashionable swim wear, etc. As in the Von Stroheim films, the characters and forces at the resort test the couple's petit-bourgeois values and momentarily cause them to lose touch with their convictions. At the center of their seduction in this realm is an entourage around the Marquis Mercier, who in fact resembles one of Von Stroheim's more decadent interlopers, and the wheel of fortune at the hotel's casino. In the young man's delirium at the casino (mid-way through the film), Camerini uses an overhead shot of a whirling roulette wheel (another sign of transition and circulation that was previously suggested by the spinning wheels of the train) followed by a dizzying, refracted vision, from the young man's perspective, of the game board and chips. Both of these images contribute to the sense of instability and the carnivalization of this hall of mirrors. The couple's commitment to one another is shaken by the Marquis's attempts to seduce the girl and the young man's failures at the roulette wheel; the fact that the Marquis begins to lend the young man money (to buy the girl) only hastens their circle of despair. Again the lovers find themselves alienated and unfulfilled in their hotel existence. Unable to communicate with her withdrawn lover (again, the movie's strategic use of silence), the girl goes to the Marquis's room to "repay" for enough money to leave the hotel. At the same time, the young man (in a scene reminiscent of Alfred Hitchcock's *Rear Window*) gazes from his hotel window at other families in apartments across from his room. His late-night vision of social stability and productivity (an architect working at his drafting table, a middle-class family seated around the dinner table, a father reading his newspaper, a mother sewing, and a young boy asleep) suddenly compels him to return the Marquis's money, retrieve his fiancée, and flee the hotel.

That evening, in the final part of the film, they sleep outdoors, in a public park. Here, free from a world of façades and of a desire for status, the couple wake to a new day and experience the natural pleasures of washing their faces (including the girl's lipstick—her mask) at a simple fountain. And as they embrace, puffs of smoke from a train appear just over a hedge. On the way back to their city, they ride in an economy car filled with working-class travelers. This scene is replete with point-of-view shots of the weathered faces, the unabashed and unselfish demeanors of these working people: a mother nursing a baby, a little girl sharing her apple with the young lovers, and the young man sharing his cigarette with the little girl's father. The film closes with a shot of the lovers embracing outside a factory at the end of a working day. The sound of the factory's whistle conjures the whistle of the train throughout the movie. Having discovered their "true" place in society and having found value in a "different" view of leisure (the factory having an ambiguous correspondence with the previous hotels), the couple walk arm-in-arm down a street at sunset. What becomes problematic about this last image is in deciding how the couple have finally reached an understanding of things that is somehow not mediated by popular mythologies, as is the case earlier in the film when Camerini artfully ties the couple's desires and dreams to the iconography—the posters, etc.—of popular culture.

In *Rotaie*, as in *Grand Hotel*, the *hôtel de luxe* is an extremely unstable domain wherein fortunes and lovers can be lost in games of chance; it is also very illusory—again, a sort of hall of mirrors which enables the characters "to see themselves." Moreover, parts of the central stage of the narrative (scenes along the road) use highly stylized camera work to convey the fragmentation experienced in the *bel mondo*. The lifestyle of which the Grand Hotel is emblematic is seductive—an option not unlike the Death which they meditate. Though the lovers avoid suicide, they do pass through an other-worldly zone—the world of jaded bourgeois myths, of omnipotence, and of silent cinema's extraordinariness. This world of absolute leisure, however, prepares the couple to understand their place in the social system; in this sense, their experience at the Grand Hotel enables them to learn about "value." They are not simply returning to the urban routine that had alienated them and precipitated their fatalistic anxieties; rather, their experience as members of the leisure class makes the social and economic realities to which they return seem fresh and whole—a place where they seem to belong. Though the couple reject the deviant nature of the domain of the Grand Hotel, they are emotionally charged by it. Thus, the "social realism" of *Rotaie*'s finale, i.e., the return to the city, the factory, etc., is based on a nonmaterialistic and utopian ideal. The couple do not simply resign themselves to return to a mechanized routine; instead, they bring with them a vitality that literally illuminates their surroundings. And, for *Rotaie*'s Italian audiences, leaving the theater at the end of the film may itself be a step toward a "new" kind of *bel mondo*. Still, the power of the ending is bound up with the parodoxes and tensions produced by correspondences between the couple's embrace at sunset, after work, and the film's previous use of night imagery and its portrayal of leisure time as backgrounds for despair, resistance, and flux.

Il Signorino Gianni and *Il Signor Max*

Camerini's *Rotaie* not only denigrates upper-bourgeois manners, it attempts to reveal as well the delusions of petit-bourgeois aspirations. Therefore, when the couple return to the positions that seem fated or ascribed for them by an unnamed author, their lives seem free of delusions. Camerini employs this strategy in most of his succeeding films but especially in *Il Signor Max* (1937).[6] *Il Signor Max*, like *Rotaie*, can be divided into three stages. The first part concerns the youthful Gianni's (Vittorio De Sica) odyssey "to learn about the world"— actually the world of the Grand Hotel. His trip, paid in part by his parents, is intended to be a sort of *rite de passage* through which he will learn to be a "*signore*" (in every sense of the word). After having ardently saved enough money for his journey, he wishes his family goodbye, leaving with only a single suitcase, a borrowed camera, and some American magazines (which, he tells his uncle, should make him seem more of an English journalist and adventurer). At the station in Naples, Gianni observes a group of affluent tourists deboard a luxury bus. As he drops his *Time* and *Esquire* magazines, a couple of young women from the bus note the magazines and the American brand-name of his camera, and, after he acknowledges them in rather broken English (which he has also learned from reading foreign magazines), they assume he too is a world-traveler: "*prestigioso quel signore.*" They invite him to a party on board their liner, which is sailing for San Remo, and thus begins Gianni's brief new life as Signor Max.

Living beyond his means, Gianni quickly exhausts the limited stipend he has alloted for his journey, and he returns to his family, who are shocked to realize that he got no further than San Remo. Caught between his rejection of his family's image of him as a child and spendthrift and of their condemnation of the "loose morals" of the leisure set on the one hand, and his desire to remain Signor Max on the other, he returns to work at his newsstand. This middle part of the narrative essentially concerns Gianni's desperate attempts to overcome his alienation. Like the lovers in *Rotaie*, whose desires are first realized through popular mythologies, Gianni turns to the popular images that surround him every day at the newsstand. In fact, his transition here is cinematically charted by bridging shots of magazine covers (all English) from consecutive months. This part is replete with match cuts from Gianni's perception of a magazine image—a tennis match, for instance—to a scene wherein he attempts to emulate the image. Thus, Gianni tries his hand at tennis in July, at golf in September, etc. In this fashion, Camerini dramatizes the ideological allure of photographic (cinematic?) images in popular texts. Max, Gianni's grand delusion, is an alter-ego constituted by a collage of popular images.

As in *Rotaie*, Camerini ridicules upper-crust snobbery as much as he does Gianni's unfamiliarity with "the rules of the game" and his futile pursuit of Max and the *bel mondo*; much of the ironic humor in the film results from Gianni's awkwardness at the bridge table, on the golf course, on horseback, and so on. When Donna Paola and her entourage arrive at the Grand Hotel in Rome and soon thereafter notice Gianni (Max) at the newsstand, his efforts to maintain his double identity and to consummate his relationship with Donna Paola and her world become more hectic and, consequently, more humorous. In the midst of this comedy of confused identities, Donna Paola's maid servant, Lauretta (played by Assia Noris), suddenly recognizes Gianni's "true" self; they are, after all, cut from the same social fabric. As Max, Gianni continually deflects her queries about his identity, but as a magazine vendor he develops a more intimate relationship with her. She, who is constantly on the road, admires his family, his homespun values, his singing in a local Dopolavoro group. (And, because Lauretta's attraction to Gianni is bound up with the charm of a community infused with the spirit of the Dopolavoro, she experiences the "allure" of Fascist activities at the social level where it was most dynamic—a local, communal one.) But, when they finally kiss, it is obvious that the intensity of her emotion is

De Sica's two masks: "Signorino Gianni" . . .

. . . and "Signor Max" in *Il Signor Max* (d. Camerini, 1937)

sparked by her inability to dissociate Max's image (as Signore) from the lesser Gianni.

The final stage of the narrative occurs on a train leaving Rome. Lauretta is upset because she has had to leave Gianni. Furthermore, Gianni, who is on the train as Max, becomes disillusioned with Donna Paola and her cronies because he is emotionally shaken by his experience with Lauretta. They, in turn, rebuff him for his continued ineptitude at the bridge table, and he leaves the first-class car to find Lauretta. After they embrace, Gianni attempts to persuade her that he is actually Gianni; but she becomes outraged, refusing to believe him, and leaves the train at the next station to return to her Gianni in Rome via a second-class car. Gianni, finally recognizing his delusions, also returns to Rome, where they meet to begin their own family.

The ending of *Il Signor Max* demonstrates that, though Camerini ridicules petit-bourgeois delusions, a sense of an ending depends upon his exalting its ideology, e.g., work, family, conservative morals, etc. The *bel mondo* of the Grand Hotel and Donna Paola lure Gianni, but the film's more profound seductiveness would seem to be the unspoken magnetism of Lauretta. Still, without Lauretta's metaphorical double, Donna Paola, Lauretta's virtues would have remained obfuscated or simply dull. Once again, the social realism of Gianni's existence on the streets of Rome (though admittedly social realism in this film is somewhat less evident than in *Rotaie*) is contingent upon Gianni's attempt to maintain his double identity as Max, the Signore. Also, around Lauretta, Gianni does in fact seem self-assured (a Signore), while in the presence of Donna Paola he appears insecure. In some ways, De Sica's stardom and popularity enable him to move "naturally" between these two worlds; his celebrity status both enhances his mythical persona as Everyman and his privileged role as Max. But this was a double role that, like many of the American comedians of the 1930s (and I am thinking particularly about Capra's screwball comedies or Astaire and Rogers's musicals) often involved a symbolic marriage between the petite bourgeoisie and a mythical aristocracy. Camerini's comedies (with the possible exception of *Darò un milione*) always reject the upper-crust lifestyle. In so doing, they decry the false magic of that lifestyle and promote the social and political idealism of petit-bourgeois ideology. In light of the film's conclusion, it is evident that the *bel mondo* is a dramatic means of amplifying and testing middle-class values; by exaggerating that which is not communal, the film enables its audience to see more clearly the ideological imperative as common sense.

Working the Grand Hotels

The last of Camerini's movies in the 1930s to invoke the myth of the Grand Hotel is *Batticuore* (*Heartbeat*, 1939), starring the American John Lodge and Camerini's then wife, Assia Noris. Set entirely in Paris, this film concerns the comic romance between a female pickpocket (Noris) and an English Ambassador (Lodge). Like *Rotaie* and *Il Signor Max*, the film's dramatic conflict, and especially its screwball comedy, turns upon a series of complicated role reversals and confusions of identity—here repeatedly questioning the sacredness of private property. Like the American screwball comedies of the 1930s and like the previous comedies by Camerini, the central couple's antagonisms and romance result in part from their class and cultural differences. And in some ways, *Batticuore* parodies some of the codes of popular romances and treats ironically the idea of the theatrical double and "acting" in the world of the Grand Hotels.

The title of this section is a glib reference to the occupation of Arlette, a pickpocket, and to the parodic impulse in this later example of Camerini's Grand Hotels. Arlette, from the beginning, appears to make up for her shortcomings as a petty thief with her histrionics in tight situations, which she demonstrates in the opening scenes that introduce the male pupils in the "pickpockets' school" she attends. (The pickpockets' school is itself a theatrical space where the crooks comically practice with mannequins.) In these scenes, it is readily apparent that her role-playing is her way of delaying the inevitable act of stealing; she would, it seems, prefer a more honest occupation. During her first pickpocketing attempt, which occurs in a crowded elevator, she lifts a brooch from an elegantly attired man who turns out to be a Count. The Count, realizing her ploy, follows her into a movie theater, where she has sought sanctuary. When he confronts her, she once again launches into her dramatic repertoire of alibis; their dialogue, however, is viewed against the backdrop of a movie screen where an analogous scene is occurring (a movie with Astaire and Rogers). As in Camerini's previous films, the petit-bourgeois consciousness is tied to a popular mythology; but in this instance, the differences between *Batticuore*'s inept heroine and the polished dancers behind her are parodied.

Instead of taking her to the police, the Count escorts her to the Stivonian Embassy, where she is elegantly dressed and invited to attend a reception by the Baroness of Stivonia. Here she becomes embroiled in international intrigue and matrimonial jealousies, being blackmailed by the Ambassador to steal the watch of Lord Jerry Salisbury (Lodge), who is with the British delegation. The Stivonian Ambassador believes that the watch contains a picture of his own wife (which, in fact, it does), but Arlette notices the picture and removes it before she hands the watch over to the Ambassador, thus allaying the Ambassador's suspicions. In her attempt to replace the watch, however, Jerry notes her maneuver and, without letting on, continues the game by asking to accompany her home. Since she is afraid of abandoning her mask, she leads him to a Grand Hotel, where she signs under another name associated with the Embassy. Afterward, Arlette and Jerry pass the rest of the night at the Lapin Rouge, and, there in a garden, Jerry warns her that he can read any lies in her eyes.

From this point, the comedy of identity continues. A young colleague of Arlette's is jailed for stealing Jerry's watch a second time; when Arlette appears at the jail to vindicate her friend, she is accused of stealing the Count's brooch earlier. The Count, however, arrives to show the brooch to the police ("It's an affair of espionage," he tells the police chief) and her young colleague denies he knows her. Meanwhile, Jerry has courted Arlette. He buys her a new wardrobe when she complains that she has nothing to wear because her trunk has not arrived at the hotel, but it is not until she is once again ordered by the Count and Ambassador to steal Jerry's watch that she discovers there a photo of them at the Lapin Rouge; she recants and reveals her past to him. In the end, she and Jerry are married in a wedding attended by both high society and the pickpockets. And, while the pickpockets are tempted to go to work in such a profitable environment as this, their "professor" instructs them to restrain themselves (unless no one is watching).

Camerini, however, is not the only Italian director to invoke the myth of the Grand Hotel as matrix for ideological and sexual conflict.[7] *Una donna tra due mondi* (*A Woman Between Two Worlds*, 1938) reworks a comic formula of mistaken identities similar to that in *Il Signor Max* but here reversing gender roles in the romantic triangle to which the title alludes. The story involves a lower middle-class girl (Mira, played by Isa Miranda) who must decide between an Indian Maharaja, visiting the Grand Hotel where she works as a singer–pianist, and a cellist for the orchestra at the hotel. The film also draws upon traditional narrative formulas of theatrical comedies and silent films, in particular Achille Consalvi's *Champagne Caprice* (1919), wherein a young princess, who has been separated from her real parents during carnival and has been adopted by a moralistic bourgeois family, temporarily forsakes her vows to a young doctor when she is seduced by a gypsy violinist and nearly debauched at his luxurious villa. But, beside these comic conventions, the movie also engages some of the most enduring Gothic situations: virginal heroine imprisoned and terrified by a perversive and treacherous aristocrat.

Whereas Camerini's film treats an urban, working-class world outside the lobbies of the Grand Hotels (though a world which is nonetheless idealized), the action in *Una donna tra due mondi* is restricted entirely to the hotel itself and to the boudoir of the wealthy Maharaja. In fact, the nationalities of the protagonists are never clearly revealed or important to the action, which is not really the case in *Il Signor Max* but which is generally common in most of the films whose action occurs around the Grand Hotel. In addition, moreover, to the international or cosmopolitan nature of some of its characters and its setting, *Una donna* is based upon a German romance ("Die weisse Frau des Maharadscha") and was shot and released in two versions—a German version directed by Arthur Rabenalt and an Italian version directed by Goffredo Alessandrini.

At the outset of the film, all the employees of the hotel spare nothing to accommodate the Maharaja, who is conducting international business dealings with Western investors in his lavish suite. He is distracted, however, by music that the orchestra is playing with their rehearsal. When the orchestra is reprimanded by the hotel manager, they become annoyed and disperse. Mira protests and is subsequenty noticed by the Maharaja; claiming that she reminds him of his deceased wife, he immediately becomes infatuated with her. Mira returns to placate and reassemble the musicians—one of whom, Stefano, she fancies (though he is more intent on cultivating his skills as a musician). The central part of the narrative involves the Maharaja's attempts to seduce Mira. When the Maharaja invites Mira and Stefano to his villa, she is enthralled by its exotic

Eastern decor; and, as Stefano performs for them, the Maharaja discloses secretly his love for her. Mira demurs, saying that unlike him she lives a "hard life." Several days later, however, when a jealous Stefano rebuffs her, she begins to find the Maharaja to be a more attractive alternative: "A woman has to feel that she is loved." After Mira deserts the orchestra for the Maharaja's company, the musicians chastise Stefano and point out that "a woman's touch" is now lacking in their performance. Meanwhile, at the Maharaja's villa, Mira (in a shadowy, almost Gothic scene) also realizes that she has simply become a surrogate for the Maharaja's dead wife; simply another of his concubines. When he invites her to return to India with him, she responds, "I am a woman of my people—those who love me." Thus, in the end, Mira and Stefano each recognize that they are incomplete in themselves. Their ultimate reconciliation and reunion is celebrated when, as Mira returns to the hotel, Stefano and his orchestra pick up the tempo of the maudlin melody they are playing in order to encourage her participation in a swing tune. One could say that, through the couple's experience, the group not only realize their harmonic potential but do so through a popular musical style.

As in *Il Signor Max*, the "harmony" of this ending results when the protagonist (here a woman) rejects that which appears to be somewhat perverse, antisocial, and, literally, foreign. In *Una donna tra due mondi*, however, the Grand Hotel is the matrix for the social realities of the central characters, and their actions are given to finding an identity in such a cosmopolitan environment as the hotel—a situation that, to hear Alessandrini describe it, strangely resembles the circumstances of the relationship between the Italians working on this film and their German producers. At one point in the film, Stefano (one of the "worlds" between which Mira finds herself) does go to a pawnshop to hock his violin, but this vision of poverty and of an alternative to the Hotel existence can hardly be called social realism, since he transforms the shop into a one-man orchestra by improvising with its available instruments as a phonograph plays. But also it is only here that Stefano truly seems a master of his environment. Because Stefano and Mira are performers, the film has only to dwell on the more transcendent nature of their occupation; again, work, family, and community are promoted, but amidst a grandiose and lyrical setting that both romanticizes and exaggerates the stakes involved in their social and gender conflicts.

Not every film of this period which conjures up the myth of the Grand Hotel maintains as clear a distinction between social groups as do *Rotaie*, *Il Signor Max*, *Batticuore*, or *Una donna tra due mondi*. In Mario Mattoli's *Ai vostri ordini, signora!* (*At Your Service Madam!* 1938–39),[8] for instance, illusory and carnivalesque properties of the Grand Hotel become much more central to the dramatic action. Nevertheless, this film does draw significantly from some of the proven successes of these earlier comedies. It exploits De Sica's screen persona in earlier Camerini comedies (*Il Signor Max* in particular); here De Sica plays a penniless "little man," Pietro, who feels (and appears) more in his element among members of the upper class. *Ai vostri ordini, signora!* bears a marginal similarity as well to Gregory La Cava's *My Man Godfrey* (1936) in that its story concerns a blueblood who is compelled, due to a conflict over his inheritance, to live as a servant to the rich for nearly the duration of the film. As in La Cava's film, the central characters and the audience (as a result of De Sica's established screen persona and star status) recognize Pietro's "special" qualities from the outset—those qualities that distinguish him from other lower-class characters. However, as in the aforementioned films, he cannot accept the sham and decadence of an upper-bourgeois lifestyle; this liminoid status imparts to his character a heroic vitality that is absent among those who are more entrenched in either a work routine or eternal leisure. Unlike the conclusions to Camerini's comedies, where the petit-bourgeois character expiates his delusions about the *bel mondo*, Mattoli's film arranges a marriage between characters who at least seem to come from different socioeconomic backgrounds.

The point of departure for *Ai vostri ordini, signora!* is the opening of a Grand Hotel somewhere in France. However, in an almost Pirandellian fashion, the audience is encouraged to mistake the hotel's lavish decor, which crews of workers and directors are scurrying to complete, for the props of a stage production that is about to begin. This ambiguity is reinforced when the central characters—a group of potential employees for the hotel (of whom Pietro is one)—first appear for a screening by the hotel manager as a sort of traveling company of performers, e.g., one has been an actor, another a musician, etc. The manager, after scrutinizing them, assigns each one a duty and a room in the hotel. Thus, from the outset, the workers appear to those who have no previous experience with their respective chores but who are simply playing them as actors. Yet, as the hotel manager briefs them on their responsibilities and the hotel's priorities, he also implies the rules of decorum by which they should act with respect to the affluent clientele whom they will serve. In this sense, the Grand Hotel again reduces a general social structure to more intimate and erotic confines; it transfers the prevalent codes of social conduct to a realm where the emotional stakes of social action are heightened. It also serves as an illusory and comic realm where image and identity are confused and where characters are often duplicitous.

When Pietro appears the next evening as the guests arrive and is outfitted in a white dinner-jacket instead of his designated dark suit, the hotel manager protests. But when Pietro is subsequently caught hobnobbing at the bar with an old friend who is one of the guests and later is observed eating at a table as if he were a guest, the manager becomes incensed and threatens to dismiss him. His position is saved (or "displaced") when a wealthy woman (Manon), noting his attire and demeanor, mistakes him for a guest; after explaining to her his financial situation, she offers to hire him to play the role of her husband. Thus Pietro's role as manservant is turned to an even more intimate and private end; and the irony of the subsequent action is augmented when it is revealed that Manon's mother, who lives in the same house, is also a paid actress. In Manon's home as well as in the Grand Hotel (both of which are highly illusory settings), social identities are constantly renegotiated. Dramatic conflict in the Grand Hotel appears to result from Pietro's inability to establish clearly a social identity, i.e., with respect to the rich and the workers; and in Manon's quarters, conflict arises from Pietro's inability to acquire a clear "role" in the family, i.e., as true provider and *signore* or as imitation and gigolo. By moving their relationship at the hotel to her boudoir, the obstacle (social taboo) that separates them also becomes more prominent. Ultimately, Pietro leaves Manon, saying that he loves her but that he is not worthy of her "status"; he then goes to Paris where he works in a restaurant—*hôtel de luxe* for six months. But, in the finale, Manon appears (she is about to be married in his hotel) and the couple realize their suppressed desire for one another. As they leave her wedding party to create their own, news arrives of Pietro's inheritance; but the messenger, after noting Pietro's happiness, decides to relate the news the next day: "He should think he's poor for one more night."

In one respect, *Ai vostri ordini, signora!* capitalizes on De Sica's earlier success in Camerini's films as petit-bourgeois comic hero. As Mattoli explains in a more recent interview, "I am unable to defend this type of comedy [referring here to *Ai vostri ordini, signora!*] because it was the kind of thing that producers from that era tried to do with successful actors and actresses."[9] But, unlike Camerini's films or the American screwball comedy, it lacks an accentuated material dialectic that is played out through the dramatic conflict. As in *Una donna tra due mondi*, the film's action occurs in the Grand Hotel and in a French boudoir— more reminiscent of twenties romantic comedies and melodramas.[10] Even the employees of the Grand Hotel are presented more as actors or performers than as workers, and the hotel imparts to these characters a more ironic than tragic significance. All accept their position except De Sica's Pietro, whose wealth and value have simply been deferred until the film's conclusion. Consequently, Pietro must vicariously relearn the "roles" of high society by playing the part of a gigolo. And, because of the narrative centrality of Pietro's perspective, the audience may well be induced to reject the snobbery of that class and hence to purge their own desire for it. The interval during which Pietro works at the restaurant is necessary because it enables him (and the audience) to reaccept Manon, the object of his desire for higher status, value, and meaning—but only insofar as his true value (signaled by the news of the inheritance) is no longer contingent upon her.

In *Ai vostri ordini, signora!* the lifestyle of the luxury hotel is not wholly admonished; Pietro and Manon's reunion and probable marriage seem to intimate an inevitable return to it. But in no way does their reconciliation indicate a return to the same delusions—the more traditionally decadent ones of the world Manon dominates. The "real" family which they will begin will be one informed by Pietro's temporarily detached perspective, though his attitude has not ostensibly been aligned with working-class values. The happiness that results from Pietro's *popular* ideals can only be realized as the messenger's observation attests, to such fleeting illusions of communality celebrated in the film's final festivities.

Because *Ai vostri ordini, signora!* marginalizes Pietro's experiences outside the *bel mondo*, it masks or glosses (to a much greater extent than the other films I have discussed thus far in this chapter) the material dialectic or class differences that have, in part, generated the dramatic conflicts. As in *Una donna tra due mondi*, however, this brief "outside" experience is necessary for his *conversion*, as an upper-crust character, to *popular* ideals. Another of Mattoli's films, *La dama bianca (The Lady in White*, 1938) and Enrico Guazzoni's *Ho perduto mio marito!* (*I've Lost My Husband*, 1937) are sexual comedies whose protagonists are both from the upper social echelon. In these two films, the luxury hotels where the action occurs allow the films' central couples to reverse or suspend their normal social duties; but the female is not overtly related to an inferior social caste. Instead, Nino Besozzi (who is the male lead in both movies) plays rather foppish characters who are continually duped and outwitted by the female leads. It is sufficient to say that in *La dama bianca* the hotel is seen by the husband as an insane asylum, a place where all social and even physical laws are suspended, where he cannot distinguish his dream (the myth of the White Lady) from reality (his wife). This more radical carnivalization of the hotel setting may attest to a more widespread familiarity at this time with its *aura* and its place in popular film culture. Due to the hotel's magical properties, the couple's sojourn becomes a means of revitalizing their marriage, which is threatened by the husband's inability to suppress, on the one hand, his superactive libidinal impulses to chase other women and, on the other, to gratify his desire to meet his ideal woman ("*la dama bianca*"). It is more relevant here, however, to examine Guazzoni's film because its theme more clearly concerns the *bel mondo*, which is at the center of the myth of the Grand Hotel.

In *Ho perduto mio marito!* Besozzi appears as a Count who has not left his estate for five years because, as we learn later, he laments the marriage of his cousin, with whom he has been enamored. After five years, though, she calls to tell him that she has been abandoned by her husband and now, for purposes of "consolation," would like to meet him at a hotel in Florence. In the end, she reveals to him that she was never married, but meanwhile the unspoken taboo against adulterous and incestuous sex makes for comic situations and an intensification of desire. Their kinship and his belief that she is married licenses them to sleep under the same roof but, for the very intimacy of the situation, calls attention to the taboo which separates them. Consequently, their odyssey from one hotel to another ritualistically reaffirms the taboo—the only obstacle that prevents them from consummating their desire and resolving the dramatic conflict. The other factor that propels the film's narrative is that they play the role of married couple each time they check into a hotel. Thus, the anonymity afforded by their flight from one hotel to another confers upon them the image of family without the restraining "moral" obligations implied by this bond. The film's paradox is that the couple can remain apart and not only suffer unrequited desire but remain solitary and antisocial, or that they can gratify that desire but violate a social taboo. This paradox is managed only through euphemisms and a metaphorical language. At the end, when Giuliano (Besozzi) discovers that Valentina (his cousin, played by Paola Barboni) is not married, he drives to Rome to retrieve her. He forces her into his car; and, when she demands to know where he is taking her, he merely replies: "To your husband." Her response: "Why not!"

Ho perduto mio marito!, an ostensibly apolitical, sentimental comedy, conveys some very subtle messages about social and political institutions. Most of the film's action occurs either at the estate of the Count, at Valentina's plush art-deco apartment in Rome, or in hotels. Moreover, the drama lacks the sharp class conflict that appears in Camerini's or Capra's films. The Count's only activity seems to be bird-hunting, and Valentina's occupation is never specified. The only (yet singularly significant) occasions in the film when work and a lifestyle other than that of the protagonists become even a peripheral issue occur when the couple visits a rural *osteria* and when they visit a factory in Rome. However, in each case the audience is encouraged, in part because of the film's emphasis on Guiliano and Valentina, to view the *contadini* of the tavern or the proletariat at the factory only in terms of the *bel mondo* (the world of eternal play) to which they belong. In fact, they only arrive at the factory as the workers are leaving. Here, they are taken on a tour of the "recreational" facilities: a commodious bar, huge Olympic swimming pool with a series of high-diving platforms, and an adjacent gymnasium. In a subsequent scene, they are escorted through the factory's well-ordered nursery, where children are being fed; later, a group of uniformed children are shown at play—though their activity is rather regimented and choreographed. Obviously, these are all modern reforms instituted in the spirit of the government's Dopolavoro program; but the audience (through the couple) never observes actual production and is left with a feeling that this factory manufactures dreams rather than more tangible goods. In this sense, the factory is itself a sort of Grand Hotel at which the couple have stopped along their journey. It is also possible to understand how such an otherwise abstract and contradictory economic theory as Fascism's "corporativism" is concretized or documented for popular audiences through a film such as *Ho perduto mio marito!* The imaginary realm (diegetic world) provided by this film's narrative lends presence to the *organic* nature of a "corporate" state by reducing the disparity between social lifestyles to a common and popular image of leisure activity.

Italy as Grand Hotel

Whereas the factory in *Ho perduto mio marito!* seems to be a replication of the Grand Hotel (in context with the hotels where the rest of the dramatic action occurs), in Augusto Genina's *Castelli in aria* (*Castles in the Air*, 1939), all of Italy appears as a land of Grand Hotels, as a playground for the wealthy, and as a locus for the romantic mysticism of the film's two lovers. It offers an image of a unified Italy (one without significant regional distinctions) by displacing the action to a lyrical level where it *can* be unified. *Castelli in aria* differs from the rest of Genina's films made in Italy during the late 1930s and early 1940s, e.g., *Lo squadrone bianco*, *L'assedio dell'Alcazar*, and *Bengasi*—all of which have moved some critics and historians to describe him as Fascist Italy's "warrior bard." Yet the movie is very much the product of a director who traditionally worked in a number of countries outside Italy. In considering the ideological implications of this film, it is also difficult to ignore that it was filmed in two versions (German and Italian) at Cinecittà in 1938–39—a period when Adolf Hitler's celebrated trip to Rome was supposed to herald a new era of solidarity between the two countries and a period following a 1937 "film treaty" between them. From a production standpoint, *Castelli in aria* can be understood as the fruit of LUCE's attempt in the late thirties to make the Italian film industry more competitive by promoting international distribution. Genina's international experience makes him an ideal director for such an agenda. Also, in the spirit of the new Italian–German relationship, the producers assign the leading roles to Vittorio De Sica and Lilian Harvey (each extremely popular stars in their respective countries and abroad). From a consumption standpoint, however, it is necessary to recognize the somewhat diverse repertory or cinematic personae that De Sica and Harvey bring to bear in this film and that make it a valuable text for understanding a widely disseminated image that Italian audiences viewed of themselves and that the industry exported to other audiences.

Castelli in aria in many ways is characteristic of the operettas that Harvey had helped popularize in Germany and throughout Europe in the early 1930s, especially *Der Kongress Tanzt* (1931), wherein she plays a flirtatious Viennese girl who becomes involved in affairs of state. But De Sica too had become a popular singer in the Za Bum group and also in films (*Napoli d'altri tempi, Amo te sola,* and *Due cuori felici*); and there had been a number of Italian sound films that, while not exactly German operettas or Hollywood musicals, frequently integrated musical numbers or used a song for narrative continuity (*La segretaria privata, La canzone dell'amore, Rubacuore, Nina Falpalà, La telefonista, Gli uomini, che mascalzoni, Darò un milione*). In any case, De Sica's character may well have helped naturalize or domesticate the film's narrative formula and use of dance for Italian audiences through his previous roles as singer and through his familiar personality as the "*bravo ragazzo,*"[11] which he especially cultivated in Camerini's films. In *Castelli in aria* (as in *Darò un milione* and *Il Signor Max*), he again plays a character who is believable as either petit-bourgeois or aristocratic and other-worldly, as one who appears insensitive and superficial yet who is actually romantic and generous:

> . . . [W]ith *What Rascals Men Are!* DeSica became a movie actor; but more than that, he became overnight the number one male *star* of our cinema. Since then he has become his own character . . . a sincere, Italian character. A sentimental young man, with simple pleasures and docile, used to hard work, and after work finding familiar and tranquil places. A really fine fellow. The shy gentleness of that young man is every bit Italian. A candor of the streets and of an unpretentious life; a lovingness one encounters by chance, genuinely, without complications.[12]

Through these two actors, *Castelli in aria* integrates narrative formulas and cinematic types of two national mythologies (though in order to clarify this point, it is necessary to analyze the film's narrative).

Castelli in aria adopts a narrative formula at least as old as Camerini's *Rotaie*: two "little people" (petit-bourgeois, young, etc.) temporarily live the life of the *bel mondo*, only to become disillusioned with it and to reaccept the values to which they were initially insensitive or which were hidden from them. The "twist" is that this story begins in a contemporary German city where Lilian Harvey, Annie, works in a theater as a seamstress and wardrobe lady to the chorus girls. Dissatisfied with her lot in life and desiring a more exotic environment, she accepts an offer by a wealthy German industrialist, Foster (a veritable father-figure), to accompany him to Capri. Attempting to fulfill her dreams, he tells her that he has arranged for them to be accompanied by a friend of his who is an actual Prince. De Sica, on the other hand, plays an unemployed Neapolitan violinist in the same German city who has, coincidentally, decided to return to Italy on the same train. On the train, Foster becomes agitated because the Prince has not yet arrived. But, in passing a second-class compartment where the violinist and a friend of his are seated, he overhears the musician pacify a crying German child by singing him a German lullaby. (In a cross-cultural context, this scene is significant since De Sica begins to sing the child an Italian song but is reminded by the others in the compartment that the still-crying child is German.) Both Foster and the people in the compartment are impressed by the Italian's resourcefulness and his "natural" talent in resolving this crisis. Therefore, Foster immediately offers to employ him to play the role of the Prince and to escort Annie (who he says is his daughter) during their vacation to Capri. The violinist declines, expecting the girl to be cold and unattractive, but he readily consents when he is introduced to her; having noticed her the previous day in a department store where she was sent on an errand with a beautifully groomed dog, he is under the impression that she too is wealthy. At one point, he gallantly defends her in public after, in a moment of hysteria, she pulls the train's emergency-brake cord. The audience is led to presume that had they met in their ordinary roles, they would not have recognized the value (partly a monetary one) of the other, but that here, on the road where they only see the *mask* the other has donned, their affections blossom.

The middle part of the narrative concerns their momentary interludes in Venice, Florence, and finally Capri. Each location appears less as a city (in terms of social realism) than as a rich and baroque encyclopedia of myths and legends related to Annie by the Italian musician/Prince. His new role as consort enables him to become not only an intimate and friendly tour guide to Italy for the German Annie, who has never been there before, but it also invests the Italian Prince with certain oracular powers, since he brings to life all of her fantasies (and his own) about these places. In Venice, for instance, the couple stand in Piazza San Marco as Annie recites to him various legends of Venice. Then, while gliding along the canals in a gondola, the imposter fabulates about the royal ladies in his aristocratic lineage—all the while intentionally confusing them with stories of famous lovers in Venice. (One of his tales involves a youth who rescued his beloved from drowning in a canal—a tale which alludes to the earlier episode on the train in which he publicly defended her.)

Naturally, their excursion through the *bel mondo* would not be complete without staying at Grand Hotels; after all, there is, as indicated in Goulding's film, a Grand Hotel in every city of the world. The counterfeit Prince having seduced Annie in Venice with tales of romance, the couple move toward consummating their relationship in Florence. Here the emotional vortex into which they have plummeted is conveyed in an absolutely lyrical fashion. After the musician borrows enough money from Foster to fill Annie's hotel room with bouquets of flowers and packages full of dresses—unequivocal signs to her of his Princeliness—she erupts into song and dances over the dresses and amidst the flowers. The lyricism of life in the *bel mondo* is further enhanced as the couple venture that evening to an abandoned castle in the country, which the counterfeit Prince claims belonged to his family. In its courtyard, intoxicated by her belief that she is in the presence of one who can fulfill her desires (sexual and economic), she dances around fountains. After her dance, the musician/Prince sings to her in Italian and they enjoy their first kiss. Here, song and dance enable them to surmount any cultural differences (which have admittedly been reduced from the outset by the fact that the entire cast speaks Italian) and to realize the meaningful and abundant world to which they have aspired. After establishing the mood of this place, they enter the castle to feast in a late-night picnic. Through the "magic" of a lap dissolve, the dusty table on which they place their meager meal becomes a splendid banquet board and the room is soon filled with characters dressed in Renaissance costume. The subsequent action is rather mystical and surreal. Foster, Annie's patron, appears as a kind of master of the castle, explaining that he is the Prince's great uncle. Replicating their actual relationships, Foster, the Lord, transforms Annie into a Princess adorned in lavish gowns (he is, after all, the one paying for her furs and her fantasy). Annie, in turn, transforms the violinist into a real Prince. Having thus invoked the divine origins of his lineage, and celebrated by the ghosts of his ancestors, the couple are again transformed through a lap dissolve, this time into an eighteenth-century lord and lady dancing a minuet. The camera dollies away from their dance, and De Sica leaves her performing on a stage for a room full of spectators. Finally, in the midst of this dance, another lap dissolve returns them to their "regular" clothes and the castle's empty room. Infused by the euphoria of this vision, the Prince closes the scene with a more contemporary jazz number. In this hyperbolic realm where the couple sing and dance instead of speaking, they seem made for each other; their present roles and their relationship appear to be preordained by Nature and tradition. Moreover, this sequence demonstrates the German stylistic impulse in the film; it is one of the rare Italian films of the thirties that involves spirits and other supernatural occurrences. Conversely, this kind of radical displacement serves as a pretext for song and dance; thus Annie, who is actually a frustrated performer (having to work "backstage") is able to unleash her latent virtues.

Emotionally deflated by their experience at the castle, the couple arrive at

Capri. Here the musician becomes disillusioned with his charade and asks Foster to release him from his role, claiming that he has become simply Foster's invention. Foster complies and so ends the couple's "three days in paradise." De Sica's musician presumably remains in Naples, and Annie is left distraught and wondering about his disappearance. As this scene fades, the action shifts back to the theater in Germany, where Annie works frantically to ready costumes for that day's rehearsal. Foster appears backstage and explains De Sica's disappearance, his own motives, and his regrets about her lingering unhappiness. All is not lost, however, as the violinist (in a cross cut) appears in the lobby of the theater to audition for the orchestra. The couple rediscover each other in the auditorium during a break between rehearsals. At the moment when they realize their love and social equality, i.e., that neither is really wealthy, the cast pours into the auditorium through the lobby exits and forces the couple onto the stage. When the director angrily demands to know who they are and what they are doing at "center stage," they both grin sheepishly and explain that they are the proverbial ideal couple and are about to be married.

This finale is somewhat Pirandellian and very much in the spirit of the Hollywood "backstage musical," where stage performances ironically redouble and redress the dramatic conflict offstage. On the one hand, this diegetic strategy calls attention to the fictive nature of the film's characters, to the formulaic nature of the narrative, and ultimately to the theatrical *magic* which has reunited them. On the other hand, the strategy undercuts any predisposed distinction between the stage and that which lies beyond the lobby—between cinematic illusion and social reality. Because the audience has been encouraged to identify with the couple's suffering and euphoria, they too (vicariously, of course) are compelled from the auditorium to *center stage*, where their vision and values are galvanized by the flood of the spotlight that illuminates the couple. They too become *actors* (in every sense of the word); their "natural" talent and lyricism, which have remained private—if not frustrated and obfuscated—throughout the film, are here recognized and applauded. The film's narrative does not concern a struggle of Good against Evil as much as it is a celebration of bourgeois consciousness and its system of representation and entertainment (popular songs) by rediscovering its mythical origins through classical song and dance. Here the myths of Italy and De Sica's imagined pedigree appear to legitimate the social identity of the couple in the finale. They have not really overcome their desire for transcendence (Foster in the end is a benign figure), but they have shunned the role-playing which he has prescribed. No longer *his* puppets, they believe that their actions are autonomous; yet they are still emotionally charged by their image at the castle in Italy. Thus, in the end, they become the *protagonists* of everyday life—models on a stage for the film audience to celebrate.

At an ideological level, *Castelli in aria* is a rather slippery subject for analysis simply because it was, from the outset, produced for audiences of two countries. I have already mentioned the popularity of the film's stars in their respective countries, but it is easy to understand how a movie such as this disseminated the myth of a working cultural alliance between Italy and Germany. From a German standpoint, De Sica's lineage and Italy as a sort of Green World (to borrow a term from Northrop Frye) are the perfect *backdrop* for Harvey's arias. From an Italian perspective, Harvey would seem to invigorate Italy with her song. These levels of meaning are never actually articulated but are suggested by the choreographed whirl of the couple as they dance. Moreover, on this lyrical level, Italy (Venice, Florence, Naples) seems regionally unified; the film's absence of social realism in depicting Italy enables the characters to harmonize effortlessly—without being impeded by regional dialects and the like.

Fascism and the Mood of the Grand Hotel

Perhaps, however, one of the most confusing aspects of *Castelli in aria*, as in many of the films that invoke the myth of the Grand Hotel, is that its comic element (lyricism, role reversals, mistaken identities, "renewal") would seem counterproductive to the political consensus which Fascism attempted to instill. This theme has been upheld recently by Ernesto Laura, who believes that the historical "failure" of Italian Fascism resulted from its not having succeeded entirely in creating a political consensus.[13] He argues that the necessary consequence of a political consensus would be the creation of a common, model citizen who responds to the system and is able to integrate himself in it homogeneously—to become, in other words, a "Fascist man." However, he sees comedy and humor (particularly in the theatre, the cinema, and even literature) as having produced an image of man who is alien and really antithetical to the Fascist universe—one who pretends not to recognize it. Laura's observation is rather convincing with respect to the ideals of the comic film talents whom he cites, e.g., Campanile and Zavattini's contributions as writers, the antics of Totò, and, eventually, the Fellini and Fabrizi line. But I would certainly question or qualify his criteria for emphasizing playwrights and actors who can more easily be tied to post–World War II styles and his assertion that Zavattini's desire to address the humanity around him, outside of the official political forms, was somehow outside of a popular ideology. First, the popularity of Camerini's comedies—ones that Laura does not include in his group and that Zavattini (though he co-wrote the script for Camerini's *Darò un milione*) sees as different from his own conception of comedy—should not be an indication of their inferiority or "regressiveness." Viewing their popularity against shifting audience expectations and traditional forms, one may better appreciate how comedies such as *Il Signor Max* demonstrate the incongruities of popular mythology and how they *decompose* (to use Pirandello's expression) both their popular heroes and the *bel mondo* by calling attention to their pretenses to reality. Second, moreover, comedy and laughter, as Henri Bergson has explained, are not disinterested (as Laura has indicated). For Bergson, comedy organizes and directs laughter; this accounts for its rhetorical and ideological force. Laughter, he explains, is inseparable from social life, although insufferable to society . . . it is, above all, a corrective . . . being intended to humiliate, it must make a painful impression on the person against whom it is directed. By laughter, society avenges itself for the liberties taken with it. It would fail in its object if it bore the stamp of sympathy or kindness.[14]

Furthermore, a comic hero is profoundly ambiguous; though the comic hero is an Imposter, one who profanes or seems to ignore accepted social conduct, his misconduct calls attention to social taboos and invites condemnation and expiation. Popular comedy, as Bakhtin notes, is a dynamic agent in changing cultural orientation; and the comic spirit of the films discussed in this chapter is part of the Grand Hotel's romantic aura and what enables parody of life outside its walls. In turn, the humor of these films often results from the paradoxes of the Grand Hotel and the ambivalence of laughter at actions there. In one sense, the *hôtel de luxe* conjures traditional theatrical settings, the decorum and snobbery of the *bel mondo*. In another sense, however, the hotel—as public and carnivalesque space—actually enables characters such as De Sica's Gianni to parody what is institutional and traditionally proper through his own bumbled efforts to be part of that world (i.e., to be Max).

Laura's belief that the antics of the comic hero in Italian 1930s films made the hero appear either revolutionary or disinterested seems tenuous if one considers these comedies as rites of purification for the overwhelmingly Catholic and conservative lower middle classes—a group whose economic insecurity demanded an image of impregnable, "sane" values. The comic hero, in this case, would be a kind of "diplomatic artist," who vicariously manages social conflict and deviance by "purging" that part of him which was truly disinterested and snobbish. For instance, in Camerini's *Il Signor Max*, De Sica's ambiguous hero (Gianni) ultimately casts a cynical eye on Max, the old Bourgeois myths, the *bel mondo*, etc., and embraces family and communal values. Although Besozzi's character in *Ho perduto mio marito!* belongs to the upper crust, he too overcomes his initial solipsism. Like Foster, the German industrialist in *Castelli in aria*, Besozzi's Count Giuliano provides a friendly and harmless image of upper-crust society. The conclusion of *Castelli in aria* allows De Sica's character to reject Foster's manipulation (that which obfuscates the violinist/Prince's *true*, whole self) without excluding Foster from the comic society. The domain of the Grand Hotel highlights the value of the common man, which has been tarnished in a daily routine in the impersonal urban environment where he lives. The Hotel offers a marginal dissociation from obligations that allow for recognition of his virtue; once his virtue is realized, he can bring to the world of necessity a spiritual and emotional verve as well as a sense of communality and wholeness. Perhaps the audience's desire for transcendence, for the absolute leisure afforded by the *bel mondo*, is not entirely quashed; in fact there is every reason to believe that the flames of desire are fanned by such a decorous image of transcendence as the Grand Hotel offers. However, the work ethic in such films as *Rotaie* or the family inheritance in *Ai vostri ordini, signora!* prove to be the most accepted means by which this leisure can be obtained.

In many ways, the myth of the Grand Hotel is at the root of the political paradox concerning the politics of Fascism during the late 1920s and throughout the 1930s. The problem faced by film critics of this period was to discover a rhetoric that reconciled an aesthetic bias against seemingly apolitical cinema, i.e., "escapist" films, with a populist ethic. On the one hand, critics such as Luigi Freddi in "Arte e popolo"[15] and Luigi Chiarini in *Il cinematografo* express the merits of arts which address the sensibilities of the public. Chiarini agrees that "it [Italian cinema] will not be a bourgeois cinema with movie idols . . . but a realistic cinema, in the sense of a spiritual reality . . . cinema by people and for people in a human and not demogogic sense—in our tradition of popular arts."[16] He sees this public in opposition to the corrupt and decadent world associated with the upper classes:

> The People don't go to the cinema to amuse themselves frivolously with the legs of girls . . . the People go to the cinema to be moved, to take in, to penetrate life more deeply. . . . The People love a strong and open diet, and they detest the delicate and insipid sauces which are so dear to sour stomachs.[17]

He also sees it as anti-intellectual and anti-literary, as is evident in a later article for *Bianco e nero*.[18] The critical contradiction occurs when Chiarini denounces "escapist" cinema; his aversion to escapist cinema is perhaps one of the only times his position coincides with a more anti-populist critic such as Umberto Barbaro.

To Umberto Barbaro (one of the early champions of Italian Neorealism), Genina's *Castelli in aria* and the film comedies of this period were "decadent" simply because they were conventional, because they were derivative and not didactic:

> This genre is a product of decadence and of the type of turmoil that occurs when one places blind faith in a little quick dialogue which is indicative of a hasty production—one whose sole intention is to make money because it employs without shame the most banal means of pleasing its audience and whose only purpose is to amuse.[19]

In his review of the Biennale di Venezia for *Bianco e nero* in 1939, he laments the popularity of *Castelli in aria* and Camerini's *Grandi magazzini* (another "sentimental comedy"): "It's amazing that Genina is capable of this kind of trifle, *Castles in the Air*; it is so damaging to the director's reputation which is solidly grounded on such films as *Cirano*, *Corsaro*, and *Miss Europe*."[20]

It is difficult to determine whether, by condemning these films as distractions, as pure recreation, and as "*solletiche per le siete del pubblico,*" Barbaro ignores their ideological value for political or for aesthetic reasons (especially in light of his later aesthetic, which itself was political). But, with respect to Chiarini's populism, it is evident that the general critical debate concerning how best to reconcile political and aesthetic standards with popular tastes results from their failure to recognize (or at least to articulate) the complex relationship between ideology and comedy, and an inability to recognize that these Grand Hotels were not simply escapist but necessary constructions of national sentiment. These "castles in the air" offered an imaginary celebration of social harmony and change and of Italian Fascism's myth of State. They offered an illusory and ambiguous arena in which ideological conflict could be expressed, celebrated, and safely challenged. The romance and intimacy of the hotel, i.e., throwing socially and economically diverse characters into highly interpersonal situations, actually amplified ideological conflict. But the erotic and nonmaterialistic aspects of hotel living usually guaranteed that differences could be surmounted.

The Epochalist Impulse in 1930s Italian Cinema

The desire among the burgeoning Italian consumer classes for the *bel mondo*—a desire which is demonstrated in films disseminating the myth of the Grand Hotel—is at least in part produced by a cultural need to establish a more clearly recognized international identity (a subject I examine more fully in the next chapter). What makes cosmopolitanism so attractive to these classes is its promise, on a cultural level, that they can be part of that which is future-oriented, modern, and (in its modernity) "transcendent." It indicates a desire to bridge regional differences, and it indicates a collective willingness to accept values alien to what might be considered an "Italian" tradition.

Basically, this futurism and internationalism are characteristic of what Clifford Geertz has described as cultural "epochalism." Geertz sees this epochalist impulse as a part of the contradictory nature of *nationalistic* movements and of modernizing societies. Nationalism, considered as a cultural event as well as a political one, is paradoxical. On the one hand, nationalistic and modernizing countries exhibit a desire to become part of a larger international community; yet foreign values appear, at the same time, to threaten "traditional" values— what Geertz describes as cultural "essentialism." These two contradictory impulses are bound up with the kind of cultural identity crisis which each developing nation experiences. In these countries, cultural production serves to *manage* the tensions and strains produced by these contradictions; yet it is only through popular rituals, ceremonies, and spectacles that, in being formalized, ideology and consensus are tested and opened to questioning.

In Fellini's *Amarcord*, the small town (despite its internal political differences) collectively celebrates national spectacles which briefly touch it, e.g., the Mille Miglia which passes through the town or the majestic Rex that glides etherially through its waters one night. Though Fellini's depiction of Italian Fascism is set in the provinces—the bastion of "*ruralismo*"—he shows the strain in the fabric of the community induced by the glamor of these foreign spectacles and by the guests of the Grand Hotel (a strain that is also apparent at the beginning of *Roma* but that is even more crucial in *I vitelloni* or *Lo sceicco bianco*). The town in *Amarcord* seems to *turn* on the impetus of traditional rituals and its desire to participate in events outside the provinces—events made accessible through the cinema. Cinema, as an emerging cultural form, was regarded in a paradoxical manner. It was seen as one of Italy's most modern cultural forms capable of disseminating images of an unprecedented national popular spirit. Yet it was also considered to be capable of presenting a *true* national popular heritage—one obfuscated by the very technology of more traditional cultural forms. It was regarded as a medium and commodity that, from its inception, had been shaped by an international marketplace and that was capable of extending Italy's cultural domain. By the mid-1930s, the creation of the Mostra cinematografica di Venezia, Mussolini's encouragement of a variety of international conclaves in Italy, and the initiation of film journals such as *La rivista internazionale del cinema educatore*, all attempted to place the Italian cinema in a more international orbit than had been the case in the previous decade.

In the following chapters, I intend to examine some of the more common epochalist and essentialist themes. Because the cinema is indeed the most international of the popular arts or mass-cultural "language" in Fascist Italy, it inevitably is inscribed with signs or traces of these ideological currents. The next two chapters, on the myths of America and on the urban, industrial myths, express most clearly the epochalist impulse; the following two chapters, 4 and 5, on the ruralist myths and the myths of divine origins, are given to more essentialist codes. It is necessary to recognize, however, that because the dramatic conflict in any of the films I discuss involves a confrontation between epochalist hope and essentialist pride (and for that matter between Culture and Nature), the distinction between these categories is provisional and each category itself is multi-faceted.

2 "Cose dell'altro mondo": American Images in Fascist Italy

> "I want to go far away, on a luxury liner . . .
> to go to America . . . to see the World."
>
> —A young lover in *Il Canale degli angeli*
> (1934)

Gradisca "Gets Her Gary Cooper"

In a recent interview (one which I have cited in my preface), Federico Fellini indicates that the world outside the town where he was reared took shape largely through the cinematic images of American movies. "America, democracy," he explains, "was for me Fred Astaire who danced on highly polished terraces or Greta Garbo who looked at us with that melancholy air, like a headmistress."[1] As a cultural exploration, *Amarcord* dramatizes the American cinema's subtle yet pervasive effect on the sensibilities of a relatively provincial Italian movie public.

Generally, it is the townspeople's apparent unawareness of the imported cinematic images that confers to their actions an ironic significance; as Titta's mother's funeral procession passes somberly through the town's streets, the carriage pauses momentarily before a wooden promotional effigy of Laurel and Hardy ("*Stanlio e Ollio*"). At other times, the townspeople spontaneously construct reality from their experiences of watching American movies. For instance, as a carriage arrives laden with the town's new supply of prostitutes, one of these ladies can find no other superlative to describe an ex-paramour than that he resembled Wallace Beery. And then, of course, there are less impromptu conjurations of American cinematic personalities, such as the suave proprietor of the local cinema, who is known to all in the village as Ronald Colman. Gradisca herself is more ostensibly entranced than anyone in the town by her semiprivate interludes with American film stars. She seems to lack sexual passion, and lives instead in a more vacuous climate of sentimental affection—occasionally directed at Ronald Colman (whom she frequently accompanies in public) and once at Gary Cooper's larger-than-life visage on a movie screen. Only in the film's finale does Gradisca, as one of the revelers at her wedding banquet so

The town cinema and its American movies as backdrop for public life in *Amarcord* (d. Fellini, 1974)—The Museum of Modern Art/Film Stills Archives

poignantly puts it, "find her Gary Cooper"—a local *carabiniere* who is hardly even a meager facsimile. How, Fellini seems to ask through Gradisca's marriage, does one realize an ideal outside the movie theater?

The centrality of the town's movie theater (as a matrix for communal experiences) is ironic, since the images that create a cinema culture for the townspeople have been imported from America. Their ability to appropriate these images and to assimilate from them more personal meanings indicates a significant (though perhaps for some, ironic) connection between the value systems of these two countries. More importantly, however (and here Fellini's film is a convenient correlative), it is necessary to consider how the spirit of American cinema, both on economic and ideological levels, did much to *validate* or impel political and social action in Italy at this time. Fellini states that America, as the outside world, was glimpsed through its movies. It stands to reason that these cinematic images in turn imparted to America a grandiose significance: *through* the movies America *became* the World (as the young sailor in *Il Canale degli angeli* seems to verify). And if America was for Italian movie audiences a mythical, almost sacred, domain beyond its own cultural vista (yet a domain that, because of its exoticism, provided Italian consumer culture with models for living in a modern world), Hollywood was the Mount Olympus where its heroes, its *divi* and *dive*, abided. For many Italians whose primary means of garnering information about American culture was through the cinema and other imported popular cultural forms, the diegetic world of Hollywood film production became a mask for America itself.[2] To say, however, that America (through Hollywood) attained a sort of sacred status in the Italian ethos is not to suggest that Italian sentiment for America was always one of veneration; and often America was emblematic of an unequivocal Evil characteristic of modernity and commercialism. The important point here is nevertheless that, whether revered, parodied, or derided, Hollywood's cinematic images invested America with an almost divine *power* which during the twenties and thirties captivated Italian audiences. Mario Soldati, literary author and film director, explains: "The United States is a sublime myth: the supreme crown of all human enterprise can be achieved only in the States . . . everyone is wealthy, refined, gentlemen—this is how a young, European emigrant would have perceived America."[3]

American Movies in Italy and the Formation of Cultural Policy

The popularity of American cinema speaks primarily to the epochalist impulse in Italian culture during an age of rapid industrial development; Gian Piero Brunetta observes that America's films made this country appear in Italy to be the epitome of modernization. Undoubtedly, the lure of Hollywood images results in part from a desire among Italian audiences to be a part of the cultural fashions promulgated through those films. The newspaper advertisements for American films used such descriptive superlatives ("the greatest," "gala event," "superfilm," "colossal success from America," etc.) that they were bound to impart to the films a grandiose aura, even by the time they reached second-run houses. Conversely, essentialism (and even Italy's own imperialistic needs to assert its culture abroad) could be said to have resulted because of the overwhelming popularity of American films. In other words, the influx of "alien" values appeared to many Italians to have diluted and possibly corrupted the traditional foundation of Italian culture; essentialism and imperialism thus occurred as stabilizing reactions to the pressures induced by Italian audiences who had been exposed to foreign models.

Cyril Black sees the problem in terms of material modernization itself; later modernizers, he argues, must undertake the process not only under conditions of greater strife and instability but also under the urgent pressure of seeing before them "models so much more advanced" that the desired goal seems almost unattainable.[4] Black adds, however, that the international effects of modernization are also mutually beneficial, i.e., the benefits of material modernization in one country enable the diffusion of these benefits in another country— relieving less modern societies of costly experimentation. One of the subjects that I intend to examine in the course of this chapter is Italy's historical obligation, as a result of its modernization, to develop a "cultural policy." As Black explains, modernization tends to invest the governments of all societies with increased authority while, at the same time, it makes them more interdependent:

On the one hand, the increased authority of governments has been promoted by the need for society-wide controls in the economic and social realm in order to establish the mobilization of resources, order, consensus, and institutional uniformity called for by the requirements of modernization. On the other hand, many forces—improvement of means of communication, the universality of modern knowledge, the expansion of the area within which goods and services are exchanged, the migration of many millions of people from one society to another, the emergence of international associations of functional groups, the economic specialization of regions and even of whole societies—have tended to make societies more interdependent.[5]

The plight of Italy's film industry during the twenties and thirties was perhaps one of the clearest examples of how the economic interdependency that resulted from modernization necessitated the implementation of a cultural policy. However, one important point which needs to be emphasized here is that, despite the economic nature of relationships between film industries in Italy and America, Italy's lack of technology and weak infrastructure were not any more responsible for the demise of its film industry during the twenties than were the worn-out thematics of its own movies, together with the growing attractiveness of American images and narrative formulas. Consequently, Italy's attempt to formulate cultural policy may be seen not only as an effort to achieve a financial stability for its film industry but also to preserve and at times assert its own cultural identity in an age when the forces of modernization seemed to threaten its autonomy.

While the demise of the Italian film industry in the early 1920s may be attributed to a number of economic, political, *and* cultural changes and crises, this demise is inextricably bound up with four American-related factors: (1) expanding American distribution networks (and, I might add, the way that, on a much broader level, industrial growth and the banking infrastructure had been tied to American investment and loans);[6] (2) increasing reliance in Italian movie production and exhibition on American raw film, technology, and service (especially with the advent of sound, when Italian exhibitors were often obliged to sign service contracts; (3) American studios' ability to sell their films more cheaply abroad due to the extent of their domestic sales in the U.S.; (4) and (perhaps most important) the overwhelming popularity of American films, with their ability to address the felt needs, fears, and desires of Italian middle and working classes—those most acutely experiencing the tensions and instabilities resulting from modernization and industrialization. These factors were in large part responsible for American films' having constituted roughly 80 percent of films seen (around 225 films from America each year) in Italy in 1925–30.

In order to demonstrate these points, it is first necessary to conduct a brief historical review of the increasing interdependency between American and Italian film industries during these two decades, acknowledging their cooperation as well as discord. Almost from its inception (as early as 1911–12), the Italian film industry became embroiled in competition on an international scale. From its more successful period immediately before World War I, the Italian film industry relied on the services and contacts of American distributor/entrepreneur

George Kleine to market its films in America and some other foreign countries. In the first decades of the twentieth century, Kleine, recognizing in feature-length Italian spectacles a lucrative investment prospect, began to co-produce Italian films; by 1914, he had financed the construction of his Photodrama Production Films of Italy—a relatively extravagant production studio outside Torino. The successful inroads made in Italy by American production/distribution companies (specifically Fox, MGM, Paramount/Famous Players–Lasky, and Warner Bros.) were enormously facilitated by the early efforts of George Kleine. Immediately before World War I, the Italian film industry's historical spectacles had achieved immense popularity throughout Europe and South America, in Russia, and in the United States.[7] Partly due to the success that it had enoyed before the war, the Italian film industry afterward became conservative—attempting to sustain styles, images, and themes which by then failed to address the concerns now generated by industrialization and an urban, consumer experience.[8] The numerous regional (provincial) production houses, such as those in Naples, were unable to create films which addressed *national* concerns in an era when mass-media networks were providing Italians with a new sense of cultural domain. Moreover, whereas America had before the war begun to institute cultural policy through sanctions imposed on film and other imports, Italy lacked a clear cultural policy. Instead, the government imposed high taxes on film distribution and on theaters, a practice that continued throughout the twenties and early thirties. Thus, as was the case in most European countries during the twenties, American distributors began to establish successful commerical avenues for marketing American films in Italy. By 1918–21, Italian distributors had begun to market American serials;[9] in 1920, Italy's first production company (Cines-Seta) was sold to an Italian–U.S. venture; and, in 1921, Fox Films became the first major American distributor of American films in Italy. Through the publicity efforts of these distributors (both Italian and American), the images of America suffused Italian printed media and adorned its buildings. (The ubiquity of this publicity was significant because it established a vital connection between the movie public's experiences in the movie houses and outside them; in many ways, the publicity made the meaning in these films more accessible to Italian audiences by addressing them directly.) A rather ironic example of the profound cultural impact of American images in Italy occurred in a 1924 issue of *Il Tevere*, the Fascist newspaper in Rome, wherein large advertisements for films of Tom Mix and John Ford accompanied anti-American editorials. As in the Fellini film, the iconography of American cinema at times seemed to form a backdrop for more immediate political rhetoric and contestation.

Policy in Italy developed, then, as a response to the perceived threat of media imperialism, yet the faltering film industry was compelled to rebuild *through* the American monopoly, distribution networks, and technology. The years 1925–26 marked the nadir of postwar Italian film production (only four films), while MGM came to Rome to film the very successful *Ben-Hur*. In those same years, American film distribution in Italy surpassed the number of imported German films; American films now garnered the largest percentage of movies shown in Italy.[10] Appendix B, on Italian film production, and Appendix C, on the distribution of American movies in Italy, reveal that, as Italian film production fell after the war, the number of American films in Italy began to rise. In 1928, moreover, box-office revenues increased 3,000,000 lire over those in 1927, while the average price of admission actually dropped (in some theaters by as much as half).[11] This overwhelming domination of an increasingly lucrative Italian market by American films produced, by the late twenties, an ambivalence among Italian critics, producers, directors, and policy makers about the Hollywood success story—an ambivalence which lasted throughout the thirties. On the one hand, there were those who envisioned a road to recovery patterned after a Hollywood model; certainly this sentiment was most widely articulated during the late twenties, though it continued throughout the thirties among many of the young filmmakers. Already in 1926, Alessandro Blasetti, who would become one of the most prolific and renowned Italian directors during the thirties, lauds Hollywood's organizational and "propaganda" skills.[12] On the other hand, there were those (including Blasetti himself), who, some three years later, came to consider the immense popularity of American films to be a form of media imperialism which threatened to devastate Italian film production.[13] This ambivalence, which continued to manifest itself in both the economy and the textuality of Italian film production, contributed to the restructuring of the Italian film industry.

In 1926, bidding against Paramount Studios, Torinese producer/entrepreneur Stefano Pittaluga (who was often regarded as being the Italian version of American producers) purchased the faltering Unione Cinematografica Italiana (UCI) and established his own company—the Società Anomina Stefano Pittaluga (SASP). It was the efforts of Pittaluga, who, before he gained ownership of some 2,000 theaters in the UCI deal, already owned about one-eighth of the theaters in Italy, which provided the first real challenge to American companies; and it was eventually through his pressure on the government, and because his investments were so tied to Italy's major banks, that successive measures were taken to restabilize the Italian film industry.[14] By the late 1920s, the government, through the newly formed LUCE organization, attempted to assist Pittaluga's efforts to facilitate subsidies from commercial banks and private investors. And, in 1927, LUCE also went so far as to limit for the first time the number of *foreign* films projected in each theater. This sanction, however, was never entirely successful, since Italian production was by no means substantial enough to compensate for these restrictions. Nor was it strictly enforced, since its imposition probably would have crippled the financial stability of Italian cinemas—a stability necessary for the dissemination of Italian films. Furthermore, in 1927, American distribution networks became entirely autonomous, bypassing Italian distributors and promoters altogether.[15]

By 1929, through the promptings of Pittaluga and film producer Gino Pierantori, the government sponsored a semiprivate financial organization known as ENAC (Ente nazionale per la cinematografia) that, through state assistance, was designed to mediate distribution rights between American and Italian producers and to negotiate joint marketing and production deals with other than American foreign companies, primarily German.

Because the foothold of the four American majors was so formidable, ENAC never really succeeded. However, its failure and some of the first government surveys of film distribution and exhibition practices in the early 1930s prompted the government to offer relatively more concerted assistance in 1933. (Some of this government action resulted from formal complaints filed by Milanese exhibitors over MGM's attempts to require them to sign minimum revenue contracts for *Ben-Hur* and *City Lights*.) This was the year that Luigi Freddi, who would be appointed the next year as the General Director of Cinematography in the Ministry of Popular Culture, returned from a lengthy trip in America touring Hollywood production facilities. Freddi advised Mussolini about specific strategies for state intervention in the Italian film industry. Also in 1933, the government imposed limits on the number of foreign films exhibited in each theater, and it limited the number of films not dubbed in Italian and levied a tax on foreign films imported into Italy. Because the money from this tax was routed to Italian film production, foreign films began to subsidize filmmaking in Italy, and thus Italian production grew more dependent on American film. The next year, an agreement between Will Hays and Galeazzo Ciano, then Under-Secretary of Press and Propaganda, established a quota of no more than 250 American films to be exported to Italy each year. But the accord also tended to institutionalize an American cultural presence in Italy. Despite the restrictions of the previous two years, however, American distribution networks were still open, and American technology, through RCA Photophone, still dominated in Italian movie-houses and studios. Also, American majors had begun to produce Italian versions of their own films in order to circumvent new government sanctions. As Jean Gili notes, the American dubbing tended to ignore linguistic nuances in favor of a more homogeneous national cultural "Voice."[16] As Appendix C demonstrates, the percentage of American films in Italy had decreased slightly during the early 1930s, though American films continued to be the most popular fare; some of this decline may be attributed to the increased costs of dubbing sound films and to the prohibition against spoken dialogue during 1929–31. By 1935, however (as the Italian film industry became more productive), the Italian government began to pursue more rigorously its quotas on the importation of foreign films.[17] Therefore, in 1935, when Mussolini threatened to limit the amount of money which American film distributors could take out of Italy, American distribution companies clamored for Will Hays to visit Italy to discuss a compromise. During 1937–38, as a result of the Hays visit, the percentage of American film imports again escalated to a level that nearly equaled that of the mid-1920s.

By the late 1930s, Italian film production had increased seven times its output of the mid-1920s; Italy had even begun to export films to America (although through small Italian-American distribution companies). Also by the late 1930s,

Italy had made substantial progress in claiming control of and strengthening the financial underpinnings of its movie theaters through a semiprivate organization known as ENIC, which, because it was subsidized by the government, became competitive by procuring the most lucrative films for its theaters. Again, however, these lucrative films were mostly American. When in 1938 the Alfieri law passed, prohibiting distribution of foreign films in Italy, American film importation gradually diminished and did not flourish again until after the American occupation. Despite the impasses that had necessitated such action, Italian audiences did not overwhelmingly support it, and some Italian officials worried about its implications. Freddi, for instance, saw American films as the most compatible with the needs of the national market and with Fascist ideology:

> One of the consequences of the Monopoly's intervention was the exclusion of American films which were ten times superior to French, English, or German films. . . . The American film industry produces films that are youthful, serene, honest, optimistic, enjoyable, generally of a high moral value and most often of a noble meaning.[18]

When Stefano Pittaluga died in 1931, Italy suddenly lacked the kind of entreprenuerial figure that Zukor or Warner had brought to American film production. And, while the Italian government may have wanted to emulate Hollywood, it was not prepared or willing to replace Pittaluga. The dilemma of the struggling Italian film industry, with respect to its American competitors, is responsible throughout the 1930s for the widespread ambivalence about American films among Italian filmmakers, intellectuals, and policy-makers. Pittaluga was lauded by Italians as a savior of the film industry, but he was just as frequently compared with the successful American producers. Emilio Cecchi, who replaced Pittaluga on his death as head of Cines in the early 1930s, was one to exhalt Buster Keaton and Frank Capra while seeing in Disney's *Snow White and the Seven Dwarfs* (one of the most popular films in Italy during 1938–39) the most abominable manifestations of American talent. After returning from Hollywood in 1933, Luigi Freddi proposed to Mussolini a new agenda for the Italian film industry that called for intervention of the state, while at the same time seeing in Hollywood a model for its development. When Vittorio Mussolini, the son of the Duce, visited Hollywood in the late thirties he was largely rebuffed by its directors and moguls;[19] but he and other young intellectuals who associated themselves with *Cinema* (which, like *Bianco e nero*, was one of the first publications concerned with Italian film culture) argued adamantly that the Italian film industry's success lay in emulating the example of Hollywood. In 1936, the young Mussolini's ideas sparked one of the more revealing ideological debates of the time in the pages of *Cinema*. In his article "Emancipazione del cinema italiano," Mussolini described European industries as flacid, feeble, and jaded, while he characterized American production and Hollywood's organizing skills as "youthful" and "fresh"—attributes, by no coincidence, often associated with Fascism:

> I might say . . . with the greatest earnestness . . . how dangerous and damnable it
> would be for the newly flourishing Italian film industry to align itself with
> European production standards, instead of following the example and the
> method of the Americans. . . . For our film industry, following the American
> example would be most advantageous. From a moral point of view, our youthful
> spirit logically finds a chorus line of a hundred beautiful girls less vulgar than the
> trite farce (in both senses) typical of the French—usually full of double mean-
> ings, of poorly concealed nudity, and of sterile intellectuality.[20]

Mussolini's article is followed by a series of others whose authors, though they
offer some tame objections, generally support its spirit.[21] Some of these succeeding essays go on to indicate the contributions by Italians in Hollywood and one
(by Giorgio Vigolo) even attempts to cite the historical and geographical affinities between Rome and Hollywood.

In either case, Hollywood and its movies became an emblem of American
success—a success inscribed in American films themselves, celebrating, through
their silent heroes of the 1920s or their urbane and sophisticated heroes of the
1930s, an American Dream of Success;[22] it was a success that Italian intellectuals,
movie-makers, and government spokesmen admired and feared. It is no wonder
that when Cinecittà was inaugurated in 1937 much of the rhetoric about its
opening described the facility as another (though smaller) Hollywood and as a
rebirth of Italy's film industry.[23] The inauguration of Cinecittà, a celebration of
the Italian film industry's "new beginning," signaled on the one hand a desire to
emulate the modernity and youthful spirit that Italians perceived in America,
and in Hollywood as the wellspring of this spirit. On the other hand, Cinecittà
was also seen as an antidote to American cultural forms, i.e., as a means of
expressing and disseminating a national spirit and as a *weapon* for combatting
media imperialism.

American Cinema in Italy and Media Imperialism

Italy's long history of domination by foreign invaders and its rich diversity of
foreign cultural influences make it an interesting case study of media imperialism
in the twentieth century. But, while it is necessary to recognize the economic
stakes involved in the political and industrial conflict about the influence of
American movies in Italy, and to consider the more significant policies imple-
mented as a result of this conflict, a material or economistic approach to Italy's
cultural policy does not fully account for Italian ambivalence toward, i.e., fear of
and attraction to, American cinema. In light of the rhetoric of filmmakers, as
well as of film critics, it seems that the Italian film industry was determined to
produce films that could rival those from the United States. This competitive-
ness, however, was intended to occur more on a national front than on an
international one. Although Italy struck an agreement with an American distributor, ESPERIA, to market Italian films in America in the late 1930s, it was

more interested in "conquering" American films at home.[24] One essential concern that appears to have directed policy in Italy's film industry was that American cinema would create a cultural hegemony. Part of this fear seems motivated by financial interests, many of which I have enumerated. Yet policy seems to have been based more on fears of a *cultural* bankruptcy, fostered by American media inroads in Italy. Often, these concerns about Italian culture assumed a political tenor; Guglielmo Giannini states, as early as the mid-1920s: "Filmmaking is considered to be a political industry and it is sustained politically. . . . It is the American spirit that diffuses itself in those films; we too must diffuse the Italian spirit."[25]

It is necessary to acknowledge the economic and cultural interdependency between Italy and America during these two decades. But far from creating a cultural hegemony, this interdependency amplified the contradictions between their cultural institutions. "Cultural invasion" theories (common among Marxist theorists and political economists such as Herbert Schiller, who hold that changes in common thinking, feeling, and believing are externally forced) often tend to gloss over the conflicts and continual policymaking that are prompted by the intercultural dependency. These scholars have applied Marx's theories about hegemonic processes in society to discussions of international media effects—directing special attention to the manner whereby one "dominant" country attempts to disseminate its system of beliefs throughout the world in order to maintain an ever-lucrative market. Theorists of international communications effects argue that the commercial imperative of mass communication presents itself in a twofold fashion: while products and services are "sold" to consumers through advertising, the mass media create audiences that are sold to advertisers and sponsors.[26] Often, these same scholars attempt to explain the manner in which foreign productions alter or rearrange symbolic meaning in a culture. Chin-Chuan Lee, for instance, in his analysis of the international effects of television, indicates that foreign productions significantly affect the stability of a society, that foreign images present an exaggerated attractiveness for certain goods and products, and that media productions of more modern countries change value structures and foster a "false consciousness."[27] It seems just as important to recognize, however, that this view of imperialism avoids the dialogic nature of any international network of media distribution. It is an attitude that presupposes a passivity on the part of the "invaded" country. It sees cultural interdependency and its inherent conflicts (as was the case in Italy) as merely a cultural *dependency*, and, as in traditional American media-effects studies, tends to assume that the processes of reception are uniform. What is lost in intercultural domination theories is a sense of the many economic and textual processes of *translating* (of encoding and decoding) cultural forms. This perspective tends to be reductive in two important areas: it tends to ignore the contradictions and historical necessities of the myths of the "invading" culture; and it often minimizes the unevenness with which the symbolic meanings of exchanged texts are absorbed or translated by the "invaded" nation. To avoid this sort of reductionism in discussing the cinematic myths of America in Italy during the Fascist regime, it is necessary to explore the significant variations and transformations of themes in American movies which are popular in Italy and to investigate the manner whereby these diverse and changing themes were themselves assimilated and reworked by Italian audiences and filmmakers.

An awareness of the complexities of a comparative cultural analysis is crucial since, as James Halloran has suggested, a critic cannot easily escape projecting his own value-system onto that of another culture (and here, of another historical period). While I have tried to respond to some of these concerns in my introduction, it should be sufficient here to remind the reader that the power of American cinema and culture in Italy cannot be easily extricated from the constellation of competing myths that I have attempted to map out through the organization of these chapters. The ambivalence that pervaded Italian film production manifested itself in policy-making, in critical reviews and theorizing, in advertising (in short, among a variety of corresponding discourses) *as well as* through the construction of these films. Therefore, it is necessary to consider areas in which the codes and formulas of American and Italian films from this period converge and diverge. The historical context of this analysis certainly helps focus attention on the limits or range of intercultural overlay and competition. But, in charting historical transitions of a national culture, one is always obliged to defer tying codes and formulas to stable ideologies or world views. The examination of cinema's changing/emerging role in representing "popular" sentiment is, for instance, complicated by the experiential differences between sound and silent film styles or techniques.

Although technological innovation as well as socioeconomic conditions circumscribe the period of silent films as a body of texts unto itself, few of the genres in it are complete. William Everson explains the difficulty in examining silent films: "One of the complexities of the silent film is that, while one can discuss it as a total and fully realized art form, discussion of individual films involves hesitations and reservation, and an enforced comparison with what came after, a critical stance almost unique to film."[28] While this assertation applies to Italy as well, it is complicated by differences between the two film cultures. Because American *silent* movies, for instance, comprised much of the cinematic entertainment in Italy into the 1930s (a point I develop below), it is necessary to consider the significance of the continued repercussions in Italy of films which were already rather "outdated" in America.

The Diversity of the "Dominant" Ideology

A weakness of some traditional Marxist (or non-Gramscian) analyses of culture and the popular arts is that they tend to encourage the notion of a "dominant" ideology while ignoring or glossing over the diversity and historicity of cultural values. "Media imperialism" stands on the belief that a dominant nation extends a *system* of values and a *way* of articulating these values which are, often as a result of a critical reductionism, understood to be monolithic. Gramsci's brief but evocative formulation of a typology for popular romances calls attention to the multi-vocality of national mythology. A more recent attempt to acknowledge the heterogeneity of a particular mode of cultural discourse is Robin Wood's essay "Ideology, Genre, Auteur." Of particular interest here is his list of twelve "components" or myths common in American cinema. While this list is (by his own admission) fragmentary and transhistorical, it does serve as a reminder of the critic's responsibility in examining an array of interacting cultural signification.

In some very basic respects, American films during the twenties and thirties demonstrated the same ambivalence to modernization that one finds in Italian films of the same period. As Garth Jowett indicates: "America in the 1920s was a paradox, for while there was an obvious change in the moral outlook of the younger generation, there also existed a strong reactionary attitude in political and economic life."[29] Not only did the industrial revolution and ensuing economic boom in America create a more consumeristic society, but American value-systems shifted too—a new morality arose, one which "rejected the old morality of Victorian idealism for a fashionable materialism which emphasized wealth, sensation, and sexual freedom."[30] As both Jowett and historian David Cook acknowledge, however, American films never entirely succeeded in rejecting this old morality. Many film historians (Jowett, Cook, and Sklar) have cited DeMille's, Lubitsch's, and Von Stroheim's abilities to concoct in their films a mythical realm of upper-crust leisure and cosmopolitan lifestyles; through this kind of displacement, however, the sexual desires and social fears of middle-class audiences could be amplified and acted out. For this reason, these films did celebrate images of social order and conservative respectability—populist values—even though they dealt with upper-crust subjects.

Not only was America's ambivalence about modernization encouraged by the messages of its films from the 1920s, but this ambivalence was also manifested through an assortment of narrative formulas or genres. It is perhaps most important to consider, beside the aforementioned romantic melodramas and comedies, the ethos of slapstick comedies, Westerns, and adventure films (especially those with Douglas Fairbanks)—since all were widely disseminated and stirred an enduring interest among Italian audiences. Though these different genres may have responded to similar historical pressures, namely those engendered by rapid industrialization and postwar cynicism, the genres offered a gallery of symbolic models about their age. For instance, it is difficult to equate the epic–heroic image of the Westerner with the comic or sympathetic heroics of such "visual" comedians as Chaplin, Keaton, or Lloyd. Both genres concerned the great themes of Modernization—civilization vs. nature, machine vs. man—and both emphasized (as products of the silent age's lack of dialogue) individual action, hyperbolic gesture, and stunts rather than the rapid-fire verbal sparring, punning, and witticisms, i.e., the collective discourse, of sound film. Yet, whereas both the Westerner and the sight-gag comedian experience the violence and periods of traditional culture's collision with the demands of industrialization/urbanization, each character gives presence to a different mood in America about this conflict. The Westerner upholds his code by self-assertion, the slapstick comic through self-immolation.

By the late 1920s and early 1930s, two principal events—the worldwide economic crisis and the development of sound films—had created a new sense of American film culture. Not only did these events alter the character of American film comedy and Westerns, but they also gave rise to another American genre, the film musical. Film musicals were extremely popular—if not *the* most popular genre—during this transition period; and their popularity was not restricted to the United States. Their emphasis on musical performance seemed to celebrate the arrival of sound itself, and their self-reflexive qualities repeatedly reminded audiences of a rich legacy of *popular* performance.[31] In fact, more than any other film genre of that period (or before), film musicals *called attention* to America as a locus for popular entertainment. The *Broadway Melody* series (begun in 1929), for instance, underscores (through self-reflexive musical numbers) the mythical qualities of New York, as a real and imagined stage for success and transcendence in a modern age. And there were plotless film musical revues highlighting the luminaries of American movies: *The Hollywood Revue of 1929*, with Greta Garbo, Conrad Nagel, Joan Crawford, Norma Shearer, John Gilbert, Buster Keaton, and others, or *Paramount on Parade* (1930), with Leon Errol, Jack Oakie, Warner Oland (*as* Fu Manchu), Clive Brooks (*as* Sherlock Holmes), and William Powell (*as* Philo Vance). Film musicals brought to the screen the lyricism and plasticity of the silent films, and they incorporated these features into an otherwise dialogic medium. The physical agility of Fred Astaire, for instance, conjures the spectacular feats of Fairbanks, Mix, and Keaton. In film musicals, however, the animistic world of silent movies generally became an act upon a stage; the action that occurred "backstage" (and which comprised most of the film's narrative) was understood to be somehow more naturalistic and conversational. This film realism (illusion of proscenium for song and dance, less hyperbolic action, more conversation, complex and multiple interpersonal relationships, etc.) seems the product of both the introduction of sound and themes concerning economic hard times.

Hollywood's urban realism pervaded virtually all its film genres during this period. Some critics see the topicality of urban themes to have been responsible for the temporary demise of Westerns and for the appeal instead of gangster movies. As Thomas Schatz notes, "the civilization which the Westerners held at bay now overwhelms the gangster-hero; the cowboy's distant fears have become the gangster's daily *angst*."[32] The gangster film in many ways dramatizes American society's insecurities brought on by the collapse of 1920s prosperity: "Whereas the Western depicts the initial and tremendous struggle to establish social order, the gangster film deals with an organized society's efforts to maintain that order"—order, one might add, in a nation where all sense of order seemed to be disintegrating as a result of the economic collapse.[33] The film gangster, unlike the 1920s Westerner or frontier adventurer, seemed to represent the perverse alter-ego of the ambitious, profit-minded American male:[34] and, as the embodiment of popular attitudes, his character called into question earlier

American values and gave presence to the frustration among American movie audiences about their own material instability. Nor did the gangster enjoy the freedom of action of his early Western counterpart. If anything, his acts of violence seem to issue from repressed desire and frustration in an overly restrictive environment, and he lacks the inexhaustible physical agility of the 1920s Westerner. The gangster is given instead to witticism and verbal *savoir faire*; one need only consider Edward G. Robinson or James Cagney—both of whom express their characters (e.g., Rico "Little Caesar" Bandello or Tommy "Public Enemy" Powers) through unforgettable *verbal* stylizations.

Beside being a part of the Western's transformation into the gangster film, the 1930s urban realism also begins to inform romantic and early "screwball" comedies (not to mention late silent films such as *City Lights*). The extreme and often violent physical expressions of slapstick comedy are greatly diminished in the new comedy; screwball comedians such as William Powell, Cary Grant, or even Fred Astaire use slapstick only to offset the suavity of their characters. Much of the dramatic conflict and humor in the romantic comedies of the late 1920s and early 1930s occurs through crisp, well-orchestrated banter among small congregations of characters brought together in intimate settings, e.g., Lubitsch's *Trouble in Paradise* and *Design for Living*, Cukor's *Dinner at Eight*, and Howard Hawks's *Twentieth Century*. All of these comedies manage to derive their humor from the foibles and stale mannerisms of America's leisure class.

While the screwball comedies operate with the same carefully syncopated exchanges of wit that one finds in the very early sound comedies, dramatic conflict and comedy are nurtured more than ever by social differences between main characters. A pivotal film in this regard is Capra's *Platinum Blonde* (1931) whose populist lead character gradually becomes disenchanted with his dreams for success and social mobility and (as in the Marx Brothers' films) repeatedly mocks traditional, Old World codes of decorum. Capra's *American Madness* (1932), on the other hand, celebrates America's grassroots faith in a wealthy, charismatic figure whose own magnanimity toward the "little man" and family values helps stabilize a major metropolitan bank. And in Capra's *It Happened One Night* (1934), the battle between the sexes becomes a means of enacting and redressing social conflict. The socioeconomic attributes attached to the two principal characters in this film form a subtext of signification through which upper-bourgeois values are simultaneously ridiculed and made laughable. The "resolution" to the film's sexual/class conflict occurs as a marriage. The romantic relationship in this formula was attractive to Depression-era audiences in part because the lower-class characters are promised a certain degree of financial security in the marriage (though he or she never seems to have desired it) and because the decadent upper-crust characters are charged with a sense of vitality and an awareness of the "moral" responsibilities of their power. Some of the more obvious variations of this formula during the 1930s include LaCava's *My Man Godfrey*, Capra's *Mister Deeds Goes to Town*, Mitchell Leisen's *Easy Living*, William Wellman's *Nothing Sacred*, and (to a certain extent) Cukor's *Holiday*.

One final observation should be made here about the evolution of the dramatic styles in American sound comedy and in early Hollywood musicals. After World War I, Europe became more than ever, for American film audiences, a "liminoid" space, an illusory realm wherein the duplicitous and darker sides of human nature lurked beneath the luxuriant decor of Old World elegance. As I have already mentioned in the chapter on the myth of the Grand Hotel, silent films by Von Stroheim did much to disseminate this image of Europe. In *Foolish Wives* (1921), for example, the Von Stroheim warrior of his earlier films is transformed into a seducer who attempts to take advantage of an American diplomat and his wife vacationing in Monte Carlo. In Wellman's *Wings* (the first film to win Best Picture in the Academy Awards, 1926), the horrors of war are experienced by two young American aviators as much in the open skies over European battle zones as during their drunken revelry at a Parisian cabaret—depicted as an orgiastic inferno that threatens to swallow the American heroes. Often, American films set in Europe did not involve American characters—particularly Lubitsch's silent comedies (*The Marriage Circle*, 1923) and his operettas (*Love Parade*, 1929; *Monte Carlo*, 1930; *The Smiling Lieutenant*, 1931); nevertheless, they too upheld an image of Europe as a domain inhabited by an eccentric leisure class and treacherous charlatans or sirens. And, with the coming of sound, the 1930s saw a remarkable escalation in the number of horror movies wherein evil and horror seemed to be confined more to Europe and Old World settings than to America. In light of these trends, it is safe to say that, in American mythology during the 1920s and 1930s, Europe became a kind of rhetorical correlative against which to highlight the natural and virtuous aspects of American values. In 1930s screwball comedy, the rural/urban opposition was paralleled with a working-class/leisure-class opposition; and, as Schatz observes, a hero's or heroine's traditional, homespun values and attitudes are attributed directly to their rural backgrounds and small-town sensibilities. By extending Schatz's rationale to this discussion of European images in American films, it is evident that American films helped instill in American audiences a sense of cultural domain.[35] Efforts by American movie distributors may have done much to further cultural expansion; but, for most Americans, the vital realities and themes of a uniquely American culture were gleaned through its more popular cinematic images, narratives, and musical scores. Thus, as historian Warren Susman explains:

> It was during the thirties that the idea of culture was domesticated, with important consequences. Americans then began thinking in terms of patterns of behavior and belief, values and lifestyles, symbols and meanings. It was during this period that we find, for the first time, frequent reference to an "American Way of Life."[36]

As a postscript to Susman's observations, however, it is necessary to note that this American way of living, while often invoked in political rhetoric of the time as a verbal image of solidarity, was also contradictory and replete with semantic tensions—tensions which found an outlet in part through popular forms such as the movies.

Decoding American Films in Italy and the Role of the Audience

In "Six Characters in Search of an Author," Luigi Pirandello exposes the illusion of authorship/ownership; the play seems to suggest that once an author breathes life into his characters they are no longer his—but seem instead to take on a life of their own. More recent structuralist and "reception" theories would carry this rationale one step further by indicating that these characters or images become the world of their audiences—continually transforming themselves like ideological chameleons. If in fact Americans developed through cinema a sense of cultural space—of an "American Way of Life"—how did Italian audiences perceive and negotiate the ideological *imperatives* in these movies? The answer is admittedly complex and would seem to elude a strict empirical examination. One could survey the more popular American movies in Italy at this time to ascertain which ones Italian audiences found most appealing. However, this type of study does not adequately explain how Italian audiences altered the semantic field of these more widely circulated films. Therefore, it is also neces- sary to concentrate on the process of translation itself, to consider how Italian audiences privileged or reduced in their own representations certain aspects of American films to easily recognizable myths (themselves contradictory).

One important consideration in discussing the most popular American movies in Italy at this time is that a film's popularity is not necessarily a result of production costs, of extensive ad campaigns, or of its critical acclaim. For this reason, it is erroneous to believe that simply by amassing lists of, say, the ten "most popular" films each year—based on findings of an American or Italian trade journal—one can actually realize which of these films most profoundly affected the collective attitudes of Italian audiences. Admittedly, this type of research is helpful, but its limitations should be recognized. Often trade journals tend to base their findings on box-office revenues; and, if a very few (though spacious and high-priced) theaters receive respectable earnings on a film, that film would make this list but ultimately fail to attract an economically diverse audience. Therefore, in order to talk about Italy's mythology of America by means of American cinematic models, it is just as important to acknowledge both the range of films going into Italy and the difference between watching films in Italy and in America.

The reason that I feel compelled here to qualify the term "popular"—as it applies to films during this period—is that, for quite a number of years, *most* movie theaters in Italy did not always exhibit movies that may have done well at the more elegant, first-run theaters. In fact, of movies shown in Milan between 1928 and 1939, the type of films run at the larger, more expensive movie houses there differed significantly from those at the second- and third-run theaters.[37] I select Milan as a locus for this investigation because it is centered in a region where theaters were most plentiful (see Appendix D) and because it provided the most diverse range of movie theaters and movie audiences. By 1934, Milan had approximately forty "full-time" commercial theaters, those which did not double as cabarets, etc. Of these theaters, about ten were first-run houses. Here I assume that those films which were common in second- and third-run Milanese theaters represent popular viewing trends in the more provincial regions. This assumption is based on two factors: that the larger theaters (the first equipped with sound) were more common in large urban areas and that during the 1920s the lower middle class and working class in Milan were generally those who had either only recently moved to the city or who still had close cultural ties with provincial lifestyles.

The division in Italy between first-run movie systems and lesser ones (known as "*i cinema della periferia*") occurred in three ways: through admission prices, through the popularity of certain film genres, and through the availability of sound films. The admission prices at most of the first-run theaters in Milan (Corso, Reale, San Carlo, Impero, Odeon, etc.) during the early 1930s were generally two or three times higher than those of the lesser ones; occasionally, when a film had already gained international recognition, the admission was four times higher. Movies were exhibited at these theaters for at least five to seven days, and frequently for longer periods. These theaters often accommodated orchestras, and even during the early 1930s, often offered live stage performances before and after the film. One of the foremost attractions at these theaters in the very early 1930s was of course sound films; one of the first experiments with sound films in Italy occurred at Milan's first-run theater, the Corso. (This gala was initiated by Tomaso Bisi, president of ENAC, who spoke about the advantages of sound film, and by a xylophone exhibition, marionettes, a jazz orchestra, and a performing bear.)[38] By 1930, Italy's first sound film, *Canzone dell'amore* (*The Song of Love*), was advertised as being "100% Italian." And, by the fall of 1930, American film musicals were beginning to be dubbed in Italian; the film musical revue *The King of Jazz* was advertised in November as having some of its scenes dubbed in Italian. Not only the admission price (and the socioeconomic class of customer who could afford it) but the size of the screen and the availability of sound in these theaters encouraged certain film genres. Musicals, for instance, were almost entirely restricted to first-run theaters during the early and mid-1930s. During late 1930 and much of 1931, most films screened at first-run theaters were musicals (mostly American); yet, by the late 1930s, when the second- and third-run houses became wired for sound, the musical had lost much of its initial novelty and was no longer such a dominant genre. Besides viewing a number of musicals, the audiences at first-run theaters also saw relatively more romantic melodramas, romantic/screwball comedies, and epic spectacles than did audiences at second-run theaters.[39] As in other European countries, American sound comedies did not fare as well as other genres—particularly because of difficulties in translating a largely verbal humor; most of the American screwball comedies, however, appear in first-run theaters. Also, movies at these first-run cinemas were often advertised by director and by genre—evidence of an audience that had already begun to develop aesthetic attitudes about film. More frequently, they were advertised by production company, the name of which became a shorthand for the film's American origins. Although Western and silent slapstick comedies did continue to appear in first-run movie houses into the early 1930s, they were not as widely recycled as in the small theaters. While it is unnecessary to belabor the significance of the types of films these audiences preferred, it is worth noting that the romantic melo-dramas, musicals, etc. which they did watch generally offered the most modern images, settings, and popular musical scores. Furthermore, these films provided their audiences with a somewhat different, certainly more urban, vision of America than did the adventure films and Westerns (whose popularity, along with slapstick comedies, continued into the 1930s in smaller theaters). In many ways, "*i cinema della periferia*" and their type of entertainment constituted an almost unnoticeable *backdrop* for social action in Italy.[40] (These neighborhood theaters also seem closer in spirit to the local cinema—the Fulgor—in Fellini's *Amarcord*.) They lacked the gaudy sumptuousness and formality that made the first-run theaters shrines for exotic bourgeois spectacle. Here, movies were quickly recycled (some not lasting more than a couple of days) and often "brought back by popular demand." In 1937, an article in *Lo schermo* exalts their often-overlooked value in Italian society as family-oriented institutions:

> Cinemas for everyone, but especially comfortable cinemas, ones close to home, where features change every other day and the LUCE newsreel arrives only a few days later than those at the first-run houses; where husband and wife, interested in following the film's drama, don't have to worry about a lively child moving an adjoining folding chair up and down, disturbing another couple who, ignoring the drama on the screen pacify him with a soothing song. Suburban cinemas, between one part and another, children and adults eat caramels and other mor-sels, where everyone is friendly and content because they all know that the show only costs a lira—a simple lira which, in its modesty, can make everyone equal.[41]

Not only were these theaters convenient but they were also (as the article suggests) less expensive; and by the early 1930s the OND had established special reduced prices for its members. The audiences who frequented these cinemas were less knowledgeable about production houses or about film genres than were their counterparts in more expensive theaters; they were usually attracted to particular stars, whom movie ads always made sure to mention. (Fellini wryly remarks that Garbo and Astaire were his only images of the outside world.) Because these smaller theaters continued to present silent movies well into the 1930s, and perhaps because of the ideological sensibilities and preferences of this class of audience, the most common genres were slapstick comedies, Westerns, and the acrobatic spectacle or adventure films that Fairbanks popularized. These were stories of heroism (farcical or melodramatic) in which Tom Mix held an encroaching civilization at bay or in which Buster Keaton's mild-mannered characters dramatically eluded the perils of an increasingly mechanized world. These characters were also more consonant with the strongmen whose stable presence and physical dexterity were valorized in the few successful Italian silent film during the 1920s. The heroic feats of these film personalities, especially those of Fairbanks's characters, helped nurture a model of social action that one associates with "supermanism" (a trope which flourished especially among Ital-ian veterans after the war through D'Annunzio, Marinetti's Futurism, and Ital-ian Fascism). But, by the late 1930s, American screwball comedies, musicals, and gangster films, which had begun to filter into the neighborhood cinemas, were quickly accepted by working-class and petit-bourgeois culture. Classical Hollywood cinema's tendency to encourage identification with a populist, homespun hero also helped concretize for these lower-income Italian audiences some of the political rhetoric which had cast the bourgeois consciousness as an impediment in the realization of a Fascist state.

Despite the differences between these two classes of theaters in Italy, and in the type of American films that their audiences enjoyed, one form of American entertainment seems to have appealed to both audiences: the animated cartoons of Walt Disney. As early as July 1929, the Corso (one of Milan's oldest first-run theaters) presented cartoons with its main feature. And, by the end of 1930, the Corso and other theaters began to advertise the cartoons of Mickey Mouse (known as Topolino) along with their other movies; some of these early Disney animations included "Topolino pianista" ("The Opry House"), "Serenata di Topolino" and "Topolino ama il jazz."[42] Although these early sound cartoons were, for technical reasons, more common in first-run houses, by 1933, Topolino had become familiar to Italian moviegoers at all levels—so much so that, in the early 1930s, when Fiat was asked by the government to produce a car that would be affordable by most Italians, the new automobile was christened the Topolino.

Disney's animated feature-length fables enjoyed a similar success in Italy, and they were the subject of considerable theoretical discussion during the mid and late 1930s in Italian film journals such as *Bianco e nero* and *Lo schermo*. In 1934, *The Three Little Pigs* is open to varying interpretations, and a discussion of the fable's ideological connotations reveals much about its popularity in Italy. One can cite, as does Richard Schickel, the one pig's self-reliance, hard work, and self-denial as virtues that enable him to survive the vicious onslaught of apparently indomitable odds. Yet it is just as plausible that, as Robert Sklar suggests, "the most effective pig is the one who does not minimize the fact of crisis and builds with modern tools."[43] Both explanations could be extended to elucidate Italian readings of this film; I have already pointed to Italian films which promote either of these themes. (The dramatic conflicts in some of Camerini's films, for example, concern characters who learn about the futility of chasing "*castelli in aria.*") In many ways, the conflict in *The Three Little Pigs* could be attributed to the pressures of modernization itself (and an interpretation of the fable as an Oedipal drama does not entirely contradict this theory); in this sense, the film valorizes the organizational abilities of the pig who builds an impregnable fortress against the uncertainties of the future. One other explanation, however, which seems equally credible in Italy's case, is that Italian audiences (through their identification with or admiration of the successful little pig) recognized their own past "victimization" with respect to larger, more powerful nations. Because the film appeared in an era when Italian nationalism was most intense, this explanation should not be ignored. Although an anthropomorphic animal cartoon is in many ways more accessible to the sensibilities of foreign audiences, Disney's films were, for Italian moviegoers and critics at that time, unmistakably American; and this fact alone would seem to guarantee that the film operated, at least in part, on this level of connotation.

In late 1938 and early 1939, Disney's *Snow White and the Seven Dwarfs* was considered by American distributors to be one of—if not the—most popular movies in Italy. The film won a prize at the Venice arts festival and was used as the cover illustration for the July 1938 issue of *Lo schermo*. *Snow White* is much more than its surrealistic predecessors, a fairy tale for middle-class audiences of the 1930s. The visual and narrative world of Snow White is pure idealism, radically less surreal or grotesque than were those of the early cartoons; this style is important because it enables the tale to point to a morality which is more clear-cut than in the early Disney shorts and the Fleischer brothers' cartoons. Understanding how Italian audiences interpreted Disney's Technicolor version of this Grimm's tale, however, is complicated by the two "levels" of protagonists, Snow White and the Dwarfs; and one should decide whether the film encourages identification with the plight of Snow White or with that of the Dwarfs or with both. If an audience identifies with the Dwarfs' experience, the film becomes (on an ideological level) a conflict between Little People and a more arrogant image of Power, both of which vie in their own ways for a virginal (and highly sanitized) ideal, i.e., Snow White. Through their gallant "little" efforts, the Evil is frustrated but finally seems to have won—until the Prince (a sort of mythical warrior and savior/superman) accomplishes what they had desired to do all along.

Although I hesitate to draw more precise connections between historical events in Italy and the film's narrative, it should be apparent that Disney's fable does reaffirm a faith in charismatic protectors. Moreover, the ability of the Dwarfs to reconcile themselves to the more "lofty" desires of the Prince is certainly in the spirit of the myth of corporativism or collective social action. In Italian audiences' identification with the plight of Snow White, on the other hand, it would seen that she becomes an ideal to be protected by all levels of a society given to traditional male codes. Throughout the 1920s and 1930s, the popular image of Italy by Italians was that of a woman protected by her male guardians. This myth is borne out in *Snow White* when the heroine becomes a pristine ideal that inspires in the otherwise heterogeneous and often antagonistic group of Dwarfs a sense of collective self-worth that serves as a model of efficient organization. She is, after all, a civilizing or domesticating force which seems to enable the hard-working but feral bumpkins to realize a sense of purpose about their production at the mine. It is also a film in which the Prince's heroic image brings together the fragmented and grotesque personalities of the Dwarfs and, in so doing, preserves the sanctity of their ideals. One could attribute the cross-cultural appeal of the film to some of its more prominent archetypes; the fable itself does evoke some of the same melodramatic elements common in certain nineteenth-century Italian historical novels, such as Grossi's *Marco Visconti* or d'Azeglio's *Ettore Fieramosca*, and some of the motifs of nineteenth-century Italian oral tradition. (In fact, during the late 1930s and the 1940s, Italy produced modern film versions of both of these novels; and the popularity of historical and costume films at the turn of the decade seems to account in part for the appeal in Italy of Disney's chivalric fairy tale). Disney's version, however, involves social and psychological tensions which had become more a part of twentieth-century petit-bourgeois experience, and its appeal to 1930s Italian audiences (whether in the first-class theaters or in the smaller ones) must be related to its ability to amplify ideological pressures of Italian society and Italy's popular culture.

It is safe to say that audiences at first-run theaters, due to their greater economic resources, education, etc., participated more directly in the cosmopolitanism that the worldwide distribution of American films did much to create. It is also rather likely that these audiences, especially by the late 1930s, were more attuned to the variegated styles and themes of American films. Being *Italian* audiences, however, they certainly could not read into American films as richly diverse a field of signification as did American audiences. Cultural distance appears most easily bridged by Disney's animated features generally because of the nonliterary and highly lyrical language of his films and because of the almost archetypal resonance of their landscapes or settings in Western culture. (Disney's next feature-length animation, *Pinocchio*, 1940, is in fact based upon a well-known Italian popular tale.) Caricatures reduce a broad range of meaning to a visual essence that, in this case, is easily recognizable not only among audiences of two different cultures but also of two socioeconomic levels.

Translating the American Dream(s)

While a film's image, narrative, and music may be enjoyed in different cultural contexts, the film is remade in this process. Conclusions about what Italian audiences perceived in American films are somewhat speculative; instead, I have chosen to concentrate on *how* they perceived American films. To elucidate the *process* of signification and perception, it is necessary to discuss it less as a passive experience for Italians and more as *translation*, i.e., to examine the re-presentations of America by Italians. It is not the Italian public's acceptance or refusal of the ideological *content* that most bears upon my analysis here, but more the restructuring of American films and the production of new frameworks of interpretation to facilitate the broadest public reception—especially since only through these interpretive frameworks may public acceptance or refusal occur. Basically, this process of re-presentation occurred in four ways: in advertising, in the practical "dubbing" of American films by Italian studios, in stereotypes or roles of Americans in Italian commercial films and newsreels, and in film criticism of the day.

Advertising

For marketing purposes, movie advertising at that time attempted to clarify, through a highly elliptical, condensed, and emblematic language of verbal slogans and photographic/graphic images, one film's relationship with a field of competing films. As a process of *translation*, however, movie advertising also involves producing an image of the film and integrating that image into a cultural/textual milieu. Advertising for American movies appeared in a variety of "readerly" contexts in Italy (street posters, newspapers, film journals, celebrity magazines). And occasionally, as is the case with the Tom Mix ad that I cite earlier in this chapter, its messages may well conflict with the messages of surrounding texts; Fellini's ironic use of the full-sized cutouts of Oliver and Hardy outside the town cinema makes much the same point. (To point only to the expanding American distribution networks in Italy may account for the sheer abundance of American movie ads over those from other nations, but it cannot really explain what kinds of clarifications were necessary to make American films interesting and accessible to the sensibilities of Italians.) While the major American studios disseminated advertising packages in Italy, theater owners were given considerable latitude in handling advertising materials; and ads occasionally varied significantly from one locale to another.

Certainly, the cinematic personality of a movie star helped clarify/advertise a film for an audience, especially since the star's personality transcended any one film (or, rather, was an aura generated through previous roles). Consequently, many of the Hollywood ads (foreign and domestic) foregrounded the movies' central actors; and, in Italian newspaper ads, American movies were occasionally advertised by their stars rather than their titles. Because the copy of an advertisement does much to establish the parameters for reading its usual image, much of the translation of the American films occurred through the Italian titles in these ads. *Wings,* for instance, is described in a 1928 Italian ad as a film "dedicated to the glorious Heroes of the sky from every nation,"[44] even though it concerns the adventures of two American pilots. And a half-page newspaper ad for *A Woman of Affairs* with Greta Garbo and John Gilbert explains that the film presents "a savage love suffocated by traditionalism . . . an interesting study of a spirit caught in the whirlpool of modern life." Directly under the two stars' names is an addendum which, ironically, pronounces that "*A Woman of Affairs* is the first film that does not attempt to make its fortune on the popularity of its principal actors, but still uses the best *artists*—all of whom sacrifice their own pride for the success of their work."[45] While the exact motives of this description are not known, its messages do pay lip service to the *mythos* of American films and their appeal for Italian audiences (i.e., its cosmopolitanism), and the latter pronouncement adheres to the political rhetoric and ideals of Italian Fascism.

Although most of the titles of American films were translated quite literally, some were significantly modified to emphasize an aspect presumably more interesting or suitable to Italian sensibilities or to play to audience familiarity with the film's generic codes. An example would be a film with Tom Mix, identified in 1929 as *Come Don Giovanni,* perhaps because it comes on the tail of Fairbanks's film. Just as often, however, American films were advertised with American words or with the original American title: *Broadway, Knock-out, Poker d'amore,* etc. In this case, the Americanisms serve as signs of a mythic world which would seem to be untranslatable, of a signifier and meaning so grandiose that they are ineffable.

Dubbing and Deleting

During the era of silent movies in Italy, American films were rarely prohibited or cut by Italian authorities, nor did translating the text or "intertitles" of American movies ever become a real political issue. According to Mario Quargnolo, films with Rudolph Valentino were banned in Italy in 1925 because of his supposed anti-Italian ideals, yet, by the late 1920s, Valentino's *The Eagle, The Sheik,* and *Son of the Sheik* were all appearing in Italian theaters because of popular demand.[46] Some of this translation work was done in Italy, although most American companies (especially during the early 1920s) were allowed to circulate their own translated versions. In 1936, Arrigo Benedetti remembers, with wry affection, how Italian audiences would watch these films with "*bellissima libertà*".[47] In what now seems an ironic allusion to the blind accordian player in *Amarcord,* Benedetti recalls the blind piano player at his neighborhood theater, who would provide the musical accompaniment for silent films. What seemed remarkable to Benedetti was the blind piano player's interpretation of a foreign film through popular Italian songs (the only ones he knew). At times, he explains, the piano player became a sort of mystic medium—listening to the voices of the small audience as they read the text out loud in unison. However, as sound films became more common among the popular movie houses, direct audience participation diminished greatly; and, as Benedetti notes:

> Today one enters a cinema in an unruly fashion—almost, I would say, without respect. This wasn't the case back then; the silence of the screen demanded one's attention; and the chorus of the inter-titles, read out loud by the spectators, resembled a kind of liturgy [literally, an "oratory"]—one more sacred than those in church.[48]

Between 1929 and 1931, American (and other foreign) sound films released in Italy had their dialogue suppressed, although sound and music were available. The Commission for Censorship argued that Italian audiences would be encouraged to learn languages other than their own.[49] Some of these films were intercut with translations of the spoken dialogue, but the strategy proved to upset the rhythm of the narrative. Some of the American films released in Italy without spoken dialogue were *Cimarron* (1930), *Hallelujah* (1929), and *Dirigible* (1930).[50] By 1932, the Commission revised its position on the ban, largely as a result of protests from American producers and from Italian audiences and exhibitors; but the question of dubbing was increasingly becoming part of a politicized debate about film language, literacy, and national identity.

In 1933, Mussolini imposed a tariff on films dubbed outside Italy, though this action was seen largely as an attempt to protect Italian dubbing studios. By 1936, the political ramifications of dubbing sound films were widely discussed by Italian officials and critics. Raffaello Patuelli, for instance, argues that translators should recognize their "moral" obligation to Italian popular audiences: "Immersed in the atmosphere of the original film, the translator lost not only his feeling for the Italian language but also for our customs, for our way of life. He forgot that, whenever possible, the *naturalization* of the film depends on his judgments"[51] (italics mine). He condemns the American "jargon" in these films, which he fears will undermine or dilute traditional Italian values—a feeling shared also by Freddi.[52] Patuelli's article also calls attention to the shoddiness of dubbing efforts by Italian studios at this time; having seen *Captain Blood*, for instance, he is annoyed that "Blood" is pronounced in four ways by different characters and that the significance of the pirate's name is lost entirely in the Italian version. In 1937, Ettore Allodoli remarks that the questions surrounding dubbing of foreign films reflect a crisis in Italy over the Italian language itself and the Italian public at large; films dubbed in Italian, he argues, would open foreign films to a broader public since through "'film language' . . . more than books, there is a more direct bond between language and culture."[53] Like Patuelli, he cites instances (*Uomo d'Aran*) in which foreign characters are made to speak in Neapolitan dialect, and he condemns the lack of clear alternatives for dealing with what he feels is a fundamental contradiction in Italian popular culture.

Related to the debate over dubbing foreign films and the perceived crisis of the Italian language in film are the few attempts to ban or to delete portions of foreign films. American films banned or cut during the 1930s include the following: *Scarface* (1932), because the gangsters are of Italian origin; *A Farewell to Arms* (1932), because it evoked the military retreat at Caporetto in World War I; *Green Pastures* (1936), because paradise was depicted as a place populated entirely by Negroes—something that raised the ire of some Italian cardinals; *The Life of Emile Zola* (1936), because it devoted too much attention to the Dreyfus case and took a position against antisemitism; *Dead End* (1938), because it dealt with juvenile delinquency; *The Adventures of Marco Polo* (1938), because the explorer was not treated with enough respect by American filmmakers (the film was re-released under another title, *A Scotsman in the Court of the Gran Kan*); *Paid to Dance* (1938), because it dealt with white-slave traffic; *Wings over Honolulu* (1939), because its representation of a divorced couple went against Italian ideals about marriage and family; *Hurricane* (1939); *House of Rothschild* (1939); and *The Woman I Love* (1939), which was withdrawn after several hundred Italian students, shouting "Down with France!" invaded a motion picture theater in Rome.[54] American movies wherein objectionable footage was deleted include: *The Garden of Allah* (1936); *Romeo and Juliet* (1936), in which the double suicide bothered censors; *Lost Horizon* (1937); *Robin Hood* (1937); *Penitentiary* (1938), from which censors cut the scene in which Hawkins spits in the face of a warden; *She Married an Artist* (1938), from which censors cut three meters showing placards in a port strike and replaced them with three meters showing the port of New York; *A Night at the Opera* (1938), from which cuts were made to remove inferences that the characters were Italian; *Holiday* (1938), from which three meters were cut because characters mock the Fascist salute; *Conquest* (1938), from which parts of the third reel are cut in which Napoleon explains to Waleska how "victories breed revenge, wars of revenge breed wars of reprisal, an endless cycle of bloodshed," and then expresses hopes for a United States of

Europe that fosters "a new idea abroad in the world—the idea of Democracy"; *The Bride Wore Red* (1938), from which cuts were made to remove any inference that the setting was Italy; *Women of Glamor* (1938), from which in reel two the entire telephone call between a "sugar daddy" and Fan and Gloria is cut; *The Girl from Scotland Yard* (1938), from which all scenes of the British coronation are cut; *Mutiny on the Bounty* (1938), from which scenes of the British flag and the line "We're off to the Mediterranean, lad. We'll sweep the seas for England!" are cut.[55] As Gili has noted, Chaplin's *Modern Times* (1936), despite its politicism, is not banned or cut, because Freddi sees it as a "ferocious satire of socialism and communism and demonstrates how striking workers quickly line up behind a demagogue they know little about."[56]

Although most of the Italian versions of American films have been lost (a loss which prevents a more careful analysis here), it is necessary to acknowledge that, by the late 1930s, Italian officials and critics clearly realized the political, cultural, and aesthetic importance of practical film translation. It is equally necessary to admit, however, that only minor attempts were made at this level to reconstitute, through dubbing, the images of Americans in their own movie versions.

American Roles and Stereotypes in Italian Films

Through a review of Italian films, on the other hand, it is easier to assimilate a kind of cinematic mythology about America. It is also *through* Italian films that one is better able to observe the ambivalent attitudes about American culture. During the 1920s, the few Italian films that were produced generally exhibit a tendency to emulate the narrative and stylistic conventions of Italy's prewar successes. The one genre that maintained its popular appeal at this time was the Italian acrobatic/superhero film—the most prominent star of which was Bartolomeo Pagano (alias Maciste).[57] The heroes of these films were, as I have already explained, in many ways Italian versions of their American counterparts, Mix and Fairbanks, whose films were screened well into the 1930s. In fact, one of the later Maciste films, *Maciste e il nipote americano*, concerns a fragile alliance between the Italian superhero and his American nephew—a relationship that, interestingly enough, displaces and inverts some of the popular myths and the attitudes in the Italian film *industry* about America. Later sound films, however, invented an array of American characters, whose attributes reveal a great deal about Italian myths of America.

Most all of the Italian films that involved American figures were romantic and screwball comedies whose conflicts and humor result from role reversals and confusions about identity. In 1932, two Cines films, *Due cuori felici* (*Two Happy Hearts*) and *La cantante dell'opera* (*The Opera Singer*), both concern romantic relationships between Italian girls and wealthy American men (again personifications of the successful and urbane heroes of American comedies and musicals from this period). In *La cantante dell'opera* (a film shot entirely in Venice), a struggling, middle-aged Venetian waiter is rewarded when his beautiful daughter, who has studied music to become an opera singer, is believed by a rich

American boyfriend to be the descendant of an aristocratic Venetian family. Here the girl's stardom, and her coupling with an American, appear as the fruit of the father's labor and his unselfish nature.

In *Due cuori felici* (directed by Baldassare Negroni in the Italian version), the successful American figure of Hollywood musicals is reworked through the Vittorio De Sica character Mr. Brown, who is the son of a wealthy American automobile tycoon.[58] In this briskly paced musical comedy, the young American's first trip to Italy becomes for him a realization of values and of a part of himself (since we learn at one point that he is really an Italian-American, his family having changed its name from Bruni) that had eluded him in the United States. The film opens at a Brown outlet in Italy, with a frantic supervisor, Signor Fabbri, instructing his workers about the proper way of conducting themselves during Mr. Brown's visit. His comic efforts to teach them to say "How do you do, Mr. Brown?" (in English) become the pretext—as in Hollywood musicals—for the film's first song, parodying and celebrating the American greeting.[59] The song so animates the employees that when Mr. Brown arrives unexpectedly he encounters a lively chorus of singers and dancers. The comedic role reversals and identity confusion accelerate when Mr. Brown visits the superintendent's brightly lit, art-deco–style apartment that evening and mistakes Fabbri's secretary, Anna (Rina Franchetti), for the superintendent's wife when she emerges from his bedroom with only a bathrobe because she has accidentally gotten her own dress wet. Fabbri's real wife, Clara (Mimi Aylmer), who prefers the company of her dog to that of her simpering and foppish husband, is meanwhile attending a movie with her canine escort. From this point, much of the film's humor turns upon Mr. Brown's growing infatuation with the woman he believes to be Fabbri's wife and the other three characters' efforts to continue the charade. But occasionally humor results from the comic overlapping of the two societies. When, for instance, Mr. Brown states that Americans do everything in a hurry, Fabbri wonders out loud whether in such a mechanized society man has not been replaced by the machine; to this, the secretary, Anna, coyly inquires, "Even the secretaries?"

Like the early RKO, Warner Bros., and Paramount musicals, *Due cuori felici* integrates song and dance in ways that repeatedly displace and momentarily redress the film's central conflicts and contradictions. When Anna first preens in front of a mirror, admiring her appearance in Clara's fashionable clothes, she is so happy that she bursts into song. In the supervisor's apartment, Anna (as the supervisor's wife) attempts to ease tensions through a song at the piano. As in American musicals, her ability to make music enables her to express to Brown her latent potential—her *true* identity; and her music, in turn, induces Brown to join her in song and then in dance. And later, after the two women argue about having switched roles, they manage their differences through song.

The music in this film is generally popularized European jazz numbers, except on one important occasion when Brown and Clara visit a working-class tavern. The four characters have gone to a nightclub, where Anna, tired of her false role, takes her boss aside to complain, and where Brown, believing the married couple have left, decides to escort Clara home. After wandering in the working-class neighborhood where Clara is supposed to live, they cool their heels at a local tavern whose intimate ambiance is purposefully juxtaposed with that of the exclusive and ornate nightclub. Brown immediately remarks that this tavern "is much more characteristic, nothing like America"; and, instead of ordering champagne, they enjoy a bottle of the local wine. Through cross-cutting, the film then ties these two social/entertainment styles together. When Anna begins singing the film's title song with her boss at the nightclub, the film cuts to the maid and cook at the boss's apartment singing the next line, and then to Brown and Clara at the tavern singing another line. At the tavern, Brown and Clara lead the intoxicated patrons in a jubilant refrain, and, as he orders wine for everyone, the people at the tavern stand to salute him and his "wife." Furthermore, just before he and Clara leave, Brown sings for these working-class patrons an American song, thus appearing to reconcile any cultural or social differences through his music. However, later that evening, when he asks his Italian chauffeur what he thinks about the quality of the Brown automobile he drives, the chauffeur (not realizing Brown's identity) complains that it is "rubbish"; only when Brown introduces himself and the chauffeur realizes that he is biting the hand that feeds him does he apologize to Brown.

The following day, in the film's finale, Brown states that his sojourn in Italy has made him more enamoured with Italy's customs and women. But, when he implores Fabbri to allow him to return with his "secretary," the supervisor offers Brown his "wife" instead, explaining that he has been having an affair with his "secretary." Just when Brown begins to understand the charade, Anna walks into the room dressed in her original plain dress; and Brown, admitting that he cannot tolerate lies but recognizing that things have worked out to his advantage, asks Anna to come to America with him. As the couple leave, the Fabbris and their maid sing "How do you do, Mr. . . . . Mrs. Brown."

In both *La cantante dell'opera* and *Due cuori felici*, American wealth, success, and modernity are connoted qualities in their leading characters. In the films, these qualities impart to the characters a seductive aura, which is played out as romantic love. The anxieties experienced by the female leads in both films result from their desire to negotiate some kind of balance between a more prosaic, traditional lifestyle and a more cosmopolitan and modern one made possible by their double identities and their affiliations with American boyfriends. In the following year (1933), however, the seductive power of this American image is called into question by Palermi's *Non c'è bisogno di denaro* (*Who Needs Money?*). This film concerns a small provincial bank (on the verge of failure) which nominates as its president a man who just returned from America—but broke. Because of his American background, word gets around that he is a millionaire; and as a result of this rumor the money begins to pour into the bank. Not only does this situation offer optimism in Italy's period of economic crisis, but it also inverts what in Capra's *American Madness* (released the previous year) appears as the instability of banks when faced with exaggerated rumor. The American bank president's double identity serves here to create a series of comic situations.

Unfortunately, the day the town prepares to unveil a bust of the new hero in the main square, news arrives from Chicago that one of his checks has bounced. Realizing their own delusions, and not knowing what else to do, the town goes on with the ceremony, proving that (as Francesco Savio glibly observes in his brief critique of this film) "money's worthless; it's *credit* that counts." It seems, however, that in exposing the American mystique, the film can do little but draw humor from misfortune.

Another film that expresses a theme similar to that of *Non c'è bisogno di denaro* is Gennaro Righelli's *Fuochi d'artificio* (*Fireworks*, 1938). This film also affirms that not all who return from America are wealthy. The story is that of a young man who, because he is returning from America, is believed to be rich. This double identity serves again to produce dramatic conflict; but finally, with the assistance of his secretary (who is a bit of a profiteer), he achieves his wealth. What is interesting about both *Fuochi d'artificio* and *Non c'è bisogno di denaro* is their ambivalence about American society and its presumed affluence. Both films affirm the transcendent nature of America—a land where people *can* get rich quick; this myth, after all, creates enough excitement in the town in *Non c'è bisogno di denaro* that the inhabitants rush to the bank to deposit their money. Yet both films also suggest (as does *Due cuori felici*) that there is no place like home, that only in Italy can the true value of an Italian-American be appreciated.

The Italian film representation of Italian-Americans was not always that of one who had failed in America. In *Chi sei tu?* (*Who Are You?* 1939) a young woman is attracted to the magnetic personality of an Italian-American actor (alias Man Rowel) who visits a small hotel she has established. In this romantic comedy, the actor's occupation and American background are emblems that arouse in the girl an immediate interest. This story, however, is more about the girl's attraction than it is about the actor's attractiveness; she has created her own stage (the Hotel of the Chimeras) onto which has walked her Prince Charming. In another film, Carlo Borghesio and Mario Soldati's *Due milione per un sorriso* (*Two Million for a Smile*, 1939) an older Italian who has made his fortune in America decides to finance a film in Italy about his first romantic love—realizing that he will never find a woman who could replicate her image. However, the young Italian director whom he hires for the task does fall in love with an aspiring young actress; and the older producer, having been vicariously gratified by their happiness, returns to America. By casting the Italian-American figure as a film producer, this movie plays upon the Italian mystique about the American film world to assure a happy ending. Although the image of the Italian-American is in this case that of a truly self-made man, the movie reaffirms the myth that only in Italy can this expatriate recover an ideal from his past and thus realize his true value.

Besides the fable of the American in Italy or of the Italian-American who returns home, there is also Mario Camerini's image of the Italian who desires to live out fantasies about American success and mobility. In Camerini's *Il Signor Max*, Gianni experiences the allure of American modernity and wealth, and ultimately learns about the reprehensibleness of this desire; a less positive value is attached to America than in the films of the early 1930s, although there is still evidence of an Italian ambivalence about the glamor of American culture. Here America becomes a part of the cluster of signification—the *bel mondo*, decadence in unlimited leisure, lack of family and cultural roots, etc.—which the traveling entourage in this film connotes. It is important to realize as well that Gianni has learned about America through the magazines and popular reading that he sells; he has become so absorbed in popular American iconography that, like the unfortunate banker in *Non c'è bisogno di denaro*, he is mistaken as an important personality because he surrounds himself briefly with American emblems (*Esquire* magazine, an American camera, etc.). It also seems that De Sica represented for Italian audiences a personality who was able to play both sides of the cultural/economic fence—performing the role of the wealthy American, Mr. Brown, in *Due cuori felici*, of the petit-bourgeois, Italian Bruno in *Gli uomini, che mascalzoni!* in 1932, and of Gianni (a composite) in *Il Signor Max*.

By the very late 1930s, as Italian trade sanctions against American film distribution begin to take effect, there appears what is undoubtedly one of the oddest *homages* to Hollywood that was produced in Italy at this time: Nunzio Malasomma's appropriately titled *Cose dell'altro mondo* (*Other Worldly Things*, 1939). In this screwball comedy, Malasomma attempts to parody Hollywood's prison movies—a strategy which attests, on the one hand, to the extreme familiarity of Italian directors and audiences by this time with certain narrative formulas and characterizations in American movies and, on the other hand, to a desire by Italians to refashion these foreign generic codes. The story takes place in an American prison, where three conspicuously refined prisoners, a man and two women, obtain from the daughter of the prison director means of escaping for a brief period.[60] The prison warden, having learned that the three escapees are notorious gangsters and fearing a scandal, substitutes his own daughter, his wife, and another prisoner in their place. Ultimately, the three escapees return, and the prison director realizes that they are actually an inspector, his wife, and her cousin. The success of this type of humor is rather dubious, considering the disparaging remarks of Italian movie critics at the time of the film's release. As Francesco Callari writes:

> There is a continuing insistence to present movies about men and events of other countries—ones unfamiliar with our customs (these films are the perfect evasion). . . . Nunzio Malasomma . . . with the intention of ridiculing or parodying the penal systems in the United States, has only succeeded in glossing over the paradox (prisoners who come and go freely).[61]

But Callari's review itself underscores the very ambivalence of attitudes toward America. Malasomma's film does indeed ridicule the conventions of the American prison genre, but it also inadvertently represents America as a land of screwballs—a place where prison is farce.

A few years later, however, America and the dream of success became the subjects of a more tragic and cynical filmic treatment in Carmine Gallone's *Harlem* (1943), produced the same year as Visconti's *Ossessione*, which is itself based upon James M. Cain's novel about an American nightmare, or dream gone sour (in fact, Massimo Girotti stars in both films—as the young vagabond in *Ossessione* and as a boxer in *Harlem*). *Harlem* is set entirely in an urban America. The film's screenplay, written by Emilio Cecchi, who had spent considerable time in America and had written about American culture, concerns a young Italian man who visits his older brother in America to further his aspirations for becoming a prizefighter. In this sense, *Harlem* borrows generously from Hollywood boxing and crime films from the 1930s—a fact not lost upon Italian film critic Antonio Pietrangeli, who reviewed the film just after its release.[62] While the young man's optimism and courage enable him to realize his dream, his road to success is punishing and tragic; his older brother (a New York builder) becomes falsely accused of homicide and winds up in jail. When the young boxer wins a bout against an American Negro fighter, he pays for his brother's release from jail; but soon thereafter, the older brother is shot and killed by rival gangsters. As he lays dying, he insists that his young brother give up boxing and return to Italy, since nothing good will come to him in America.

Harlem was made during the years when *official* animosities toward America were widely proclaimed in Italy. The black boxers and white extras in the film were actually inmates from prisons in Rome. Unlike the previous films that used American characters in Italy, *Harlem* exposes that myth by setting its dramatic action in America; here America is not a far-away dream but a "new reality" captured through a vision of blood and sweat. The movie once again depicts America as a land where success is attainable for those who are special, but here through the young Italian fighter who forges his fame despite an inclement and unsavory environment. One cannot easily attribute these changes entirely to political and international circumstances, especially since the film's *realism* speaks to an aesthetic impulse already evident in Italian cinema and since its messages about the American dream are generally congruous with those of early Hollywood *film noir*. What this film's realism and demystification demonstrate, however, is that America is still a myth—here Harlem and New York, places that readily evoke a pedigree of other Hollywood formulas and models. Amedeo Nazzari, who plays the older brother in the film, has recently related an anecdote that vividly amplifies this point. He explains that after shooting *Harlem* he complained to Luigi Freddi that he resented his denigration of Americans. At one point, for instance, he stands looking out a window at the people below and says, "These are despicable and corrupt people. . . . " The line appeared in the film's original release; but, after the war, Nazzari remembers seeing another dubbed version in which, standing at the window, his character is now heard to say, "These marvelous people, this stupendous race, this society which creates progress in the world. . . . "[63]

American News/Italian Newsreel

As Italy became increasingly involved with American movie producers and distributors during the 1920s, the state also relied upon American sources for

America as movie spectacle (from a title-shot of a feature in a LUCE newsreel)

newsreel footage. As I explain more fully in chapter 7, the LUCE newsreels from the late 1920s and the 1930s frequently included material from foreign countries in order to place images of events in Italy in an international context. In the very first LUCE newsreel in 1927, for example, American sources supply four of the six features; two of the features (one about the Lindbergh flight and another about the flooding of the Mississippi at New Orleans) concern events in America. Until 1940, an average of about one American feature appears in each LUCE newsreel. This fascination with events in America can be attributed in part to what Mino Argentieri describes as the United State's representations as "a gay circus populated by eternal children."[64] There were, among others, rodeo exhibitions (#23), handstand races (#1170), soapbox derbies (#1578), a miniature Dutch town in Ohio (#11), a freckle contest (#1572), motorboat racing (#1600), air stunts at the World's Fair (#1606), an amusement park in San Francisco (#1480), water sports in Florida (#443), and rubber-horse contests in swimming pools in California (#6). But, in addition to these representations of frivolous leisure activities, found less often in newsreel footage from Italy or from other countries, American footage also featured more cataclysmic events: tornado damage in Georgia (#9) or a train derailment in Nevada (#1575). And, by the late 1930s and early 1940s, LUCE newsreels include frequent scenes of American military exercises, described in some of the Italian newsreels as the "two faces" of America (#7, March 1940, wherein a feature entitled "The Beautiful and Ugly in America" juxtaposes coverage of gymnastic routines by naval cadets at Annapolis with another sequence about a hairy and obese wrestler named Angelo, "who's not afraid of being called the ugliest man in the world").

Like the more commercial feature films, the state-produced LUCE newsreels are inscribed with an ambivalence about American popular culture and its appeal for Italians. In fact, as I explain further in chapter 7, these images of a world "beyond" the cultural vista of Italian audiences (and the "other-ness" of these representations must be qualified) provided a crucial strategy for clarifying and legitimizing the featured events and images of Italian national character constructed through LUCE newsreels. And at the same time, the Italian features, music, narration, etc. that accompanied the scenes from America helped both to naturalize and to distance these American images. Whereas narrative films may have enhanced America's figurative power and its mythic significance through fictional characters/stars and fables, the newsreels helped ground their reality in expositions on *historical happenings*. That newsreels were watched along with narrative films only makes this connection more important to recognize; although an expository mode, newsreels relied heavily upon the evocative resonance of the narrative forms. Two particularly interesting cases in point would be LUCE #12's 1940 feature commemorating Hollywood movie star Douglas Fairbanks or the exhibition in April 1930 at a first-run Milanese cinema of a LUCE monograph about the marriage of Mussolini's daughter, Edda, followed by Dolores Del Rio in *Evangeline*.

The Critic's Translation

Up to this point, I have referred frequently to the praise and warnings by Italian film directors and critics about various aspects of the American film industry. There were, as well, a number of Italian books written in these years about Hollywood films and stars.[65] While it is true that Italian films in this period convey more popular or common sentiments about America than do critics (the critic's activity *generally* being less a function of popular tastes), the observations of Italian critics and political ideologues about American film are not entirely without the same stereotyping that one finds *in* popular forms. First, even for Italian critics and political figures, the ubiquity of American films made it difficult to understand America other than in terms of its cinematic images. Second, it is equally necessary to remember that critics and political ideologues themselves, when discussing America, often wrote *for* a popular audience (through newspapers as well as film journals with more limited circulations); their own rhetoric required vivid and concise images—ones which could be readily apprehended by mass audiences.

Although the more educated and traveled critics may have understood the variegations of American cinema and American culture, their own discourses frequently adopted many of the same myths that were common in Italian films about Americans. Perhaps one of the clearest examples of American myths in

Italian criticism is Alberto Consiglio's and Giacomo Debenedetti's "Il senso dell'avventura" (1936). These two authors characterize America as the ultimate frontier, the land of the pioneer; and they relate all American film genres to this metaphor. For example, they see Tom Mix and Clark Gable (in *It Happened One Night*) both as wandering cavaliers in search of fortune and adventure. Then there is the ganster, who "bears adventure through the 'streets of the city'." They note that Lubitsch, who would seem to evoke themes antithetic to those of Westerns, is himself a kind of "pioneer" in visual stylization.[66]

Critiques or reviews of American films in the 1920s and early 1930s generally addressed two concerns: the aesthetic or stylistic qualities of the film (usually its *theatrical* qualities, e.g., acting, style, set design, etc.) or the audience's responses to it. Unlike the Neorealist theoreticians after the war, Italian 1920s and early 1930s critics paid little attention to the relationship between the filmmaker and his film. This attitude among Italian critics toward cinema is indicative of the general role of intellectuals in Italian society during the regime. As Anna Panicali has observed in a recent essay, the function of intellectuals at that time was to bridge art and popular culture and to level any differences between themselves and their audience. Although there were Italian film critics during the 1930s who discussed films in terms of their directors, they belonged to and wrote for a very limited group of cineasts. Examples of their perceptions about American directors would be Margadonna's discussion of King Vidor as "poet"[67] (also see Consiglio's or Fabrizio Sarazani's essays on Vidor[68]) or Emilio Cecchi's article on Capra.[69] These early writings by the more "literary"-minded critics inspired the younger generation of Italian film critics who, through programs sponsored by the GUF, developed a sophisticated vocabulary of cinema and, in many instances, became filmmakers themselves. During the 1940s, these younger theoreticians/filmmakers generally rejected American cinema as "escapist," although they lauded works by certain directors such as Orson Welles.

The point here again is that Italian film critics were a historically diverse group who reviewed American films according to different critical paradigms. Despite the heterogeneity of their approach, however, there remained a fairly limited set of stereotypes and myths about America—ones they shared with the larger Italian film audience.

One of the more interesting and ironic examples of the effects of American myths on Italy's critical and political "elite" concerns an essay by Luigi Freddi about the Duce's own movie tastes.[70] In some cases, movies not yet released were sent both to the state review committee and to Mussolini's private screening room. Freddi notes that Mussolini was given to watching at home on a regular basis the LUCE newsreels and, usually on Fridays, a feature-length film. Freddi characterizes the Duce's preferences for feature films as follows:

> The films which he preferred were, above all, those with a social content, musical film, and those which reflected aspects and customs of other countries. He gave himself completely to certain comic actors, in whose presence he became really just another spectator amidst the general public.

Films of Laurel and Hardy were of particular enjoyment to him, and he was heard to have exclaimed, "*mi hanno rovinato il 'grasso' e il 'magro'!*" According to Freddi, he never wanted to view detective or gangster movies, nor did he express a preference for certain actors or directors. What is perhaps most significant about Freddi's exposition on the Duce's movie habits, however, is his final anecdote about Mussolini's ability to distinguish cinematic reality from real life. It seems that while watching *Desire*, with Marlene Dietrich, he became disconcerted about a scene wherein Dietrich, who is seated on a divan, converses with the male lead; the scene is shot in a series of close-ups from different points of view which present either the actress or the actor, or both together. After the film, Mussolini is reported to have asked Freddi, "Why during the conversation on the couch was the actress's handkerchief positioned at times in one way and at other times in a different way?" After Freddi explained to him that it was probably an error by the script-girl, the Duce replied, "Well, even the Americans make mistakes!"

Conclusions

The anecdote about Mussolini reveals an important point about the manner in which popular audiences watch and understand foreign films; foreign audiences tend to *literalize* a film's "national accent." The meaning of America's power was, therefore both real and imagined; the ubiquity of its movies enabled each film to draw upon an existing storehouse of cinematic models and, thus, to mean more fully. But these meanings were necessarily mediated by a shifting Italian infrastructure and an emerging cinematic literacy—processes that problematize the signification of power and necessitate careful consideration of its textuality. Hollywood film styles during the 1930s can themselves be described as realistic, since they make little effort to call attention, in an ironic way, to their own cinematic strategies; and one should also recognize that the mimetic qualities of the cinematic image and of sound synchronization by the early 1930s provided the illusion of nature reduplicated. Abroad, however, Hollywood movies could easily be mistaken as "mirror images" of America and its lifestyles. For Italian audiences, America literally was Hollywood's images.

These images were not semantically uniform, and their translation by another culture often altered the semantic field of the films' "preferred" messages elsewhere. Among Italian movies that involve American characters, it is evident that the set of Italian myths about America was rather limited, e.g., the wealthy American, the American woman, a cosmopolitan America, etc. These myths, as Levi-Strauss would indicate, give presence to contradictory attitudes about America, and the Italian films about American characters dramatize this ambivalence. In *Per uomini soli*, for example, a wealthy American actress's "imaginary" affair with an Italian opera singer forces him to realize the value of his former Italian girlfriend; here the American appears as both temptress and the way to salvation. It is also significant that in *Per uomini soli*, as in a number of Italian movies about Americans, American characters are directly linked to the cinema—an occupation which makes these figures appear even more remote and symbolic. In a LUCE newsreel, a feature about America is introduced by an art-deco tableau of the Manhattan skyline framed with what appears to be the lights around a Broadway marquee. The cinema, cosmopolitanism, commercial success, and frontier adventurism are all themes nurturing Italy's "epochalist" impulse.

If, as Peter Brooks has suggested, the modern imagination attempts to articulate (in a bourgeois and "democratic" world—a world which otherwise lacks a sense of an absolute Other or a sense of sacredness) the transcendent value of events through public spectacle, it would seem that America had become for Italian audiences an emblem of this transcendence. Certainly, in many of the Italian films about America, American characters enable Italian characters to realize an other-worldliness which both threatens and confers value—often comically—on their Italian surroundings. Their ambiguous roles, as film personalities or as Italian-Americans, make them seem both alien and a part of Italian society. The images of American popular entertainment were able to expand the cultural horizons of foreign audiences ("*gli States sono un mito eccelso*"); but they also presented this other world in intimate, family-oriented situations and through a "populist" perspective. They gave a cinematic presence to a realm beyond that of Europe: "That sense of a different lifestyle that our grandfather's sought in Paris, or as far as London or Berlin, today lies on the other side of the Ocean and really can't be found any closer to us than New York."[71] But Italian audiences could also find in America a celebration, in *modern* images, of spiritual community and conservative values. America's mythical status produced both desire and fear—emotions which for about twenty years helped transform Italy into a stage for ideological conflict.

3 *Grandi magazzini*: *Stracittà* and the Department Store as Temple of Consumer Culture

What's left of Vulcan in comparison with
Roberts & Co., of Jove in the presence of the
lightning rod, of Hermes in the presence of
Credit mobilier?

—Karl Marx

Any discussion of a popular or mass culture in the early twentieth century must address the relationship of industrial capitalism to public culture and also to the growth of urban commerical centers and the social classes which accompanied this growth—in short, the common symptoms of social "development" and "modernization." Anthropologist Clifford Geertz describes modern culture in terms of its ideological formations and social rituals—the implementation of belief and value systems which are both organized/unorganized, rational/irrational, material/occult. Ideology, in a sense, mediates these dialectics, which are, by and large, symptomatic of modern, industrial societies. Though ideology provides a society with a sense of collective self-worth (of its own *sacredness*), these ideals remain bound up with material conditions. Alvin Gouldner notes that in modern societies, as a result of what he describes as the historic "splitting" away from a Tragic, hierarchical vision of things, ideology secularizes transcendence. It is ideology's role, according to Gouldner, to serve as the necessary social *glue* between what is real and what is ideal: "In the tragic vision . . . the world and the ideal have the power to help by reconciling men to What Is, to an essentially unchangeable fate. . . . In the ideological vision, the word and the ideal are seen as having the power practically to change What Is, here in the world, and it intimates that this world is all there is."[1] Ideology thus generates *myths*, but ones which are, because of the available technology/technique and a public literacy, very much a part of a historical moment and a particular society. Hence Marx's rhetorical question about the exact location of

Mount Olympus or of those places where modern man worships. In an urban and commercialized milieu, where does one discover *transcendence*—if not, as Walter Benjamin suggests, through the manufactured image itself? The towns-people in Fellini's *Amarcord*, for example, seem to have assimilated this merging of the Ridiculous with the Sublime; they pass every evening before a shop whose windows are packed with seemingly myriad manufactured reproductions (in all shapes and sizes) of the Virgin Mary.

Traditional political economists such as Cyril Black have argued that modern-ization, while providing new opportunities and prospects, does so at a high price in human dislocation and suffering. For Black, modernization gives way to uncertainty and instability; it tends to atomize society, "depriving its members of the sense of community and belonging without which individual fulfillment cannot be satisfactorily achieved."[2] However, ideology—through cultural pro-duction—is comprised of models for managing social tensions and the in-stabilities of historical change. Certainly, for those social classes created by industrialization and most affected by modernization, e.g., the urban middle classes and proletariat, cinematic images and narratives (rather than those of the traditional arts) offered provisional frameworks for understanding and solving their vaguely defined and rapidly changing cultural and material environment. Actually, the problems of modernization, brought on by industrialization, oc-curred later in Italy than in America and other European countries. The Italian historian R. Morandi notes that

> it is necessary to recognize that the fifteen years that transpired from 1898 to 1913, if they did not give to Italy an industrial system that had real consistency, and above all that minimum of completeness necessary to secure for the country a certain economic autonomy, did nonetheless signal a noteworthy moment in the evolution of the social environment, characterized by the modern *industrial spirit* which manifested itself there.[3]

Although this "industrial spirit" had begun in Italy before the Fascist regime, its consequences were not fully experienced there until the 1920s and 1930s. In fact, as Nicos Poulantzas observes, industrial development in Italy was more a part of the Fascist period:

> Industrial recovery between 1922 and 1929 [in Fascist Italy] was the strongest in capitalist Europe . . . and the recovery after the crisis was quite spectacular. . . . It represented industrial development, technological innovation, and an increase in the productivity of labor.[4]

In light of this rapidly changing material environment, it is not surprising that collective values and ways of celebrating or challenging them were changing as well—that the search for transcendence was to be expressed through new mod-els and new technologies. It is important to remember that cinema itself was a feature of modernization in Italy and that it served as a *forum* for ideological conflict. The cinema was one of the first cultural forms to become an industry, dependent upon expedient, far-reaching distribution networks and upon skilled technicians, and a type of spectacle that primarily addressed the concerns of an audience created by industrialization and the growth of urban trade centers. Moreover, as I have indicated in the last two chapters on the myth of the Grand Hotel and the myths of America, the networks of foreign distribution placed Italian audiences in the presence of models of "modern" and cosmopolitan lifestyles—ones that, due to the growing ubiquity and accessibility of the cinema and to the mimesis of film imaging, appeared to be seductively plausible.

The Modern Myths

Through foreign movies, a relatively more provincial Italian movie audience witnessed and was compelled to come to terms with some of the primary Modern themes of twentieth-century Western experience—the most prevalent of which, as Monroe Spears has noted, concerned the arrival of Dionysus in the City: "the literal and physical city which dominates the modern environment and is both cause and symptom of our characteristic maladies. . . . It is the background which produces the typical modern man and the stage upon which he acts."[5] For Spears, the arrival of Dionysus in the City refers to the changing nature of myth (to that which has come to be described as ideology); for Modernists, urban culture provided new subjects, new images through which to ponder the human condition. Of course, these images were more transient than those that had been found in Nature (or in nineteenth-century Naturalism and Neoclassicism); thus they often produced a more ironic and fragmented vision of the human condition. Roberto Tessari provides an eloquent appraisal of the aesthetics and sociology of Modernism in Italy:

> Places at the fringes that separate country and metropolis, present and past. Our writers, meanwhile, suffer severely from the cultural crisis engendered by industry; they lift the banner of myth and of mythopoeic action in order to make themselves healers of the modern public—prophetic trustees of a linguistic magic that attempts to reconvey the ancient orphic chant, taming with new melodies the metallic "monsters" of the modern factories and streets, reshaping the new chaos into the ancient song of form.[6]

According to Tessari, Italian artists around the turn of the century reacted to the "triumph" of the machine by imparting to it a mythical significance.[7] Italian Futurism offered perhaps the most radical expressions about the mythical nature of the machine; Futurists exalted through theater, verse, and manifestos a mechanical theophany, which they hoped could transform a modern, industrial environment into a heroic stage. On the other hand, Massimo Bontempelli and some of his immediate "900" group, though they were labeled elitists by the Strapaese proponents, desired more "popular" and social myths about the machine and industry than those offered by the Futurists.[8] Yet Bontempelli's attitude toward the machine was more conspicuously ironic and grotesque than that of the Futurists and failed to appeal to the type of public that he idealized. Nowhere, however, was the transcendent nature of industry described with more florid and spirited embellishment than in a work of the little-recognized Italian author Mario Morasso, who as early as 1898 wrote:

> Industry, exactly as in the ancient dawn of heroism, has produced the material for future myths, for the new epic poetry. . . . The great works of our clerical offices, the rhythm of our motors, the driving force of our machines and finally, the supreme encounter, the ultimate duel between steam and electricity, in the spirit of that great battle between Hector and Achilles, between the black smoking Titans—horrendous and deafening progenitors of legends—the fury of Averno, jumping out from the caverns of his galleries with huge red eyes; and pure, soft Angelo—invincible, rustling in the air, armed with a mythical flaming sword forged from the eternal lightning of Zeus, a testament to a time of extraordinary ferment and of primordial chaos. And this new poetry will not be inscribed by Man, or City, but by Machine.[9]

For Morasso, industry was the divine symbol of the modern political state of humanity—a theocracy whose temples were the Department Stores:

> The holy temple, as a means of satisfying a spiritual need for a real sense of fellowship and of community, has become the Department Store or the Clerical Office. . . . The primordial battlefield is now the Department Store, the Clerical Office, the Pocketbook, Mercantilism . . . the heroic virtues return to shine with a generative splendor.[10]

The historical irony of Morasso's vision is that by the late 1920s a chain of Italian department stores called Il Duomo (The Cathedral) had been established in major northern Italian cities, and another, Il Rinascente (The Revival/Rebirth), had been established in major cities throughout Italy.

Morasso's vision of modern Italian culture, perhaps because of its highly ebullient rhetoric, demonstrates most vividly the epochalist impulse that flourished during the 1920s with the rapid growth of industry in Italy and its increasingly international commercial connections. In Walter Ruttman's 1932 melodrama *Acciaio* (*Steel*), set in and around a steel mill in Terni, the fiery, mechanized mill (as a result of Ruttman's Expressionistic depiction of events therein) evokes the kind of sacred and mystical aura traditionally associated with ritual caves or religious temples, as centers for the community's spiritual revitalization and unity of purpose.[11]

The echoes of early Modernist and Futurist rhetoric also inform, in rather curious ways, film theory, as in Guglielmo Giannini's 1929 treatise on sound in film:

> The twentieth century . . . which has heard the thunder of piston-driven engines, must harmonize their own sounds just as other centuries have harmonized theirs: the jazz-band is the foremost effect of the musical revolution—sister to the

automobile. . . . The culture of our century is therefore mechanistic, and the machine has become our poetry. . . . We need to rejoice that the machine is our culture rather than to be ashamed of it. The machine must be our artform.[12]

But, despite the intentions of Italian Futurists or those of the "900" circle to reach a popular audience through literature, theater, and film criticism, their efforts proved either too abusive (as was the case with Futurist performances) or too abstract and literary (as was the case with Bontempelli). A formulaic and image-oriented medium, more than a complex linguistic one, seemed best suited to achieving the kind of immediacy of experience that these post–World War I avant-garde groups desired. Moreover, rapid recognition and an immediacy of experience were, in a certain sense, the only means of receiving information afforded by the routine and leisure of the lower middle classes and working classes.

The illusion of familarity, of being "in touch," certainly may have also aided the government's attempt to create a *regime*, a sense of organic community, in a period dramatically destabilized by significant economic and ideological trans-formations. As de Grazia has noted, industry and bureaucratic Fascism were more successful than the avant-garde artists of the day in providing images intended to invigorate the routine of the "new middle class"—the group which experiences most intensely the strains of modernization.[13]

Corporativism and the Myth of the Department Store

After the economic boom of the 1920s, the economic crisis of 1929 necessitated the reconversion of the entire production system, part of which included the revival of the Italian film industry itself. It was at this time that, according to contributors to *Critica Fascista*, the Fascist revolution culminated in the forma-tion of a state-society, i.e., a regime. The theorizations and implementation of economic reforms become part of the Fascist government's need to express its own political modernity: "undertaking and continuing the collosal transforma-tion of a technological civilization."[14] Fascism's *corporativism* was not necessarily a new economic science or "system"; it was, however, both a highly rhetorical political model or trope (through which the lower and middle classes could presumably envision their indispensable function in a production system) and an ideal—the transcendent essence of Fascism's modernity and its *difference* from foreign systems. In 1935, Luigi Chiarini even suggested that the Italian film industry itself was paradigmatic of the corporativistic spirit.[15] As a social ideal, corporativism *depended* upon the organizing activity of bureaucrats, clerks, etc. (i.e., of the lower middle classes) and upon vivid, moral images that promoted the virtues of organization, i.e., organicism. Because it was political and rhetori-cal, corporativism required a "natural" foundation—one which upheld modern Italian culture.

In this period, one Italian movie—Camerini's *Grandi magazzini* (*Department*

The department store as cinematic space in *Grandi magazzini* (d. Camerini, 1939)—Museum of Modern Art/Film Stills Archives

Stores, 1938)—particularly succeeded in addressing the broad concerns accompanying the flux of modernization and social change.[16] Most of Camerini's films during the 1930s concern conflict created by the central characters' commitment to work and their desire for leisure.[17] However, in *Grandi magazzini*, he discovers in a department store a dramatic stage that crystalizes the economic infrastructure and brings the various levels of society into direct interpersonal rivalry. Although the concept of department store as social ladder was not introduced by Camerini (the ladder having been precariously scaled sixteen years before by Harold Lloyd in *Safety Last*),[18] it offered an inspired metaphor for its Italian audiences. Because much of the action in *Grandi magazzini* occurs in a department store, the movie evokes the myths of the Italian consumer society—myths which Morasso had dramatically underscored at the turn of the century.

The department store serves as an ideal structure or stage for spectacle primarily because of its relatively extraordinary place in Italian society, which had traditionally been catered by smaller, family-operated stores;[19] Camerini makes much the same observation in a fairly recent interview.[20] For example, a film such as *Felicità Colombo* (1937),[21] which is a remake of a nineteenth-century play, updates for Italian audiences a more familiar dramatic stage: a family-operated delicatessen. (In this film, family conflict involving the older and younger generations directly impinges upon the welfare of the shop; restoring the natural order of the family is tantamount to saving the family business.) As H. Pasdermadjian observes, department stores have historically been connected with the rise of the middle classes; department stores emphasized *customer services* and sold far less than smaller specialty stores. Department stores were actually more prevalent in northern Europe and America, where the middle classes had become a more formidable social force. It is not unlikely that Italian department stores were an emblem of modernity precisely because they regularly imparted (through marketing strategies) the "exoticism" of commerical fashion set by these foreign countries.

Besides being a locus for popular fashion and cultural modernity in Italy during the 1930s, the department store was the epitome of organizational theory and architectonics. Pasdermadjian notes that "in the eye of the public, the department store, whatever its shortcomings when judged against the background of modern management principles, represented one of the most striking examples of application of the science of organization."[22] He also points out that the systematic application of the principles of modern management to department-store operation began only during the 1920s and 1930s. Such a claim seems to be borne out by Arthur Lazarus who, in 1926, likens the department-store organization to a centralization of government; and Mussolini himself used architectural metaphors to characterize Fascism as a house of glass into which all may look.[23] A 1928 newspaper ad for the Milanese department store Il Rinascente actually reminds readers about the store's numerous amenities—tearoom, beauty salon, nursery, free train tickets to the provinces, etc.—to make it appear *more* than just a consumer space.[24] It would not, therefore, be stretching a metaphor to say that *Grandi magazzini* is in many ways the cinematic model of Fascist corporativism and a microcosm of the social order. But the spirit of corporativism runs through more than the movie's themes; it is given presence as well through the film's set design, its cinematic style, and the construction of its narrative.

One of the movie's themes concerns the consequences engendered by a breakdown in the organization of the *tribe*. This breakdown commences when Bruno (played by De Sica), who drives a delivery truck for the department store, attempts to collect workman's compensation for an injury he claims to have suffered. Actually, he is feigning the injury to extort the money; but, surrounded by the corporate heads of the store in the office of the president, Bruno arduously seeks to convince them about the severity of his injury. They, of course, are skeptical until he is able to solicit from the president an account of the president's own similar mishap. In the momentary spirit of this camaraderie, the president reluctantly grants Bruno his compensation; Bruno leaves the office congratulating himself for his cunning in obtaining this meager fortune.

Here the film comically treats the pettiness of his crime and his ideals by exaggerating the transience of fortune. Bruno leaves the office and enters the store's elevator, where he notices an attractive salesgirl. Invigorated by his sense of self-importance, Bruno silently flirts with her. But, as he descends in the elevator, he suddenly is overcome by a sense of false security. He frantically searches his pockets for the money and, unable to locate it quickly, suddenly charges the passengers on the elevator with its theft. They, in turn, become indignant as he physically attempts to recover his presumed loss from each of them. Especially angry is Lauretta, a young salesgirl (played by Assia Noris). On the ground floor, where Bruno, at the height of his anxiety and hysteria, discovers the money, she chides him for his previous posturing and subsequent outburst. Thus, in this initial episode, the ethical stability of the store seems threatened by deceit, mistrust, and egoism. Because these initial actions occur in a department store, the egoism appears prompted in part by the spiritual emptiness of an unmitigated commercialism (a characteristic commonly attached to American society and to the old Liberal or pre-Fascist order). And, from this point in the narrative, Bruno and Lauretta come to learn that there are forces at work which seek to obfuscate the virtuous nature of their system and its vitality.

Although not all of the subsequent action occurs in the store, "backstage" events influence events in the store and vice versa. (In fact, some more intimate scenes occur in the employees' dressing room at the store; that characters don uniforms/costumes imparts to their work space a theatrical quality, as though the dressing room were "backstage.") The instability of the tribal politics in the department store is redoubled in the more intimate, romantic conflicts among the employees. For instance, as Lauretta leaves the store after her encounter with Bruno, she meets her roommate (also a salesgirl in the store). Her roommate has recently separated from her husband, and they commiserate with one another about "what *mascalzoni* men are" (an obvious allusion to an earlier Camerini film starring De Sica). Their seemingly more private dialogue outside the store helps reframe and enlarge the meaning of Lauretta and Bruno's previous department-store encounter, and it deepens the emotionalism and moralism of the opening events at the store as romantic desire begins to overlap with material desires. Because much of the intermediary stage of the narrative concerns romantic conflicts between men and women, the meanings of the department store gradually become more transcendent—both for the lovers/workers and for the audience, whose understanding of the store's significance is mediated by the romantic conflicts of the central characters. In *Grandi magazzini*, the audience would have recognized immediately that, despite their initial hostilities, Bruno and Lauretta are "made for each other"; part of the *naturalness* of this couple's rapport results from De Sica's and Norris's having been paired in previous Camerini films and from ways that Camerini reworks his formula for comic effect. But beside this level of connotation, which results from the body of films they have made together, other levels cultivated in the narrative itself enhance the inevitability or "fatedness" of their romance. For one, their socioeconomic attributes (both are employees for the store) impart to their roles a certain equality which is underscored whenever either of them is courted by characters of a different socioeconomic status. A network of triangular desire develops soon after Bruno's and Lauretta's first encounter, and this network serves as the primary basis for dramatic conflict in the rest of the film. After their confrontation in the store, Bruno observes Lauretta and her roommate being offered a ride home by the store's director of personnel. (The director's car here has several functions: it is an icon that a film audience during this period would associate with an upper-middle-class lifestyle; it is a dramatic metaphor for the director's social mobility; it is a narrative motif found in Camerini's earlier film, *Gli uomini, che mascalzoni*; and it is also an indexical sign of the innovations in transportation which literally sustain department stores, outlets for the *novelties* of a modern, urban consumer society.)[25] As in *Il Signor Max*, Lauretta's appearance with the store's director only enhances her image in Bruno's eyes. Paradoxically, however, the director (and his lifestyle) seems to Bruno to be both a conduit and an obstacle in consummating his desire for Lauretta. Soon thereafter, Bruno approaches her in the store (at her counter in the sports department) to apologize and to profess his attraction for her. Her passion for him intensifies when she sees him offering a ride in a delivery truck to the female floor manager with whom she works.

Not until the film's end do Bruno and Lauretta realize that they have been beguiled by these "false" suitors and that their desires are misdirected. (The director and the floor manager, it turns out, have conspired to steal merchandise from the department store; Bruno and Lauretta finally realize that the manager's and director's ability to purchase cars and lavishly furnish their apartments results from their duplicity.) Bruno, for instance, is asked by the floor manager to be driven home and then is invited up to her apartment in order that racketeers can use his truck as cover for their scheme. The drama intensifies when Bruno accepts a weekend ski date with the floor manager to impress Lauretta. Lauretta, in turn, briefly accepts the director's request for a date (though she quickly declines, sensing that they are not suited for one another but unsure why.) Here the thievery motif (of goods and lovers) becomes more eminent and complicated. Desperate to have Bruno and to appear worthy of his presumed tastes for more elegant ladies, Lauretta steals a ski outfit from the sports department. She sits alone in the train station, pretending to be waiting for a date. Bruno is also waiting in the station for his date and finally, realizing that he has been stood up, defers his attentions to Lauretta. In a highly sentimental scene, the couple nervously decide to enjoy together their brief vacation (at a Grand Hotel in the mountains).

Instead of bringing them closer together, however, their tryst only creates further problems for them. Having returned from the ski resort, Lauretta confides to her roommate that she now *must* marry Bruno. Soon, the theft of the ski outfit is discovered by the floor manager and the director, who, in order to conceal their own misconduct, accuse Lauretta of having stolen a number of other items. This subterfuge once again conceals Lauretta's virtues in Bruno's eyes. (On a paradigmatic level, the loss of her virginity and the theft of the clothes are associated with a ruined reputation.) In her agony, Lauretta returns during the night to the store to replace the ski costume; yet so beleaguered is she by Bruno's loss of faith that she nearly commits suicide in the store. Having thus unequivocally demonstrated to the audience her moral innocence, her contentment in doing without the ski ensemble, Lauretta is ready to appear chaste once again to Bruno. Meanwhile, Bruno discovers the embezzlers' scheme. A high-speed chase ensues, after which Bruno salvages a cache of stamps with the GM seal. Again, the scheme involves sullying the "good name" of the department store by counterfeiting its image. Bruno's actions vindicate the reputations of both the store and Lauretta. To heighten the emotion generated by his release of latent qualities that the audience recognized from the beginning as virtuous and natural, Bruno returns to the store to reprimand physically the conniving director. This gesture elicits cheers and laughter from nearby customers in the store—an excitement in which the film's audience is also encouraged to participate. The source of confusion at the store having been exposed and dutifully punished, the store's festivities magically commence. Within the film's narrative logic, Bruno's action appears to rejuvenate the store and to impart to the system which it incarnates a transcendent value.

It is important to note here that the store's festivities at the end coincide precisely with Bruno's deed and Lauretta's epiphany. The celebration inaugurates a "new season" for the department store. Yet, as urban and commercial ritual, these festivities signal a new *shopping* season rather than (as in agrarian rituals) a planting season. Bruno's action seems to guarantee the success of this season. Just as an agrarian ritual ensures the success of the harvest, this commercial spectacle infuses the corporate system with a sense of *organicism* or organization; employees and employers participate in the success of the system through their cooperation and commitment and through a momentary recognition of their place in the organization.

Actually, because the inauguration of Bruno's and Lauretta's family life seems inextricable from the restoration of the corporate system, their realization of family imparts to the system an organic or tribal image. At the beginning of the film, Lauretta's intimate contact with her abandoned roommate reinforces her cynicism about family and social institutions. However, as the narrative progresses and the roommate's husband makes frequent visits to their apartment to save the couple's marriage, Lauretta learns that family strife can be surmounted. Therefore, when her roommate and her husband make public their intentions to revive their marriage, Lauretta despairs over her own misconduct, e.g., stealing the ski outfit and despoiling her honor with Bruno. The exemplariness of the couple, in her eyes, pushes her to the edge of the store's elevator shaft and suicide. Thus, at this point, only her epiphany and Bruno's grandiloquent gesture enable them to achieve a sense of family the value of which is unambiguously transcendent and emblematic of the *spirit* of the larger tribe/system. Bruno's heroic deed also vindicates his shiftlessness as a company employee. In the epilogue, Bruno is congratulated by the corporate heads for exposing corruption in the store. His reconciliation with those at the top of the corporate pyramid affirms an implicit understanding by characters and audience that a natural and vital bond can be achieved between different socioeconomic groups.

The structure of the film's narrative does much to project the image of corporate society. Its circularity, signaled by Bruno's return to his bosses' office atop the store, creates a sense of mythical time in which social problems (here the spiritual emptiness of an egocentric and materialistic world) are amplified yet, in their emotional intensity, surmounted. *Grandi magazzini* lacks the intricate interweaving of characters' actions that one finds in a movie such as *Grand Hotel*, which has a more diverse array of stars. Yet, through the narrative, there is a deliberate attempt to interweave (in a highly baroque manner) events in and outside the store as well as among the various chambers of the store itself. Editing and visual stylization also contribute to creating the illusion of an organic bond between characters' actions in the store and outside it. At one point, Bruno and Lauretta fantasize about all the items they will need to purchase for their home when they marry; the audience believes that their conversation is occurring on a couch in her apartment. The conversation continues long enough to establish this sense of place; then the camera dollies away to reveal that the couch upon which they are seated is actually one among many in the store's furniture department. From here they go on to peruse and to wonder at the appliances and other merchandise in the store. And as in Camerini's other films, petit-bourgeois consciousness is visually tied to popular mythologies. The audience's sense of cinematic space is perhaps most influential here in conjoining the realities of the store with those of the characters' private lives. This bond between actions in the store and outside it is paradoxical because the store (as public, consumer space) lacks the realism of the outside or Naturalistic world.

On the other hand, scenes of the characters' private lives exhibit the same staginess and preoccupation with objects as do scenes in the store. For instance, Bruno marvels at the accoutrements in the apartment of the floor manager; her living room, filled as it is with *nouveautés*, could just as well be a showroom in the store.

In the first part of the film, the department store evokes a surreal quality whereby the frozen gestures of mannequins become externalizations of certain characters' sentiments. At one point, Lauretta imagines how splendid Bruno would look in a ski ensemble; her fantasy is not a difficult one because the mannequin wearing the outfit is nearly an exact replication of Bruno. Later, as Lauretta attempts to steal a ski outfit for herself, she conceals herself from the night watchman by posing amidst a group of mannequins. Besides the surreal nature of the store, an Expressionistic style in the second half of the film seems to anthropomorphize the store. In her moment of delirium at having been rebuffed by Bruno, Lauretta languishes in the sporting-goods department (after attempting to return her ski garb). Here, her moment of epiphany occurs when the door to the elevator shaft swings open magically and seems to beckon her to her death.

In addition to cinematic stylization, music also confers to the store a carnivalesque atmosphere. The jazz rhythm (actually more of a sedate "businessman's bounce") that accompanies the first establishing shot of the store's expansive interior makes the activities of the shoppers resemble those of party goers. This music recurs at the end when, as Bruno punishes the director, hundreds of balloons fall from the ceiling, and the store's festivities begin. Both the cinematic stylization and the music highlight the store's potential as arena for social spectacle. In this capacity, the store tends to mystify appearances and to blur distinctions between what goes on inside and outside its doors; that which is public appears private and vice versa.

As Richard Sennett explains, the industrial revolution had two profound effects on the nature of public culture. The first effect was that it mystified public phenomena: "Fielding's world, in which masks do not express the nature of the actors, was over; masks were becoming faces."[26] The pervasiveness of commercial advertising in the public sector meant that quality was determined less by craftsmanship than by the product's ability to appear fashionable and "modern." As Sennett quite rightly adds, mystification of appearances in the public realm was accompanied by a change in the nature of privacy:

> At the end of the nineteenth century, Engels spoke of the private family as the expression of a capitalist ethos; he should have been more specific. The family parallels not the public world of capitalism, but the wholesale world; in both, secrecy is the price of continuous human contact. . . . Privacy as the realism of interactive expression—yet a culture where a stranger spectacle few men played an active role.[27]

One could add to this that cinematic images themselves participated in conferring to certain products or styles a transcendent significance.

While few men may indeed play a direct role, one should not be so quick to discount the symbolic power and collective interaction of movie characters/stars and their audiences or to ignore how public realities are constantly reworked through modern modes of mediated and vicarious experience such as the cinema. The film does much to show how this corporatavistic model, which has produced the central characters' intimate contact within this consumeristic space, is very much the cause of their jealousies and frustrations. Sennett argues that, in a world where "privacy" enters public culture, the only social action possible is that of compelling others to be more in one's own image; clearly, however, the conflicts involved in achieving that goal, and the validity of the goal itself, are a central part of the film's treatment of a society oriented toward the magic of department stores. In the film's epilogue, Bruno and Lauretta leave the store in the company of Bruno's paternal friend, Lauretta's roommate, and her husband. They pause before a store window and admire a display wherein baby dolls spin slowly on a miniature carrousel. In this final scene, the couples silently envision the *true* purpose of family, displayed as department-store spectacle. They have become insiders standing on the outside looking in; in fact, the camera captures their reflections on the windowpane as it focuses on the rotating carrousel. The couples, through their recent experiences, have learned how to become consumers; in fact, much of Lauretta's crisis and temptation results from her role as a vendor of leisure attire. Importantly, however, they have also learned that unmitigated desire endangers the system on which they are dependent. The power of this final shot is that it helps establish a bond between the characters and the audience as spectators. The characters gaze at the revolving display in silence, and their silence gives presence to an understood meaning. The emotions experienced at this moment by the audience occur through this bond with the images on the screen, just as the characters display gratification in their emotional bond with the ceramic dolls in the window display. This redoubling effect itself nurtures a myth about social action in a modern, urban, and highly illusory environment—a myth that helps to channel and manage tensions engendered by this environment.

Urban Culture as Popular Culture: A New Image for the Italian City

The epochalist impulse is, in part, a search for new models for modern living. The "new" middle and working classes—society's consumers—were created by industrialization and were the ones most affected by the pressures of the cultural instability that rapid modernization fostered. From a cultural standpoint, cinema helped to fill the spiritual vacuousness created by their rather ambiguous identity in modern society; it directly addressed their desire for a "spiritual community" and for social alliances. But gratifying this desire often entailed deriving a sense of sacredness from the City or from manufactured, commercial images. So filmmakers attempted to infuse the urban environment with a mystical value, either underscoring the darker side of the City's mysteries (as in German Expressionistic films or the American gangster films) or depicting its gayer, more lyrical side (as in American film musicals and some French comedies).

Although, in a number of Italian films from the 1930s, the City is an arena for ideological conflict, these films express a less menacing image of it than one finds in German or American cinema. In Camerini's films, for example, ideological

De Sica's Bruno flirts with Mariuccia (Lia Franca) and her girlfriends in *Gli uomini, che mascalzoni!* (d. Camerini, 1932)

conflict appears less as a violent struggle for domination than as a sentimental search for community in an environment where, as in *Grandi magazzini*, characters are continually seduced by fashion, exotic *nouveautés*, and material extravagance. Although Camerini's protagonists' suicide attempts in *Rotaie* and *Grandi magazzini* perhaps *could* be attributed to urban *angst*, the characters' suffering seems grounded more in their romantic relationships.

While the City was for Italian audiences emblematic of modernism and cosmopolitanism, it was also seen as a cultural space that had to be "naturalized" and presented through unequivocally "Italian" images. It is not surprising that, in 1932, Camerini set *Gli uomini, che mascalzoni!* (*What Rascals Men Are!*), his sentimental comedy about the love affair of a petit-bourgeois couple, in Milan, since that city most clearly characterized Italy's modernity and recent industrialization. But it is just as important to recognize Camerini's ability to present this modernity through familiar, often traditional Milanese images. The rather paradoxical treatment of Milan is affirmed by two Milanese film critics who reviewed the film at its release. According to Filippo Sacchi, well-known critic for Milan's largest newspaper *Il Corriere della Sera*,

> it is a film that in its characterization and atmosphere is profoundly our own [i.e. the people of Milan]. . . . The film is truly a ray of youth and joy for its pub-

lic. . . . This is the first time we have seen Milan on the screen. And who would have suspected that it is so photogenic? Camerini has really succeeded in assimilating with the most extreme clarity certain characteristics that unmistakably belong to the appearance and movement of Milan in order to convey to us, subtly and without the *documentary* abuses, which often reduce films of this kind to a collection of postcards of famous monuments, its local color and its industrious vitality.[28]

For Sacchi, the Milan of *Gli uomini, che mascalzoni!* is realistic and attractive, that is, "photogenic," because it does not seem constituted solely by those icons most familiar to foreigners; instead, it addresses local, popular concerns. (The "documentary" quality to which he refers may be a result of Corrado D'Errico's earlier documentary about Milan's modernity, *Stramilano*, 1929, which I discuss in chapter 7.) It seems paradoxical, however, that this "local color" is described as a new and fresh—even modern—vision of Milan. Manlio Miserocchi, writing for *L'illustrazione Italiana*, also notes:

> Italy is presented in *Gli uomini, che mascalzoni!* without pretense but demonstrating that one can indeed present a friendly, appealing and sentimental comedy in a Milan that not even the native Milanese have known to exist and for whom the film has been a true discovery.[29]

Here again, Camerini's Milan is both magical and real, modern and traditional; but, most importantly, Milan appears to Miserocchi as emblematic of a larger *national* experience.

Some of the "honesty" that these critics recognize in Camerini's film can be attributed to his outdoor shooting (about three-fourths of the action is filmed outdoors), to the authenticity of the interiors of the working-class character, and to the heroine's (Lia Franca's) relative anonymity as an actress. Most of the scenes were filmed on location rather than in studios—a strategy that was almost unprecedented in Italian films. And filming from a moving cable car is one of the first instances in Italian cinema of a camera mounted in such a way to film street scenes. Nevertheless, it seems that the realism of Camerini's film also results from its ability to crystalize one of the more profound cultural contradictions at this time, to give presence to tensions created by modernization and to the ambivalence of Italy's middle and working classes toward their changing cultural environment. The film explores the problems encountered by Italy's younger generation of workers, but it does so without the cynical and didactic tone prevalent in social realist films. As in most Camerini films, dramatic conflict results from differences between wealthy characters and poorer ones, between the powerful and the humble. Vittorio De Sica plays a character again named Bruno, a chauffeur/mechanic who in the narrative's initial stage falls in love with the daughter of a taxi-driver. From the outset, Bruno's and the father's occupations establish a bond between the two characters; and of course this bond is personified by the girl, Mariuccia (Lia Franca).

The father and his daughter live alone, and the film begins by following their morning ritual, wherein the father arrives home from driving his taxi all night to wake his daughter so that she will not be late for her job at a women's cosmetic shop (the only setting in the film that adopts the art-deco styles of more cosmopolitan spaces). This type of family seems to be a product of urban living—a family that, while maintaining a closeness and harmony, must restructure its routines to make ends meet. Having introduced this family, the action breaks to Bruno's morning duties, which he conducts under the auspices of a rotund, cigar-smoking boss. The decadence of the wealthy family for whom Bruno works is contrasted with the hard-working nature of Mariuccia's family life.

The central part of the film concerns Bruno's attempts to woo Mariuccia; and again, as in Camerini's other comedies, this romance involves a confusion of identities. As in *Grandi magazzini*, De Sica's comic hero attempts to impress the girl he desires by playing the "*signore*"—here, by borrowing his boss's Isotta Fraschini. In both movies, cars are emblematic of upward mobility and seem obliquely to perpetuate a theme which Camerini introduces in *Rotaie*, modern life as travel-oriented. The couple pass a romantic afternoon at a modest tavern on Lake Maggiore in the mountains outside of Milan; here in the provinces, these urbanites experience the simple, idyllic pleasures of country folk who seem eternally at play, e.g., men who play *bocce* all day long, older couples who dance to slightly outdated tunes. Rural Italy here seems less a peasant society than one comprised merely of an older generation with outmoded yet quaint diversions. In fact, Bruno and Mariuccia's "natural" compatibility is demonstrated when, in the presence of the older couples, they dance effortlessly to a modern song ("Parlami d'amore Mariù") on the tavern's jukebox—a song that this film helped popularize in Italy.

Bruno's charade and his budding affection in this leisurely and bucolic setting, however, are interrupted by the arrival of his boss's wife, who has come to the tavern to pass time with her upper-crust peers. Here, high society's fashion and decadence again contrast with the less ostentatious demeanor of the homespun "regulars" at the tavern. The couple find both groups fascinating yet inaccessible; thus, in the presence of these two radically disparate social groups, the couple find more pleasure in each other. Actually, their romance and its potential appeal to the film's audience can be attributed to their capability at this moment (due to Bruno's ambiguous identity) to *mediate* these two worlds. Although initially distraught at discovering her automobile, the boss's wife soon realizes the fortuitousness of her situation and requests that Bruno return her to town himself. Not wanting to reveal his true occupation, Bruno convinces Mariuccia to wait while he assists his boss's wife, whom he identifies only as a lady in distress. On his return from Milan, already late, he swerves to avoid a farmer's wagon and damages the car irreparably. Believing her wealthy paramour to have deserted her for someone of his own status, Mariuccia remains alone at the tavern and returns the next day to Milan, where she is chastised by her father for having spent the night out and having forfeited her virginity. She also loses her job and is forced to find work in a booth at Milan's "sample fair" (La Fiera Campionaria), where the latest consumer items are advertised to buyers and the general public.

The second half of the film continues the play of mistaken identities. Bruno, who is fired by his first boss as a result of the accident, takes another job as a chauffeur. Soon thereafter, he is spotted by Mariuccia; and, when it appears that his new boss is flirting with her, he quits—expressing his respect and affection for her. Out of sympathy for his destitution and out of admiration for his honesty, Mariuccia implores one of her girlfriends at the fair to arrange employment for Bruno through a wealthy industrialist friend. Although Bruno obtains the job, Mariuccia must now return the industrialist's favor by going out with him. Believing *she* now desires a more wealthy suitor, Bruno arranges a date with her girlfriend. They follow the couple to an amusement park, where, in a scene involving miniature cars (here a parody of the automobile motif), Bruno chases and repeatedly bumps into the rear of the industrialist's and Mariuccia's car to express his displeasure. Finally, after Mariuccia rebuffs the industrialist, she and Bruno overcome their jealousies—each gratified by having obtained the object of his/her desire.

Their romance thus unfolds through a series of coincidences whereby one of the lovers is mistakenly paired by the other with a wealthy figure: Bruno with the boss's wife, and later Mariuccia with the industrialist. These "false" affairs amplify the couple's ambivalence about upper-crust lifestyles; they find the wealthy images both seductive and threatening. In the film's epilogue, Bruno, who has abandoned his job at the fair, appears next to Mariuccia's father in the front seat of his taxi, ready to return to being a "chauffeur" and content to follow the father's example. In one sense, Bruno is right where he began: driving cars. Yet, importantly, his work now seems to have acquired a purpose. Having experienced the turbulence of living (acting) beyond their means, the couple realize the value of cooperation and more stable routines.

Perhaps one of the most significant features of Camerini's vision of Milan and urban Italy is his ability to transform a radically commercialized and technological environment into a dramatic stage and to infuse it with an almost mystical aura and a symbolic value. The Fiera Campionaria in Milan, for example, is a microcosm of modern fashions, a dazzling spectacle of the latest advertising gimmicks and commercial gadgets. (In *Grandi magazzini*, where Camerini substitutes a department store for the fair, the modern marketplace assumes a more central but equally carnivalesque function in the characters' lives.) Before Bruno takes a job there, he wanders as a spectator among its booths (which are not unlike sideshows at a carnival), fascinated by the spirited mood of the setting. At one point, he admires a large and elaborate perfume dispenser, from which, with great embarrassment, he draws enough perfume to spray several people. But, when he begins to work at the fair, no longer as spectator but simply as another *fixture* (a barker in the sideshow), he quickly becomes demoralized by its hectic pace and impersonal relationships. For Bruno, transcendence lies in becoming part of a family—not a traditional family, but one wherein his life and his work assume a purpose.

Another film from the 1930s that concerns the changing faces of Italian cities is Amleto Palermi's 1939 melodrama *Napoli che non muore* (*Naples Everlasting*). Palermi, known for his portrayals of southern Italy, here attempts to demystify antiquated images of Naples (and of Italy) and to redefine its place in a modern world. Unlike Camerini's Milan, Palermi's Naples could not possibly serve as a stage for the social tensions experienced by the lower working classes; while a commercial center, Naples during the 1930s did not undergo the rapid industrial development of the burgeoning northern cities. Palermi's film does share Camerini's faith in the ability of family to survive in rapid change. But the family of *Napoli che non muore* is not beset with the same type of problems nor is it redefined in the same fashion as northern families might be.

If Camerini avoided depicting Milan through its more renowned monuments (as Filippo Sacchi's review of *Gli uomini, che mascalzoni!* attests), Palermi's film made an issue of Italy's changing image. For one, Naples was steeped in a more classical Mediterranean lore that it could not shed as easily as could northern cities, which by the 1930s were becoming more in touch with the rest of Europe. Secondly, Naples' "cosmopolitanism" was of an entirely different order than one might associate with a modern industrial metropolis such as Milan. The perennial influx of wealthy foreign tourists made Naples an ideal setting for epochalist and essentialist conflict. One of Palermi's intentions in this film seems to be to debunk the notion that Naples, i.e., Italy, is simply a playground for decadent high society; he attempts to reveal the *true* Italian society that lies beneath Naple's glittering façade. What he uncovers, however, is a middle-class family who do not speak in a dialect and who appear just as *modern* as the tourists who visit their city.

At its outset, the film invites its audience to view Naples (and those aspects of Italy that Naples represents) from the point of view of a tourist, i.e., in terms of the superficial Western stereotypes about Italy that Naples embodies. To establish this perspective, Palermi begins the film with a shot of Mount Vesuvius's fiery crater above the city and with sweeping pans of the *lungomare* at night with its restaurants, small boats, and illuminated boulevard. Superimposed on this opening montage is the image of a beautiful blonde woman stretched languidly on the bow of a boat approaching the harbor. The woman, Anna, is actually a French high-society "debutante" who is sailing with a girlfriend on their friend's yacht to Naples for the first time. The initial images of Naples—an etherial city observed from *afar* at night to the sound of distant accordians—seems to be part of her fantasy. "It's Naples just as I've always dreamed," she exclaims.

Having established this "romantic," naïve perspective, the action cuts to a restaurant on the *lungomare* where Mario, a well-dressed, refined businessman (played by Fosco Giachetti), sits captivated by *her* distant image. Mario is surprised to recognize Anna's navigator, the owner of the yacht, whom he greets with, "It's been five years since I saw you in New York." Unable to take his eyes from Anna, he volunteers to be their guide in Naples; and Anna, still intoxicated by her dream come true, eagerly consents to his offer. "You should see Naples at dawn," he tells her.

But Naples by day does not lose its luster. As the four walk among Roman ruins, the owner of the yacht confides to Anna that Mario was once known by his classmates as "poet," and Anna's girlfriend reveals to Mario that Anna seems happier than she has in months. That evening, Anna and Mario sail alone, listening again to music emanating from the shore. When Anna asks him about the meaning of the song's lyrics, he invokes a familiar dictum about Naples: "When one sees Naples, one forgets everything else." And on this note, they embrace.

The middle part of the narrative concerns Mario's introduction of Anna to his family and the couple's eventual marriage. The audience at times perceives the family's lifestyle through Anna's eyes as she passes through the house, observing family members at their chores. But her presence, as a foreigner, also amplifies certain familial tensions. The family members, especially the older ones, are intimidated by her alien customs. The mother, for example, insists on serving "a 'cocktail'—what foreigners drink but we don't." And the servants discuss French idiosyncracies—"They eat very little"—and must translate certain phrases and customs for her—"What we in Italy call *emotion*." After the couple's honeymoon, when Anna continues to take her breakfast in bed, the family become more disconcerted. Anna's trifling while Mario is at work fulfills the family's suspicions that the French are a decadent lot.

Anna instead is deluded and depressed. She laments that life in Italy is becoming too real; in many respects, the Italy she discovers is not all romantic evenings spent strolling to accordian music. Bored with her domestic confines, she convinces Mario's sister to go for a cocktail. At one modern jazz bar, Anna explains to the sister that she is now looking for that Naples she had not known before. For the next few weeks, Anna and Mario's sister cavort at the racetracks and play bridge; and finally Anna enters a sailing regatta. When she returns home from the regatta in the company of men ("Boy did *she* show us men!") the entire family voice their hostilities. Anna in turn explains to Mario that she was bored because she felt neglected and that all along she really needed a place that was their own and not the family's.

In the emotional finale, Anna runs upstairs after being reprimanded by Mario. She is followed by Mario's nephew, a child who stands at her door and rebukes her. When she screams at him to desist his taunting, he turns to run away but in so doing trips and falls down the stairs. Days pass as the child lies unconscious, and Anna brings herself to pray for his recovery with the rest of the family. When the child finally opens his eyes to the accompaniment of celestial music, the camera pans to a picture of the Madonna and child over his bed. Before the doctor leaves, however, he checks on Anna, who has locked herself in her room for days. To everyone's amazement, he discovers that she is pregnant. Infused with a new sense of responsibility and now carrying a child who will actually link her to this Italian family and confer on her a role more compatible with their values, she professes her desire to begin a new life with Mario. She learns from an old professor friend of the family that Naples is in this house: "It is really you people, your experiences as a family and not simply that initial romantic image." Mario confesses that he too has learned something, that he and Anna were already a family.

Napoli che non muore does explore the consequences of the changing roles of women in Italy. But Anna's ambiguous identity and her attempt to fit into Italian society call attention to essential cultural tensions. Through Anna and her effect on this Neapolitan family, the film invites Italian audiences to renegotiate or redefine Naples—the more traditional image of Italian culture. The film does not prescribe a return to a more traditional value system, as is demonstrated by Mario's final acceptance of Anna's nature, nor does it suggest that Anna's initial tourist's vision of Naples as a playground for the rich is in any way accurate. Instead, Naples becomes an emblem of Italy's popular culture, a milieu in which Mario and Anna can start their *own* family—outside his family's house—yet still bound to the larger, traditional family.

The New Woman: Lost and Found in the City

In *Napoli che non muore*, a modern vision is predicated upon changing social roles, and here the film's heroine, Anna, gradually learns the rewards and pleasures of finding her own responsibilities within the Neapolitian view of family. The film tends to cast these rewards behind the superficiality of first impressions and façade, yet still as part of the fundamental allure of Naples. For the family, it is this more cosmopolitan female role that has loosened the family's underpinnings, which here seem screwed a bit too tightly by characters such as Mario's mother. While questions about gender roles, particularly about a woman's place in society and family, lurked throughout silent films and popular theatrical melodramas during the early decades of the twentieth century, the City—as dramatic setting and as social experience—brought new imperatives to representations of women in Italian sound films.

In many ways, the changing depictions of women in popular Italian films can be attributed to myths of America popularized through both its cinema and its theatrical melodrama. The inspiration for Giacomo Puccini's opera *La fanciulla del west* (first performed in 1910) was David Belasco's untraditional heroine, Girl, in his *Girl of the Golden West*. While Belasco's Western melodrama was certainly not the first American work to break from the conventional model of heroine as either victim or hag, it clearly reformulated a role that for over a century had become relatively standardized in popular European forms. Moreover, American silent films, especially by the 1920s, had cultivated a bevy of starlets (Negri, Swanson, Garbo, Brooks) known for their characters' frank sexuality and ability to blend integrity with a new independence (even if they were cast as Europeans). But the period of silent film had also frequently encouraged roles and images that seemed to transcend questions of a woman's place in the work force and her competition with men in an urban environment. William Everson sees this same transition in terms of the silent-film experience itself:

> Having achieved legal equality in the twenties, the woman of Hollywood aimed at, and largely achieved, a kind of goddess-like stature as well. She lost it when the talkies and the Depression came along at the same time. Not only did she have to speak, instead of merely receive adulation, but she had to compete with men, on an equal footing, in a battle for survival.[30]

In Italian silent film, female characters had also begun to lose the unequivocally innocent roles that had dominated popular melodrama during the nineteenth century. In *Cabiria* (1914), Italia Almirante-Manzini's Sofonisba rules a
pagan empire, but one that because of her aimlessness is continually presented as
a threat to and weaker than the male-oriented invaders. In *Lydia* (1910), the
heroine's desire for wealth leads her outside her middle-class values into a decadent world where she contracts "an insidious disease." Much the same situation
befalls Lyda Borelli's character in *Ma l'amore mio non muore* (*Love Everlasting*,
1913), wherein family circumstances compel her to relinquish her innocence and
Italy to become a stage actress with a questionable reputation in Paris. After the
war, in the 1920s, these representations are reworked in Italian films such as the
romantic comedy *Champagne Caprice* (1919). But generally, women (while they
may appear as prostitutes, as in *Le confessioni di una donna—Confessions of a
Woman*, 1928) are generally virtuous, passive victims or forlorn mothers. Examples would be *Miss Dorothy* (1920), wherein a mother sacrifices herself to protect
her daughter and to circumvent false accusations about her character, or *Casa
mia, donna mia* (*My House, My Woman*, 1922), in which a girl who is violated by
and forced to marry a young ne'er-do-well finally realizes her dream of a stable
and whole family when her husband, who has been seduced by an unscrupulous
female adventuress, returns to redeem himself. Then there are the "strongman"
film series, in which women become the goals of or reasons for the quests of the
male protagonists. Furthermore, the sexual conflict is usually displaced in these
films to a provincial setting (*Cenere*, 1916; *I figli di nessuno*, 1920; *Casa mia, donna
mia*; *La grazia*, 1929), to the boudoirs of nineteenth-century theater (*La donna
nuda*, 1914; *Miss Dorothy*; *Sei mai!* 1920), or to the luxurious villas of antiquity
(*Messalina*, 1923; *Quo Vadis?* 1924; *Gli ultimi giorni di Pompei*, 1926). It is not until
the 1930s that the City becomes a mythic locus for dramatic action in Italian
films. The roles of women in these movies result from social as well as cultural
changes; they are not simply *reflections* of social values but selective arrange-
ments of particular values and their relevance to specific social/dramatic roles.

One of the first Italian sound films to use as its central dramatic situation the
experience of a woman seeking work in the city is Alessandrini's 1931 musical
comedy, *La segretaria privata* (*The Private Secretary*). The film's modern concept
is based upon a German story, "Die Privatsekretärin," which had been adopted
as a screenplay by Franz Shulz and produced in separate German, French, and
English versions. But its adaptation for Italian audiences proved to be an enormous success, having the then rare distinction of playing for as long as a month
during its openings at first-run cinemas in major Italian cities.[31] The story's
broad international appeal was indubitably tied to its promise as a film musical
and to the existing social conditions; as Italian film critic Rosario Assunto
observed in 1940:

> This film was born during the height of the transformation of the social order
> and system—what has been christened "the world crisis of 1929," a time when
> every family felt a need to augment the income of its domestic budget. And
> young women closed their fashion albums, put away their embroidery, and

Elsa Merlini's Elsa is saluted by a male chorus as she dances gayly down a city street in *La segretaria privata* (d. Alessandrini, 1931)

began to study typing, stenography, and bookkeeping in order to get jobs in banks, in offices, and in businesses.[32]

One of the most significant features of the film, viewed at the juncture of Italian cinema's representations of women, is that it literally begins with the arrival of its central character, Elsa (Elsa Merlini), in a city's train station. Elsa does not appear to be overly naïve *or* experienced; she continually radiates an optimism, but also engages in marginally acceptable female behavior such as smoking and drinking.

The film's comedy and stylized representation of urban life appear to be part of the wide-eyed wonder that the provincial Elsa brings with her on her first visit to the city, where she plans to find employment. To reinforce this "feminine" perspective, the film's opening credits are even typed on office stationery that fills the screen; and the first shots involve a pan, on board the train, of Elsa's suitcase resting in a luggage rack, then down to a collage of French vacation posters, and finally to Elsa gazing longingly out a window. The first shots of the train station, taken *from* the train as it pulls in, also help establish Elsa's central role and her point of view as a newcomer. These first shots of Elsa are accompanied by light jazz music; but, as the train pulls into the station, the music begins to compete with the noises from the bustle of man and machine in the crowded station.

As a narrative bridge or framing device, the opening scene at the train station imparts to the metropolis, where the subsequent action occurs, an almost carnivalesque mood. The photography of the station emphasizes its art-deco style. The jazz soundtrack seems to enliven Elsa's gait as she steps off the train and helps legitimize the highly choreographed, excessive, and farcical gestures of the swarming male workers and dandies she first encounters there. Her experience next at a ladies' boardinghouse is just as lively and lyrical, as she quickly befriends a group of women who are already employed in various clerical positions. The women's contentment, however, appears to result more from their sense of camaraderie and mutual support than from their opportunities and the working conditions in the city; beneath their playful banter runs a pessimism and practicality that temper Elsa's idealism some.

Her search for a job the following day leads her to a bank, where she hopes to interview for a position as secretary. After being denied entrance (there are too many applicants, she is told) she is compelled to cajole the doorman and to flirt with the head of personnel, the latter of whom becomes so stimulated that he cannot resist her request. Afterward, she celebrates her fortune, dancing gaily down the street to the movie's theme song and animating a chorus line of male onlookers, who react in broad, sweeping gestures of approval. And, when she returns to her *pensione*, still singing, she is visually framed by and centered within her courtyard (as if she were the focal point of that domestic space) and is accompanied by a chorus of other women engaged in domestic chores. Her enthusiasm diminishes, however, her first day at work, where the regimental routine and order of the female secretaries is exaggerated and parodied as they march to a musical score in single file down a long, art-deco hallway and to orderly rows of typewriters. Here, Elsa must now fend off the advances of the personnel director, who expects some form of compensation for his having granted her employment. Furious when she rebuffs him, he destroys her assignment, orders her to work overtime, and insists that she begin to dress in more subdued, less trendy clothes. After a few days of increasing antagonisms with her manager, she no longer sings.

Her singing is revived only after a humorous series of role reversals involving the bank's young president, Signor Berri (Nino Besozzi). One evening, while she is working late at the office, Berri notices her fatigue and offers to assist. Not realizing Berri's position, she complains about the personnel manager as they work. Berri, enjoying these candid revelations, maintains his charade and, after they finish, invites her to a late dinner at a modest restaurant nearby. It is here at the restaurant that the social relationships between boss and employee, between men and women become skewed through drink and musical performance. Berri has chosen a restaurant where his charade and his interlude with a woman who is *really* his secretary will go unnoticed by acquaintances. He is surprised, however, to find the bank's doorman, Otello (played by the brilliant comedian Sergio Tofano) practicing with his all-male glee club. Much of this scene is given to Berri's comic efforts to play the role of an Everyman (he even instructs Otello, the doorman, to "treat him like a lowly employee") and to Otello's demonstration of his skills as a performer and conductor (*leader*) of the singing group. Popular music again serves as an expression of communality between these different social groups, as Berri and Elsa dance and sing a duet and as Otello leads the entire restaurant in a chorus. In some ways, the number continues to underscore the centrality of the bank president in this populist environment, but their revelry also necessitates a temporary suspension of role distinctions as Elsa locks arms between the inebriated Berri and Otello, kisses each of them, and then insists the two men kiss one another. Not until the couple's taxi ride home that evening does she decline his invitation to spend the night with him, saying that she doesn't want to marry someone of his social stature and vice versa. Only "their music," sung by each character later in different places but connected through cross-cutting, continues as a manifestation of their bond.

The next day at the bank brings a return to the couple's social obligations; but, due to their experience the previous night, these obligations become more problematic. First, Berri scolds both Otello and Elsa for attempting to finagle a position for her as "personal secretary"; then he invites her to his apartment, where, in a more domestic setting, she refrains from smoking and adopts a more humble posture. But when, still feigning disinterest, he suggests that they can work together without becoming romantically involved, she slaps him and storms out. Later, he attempts to retrieve her through his personnel manager, who is now so worried about his own mistakes that he eagerly obliges his boss; but, when Elsa quits her job, Berri himself confronts her and convinces her to marry him. As the lovers kiss inside Berri's office, Otello leads the secretaries outside in a chorus of the film's theme song, here transforming the bank into a stage for celebrating romance and reconciliation. While the social positions of Otello and his chorus are unchanged, and while Elsa has surmounted her anxieties in the work force by marrying a wealthy banker, music once again serves as a means of expressing a communal vitality.

A year after *La segretaria privata*, Cines studio released another musical comedy based upon a German story and film, *La Telefonista (The Telephone Operator*, 1932). This movie, directed by Nunzio Malasomma, also celebrates sound in the cinema through its romance and comic confusions surrounding a central telephone station. Through musical numbers, such as one in which the conversations of different callers become the lines in a song and the refrain is sung by a chorus of female operators, the station appears as model of social/industrial order (the singing female chorus) and comic disorder. And a public dependency and ambivalence about new technology overlap with woman's central role in the organization.

In 1933, however, Mario Camerini's *T'amerò sempre (I'll Always Love You)* explores some of the questions concerning a single woman's existence in an urban milieu.[33] It couches the plight of its heroine, Adriana (played by Elsa De Giorgi), well within the conventions of traditional melodrama: an orphan victimized by a young Count and by inequitable social circumstances; but Camerini's cinematography, and set designs by Gastone Medin, emphasize how a modern, urban environment contributes to her anxieties. And, like some Ameri-

A chorus of singing telephone operators in *La telefonista* (d. Malasomma, 1932)

Nino Besozzi (left) and Elsa De Giorgi (right) are cast as misfits and heroes in *T'amero sempre* (d. Camerini, 1933)

can maternal melodramas (such as *Stella Dallas*), Adriana's problems result from her efforts not only to make a life for her and her child, but to be both a mother and something outside the home. In this sense, the woman's place in the family and society appears problematic, and the film repeatedly sets her problems against models of social organization.

The correspondence between family and larger social organizations becomes the subject of the film's opening scene, in which documentary footage of the orderliness of hospital procedures in a maternity ward give way to a staged scene of new mothers in one ward receiving members of their families. Besides emphasizing the closeness of these families, this scene also underscores the privileged status of male children, as one father gloats over his wife's having just delivered twin boys. To amplify the significance of the man's gesture, the film follows an austere woman dressed in black and furs to the bed where Adriana lies alone. She quietly but brusquely informs Adriana that "he" is unable to come to see her. Adriana's sense of abandonment brings her to tears, and her anguish is punctuated by a quick parallel cut to a fashionably dressed man teeing off at a golf course, and then by a cut back to Adriana sobbing in her hospital bed.

Amidst her anxiety and emptiness, the film interjects a flashback, which is both a clarification of the narrative's abrupt beginning and an attempt by Adriana to remember her own childhood and to make some sense of her despair. Through her flashback, the film draws connections between her present plight and epiphanic moments growing up. She first recalls the strange men who would pay visits to her own mother, the fragments of conversation about exchanges of money, her mother's beatings by men, and finally the murder of her mother by a man who left her an orphan. She then remembers her adolescent years, isolated from boys at a girl's orphanage, where she learns those things which a woman is supposed to do (sewing, maintaining decorum in the presence of a severe headmistress) and, only because of her spying on people *outside* the orphanage, what a young woman should not do (make love). Like the heroines of traditional melodrama, Adriana imagines her adolescence as a period of confinement from Nature, and it is here that the City intrudes to reinforce her despair. After a bridge shot with birds flying into the heavens (signaling her release from the orphanage) and then of a locomotive speeding across the screen (signaling her transition and maturation), Adriana emerges into a modern, urban world—an environment established through an accelerated montage of metropolitan images (electrical power lines, the feet of crowds on a busy city sidewalk). Besides tracing her own maturation, this flashback sequence serves to place Adriana's plight amidst a tradition of melodrama—here ending with the heroine's arrival (as in *La segretaria privata* two years earlier) in the City. But, because the flashback ends with her arrival in the city, returning the audience to the present moment of despair in the hospital, the city would seem to be just as much another prison into which she has stepped. This is accentuated through a brief montage that juxtaposes images from Nature (shots of blossoming trees) and of Adriana's embrace with her first lover (part of her physical maturation and her new life) with succeeding close-up shots of her crying once again in her hospital bed. To exaggerate the grief of her present, internalized moment even more, the film intercuts another image from her past, of Adriana and her lover walking slowly in heavy winter coats along a mud-soaked road, and then to a shot (in the present) of her lover having coffee with the woman in black at an elegant sidewalk café.

The flashback sequence at the beginning of the film helps establish the centrality of Adriana's perspective (much more so than the strategies at the beginning of *La segretaria privata*). The flashback also undoes the linearity of the film's narration, making this moment in the hospital inextricable from events before or after it. From this point, the film includes a brief scene of Adriana's departure with her baby; it is shot from inside the quiet hospital to reinforce the frantic pace (crowded streets), the bleakness (factory chimneys over the buildings), and the cacophony (scream of sirens) of the world to which she is returning. Then, through bridge shots, Adriana and her child are presented some years later, in a scene that conjures her earlier recollections of her own childhood.

This second part of the film concentrates more on Adriana's difficulties in working at a hair salon than on her role as mother. Generally, she appears to be a model mother; her problems concern her attempts to ensure that her own daughter has a better life than she did. Throughout this latter part, then, Adriana seems trapped both by her past, which continually intrudes into her present life, and by the exigencies of modern society. The women's beauty salon where she works is run by an effeminate character with a French accent called only Oscar, whose vaguely non-Italian name is wonderfully suited to the phantasmagoria of female fashion and the latest technology for stroking the pompous egos of its upper-crust clientele. As a dramatic stage, the salon concretizes both Adriana's desires and her horrors; its set design highlights all that is superfluous and grotesque in modern notions of elegance. The first view of this salon, which appears abruptly after the bridge sequence in which Adriana leaves the hospital, begins with a close-up of an elaborate art-deco sign above its door, followed by a close-up of a metallic, futuristic bust of Oscar. As a kind of parody of the classical hero, a laurel wreath garlands the brow and hair of the bust, and, as the camera pulls back, the bust appears over Oscar's outstretched hand (almost like a puppet) as he glides among the women, patronizing them in French. In this female domain, there are no clearly strong male characters; besides Oscar, the husbands of the women appear meek and often of smaller stature than their wives. The other central male character here is the salon's bespectacled accountant, Mario Fabbrini (played by Nino Besozzi). The power of Besozzi's performance in this film can be attributed in part to the ways in which his restrained timidity and his almost neurotic mannerisms play against his previous role in *La segretaria privata*. Besozzi's Fabbrini becomes, in this second part of the film, Adriana's new suitor, who is forced to assert himself when the young Count returns from Adriana's past and accidentally discovers her in the salon. In fact, this second half of the film dwells on Mario's reactions to Adriana as much as it continues her centralized perspective from the opening act. While Mario idealizes Adriana from afar, the Count attempts to reestablish their relationship; the

Count's superficiality and condescension toward women are conveyed through a scene wherein, trifling away his time yo-yoing with his wealthy friends at a bar, he responds to a female receptionist's (Adriana's) rejection of him over the telephone with: "When a woman hangs up on you like that, she's bound to be ugly."

After witnessing the Count's rough treatment of Adriana at the salon, Mario invites her to dinner at his family's house. In this scene, Camerini (as in his other films) both valorizes and satirizes the Italian petit-bourgeois sensibility and family ideals. Fabbrini is ridiculed by his loud uncle for his childhood photos in the family album—photos which Adriana admires lovingly. And, seated at the center of the table, opposite Fabbrini and Adriana, who seem incapable of a "normal" family, are Mario's sister and her erect soldier fiancé—the ideal couple. After dinner, the mischievous uncle plays a romantic ballad on the family phonograph, and tension mounts in the room as the family quietly waits for the shy Mario to dance with Adriana. When Mario becomes paralyzed by these tensions, the uncle pulls Adriana from the table to dance with him and the others; here, she again becomes a remote ideal for Mario as the editing repeatedly dwells on *his* reactions to her dancing. The restraints separating Mario and Adriana (Mario because of his timidity and Adriana because of her stigma—her child, whom she has kept a secret) make for a particularly effective scene after dinner as he musters courage to ask her to marry him and she feels obliged to reject him.

The movie's conclusion involves Fabbrini's ultimate act of self-assertion and Adriana's recognition in him of a "natural" match for herself. After arriving at her apartment, she finds the Count with her daughter, an event that tends to heighten her fears of having a life outside the home and of her similar predicament as a child; enraged, she coerces the Count to leave. The following day, Mario notices Adriana walking with her daughter; when he relates the encounter to his mother, she reaffirms her fondness for Adriana. At the salon, the Count reappears and bullies Adriana, causing such a commotion that Oscar fires her. And it is at this point that Mario steps in to vindicate Adriana's misfortune, shoving the Count through some of Oscar's more ornate glass partitions. On the street, Mario invites Adriana to bring her daughter to his home, and the couple depart Oscar's salon arm-in-arm.

While the ending promises a union between these two refugees from the decadence of Oscar's factory of fashionable façades, their future family would not necessarily seem to be a "natural" one—only one that is marginally acceptable in terms of the family's ideal couple (Mario's sister and her fiancé). Nor does the film clearly resolve Adriana's ambiguous role in the family/social structure. Marriage *may* redeem her past and her social stigma as an unwed mother, but Camerini has already satirized the rituals of petit-bourgeois family life in the earlier scene at Mario's home. And herein are the contradictions of the movie's ideology. The audience is encouraged to enjoy and accept lovers who are misfits but who, in their rejection of the fads of upper-crust society, appear quite stable.

A year after *T'amerò sempre*, in Max Ophuls's only Italian production, *La signora di tutti* (*Everyone's Lady*, 1934), any kind of personal, familial, or social stability is flagrantly eroded.[34] In some ways, this movie foreshadows the narrative style and thematics of his 1955 film, *Lola Montes*. As in Camerini's *T'amerò sempre* the personality of the female lead is fragmented by her past and by the strains over her increasingly desperate attempts to recover or to piece together an identity in a modern society—here through her rise to stardom in the cinema. Ophuls, however, offers little optimism about this recovery, concentrating instead on the torturous self-immolation of the heroine and adopting narrative and photographic strategies that (in an almost Pirandellian fashion) continually foreground the illusions and transience from which her realities emerge. While, as the title suggests, the heroine (Gaby Doriot, played by Isa Miranda) is surrounded by men who desire her, their desires all seem somehow perverse and contributing to her emptiness rather than her fulfillment.

The "Modernist" overtone of *La signora di tutti* neutralizes or subverts the kind of wholeness (of characters, of plot, of meaning) that the film's repeated use of melodramatic convention might lead one to expect. The film opens with a scene involving male producers and promoters discussing the direction of Gaby's career and a current publicity campaign about her. Gaby, however, is discovered by her agent lying near death on the floor of her boudoir, the victim of an attempted suicide. All that the audience understands about Gaby in this first section is the image of her that these other characters perceive or would have the public perceive; in fact, the audience does not actually see Gaby here. After she is rushed to a clinic and placed on an operating table, the camera assumes her supine perspective, as a mask that will administer anesthesia is slowly lowered onto her/the viewer. Titles explain that under the influence of these drugs she begins to revive her past. This narrative framing device helps ground the following story in Gaby's personality, but it is a personality that is not necessarily her own and one that is destabilized by her narcosis. Moreover, the events that she remembers are conveyed through an array of melodramatic situations; but, because of the framing sequence, the melodrama of her past becomes tied to *her* perspective (as a movie personality whose identity has been produced by men). Like *La segretaria privata* and *T'amerò sempre*, *La signora di tutti* explores the emergence of the melodramatic heroine into a modern, technological milieu, but Ophuls's film does so "in reverse" and through a style that discourages a clear understanding of her role either as innocent victim or as vamp (as someone "undone" or "made-up" as a popular screen personality).

Rather than gleaning meaning and wholeness from her past in her moment of crisis, Gaby confronts her instability, marginality, and failure to fit into a family and social unit. Her past is littered with self-destructive characters who mirror her own impending demise on the operating table. When she is seventeen, one of her professors kills himself because of his obsession for her; the trauma and style of the event compel her to leave school and to move farther away from her own family. She at this point meets Roberto Nanni, a young man from a wealthy family, who also falls in love with her. But when Roberto is forced to leave, his invalid mother invites Gaby to stay at their sumptuous (though rather

Gaby Doriot, imprisoned by her image in *La signora di tutti* (d. Ophuls, 1934)

Gothic) estate. Rather than becoming a sanctuary, the family home becomes yet another stage for destructive passions. Leonardo, Roberto's father, also develops an obsession for the girl, and they become lovers. One evening, while they are in the garden, Alma (the invalid mother) plummets downstairs in her wheelchair to her death. So distraught is Gaby over this calamity that she flees from Leonardo and searches for work. Leonardo, meanwhile, is so distracted by his passions for Gaby that he forgets his business interests and gradually falls deeper into debt, and, soon after Gaby leaves the estate, his financial problems force him into prison. After being released from prison some years later, a poor man, he discovers that Gaby has made a career in the cinema. Bent on finding her, he passes into the lobby of a theater where her latest film, *La signora di tutti*, is premiering. After seeing her, however, he emerges from the cinema only to be struck down and killed by an automobile. Once again, Gaby's fortune is marred by a tragic event that prevents her from escaping her past and that surrounds her with scandal. Roberto, who had divorced himself from his father and Gaby when he learned about their affair, returns. Trying to rescue something unsullied from her past, Gaby seeks to rekindle Roberto's feelings for her, only to find that he has married her sister (Roberto's substitute for her). Finally, then, succumbing to the emotional pressures of her failures and her alienation, she attempts suicide.

At the point where her past converges with her present condition on the operating table, she expires. Once again, Ophuls returns the viewer to her supine position as the mask that administers the anesthesia is removed and she is pronounced dead. When news of her death reaches the printing press that is manufacturing poster of her, the machine slowly rolls to a halt, leaving her image beneath the metal bars of the press as if that image were imprisoned. Outside her recollections, the viewer is again left with only her manufactured personality—an image that is frozen as the motion picture itself concludes.

Certainly many Italian films produced during the 1930s lack such a bleak and problematic view of a woman's place in the family in a modern society. Still, lurking beneath Ophuls's treatment of Gaby's predicament is a sense that her failure to form a socially acceptable bond with a man contributes obliquely to her inability to enjoy her public success or career. And it is the implicit correspondence between work and family that also produces much of the humor in the "private secretary" comedies. In Gustav Machaty's *Ballerine* (1936), a ballerina is forced to choose between her career as a dancer and her love for her middle-class boyfriend, a radio announcer and journalist. When she opts for a tour in America with her company, her boyfriend breaks off their affair. After she returns, however, it is clear that her successes have not enabled her to reconcile her romantic interests in her former boyfriend. That his journalistic reviews now laud her public success undoubtedly enamors her even more.

Another significant permutation of this conflict over a woman's identity in the family and in a modern, urban environment is Max Neufield's 1939 screwball comedy *Mille lire al mese* (*A Thousand Lira a Month*). Here, a young Italian woman (Alida Valli), while listening to the gay lyrics of the film's title song over her radio, becomes depressed over her fiancé's prospects of landing a high-paying job as a technician. (The title refers to what was then a substantial income.) In order to get to the "source" of her problem, she decides to visit the radio station itself in Budapest to convince its director to hire her husband. Both Budapest and the radio station would satisfy even the wildest fantasies about cosmopolitanism, material excess, modernity, and automation. Like Camerini's department store, the radio station is also a model of organized, corporativistic industry, which, by virtue of its emphasis on organization through automation, serves as an ideal stage for comic situations. The station's involvement with the latest technology has led it into experimentation with television and has increased its demand for skilled technicians. The film dramatizes the point that a pursuit of the New creates jobs when radio technicians, who are unfamiliar with the intricacies of the station's new experimental technology, create havoc and botch the station's first television broadcast by mistakenly transmitting a performance with scantily clad dancing girls over a report about the launching of a new ocean liner. To avoid future calamities, the director agrees to have the girl return with her fiancé for an interview.

From this point, however, a series of complicated role reversals ensues. When the fiancé arrives at the station, he mistakenly becomes embroiled in a dispute with the station director. So, in order to gain the interview without being

recognized, he and his fiancée convince a friend who is a pharmacist to masquer-
ade as the technician. They pass their first assignment, the repair of the TV
transmitter, and delight the director by revealing to him over his closed-circuit
monitor a group of his employees forgoing their duties to play cards. Later,
however, despite the technician's efforts to coach his friend, the pharmacist
mishandles the equipment; and, one evening at a jazz nightclub, jealousies arise
because of the director's confusion over the relationship between the technician
and his fiancée. Only after the director, through his closed-circuit monitor, spies
the real technician operating the TV equipment, does he realize their charade
and offer him a job.

The station director in *Mille lire al mese* helps perpetuate a stereotype of an
omnipotent, and through his personal television monitor, omniscient male
hero. In some senses, he personifies the qualities imagined by Alida Valli's
character when she listens to the movie's theme song over the radio in the
opening scene. And it is her desire to remake her own fiancé in his image (or
her image of him) that leads all of them into the jealousies and identity confusions which transpire in Budapest. If her character is viewed amidst the field of
female characters which I have tried to delineate here, it should be evident that
popular film culture in Fascist Italy did not produce a uniform and unified role
model, that any one of these characters becomes particularly dramatic and interesting to an audience familiar with competing roles. What these movies should
demonstrate, however, is an impulse, a felt need, to work past traditional models
or to rework traditional strategies for characterizing changing public realities
and social conditions, and to amplify or mask some of the central, most broadly
felt crises engendered by these transformations.

To see all cultural practice in Fascist Italy as merely perpetuating a *coherent*
representation of the Fascist Woman would be to ignore ways that films such as
these challenge gender roles in the process of affirming them. According to
Alberto Consiglio, writing in the pages of *Cinema* in 1937:

> Let us show how in the European family the equality between men and women is
> not based on an empty juridical formula, but how it springs from a truly equal
> division of labor . . . the tasks of a man prevailing over the familial domain with
> regard to actions and to the network of relationships outside the home, and a
> woman managing the hearth—"mistress" of her house, mother of her children
> (even with regard to her husband, mother before wife).[35]

These films, however, often reveal the difficulties in attaining this "ideal" familial
and social role, and in some instances they question its desirability.

Conclusions

As in *Gli uomini, che mascalzoni!* technological innovations which facilitated
outdoor shooting enabled filmmakers to take dramatic action out of the "closed"

interiors of early, upper-crust boudoir comedy and to explore the *domain* of the man on the street. Yet, because urban topography lacked the "open" quality of nature, characters were still thrown together into intimate situations; only now intimacy was experienced in public places. Camerini's department store, his Milanese sample fair, and his sidewalk newsstand are examples of *public* places that are transformed into *personal* theaters for the films' protagonists. Since a cityscape is man-made, it increasingly becomes, as Richard Sennett argues, a zone where public space is made private and vice versa and where commercial, man-made images promise spiritual transcendence.

The City is an important setting for dramatic action in films from the 1930s because it enables filmmakers to address most directly the cultural, social, and psychological problems engendered by rapid industrialization and technological innovation. Camerini's films, for instance, concern the ambivalence of Italian "consumer society" toward urban fashion and to a general overabundance of products and images. In Neufield's *Mille lire al mese*, the City's orientation toward new technology and future development creates havoc while it also promises economic opportunity for its middle-class characters. The City, as a carnivalesque realm (*La segretaria privata*), is also an ideal setting for probing changes in the nature of family relationships and gender roles. Although the City becomes an obstacle to maintaining a traditional, rural sense of community, it is also a means of legitimizing change and of imparting to urban families a sense of purpose. Movies which set dramatic action in urban environments, as in the case of *Napoli che non muore*, even enable their filmmakers to redefine and assert Italy's *national* values in an age of increased international travel and commerce and, on the other hand, to demonstrate the resiliency of Italian middle classes. For filmmakers such as Camerini, modern, urban images were often a means of contextualizing traditional themes. It is in this way that the films I have discussed in this chapter participate in the spirit of what was described in Italy as the rhetoric of *Stracittà*—a subject which I examine in the next chapter.

4 *Terra madre* and the Myth of *Strapaese*

Stracittà and *Strapaese*

During the 1920s and 1930s, a number of Italian intellectuals adopted the expression *Stracittà* (or "ultra-City") to identify and to belittle the ideals of certain Italian Modernists, particularly Marinetti's Futurism or those of Bontempelli's "900" circle.[1] Essentially, *Stracittà* was a buzzword that enabled these intellectuals to legitimize their own theoretical position, which they described as *Strapaese* (or "ultra-Country"). It seemed to proponents of *Strapaese* that the early Italian avant-garde had promoted ideals consonant with "Lutheran" bourgeois industrialism and the "dehumanization" characteristic of an urban milieu.[2] These same proponents of *Strapaese* insisted on regionalism and expressed a desire to recuperate "agricultural values"; they believed their vision to be the necessary antidote to a culture that had been "contaminiated" by technological society, with its machines imported from abroad and an ideology "alien" to that of provincial communities.

Much of the critical literature of *Strapaese* appears in Mino Maccari's and Curzio Malaparte's journal *Selvaggio*. In 1927, Maccari defines *Strapaese* as follows:

> *Strapaese* has been introduced in order to defend with the sword the rural and brotherly character of the Italian people; apart from meaning the more genuine and sincere expressions of the race it also refers to treatments of the environment, the climate and the mentality through which—whether by instinct or by love— our purest traditions are safeguarded. *Strapaese* is the bulwark against the invasion of foreign values or ways of thinking and of modernist civilization, through which thought and culture threaten to repress, undermine or destroy those things most dear and familiar to Italians who in their effort to create a unified Italian State must realize their indispensable base and their essential element.[3]

Through this type of highly argumentative treatise, proponents of *Strapaese* characterized all Modernist art, with its urban and international themes, as anti-Italian and anti-Fascist:

> We are attempting, as much as possible, to distinguish early futurism—as a kind of therapeutic massage on a lifeless and feeble body—from later futurism, which

becomes merely an artistic movement that is internationally-oriented, conventional, democratic and inclined to Bolshevism, but absolutely incompatible with the Fascist regime.[4]

They preferred the traditional agricultural zones to the great industrial metropolis, regionalism to internationalism, and the past to the future. The rural peasant became for them a political ideal, and they found in the rural settings of works by the nineteenth-century writer Giovanni Verga and by the twentieth-century author Tozzi models for their cause:

> We, the younger generation, should have clear ideas about ourselves and our "novelistic" voice—one at least on par with the likes of Palazzeschi, Tozzi, and Verga. Their peasants and fishermen [e.g., *Podere* and *I Malavoglia*] are like a breath of fresh air, and they lift our spirits.[5]

Proponents of *Strapaese* argued that only through images informed by ruralist ideals could Italians discover a sense of national political culture.

Strapaese called attention to conditions that had significantly and rapidly altered Italy's demographic profile: technological innovations in travel and mass media, industrialization and urbanization, and an influx of foreign images and fashion. And, despite its emphasis on artists whose work seemed to glorify rural lifestyles, *Strapaese* (as a neologism for a *new* cultural orientation) also depended upon modern procedures for communicating these changes. The Fascist government, whose ideologues often invoked the rhetoric of *Strapaese*, promoted rural festivals, arts and crafts exhibits, folk costumes, etc. in an attempt to instill a nationalistic spirit and to create an "organic" sense of State (even though these efforts were more successful in producing popular spectacles than in orchestrating a real return to rural lifestyles). However, it would be too reductive to view simply as diabolic the initiatives intended to authenticate Fascist policy by conjuring images of Nature through traditional ritual. Every political organization must *discover* its audience and the appropriate means of addressing them, and the vitality of any policy springs from endless innovation and recuperation through whatever modes are available for communicating self-images. As Clifford Geertz has noted, "essentialist" pride (one aspect of Italian nationalism) is not merely a by-product of social change but the very stuff of social change itself. For aestheticians, for political leaders, and for some filmmakers, *Strapaese* was a means of identifying their constituency, their audience; and for middle-class audiences, the images of a rural communality promised means of managing the social and psychological tensions engendered by a society in transition.

In many respects, the debate in Italy over *Stracittà* and *Strapaese* is simply another manifestation of the epochalist/essentialist conflict that Geertz sees as characteristic of nationalisms. One could even argue that Fascism's failure to articulate a clear and consistent cultural policy resulted from its inability to reconcile these two contradictory themes. It is, however, necessary to recognize that the semantic structures of *Stracittà* and *Strapaese* are a great deal more complex than they appear immediately to be:

The images, metaphors, and rhetorical turns from which nationalistic ideologies are built are essentially devices, cultural devices designed to render one or another aspect of the broad process of collective self-redefinition explicit, to cast essentialist pride or epochalist hope into specific symbolic forms, where more than dimly felt, they can be described, developed, celebrated, and used. To formulate an ideological doctrine is to make (or try to make—there are more failures than successes) what was a generalized mood into a practical force.[6]

The *Strapaese* and *Stracittà* camps constitute two aspects of what could be described as Italy's Neo-avant-garde; unlike the prewar Futurists, et al., both of these groups desired to address and engage "popular" audiences. (How well they succeeded is of course open to speculation.) The paradox of their debate and its importance in understanding Italy's national popular culture is that Bontempelli and his group saw *modern* subjects and styles as a means of representing a national and populistic identity and of contextualizing traditional themes; whereas the *Strapaese* camp believed that, by relying upon images of *traditional* culture, the arts could more effectively convey to a larger audience messages about national integration and modernization. Both groups addressed Italy's need for a "popular culture," but they each proposed different means of achieving it and articulating it.

The rhetoric of *Strapaese* is evidence of attempts to draw political policy and a politicized aesthetic into a *cultural* conflict (and vice versa). Moreover, because this conflict was so embedded in popular tastes and the production of popular forms, there was little guarantee that the politics of *Strapaese* could completely negate or even tarnish the attractiveness of epochalism or could redirect the public's impulse toward it. Gian-Piero Brunetta argues that most Italian films from the 1920s and 1930s did not actually address the problems and interests of rural Italy:

> Notwithstanding these elements that rest on a cultural tradition and on some nationalistic models that will continue even after the fall of Fascism, the portrait of the Italian undergoes certain necessary modifications: films begin to underscore material dialectics, in what would seem to be the spirit of Strapaese rather than of Stracittà. But the Italian lower classes, i.e. the peasants, proletariat, and petite bourgeoisie (dialectical Italy), seem to desire (at least in Italy's feature films) the Stracittà image of Italy—one with a uniform and reassuring moral image of the bourgeoisie.[7]

As I have tried to demonstrate in the last chapter, Italian films whose action occurs in an urban and industrial environment do not necessarily reject traditional values in favor of a cosmopolitan elitism; quite the contrary. Films such as *Il Signor Max* or *Rotaie* denigrate the elitism of the *bel mondo* and the petit-bourgeois protagonist's desire for it. Even in these films, the tensions between essentialist self-interest and epochalist acceptance of foreign lifestyles and the technological *nouveautés* of industrial and consumer society produce the conflict for dramatic action. Conversely, as Brunetta's observation affirms, films that deal with rural characters and settings do not prescribe a return to rural lifestyles. Rather, the epochalist impulse is examined in a rural setting so that it can be assimilated and purged. In a number of these films, conflict occurs between rural and urban values—values which seem to co-exist in the narrative resolution.

The Rhetoric of *Strapaese* in the Films of Alessandro Blasetti

A number of Italian film critics during the 1930s pointed to Mario Camerini's *Rotaie* (discussed in chapter 1) and Alessandro Blasetti's *Sole* as films having engendered the two most distinct Italian film styles. Both films were produced in 1929 and were two of the very first sound films made in Italy during its industry's period of reconstruction. Both films concern the erosion of traditional, working-class values by industrialization and urbanization. Camerini's film examines the consequences of cultural instability in an urban milieu; his young lovers do not escape the city to an arcadia but to the world of the Grand Hotel. Blasetti's *Sole*, on the other hand, presents many of these same themes (rural culture vs. encroaching civilization) through rural and provincial settings.

From the rather fragmented version that exists today and from reviews of the film at the time of its release, it is evident that the dramatic conflict in *Sole* occurs between the inhabitants of the Pontine marshes outside of Rome and those who arrive to rid the area of disease and to revitalize the land. The attractiveness of this wild, rural place is enhanced when the leader of the redevelopment operation, Rinaldi, falls in love with Giovanna, the daughter of a leader of the marsh's denizens. And later, when the prerogative of Rinaldi is challenged by Silvestro, another of the local inhabitants, Rinaldi is recognized as his comrade from the war and is then accepted into the community (an awareness of a deep "national" bond presumably being the basis for their reconciliation). The film concludes with a cooperative effort between Rinaldi, an engineer, and Silvestro, who guides a plow to work this land, and with the marriage of Rinaldi and Giovanna. As a publicity notice for the film states, their harmonious enterprise "offers virgin soil, not tilled for centuries, to be kissed by the sun."[8] In his equally "poetic" appraisal of *Sole* in 1929, Corrado Pavolini praises the ways in which the film also covers new cinematic territories: "The film is called *Sole!* which is by the way a beautifully luminous and Italian title: its author is unknown, its director unknown, its actors unknown, and it is truly a revelation."[9] And in a similar review Alberto Cecchi observes: "After almost fifteen years, that have been a kind of dark and backward Middle Ages for the Italian film industry, here is a work worthy of us and of our times, worthy of the Americans, and . . . worthy of traveling around the world."[10]

As both these reviews suggest, *Sole*'s account of the reclamation of the Pontine swamps seems something of a prophecy about the rebirth of the film industry itself. The meanings of the broader social and political reforms hinted at by the film are also mediated through the more intimate romantic affairs of the protagonists; their marriage even obliquely heralds the commencement of the re-

Two scenes from *Sole* (d. Blasetti, 1930)

gime's efforts to rehabilitate this area and to make Italy economically and culturally productive. What now seems just as significant about *Sole*, however, is that
(as Blasetti himself has stated) it was a project given to discovering a popular
language and popular themes, but that it was not financially successful.[11] While
later critics note that, in its subject matter, tone, and style, *Sole* seems influenced
by Russian Formalism, Blasetti has argued that he was unfamiliar with Soviet
cinema until at least two years after he directed *Sole*.[12] Instead, he cites King
Vidor's *The Big Parade* as an early inspiration to his style.[13]

Although Blasetti's next two films, *Nerone* (1930) and *Resurrectio* (1931)[14]
(done under the urging of Pittaluga), abandon the rural setting, his *Terra madre*
(1931) resumes many of *Sole*'s rural and nationalistic themes and motifs—ones
that recur throughout many of his succeeding films and those of other Italian
directors. Before discussing *Terra madre*, however, it is necessary to consider
briefly the codes that shaped Blasetti's films as well as the popular and critical
attitudes toward them.

As I have indicated in chapter 2, Blasetti (especially during the film industry's
period of reconstruction) frequently lamented the allure in Italy of foreign film
styles; instead he preferred movies that dealt with "national" subjects and concerns. Undoubtedly, the appeal of Vidor's films for Blasetti was due partly to
their treatment of *American* events and settings and, in the case of *The Big
Parade*, to their national patriotism. Although other Italian directors and film
critics voiced some of the same concerns, Blasetti is perhaps the foremost propo-
nent of an "Italian" popular cinema—one with which he intended to raise a
political consciousness in his audience. He attempted to express through the
Pontine marshes of *Sole* and (as we shall see) through the country estate of *Terra
madre* the value of "italianità." Geographical settings in these films were less
"international" arenas for dramatic action than were the Grand Hotels or the
cityscapes of other Italian films. *Sole* was shot in the countryside around Rome
and used mostly untrained actors and actresses; the trained actors he did use
were, according to Blasetti, chosen for their lack of star-status.[15] Although
Blasetti may have described his first sound film as an attempt to capture the joys,
the travails—the spirit—of the Italian "people"[16], it should be obvious that his
representations of Italian culture were significantly different from those of, say,
Camerini, whose films often dealt with the problems of those living in an urban
or more cosmopolitan environment. In his rural films, the procedures of "spatial
modeling" offer a significantly different interpretive framework or world view
than do those of films discussed here in previous chapters, but it would be
erroneous to say that films set in Grand Hotels or in urban areas somehow
present a less "accurate" image of Italian culture in the 1930s. Furthermore,
Blasetti's images of Italian culture were not laden with more conservative or
traditional values or with political statements more Fascist than films set in
urban or foreign places. One could cite the couple's rejection of the *bel mondo* in
Rotaie as an example of a film that deals with urban subjects yet that still reaffirms
traditional, conservative values. Blasetti simply recognized that rustic images
connoted traditional lifestyles and offered easily identifiable models of commu-

nal living and collective action. Images of Nature and of provincial living may help legitimate political messages or the ideological assumptions of the film's director, but they also enable (particularly in this case) a crucial self-image for audiences. During the years of the industry's reconstruction, when Italian directors and producers were desperately seeking some recourse to the overwhelming popularity of foreign films, filmmakers attempted to develop images that might put their audience in touch with an unequivocally Italian culture. Blasetti's images of rustic and regional life seemed to impart to his films a uniquely Italian flavor—one that he hoped would be more "natural," more accessible, than foreign ones or those in Italy that might appear to imitate foreign styles. Nature in his films becomes a way of legitimating Italy's popular film culture.

Terra Madre: A Return to the Land

In 1974, Blasetti explains that the "photogenic" qualities of the country as opposed to the city, were both the subject and the inspiration for Terra madre; he also cites one of Murnau's last films, Our Daily Bread (City Girl, 1929) as an influence on his conception of this film.[17] Terra madre reworked some of the motifs or situations not only of Sole but also of some of the last Italian silent films (Senza padre, 1926, and La grazia, 1929, both of which involve the return of a noble master to his country birthright and its inhabitants). Although Terra madre was described by some critics as Blasetti's "return to the land" (due presumably to its pastoral subjects and setting, to its outdoor shooting, to its Naturalistic style, and to a revival of themes found in Sole), the film was actually more of a dramatization of contemporary ideological conflict. Leo Longanesi thus described it as "the masterwork of the ruralist rhetoric, the oleography of modern times."[18] Certainly, the peasants' costumes in Terra madre seem more romantic or "popularized" creations (in the spirit of the Dopolavoro's efforts to fabricate a "folk culture") than facsimiles of the clothing actually worn by Italian peasants. The ideological nature of the film's dramatic conflict is posed in its introductiory titles:

> Throughout the whole world the leftover grandeur of yesterday is clashing with modern progress. In Italy a glorious past of 3,000 years is threatened. Will the treasures of Old Roman civilization die or can it be harmonized with today?

One can view the rest of the film as a response to this initial question—as a model for social action in confronting this historical crisis.

Although these opening titles establish a field of signification for the ensuing dramatic action, it is still difficult to understand the connection between "the treasures of old Roman civilization" and the actual setting for Terra madre unless one continually refers to the essentialist codes that I have mentioned. The film's narrative concerns a refined yet hearty young Duke, Marco, who returns from his leisurely, urban life to the estate where he was reared. Because his father (the estate's proprietor) has died, the son sees his own return merely as a means of settling his father's affairs and of selling the land—to, as we later learn, a greedy speculator. The "harmony" of the country and of its grandiose past (mentioned in the film's opening titles) is established immediately after the opening titles through a long shot of a field of peasants singing a sort of chantey in unison as they work. The idyllic nature of this opening scene is soon interrupted, however, by the arrival of the Duke's automobile; and the musical accompaniment to the car's appearance is much more gay, more Modern, than is the peasants' singing. Even in these first scenes, the original question is reiterated: How can the cosmopolitan rhythm by which the young Duke lives be synchronized with the pastoral hymn of the peasants?

The answer seems to be in the myth of the automobile itself: as the car approaches the estate and the peasants run to greet the returning son, the auto (symbolically) becomes stuck in the mud. It is as though the earth or Nature immobilizes the very symbol of urban, industrial society and denies the Duke the one indexical sign of his wealth. This first conflict brings out in a highly elliptical fashion the temperaments of all involved. For instance, a young and sophisticated woman traveling with Marco is annoyed by the inconvenience and complains loudly about the hostile environment. The Duke, on the other hand, is undaunted and nimbly extricates the automobile (an emblem of the modern, mechanical world), demonstrating his sort of "natural" versatility. And the peasants, of course, are delighted; his action seems to fulfill their expectations about his virile potency. His feat seems to be one with which they, as agents of the Natural world, can identify.

In this opening scene, young Marco mediates the civilized world and Nature. His ability to interpose these two realms makes him charismatic (a sort of a changeling), and in turn his charisma imparts to him a license to manage conflicts between these two worlds. All that he lacks is an image through which he can recognize his "obligation" as an agent for mediating social crisis, and he acquires this needed impetus through the daughter of his father's chief steward on the estate.

Riding his horse one day not long after his arrival, Marco comes upon a group of peasants singing a dirge in an open field. As the peasants eulogize a fellow worker, the Duke is touched by the sight of Emilia (the steward's daughter); he secretly watches as she includes in her own eulogy a prayer for the Duke (whom she has not yet encountered). Upon hearing her prayer, Marco dismounts and makes his presence known. Still not suspecting his identity, she speaks candidly to him about her desire to revive the land and about her lack of faith in the young Duke, whom she feels is not of her "race"—someone no longer bound to the earth. So impressed is Marco by her frankness, her "naturalness," and, consequently, her beauty that he leaves inspired, through a growing desire for her, with a new sense of duty. In Emilia, Marco sees the virginal aspects of the land, which to this point has seemed to be merely a tomb for his late father and the dead worker.

The unsympathetic and antagonistic characters in *Terra madre* are those who cannot adjust to country life. Marco's female consort, for instance, exhibits little desire to abandon the bedroom (the domain of urban comedy). She sleeps late every morning, dresses in the latest casual fashions to stroll the estate, and is genuinely appalled by the "primitiveness" of cows being branded. Having become disenchanted with Marco (whose feet are more solidly planted on the ground), she soon develops a romantic interest in a dandyish merchant who is visiting the estate. Through these two women, the governing political and ideological opposition between the forces of Nature and Modern civilization is condensed to a romantic *tête-à-tête* in which the emotional stakes of the conflict are amplified.

Marco's function as agent of narrative resolution cannot, therefore, be separated from his role as lover. The film's narrative follows his rite of passage from the arms of the more capricious city-girl to the more steady character of Emilia; here his sexual desire for the blonde city woman is sublimated through his romantic love of Emilia. As he becomes increasingly annoyed with his traveling companion and her elitism and pretense, his own natural qualities as savior/prodigal son are made manifest. The climax of the film occurs when he breaks from the company of his upper-crust peers because he is drawn to the vitality of the peasants at the branding ceremony. With this step, Marco relinquishes his role as observer to become a man of action—here, literally taking a bull by the horns and wrestling it. His initial affiliation with the upper-crust snobs obfuscates for the peasants his true power as lord or *duce*. But his physical agility, earlier with the car and later as he wrestles the bull at the branding event, highlights his new active role; it transforms him in the eyes of the peasants (and in the minds of those willing to recognize the humble valor of the peasants) into a Fairbanksian hero over whom they become ecstatic.

The movie culminates with a folk festival in which the peasants celebrate the true return, the maturing, of the young Duke. They urge Marco to continue in the footsteps of his father, whom they consider a "true man of the earth," and to never leave his *terra madre*. The vigor of the peasants' festivities in this scene is contrasted with the decadent dallying inside the villa—idle card games, ragtime music played on a phonograph, etc. But, as in the opening auto scene, the forces of Nature are eternal and indomitable; the pitch of the revelers' songs outside becomes so feverish that it overpowers the music and the more constrained mood inside—a gesture that clearly attests to the virtues of the peasants' cause.

Amidst this celebration, the speculator finally arrives to claim his land, and his arrival sets the stage for the final demonstration of the young Duke's conviction. Not only does this intruder lack any redeeming physical characteristics (he is extremely fat and oily), but he also fails to mitigate his sexual desires for the peasant girls (sentimental and romantic affection being signs here of Marco's temperance throughout the story). The speculator, believing the land is his, begins to burn the houses of the peasants on the estate. But, charged by the flames from these homes and by a desire for Emilia and his *terra madre*, Marco expels the speculator to reclaim the land. His heroic actions in turn spur the peasants to overcome their indifference and to put out the flames and save "their" land. As he and the bewildered peasants stand amidst the charred remains of their former existence, the young Duke boldly announces his plans to remain as the protector of the land and as Emilia's husband: "The land is mine and it shall remain mine!" And in the final scene of the film, Marco appears in a field (presumably the same one as in the beginning), demonstrating to his new charges the merits of a tractor and a mechanical harvester. This young Hermes has brought the Machine to Earth.

Marco's marriage to Emilia suggests several contingent reconciliations. The Italian earth, a virginal ideal of which Emilia and her province are an emblem, gains a virile protector—the myth that Italy is a Woman, protected by male guardians. Furthermore, Marco and Emilia's marriage signals a union between two social classes—a narrative strategy quite common in American screwball comedies, musicals, and some silent melodramas but also apparent at the end of *Sole*. The resolution also promises a classless society—the illusion of a truly *popular* culture. The marriage redresses the question posed at the beginning of the film: How does one harmonize traditional values with the demands of a modern society? The film's ending obliquely conjures the Futurist myth of a world where man and Machine are one, where they operate together to resuscitate from Nature a cultural ideal. But the real answer to the question is the film itself. Its Naturalist style and rural setting create the illusion of an ideological imperative, an exemplum whose moral message seems grounded in Nature. If one accepts the film's resolution, the Utopian world exists just beyond the narrative and outside the cinema lobby.

The Rural–Urban Conflict in 1930s Films

That Marco decides to remain in the country instead of returning to the city is certainly characteristic of *Strapaese's* absolute rejection of urban and cosmopolitan values. Yet the film also affirms the peasants' need for enlightened youth and technological know-how, both of which could not have been found otherwise in the country. Both of these themes appear in different variations in films throughout the 1930s. Some, such as *Treno popolare* (1933), *Come le foglie* (1935), *Non è una cosa seria* (1936), and *Patire* (1938), demonstrate the redeeming values of country life for urbanites. Others, such as *La provincialina* (1934), *Inventiamo l'amore* (1938), *Marionette* (1939), and *Stella del mare* (1939), concern unfortunate bumpkins who are lured to the bright lights of the city; they attain momentary fame only to learn that there is really no place like home. Although all of these films underscore the Truth and innocent beauty of country people, they also stipulate that the preservation of this beauty often lies in Modern experience.

In Palermi's *Partire* (*Getting Away*), Vittorio De Sica plays a young, unemployed petit-bourgeois Neapolitan, Paolo, who is bored and disenchanted with his lack of social options. His routine seems to consist of little other than dreaming of the *bel mondo*. In the opening scenes, for instance, Paolo idly passes his time at the docks, watching liners embark for exotic lands, or at the bank, enjoying vicarious contact with large amounts of money. Later the same evening, he sings an ode to "*patire—che felicità*." And when his date asks him what he wants to do with his life, he responds only, "To get away."

His sentimental reveries suddenly seem attainable, however, when a large automobile carrying a wealthy family careens off the road in front of a *trattoria* where he is passing the time. (Although the family—a portly man, his demanding wife, and their spirited though snobbish daughter—are only shaken, the father decides to defraud his insurance company by claiming a nervous disorder; he laments that he has paid his insurance for twenty years without ever collecting.) Fortune seems to shine on Paolo when the family leaves and he discovers a large briefcase—one into which he had seen the father that morning at the bank deposit a large sum of money. The satchel turns out to be empty, but Paolo decides to return it, hoping perhaps to collect a modest reward. Thus, in the first part of the film, bourgeois life in the city (at all levels) seems motivated by alienation, petty greed, and egocentricity.

Although the film is replete with comic moments, the characters' opportunistic scheming in the first part only seems to augment their quiet desperation. Paolo is compelled by the father, through a series of witty subterfuges, to work as his personal secretary in his law office. But, although Paolo had desired social mobility, he is equally unfulfilled with his new managerial post. (At one point he does undo the office tedium by entertaining the clerical staff with a popular swing tune.) Sensing his dissatisfaction, the father sends Paolo to the country to assist his (the father's) own father at their family villa.

During his residence at this villa in the last part of the film, Paolo acquires from the land a sense of self-worth, while he in turn revives the land. Like Marco in *Terra madre*, Paolo brings with him the modern technology with which to increase the land's productivity. Not long after he arrives, he educates workers about the newest methods of cultivating a field; this scene is presented through a rather protracted montage featuring the latest farm machinery. At first, the grandfather is furious that Paolo should upset traditional methods, but, when he observes the efficiency of the machines, he decides to dedicate his land as an experimental base for all new farm equipment. The rest of the film concerns the progress and temporary setbacks of this experimental system.

This rural world seems unaccustomed to the contradictions of the bourgeois society from which Paolo has just come; it is a domain of landed gentry and of peasants—a realm of stark contrasts where Paolo can discover a personal transcendence. Paolo's moment of epiphany occurs when, during a storm of almost cosmic proportions, his own car runs off the road and he is forced to take shelter in the habitation of peasants. Here he observes the squalid though harmonious conditions in which several families live and work together. The peasants offer Paolo some of their soup. Then, because they realize that the storm will ruin the wheat crop, they go to work to salvage it, thus demonstrating to Paolo the superiority of Man to Machine. (The apocalyptic scene in which Paolo assists the peasants in harvesting the crop amidst the storm is quite dramatic, characterized by a thunderous musical score and quick editing.) Paolo, who has now seen how hard peasants work, is inspired to abandon his laziness, and (as in *Terra madre*) Paolo's recognition of his duty enables him to become a provider, to start a family of his own with the daughter of his boss.

At the outset of *Partire*, Paolo's vision of the *bel mondo* enables him momentarily to displace his desires. Through his encounter with the family who send him to the country, however, he discovers a far more gratifying state where he himself can become an organizer of men, in touch with Nature. Actually, he gets what he desired in the beginning (a chance to break away), but not in the manner he had anticipated. The florid images of vacations are ultimately transitory; only the more Naturalistic images of rural life, work, and community offer him a stable reality through which he can build a productive life. Moreover, films such as *Terra madre* and *Partire* demonstrate that rural images were ideally suited to portray, for urban audiences, collective social action.

Whereas films such as *Partire*, *Terra madre*, and (as I will explain below) *Treno popolare* foreground the experience of a city-dweller in the country, other Italian films during the 1930s highlight the innocence and Natural virtues of rural life by transposing a small-town nobody to the big city. Films such as *La provincialina* (*The Little Country Girl*) and *Inventiamo l'amore* (*Let's Invent Love*) created sentimental comedy about the experiences of provincial denizens out of their element. In Carl Boese and Ferruccio Biancini's *La provincialina* (an Italian–German co-production), a young female fan of the theater assists a director who has had an automobile accident in the provincial community where she lives. As a joke, the director invites her to accompany him to the city to play the role of Juliet. Here, as a result of a misunderstanding, the girl, Annina, is mistaken for the director's lover. Upset by these insults, she steps onstage during the middle of a performance in order to plead her innocence. But her unintended performance sends the audience into rapture, saves the show, and transforms the girl into an overnight success. One of the film's messages is that the latent virtues that she brings with her to the city are immediately recognized by upper-crust theatergoers. The Naturalness of her character makes her resilient to the attempts by the director, by his wife, and by the artifice of stage production to conceal her *true* talent.

Four years after *La provincialina*, Camillo Mastrocinque's *Inventiamo l'amore* (1938) adopted a similar narrative formula. Here, a young couple from the provinces attempt to escape the repressive traditions of their village to realize their romantic fantasies in the city. The film was based on a drama by Bruno Corra (of the early Futurist circle) and Giuseppe Achille, wherein the young lovers are exploited in the city by theater workers. But in the film version, the lovers are seduced by unscrupulous cinematographers. As in *La provincialina*, comedy is created here through the couple's exploits outside their natural domain; but, although this reversal of roles is humorous, they eventually realize that they are better off in more stable and familiar/local surroundings. Thus, in the end, the lovers recognize their delusions and return to the provinces, having learned once again that there is no place like home. Of course, their moment of recognition would not have occurred had they not visited the city. Here, however, another level of irony is produced by their escapade with the filmmakers. The couple experience the city only as spectacle (i.e., as movie actors/performance); they see the country instead as Nature—a place without the theatrical artifice or any other trappings of culture that they find in the city. Although Mastrocinque's image of rural life is a far cry from the political realism that Blasetti attempted, this film does uphold the myth of the country, and it stereotypes filmmaking as an urban and thus slightly contemptible enterprise whose fabrications confuse rather than clarify.

As I have indicated in the chapter on American films, movies *about* screen personalities often typecast these characters as foreigners or city folk, as people who trade in exotic, chic fantasy. This unsympathetic image is somewhat ironic in that it calls attention to the film's own "manipulative" tendencies. But, perhaps more importantly, this sort of self-reflexivity also helps mask the film's own rhetorical stylization. By encouraging its audience to follow the plight of the bumpkins who become actors, *Inventiamo l'amore* rounds out the popular register of its voice; its own images appear to emanate from the collective spirit rather than from an *artist*, individualist, or a director (in the literal sense—one who is dissociated from the collective will, that is, Nature). As an expression of popular sentiment, in its attempt to provide images which draw together a popular culture, it also gives presence to the ambivalence of Italian audiences toward the value of popular entertainment. Cinema appears as a spectacle that corrupts and captivates as well as one that liberates; it appears to mediate and thus transcend both urban and rural experiences.

Other films examine the more tragic implications of rural innocence corrupted by unscrupulous city hustlers. In Corrado D'Errico's *Stella del mare* (*Star of the Sea*), a young fisherman from Viareggio, who sings popular Neapolitan ballads while he works, is seduced by a wealthy siren from the city who promises to make him a recording star. Although he sings as well as an accomplished opera performer, his abilities seem to spring from his contact with Nature, i.e., with his seashore community and ultimately with the myth that all Neapolitans possess an innate ability to sing well. He abandons Viareggio, a girl of his own social status who loves him, and the songs of the sea in order to sing modern swing tunes in Rome. While he is transformed into a celebrity, Luisa (his former love) listens to him regularly on the radio at the bar where she works. Finally, she ventures to the city to reclaim him; the image of the city which she encounters is that of high-society cabarets and recording studios with lavish promotional displays of the latest stars (of Gianni, the young singer, in this case). During his important debut at one such nightclub, Gianni realizes that the recording director has only feigned affection for him in order to procure a contract. When he confronts her after the performance, she rebuffs him and leaves with a wealthier South American opera producer. The *coup de grâce* comes when her assistant director coldly alerts Gianni to his delusions: "You think you are a great man because we taught you a few songs; but you are only a record, nothing more, just a phonograph record, who repeats what he is taught." In his anger, Gianni breaks his records, vowing to give up singing altogether and to return to the simple routine of a fisherman. In the end, Luisa attempts to help him overcome this form of impotence. Her efforts are rewarded when Gianni enters the local church, sees Luisa standing next to an icon of the Virgin Mary, and subsequently, summoning his dormant abilities, erupts once more into song.

In *Stella del mare*, Gianni's songs become an expression of his naturalness—his bond with the sea. He is a "star" of the sea to begin with but simply does not recognize it until he experiences the decadence of modern, urban society and its *music*. His return to Luisa is thus a redemption of the fishing village and provincial religious values. However, the small-town routine would not appear extraordinarily special had Gianni not returned to become the town's star; his presence charges the town, in the eyes of the movie's audience, with a vitality that it might have otherwise lacked.

Much the same virtues are recognized in Mario in Gallone's *Marionette*. In this film, the alchemy of a wealthy female journalist transmutes a young country boy into a celebrated tenor. She is so taken by his vocal gifts that she arranges for his debut on stages everywhere. Unlike the relationship between Gianni and the record producer in *Stella del mare*, however, this couple are finally able to reconcile differences that occur because of his fame.

Treno popolare: The Realism of Rural Romance

For urban Italians, the country was someplace to be visited during leisure time or vacation, someplace made distant during modernization yet accessible through modern means of travel. In Raffaello Matarazzo's *Treno popolare* (1933), the country serves as a romantic metaphor for that uniquely bourgeois experience: the *weekend*. The "popular trains" of the title refer to the government's working-class discounts for weekend train travel and to the excursions into the provinces sponsored during the 1930s by the OND ("Opera Nazionale Dopolavoro," a national committee for recreational development). This travel project was initiated just over a year before the film was made and during its first years was taken advantage of by hundreds of thousands of people living in Italian cities (though after these initial years the number of passengers leveled off to about 100,000 each year).[19] De Grazia notes that the state discounts had two objectives: "to boost mass transit, thereby reducing the huge deficit of the state railroads as revenues declined during the depression; at the same time they provided the urban unemployed and poor a brief respite from the dismal depression atmosphere of the cities."[20] *Treno popolare* does participate in the flourish of enthusiasm over what is implicity a Fascist reform. But to understand this film simply as an example of propaganda, produced to promote a government program or to mask the material concerns of the state, as some have been inclined to do, would be to ignore the film's formal innovation, its satire, and its difficulty in competing with other commercial films.

Both Dino Falconi and Filippo Sacchi, who reviewed *Treno popolare* at the time of its release, praised the film for its "freshness" and its initiative; however, it is as much a celebration of tradition as of youth—the country and the antiq-

Boarding the "popular trains" in *Treno popolare* (d. Matarazzo, 1933)

uity of small provincial towns offering an ideal locus for expressing the vitality of a young generation.[21] Gastone Bosio and the 23-year-old Matarazzo, who were responsible for the film's direction, story, screenplay, and editing, and Nino Rota, who was responsible for the film's musical score (and would later go on to score many of Fellini's films), all belonged to a younger generation of Italian filmmakers. And, while the film does involve some older characters, the four central characters are also very young; in fact, theirs is an "initiation" into a cultural heritage that has been obfuscated by their urban routine, but that is recovered through the new national initiative of modern travel (as well as through the cinema).

Treno popolare differs from most commercial feature films at that time primarily because of its total lack of studio sets (most filming occurs outdoors and some, in the initial scene, inside one of the train's cars) and a lack of stars (many without any acting training at all). The film incorporates lengthy and frequent expository footage (of the train's passengers, of rural panoramas, of rural customs) that imparts to the narrative a documentary style; in fact, it is at times difficult to tell whether, in the scenes aboard the train, Matarazzo edited in documentary footage of "popular trains." (As I explain in chapter 7, Matarazzo, along with Blasetti, was involved in the production of some of the most creative documentaries produced during the 1930s by the Cines company.) The film's narrative lacks the coherence of commercial feature films. Marcello Spada, who plays one of the three central characters, has explained that some of the acting was improvised and that the narrative was assembled by Matarazzo and Bosio only after they had screened rough cuts of the film.[22] While these extemporaneous elements made the film less competitive with more polished foreign and domestic movies, they contributed a great deal to capturing the kind of vacation experience that the film takes as its subject.

In some ways, *Treno popolare* extends Camerini's glorification of the working-class passengers aboard the third-class car in *Rotaie*. Here, however, many of the idiosyncrasies of these tourists are satirized. The initial scene, at the crowded train station in Rome, establishes the *democratic* attributes of riding popular trains. The train itself first appears with all its doors open to a variety of people: single people, couples, families, young people, old people. But their rushing to board the train is made to appear humorous through caricaturing—a strategy that prevents one from reading the film as a social realist text. Within the train, its open compartments become visual metaphors for a kind of extended Family; the arrangement of its seating brings families into intimate contact with one another and precipitates a number of romantic and comic situations. Just before the train leaves, a well-dressed older woman rushes on board to retrieve her husband, who is about to depart with a younger paramour. Her chastising the shocked girl, Maria, elicits both mild indignation and laughter from the surrounding passengers. Facing one another on adjacent seats are two older men whose bewilderment is made to appear slightly eccentric. In another area, two young office colleagues, Giovanni and Lina, fidget nervously as the timid Harold Lloyd-esque Giovanni struggles to engage Lina in polite conversation. This couple's tension is disrupted by the self-assured and effervescent Carlo (Marcello Spade), whose interest in Lina generates the romantic and comic adventures that serve as the narrative thread, such as it is, for the rest of the film. As the train rambles through the countryside, all the passengers burst into song (one written by Nino Rota for the film)—an expression of their harmonic potential and ability to overcome individual pecularities or jealousies.

Once in Orvieto, their destination, the passengers wander over the landscape and admire the small community's antiquated shrines. They ride a funicular, drink from old wells, visit local churches, and listen to one of the town's women explain the history of an old bell-tower. On the one hand, the visitors' presence mediates the audience's recognition of Italy's rich cultural past. On the other hand, the spaciousness of their surroundings helps instill a sense that they are part of something bigger than themselves. In one scene, this sense of transcendence occurs as the three young characters (Giovanni, Lina, and Carlo) enjoy their lunch alone atop a mountain, overlooking an expansive valley. In another part of the town, Maria (whose clandestine rendezvous had created a scandal earlier on the train) acts reinvigorated and seems purified by her distance from the social taboos of the City. After the film follows these characters separately, however, bells ring in churches throughout the town, as if to honor the winsome travelers and to enliven their communal merrymaking as they all converge to sing and continue their picnic together outdoors.

Just beyond this scene of open-air festivity, the three young lovers engage in a more festive adventure, bicycling down country roads. At one point, Lina and

Carlo free themselves from Giovanni, and, hiding themselves at a secluded spot on a river, they borrow a rowboat to continue their amorous dallying. Here, arcadia becomes a stage for petit-bourgeois romance, presumably allowing the couple to realize desires outside the purview of the City and away from the other passengers. When, however, Carlo reaches to embrace Lina, the couple overturn the boat. As they reach the bank of the river, Lina shyly consents to remove her wet clothes, and Carlo takes the opportunity to steal his first kiss. Giovanni soon arrives and, seeing only Lina's clothes and the boat adrift (Carlo and Lina have hid from him in a cabana), he immediately believes they have drowned and hurriedly departs with Lina's dress to seek help. The last part of the film involves his comic attempts to mobilize the local peasants (engaged here in their own festivities amidst bales of hay) to help him rescue his damsel in distress, and Carlo's efforts to stop him. In the final scene, aboard the train home, Carlo and Lina make love while Giovanni courts Maria; both couples and the singing passengers return to the city with a visible sense of belonging and a sense of having formed inevitable and natural bonds.

In some ways, *Treno popolare* exploited the most classical setting and situations of comedy; here the Italian countryside replaced the enchanted forest or the travel scenario of Renaissance comedy. Yet, viewed socially and historically, the film attempted to bring comedy out of the drawing rooms and the urban settings of earlier and contemporary Italian movies. Precisely for this reason, Falconi congratulates its young directors: "They have effortlessly and joyfully brought filmmaking to its *natural* habitat—the open air, so much more lovely and dear when it (as is the case here) is the clear, fresh air that permeates the charming countryside of Italy."[23] Three years later, in 1936, Mario Mattoli also filmed a comedy (*Musica in piazza*) entirely outside a studio, in a provincial Italian community. But Matarazzo's film works more toward an integration of *Stracittà* and *Strapaese*, and, in its attempt to capture a "popular" profile, engages a curious mixture of film aesthetics. *Treno popolare*'s expository sequences verge on the social realism of earlier Russian filmmaker's "direct cinema" or their treatments of the working class. But the romantic comedy and the physical humor in *Treno popolare* align it with commercial genre films. By casting its heroes as "the man on the street," the film overturns and parodies the heroes of traditional film and theater. But these parodic and comic features of its central characters also prevent a wholesale valorization of the working class through social realism. While *Treno popolare* dramatizes the harmonic solidarity of those riding the "popular trains," their habits are also exaggerated; and, in the spirit of vacation, they become objects for satire and caricature. The country, in this case, serves as a place where traditional culture and unlimited vistas are redemptive for tourists, but also where havoc occurs because of the vacationers' disorientation and their unfamiliarity with the "uncivilized" features of the environment.

Rural Culture and Popular Culture

Treno popolare lacks a clear antagonist or anything, other than the bustle of the city (the station) or their unfamiliarity with the country, that challenges the travelers. However, some of the films discussed here, e.g., *Stella del mare, Inventiamo l'amore, La provincialina*, reject in their conclusions modern entertainment styles and entertainers' lifestyles, even though the experiences of their naïve protagonists with the practitioners of modern popular entertainment prove necessary for the realization of the film's populist values. Ironically, then, these films reject the artificial nature of their own enterprise as somehow obfuscatory. Their rejection of cinematic artifice is made to seem necessary, by the events in the film, for a more Natural vision of society, i.e., more Natural than foreign film styles or Italian ones that involve urban settings. Similarly, the open-air shooting, the rural sets, the expository sequences, the use of lesser-known actors in *Treno popolare* all help give audiences the impression of a "non-stylized" film and of one that is somehow a purer vision of Italian popular culture.

In most of these films, the country appears as an ideal image of Italian popular culture, whereas the city (an imaginary locus of upper-crust society) appears, through the eyes of the more provincial characters, as the gateway to the *bel mondo*. At times this image is alluring, and at other times it is an illusory realm that threatens to conceal or tarnish the natural value of rural community. In either case, it lacks the readily identifiable characteristics that audiences could associate with *italianità*. Although Italian popular culture depended upon models of rural culture for a sense of equilibrium in a period of social change, the city or its representatives in the country are a necessary means of recognizing the value of rural and traditional lifestyles. Role reversals—"city slickers" in the country or bumpkins in the city—are necessary to address the conflicts of trying to reconcile epochalist and essentialist tendencies in a new popular culture. These films do not insist on a return to rural lifestyles but favor the creation of a modern "popular" society based on a conservative value system and an awareness of Italy's cultural heritage. By aligning Italian popular culture with regional and rural images, these films provided Italian audiences with a cinema that was no more or less a portrayal of "Italian" culture than, say, a film such as *Il Signor Max*. Nor did the ruralist codes in Italian cinema produce a type of film that was necessarily more political than others. And in the final analysis, these films were not (as some critics and filmmakers of the day suggested) more Fascist than the others. In fact, the same emphasis on regionalism and on Naturalistic or "open-air" film styles would reemerge after the war in Neorealist films, many of which adopt clearly anti-Fascist themes. Recent film historians have acknowledged that such film directors as Visconti, whose sense of film style developed through 1930s cinema, were unavoidably compelled by these myths years later; here one only need consider their regional and rural subjects, as well as a rejection in films such as *Ossessione* or *La terra trema* of the "stylizations" of commercial cinema. It should be evident that economic "necessities" and experimentation in *Sole* or *Treno popolare* foreshadow the more full-blown postwar aesthetic. But while neorealism evoked in many ways the myth of *Strapaese*, it lacked the ideological and political impetus for continuing its tendency to glorify the past—a subject which I examine in the next chapter.

5 Historical Films and the Myth of Divine Origins

L'amore delle tradizioni e del paese non solo
dunque non crea dei limiti ma ne abbatte e
porta a vivere una vita che ha radici in altre
vite, in un passato sempre più remoto e che si
sente, per quell'amore, già vivo nell'avvenire.[1]

—Mino Maccari, *Il Selvaggio* (1927)

The mythology of *Strapaese*—its emphasis on rural and regional images presented in a Naturalistic style—continues to echo in some Neorealist films after the war, particularly those of Visconti or De Santis. Some filmmakers still found in these provincial images a matrix for cinematic expositions on family and communal values. Despite the affinities between pre- and post-war films, however, Italian film production after the war lacked the truly essentialist impulse (the preoccupation with and need to glorify or conserve cultural tradition) which had been quite common during the 1920s and 1930s. Although post–World War II films, like their 1930s counterparts, examine familial and communal conflict, these later films ground their dramatic conflict in Italian society itself; Evil is not represented as an imagined Other, i.e., a foreign model, which threatens to undermine Italian traditions. For example, postwar films with such disparate settings as those of *La terra trema* and *Ladri di biciclette* attempt to demonstrate the inhuman and merciless nature of social systems in Italy; Evil here is made to appear systemic.

Partly as a result of the desire of many Neorealist filmmakers to expose the injustices of social institutions and to examine alienation, they concentrated on fairly topical situations and settings. Gone were the lavish costume films and historical spectacles that had constituted a significant percentage of Italian film production in previous years. The historical film was certainly the clearest expression of cultural essentialism and nationalism in Italy during the 1920s and 1930s; it sprang from the social and psychological pressures of modernization in those years and it gave presence to a collective desire for international identity, which achieved fruition in war. It is easy to understand the Neorealist "revolution" in the Italian cinema as a conscious attempt by postwar directors to divorce themselves from a "Fascist" film style or to create in its stead their own highly personalized rhetorical stance. It seems just as plausible, however, that the war produced a new field of ideological imperatives, to which Italian directors felt compelled to respond.

The Legacy in (and of) Italian Historical Films

While historical novels and historical drama (with its on-stage processions, battle scenes, etc.) had been extremely popular in Europe and America throughout much of the nineteenth century, by the late nineteenth and early twentieth centuries the stages of theatrical melodrama (especially the stages of small neighborhood theaters) were no longer able to accommodate the kind of spectacle and realism that popular audiences had come to expect. In many respects, the costume film and historical spectacle film were first popularized by the Italian film companies; D. W. Griffith attributed much of the inspiration for some of his own historical films to the works of Pastrone, et al. Before the First World War, Pastrone, Guazzoni, Caserini, and other Italian directors had begun to create historical films that achieved international acclaim, partly as a result of the production and distribution enterprises of an American, George Kleine; in fact, their efforts were largely responsible for the early economic success of the Italian film industry. These early silent spectacles—*Quo vadis?*, *Gli ultimi giorni di Pompeii*, *Cabiria*, *Marcantonio e Cleopatra*—utilized florid and sumptuous art nouveau set design, the expansiveness of long shots, exotic costumes, outdoor shooting, and huge casts to underscore the films' epic nature. By enlarging the arena of dramatic action, these films also encouraged more spectacular physical feats and heroes who could perform them. It would also seem, however, that their epic nature resulted from their having been some of the first *feature-length* motion pictures. Male leads, usually portrayed as men of action, did not achieve as publicly celebrated a status before World War I as did the films' *dive* (female stars). These leading ladies brought an element of eroticism that pervaded all aspects of the film: in their dramatic gestures, in their often scanty costumes, and in themes that involved the occult and mass ritual. (Their eroticism accounts in part for the films' international success, especially in America, where their sexual appeal emanated from a "forbidden fruit" attitude toward the pagan and primitive settings.) Like theatrical melodrama and opera, which silent films greatly resembled on a narrative level (many were adaptations of stage productions) as well as in terms of acting styles (through frequent use of stage actors, hyperbolic gestures, etc.), these historical films offered to an age of Liberal democracy images of egalitarian societies wherein characters from diverse economic castes could interact through the intimacy of sexual and romantic relationships. Examples of this sort of interaction would be the slave girl's affair with Marc Anthony in *Marcantonio e Cleopatra*, or Maciste's sentimental alliance with the Roman patrician in *Cabiria*. Unlike the theatrical melodramas and operas, historical films could incorporate large numbers of characters at virtually any moment. By accommodating masses of people, often *for* whom the central characters acted, the historical spectacles seemed to address a more extensive and consolidated audience. It is no wonder, therefore, that these films became ideal vehicles for presenting nationalistic themes. Through these throngs of extras, mass audiences were given a stake in the films' action, and they were able to visualize on the screen their own collectivity. Outdoor shooting also enabled these silent historical films to dramatize international battles, in which large casts visually heightened the collective significance of these conflicts.

To explain these films in terms of their international success tends to ignore how historical film, by the early 1920s, had become part of an emerging national political consciousness. For Italians, historical films not only displaced contemporary ideological conflict but (for a growing movie public) helped legitimate a national–popular identity—especially with respect to the growing popularity of American historical films. After the First World War, the earlier successes of these films induced Italian producers to subsidize other historical films; the more obvious examples would be the remakes of *Quo vadis?* in 1924, *Gli ultimi giorni di Pompeii* in 1926, and *Messalina* in 1923. The "strongman" films from the 1920s, those with Sansone, Ajax, Maciste, et al., while frequently set in a contemporary location, also continued the early historical film's emphasis on spectacle and acts of heroism by characters who were at once mythic and popular, powerful and humble. As I have already explained in chapter 2, much of the failure of the Italian film industry during the 1920s was due to this sort of conservatism as well as to the attractiveness for Italian audiences of American films, and only the "strongman" movies, which discovered a formula for translating mythic characters to a contemporary (though just as fantastic) setting, succeeded. Although Italy's inability to compete with American distributors contributed to its industry's inertia, it is just as evident that Italian producers briefly lost a sense of their audience. Part of the allure of American films in Italy at this time can be attributed to their ability to articulate most clearly the concerns of modern audiences, and America's own *foreignness* amplified the modernity and fashionableness of its cinematic images abroad. American films did much to nurture the epochalist impulse among Italian urban and provincial middle classes during the 1920s—so much so that, by the late 1930s, Italian historical films took on a new significance for Italian audiences. They became a means of asserting, amidst the onslaught of foreign films, images from a uniquely Italian tradition and, for a faltering film industry, a means of reviving the industry's own once "heroic" status.

As I explain in chapter 7, there were a number of documentaries produced during the 1920s that charted the "historic" social and cultural reforms of Fascism. As early as 1923, however, the Fascist Institute of Propaganda helped sponsor a feature-length narrative film, with actors, dramatizing events leading up to the March on Rome the previous year. Directed by Mario Volpe, *Il grido dell'aquila* (*The Eagle's Scream*) follows the friendship and broken dreams of several Italian soldiers during and after World War I. One, Aldo, becomes a leader of a Communist workers' movement against a northern Italian factory; the others pursue less political but more cheerful lives. Among this latter group is an older soldier of Garibaldi's campaign (Pasquale) and his enthusiastic nephew (Beppino). When worker unrest breaks out at Aldo's factory and threatens to destabilize the town, these other comrades, inspired by their memories, intervene. As one friend's life is endangered in an ensuing conflict, Aldo redeems himself by saving the friend's life and, in the process, forfeiting his own. The film closes as the "heroes," the Fascist Black Shirts, converge and restore order, thus *vindicating* the *sacrifices* of those who have fought or given their lives. And among the Black Shirts marching to Rome are Pasquale, personifying the spirit of the Italian revolution, and Beppino, whose enthusiasm galvanizes and keeps alive the memory of these sacrifices. *Il grido dell'aquila* is a pivotal film in that it signals a growing awareness of an *Italian* popular heritage and ways that this popular heritage is tied to a political movement, even though the film valorizes this movement more overtly than do most later films of the 1930s.

Relatively few historical films were produced in Italy in 1930–39, although there is a slight increase during 1936–39 (about ten a year). After 1939, with the augmentation of film production and with the beginning of the war, the number of historical films climbs to roughly 30 a year through 1943.[2] Thus, if we can agree that about 720 films were produced in Italy between 1930 and 1943, historical spectacles and costume films comprise about 20 percent of this film production.[3] The resilience of historical films in Italy during these early decades seems to confirm that they were able to address vital ideological concerns engendered by modernization; they seem inextricable from Italy's struggle to realize its unification on a cultural as well as a political level. However, as a result of the popularity of American films during the 1920s and 1930s, the political nature of Italian historical films during the 1930s often seemed to be of primary significance; Italian filmmakers and political ideologues both began to adopt a highly nationalistic rhetoric in their attempt to rediscover or "reclaim" their constituency.

It is easy to cite the political overtones of Italy's historical films. These films generally dealt with affairs of state wherein political power was bound up with sexual conflict, where political conviction was inseparable from romantic involvement. For example, Giovanni de'Medici's rejection of a courtesan for a more pristine lady, in *Condottieri*, parallels his disavowal of his ties with mercenaries to fight instead for an Italian ideal. Many recent film and social historians predictably point to some of the 1930s historical spectacles as the most "doctrinaire" displays of Fascist nationalism, i.e., of the government's attempt to reeducate the public and to mastermind a political consensus.[4] There is of course some evidence that lends credence to this rationale. There were filmmakers during the 1930s who lauded historical films as "the most Fascist" film genre, i.e., films which could best serve the policy of the regime.[5] And then there was the address by Galeazzo Ciano, the Minister of Information, to the Fascist Senate in 1936, wherein he argued that Italian cinema was obliged to "chart the flowering of a powerful and new civilization."[6] Also in 1936, Senator Romei Longhena, during a speech about the LUCE Institute, remarked: "The historical documentation of our victories and of our civilizing efforts will remain for Italians an everlasting source of pride while, for foreigners, it will represent a serious warning: an intimation of things to come."[7]

With regard to the political connotation of these films, however, it is quite important to recognize that they were not simply vehicles for veiled political directives. One should not forget that production of the historical films was never rigorously "controlled" by the government; basically, they were commercial enterprises. Even though the government provided financial assistance for many of these films, the assistance did not come directly from the government but from loans it procured from commercial lending agencies. (Jacopo Comin, a film scholar of the period, observes that, of the eleven films during the 1930s that received generous financial assistance from the government, seven were historical films.)[8] Even the nature of the government's interest in these films was not clear-cut. The films' lasting popularity made them attractive investment prospects for Italian producers; and, in its effort to revive the film industry, the Fascist government was thus disposed to promote them.[9] Because these films were expected to help resuscitate the financially troubled Italian film industry, it is difficult to decide whether the awards that these films received were due solely to their "favorable" political messages or to the state's and industry's need to enhance their prospect for increased box-office revenues; the popularity of foreign historical spectacles (particularly those produced by Hollywood) had, after all, contributed to the cultural, economic, and political problems that had beset Italy's film industry. The irony involved here is that, if the government did become involved in attaching value to these films, it was through a rhetoric that actually played down their political nature. The longevity of the historical film in Italy—a genre that goes back to the birth of Italy's commercial film industry and that has survived different political ideologies—seems to suggest that the political meanings of these films were more a part of a profound cultural crisis which had resulted from modernization and the limitations of traditional cultural forms such as theater and literature in addressing national–popular concerns.

The social and psychological pressures of modernization have produced a need, in societies most affected by these pressures, to make their history more meaningful. In some ways, cultural conservation is necessary to validate and facilitate new agendas and projects. Structuralists such as Roland Barthes see this trend as a product of bourgeois ideology, which seeks to legitimate cultural values by invoking (or rather by manufacturing) Tradition, by constructing cultural models through historical images and narratives. Bourgeois society, he would argue, operates through a type of discourse which appears to make the present ahistorical, i.e., of Nature. Although this discourse is political, in that it is necessary for the maintenance of the society and its systems, it may not *seem* political, because it is couched in conventionalized practices. When I suggest that the political messages of these historical films were *directed* by cultural practice rather than by any political group, I intend to call attention to the paradoxical nature of these films as a form of social discourse. Italian historical

films during the 1920s and 1930s seem to speak just as much *about* their audiences as *for* them, i.e., they conceal their rhetorical nature through myths about historical events and figures. But, as Barthes points out, myth ripens better in some social strata and historical periods than in others: "For myth also, there are micro-climates."[10] It would seem that modernization in Italy offered the ideal climate for the historical film and Italian Fascism's affinity for it.
the historical film and Italian Fascism's affinity for it.

A significant feature of historical films is their capacity to displace current ideological conflict to a mythical setting and, in turn, to reduce history to a diegetic world wherein the present suddenly becomes charged with value. It is necessary to remember that images of the past in popular movies reveal more about the present, i.e., about their audiences, than about the past, or about the people who lived in the past. It also seems that certain historical periods were more suitable than others for representing ideological and political struggle. Of the historical spectacles and costume films made in Italy between 1930 and 1943, four films were set in an ancient period, one during the Middle Ages, twenty during the Renaissance, eighteen during the seventeenth and eighteenth centuries, twenty-eight during the nineteenth century (not including those about the Risorgimento), fifteen in the Risorgimento, twenty-two in the Belle Epoque, and three during the years of World War I (1915–18).[11] As film historian Jean Gili notes, films made about the eighteenth and nineteenth centuries, and often those about the Belle Epoque, do not ostensibly concern political subjects. However, Italian directors and audiences found in the Classical period, the Renaissance, and the Risorgemento ideal backdrops for presenting political conflict and social crisis and change. In the following paragraphs, I examine films about each of these three historical periods, and about two other periods, and I consider how each one imparted to the 1930s a transcendent value—both in the political arena and for the national culture itself.

Scipione and the Grandeur of Ancient Rome

Relatively few historical films about the ancient world were produced during the 1930s, but one in particular—*Scipione l'Africano*, which involves Scipione's (Scipio Africanus's) conquests in Africa during the Second Punic War—received substantial public attention, having been the subject of one of the more extensive promotional campaigns in the Italian film industry during the 1930s. Although the government helped procure astronomical investment capital for *Scipione* (about 12.6 million lira, the most ever spent on an Italian film before the war), the film met with only lukewarm critical reaction—both in the newspapers and at the Venice Film Festival in 1937.[12] Mussolini had taken great pride in the film before its release, once visiting the set, where he was hailed with chants of "Duce, Duce" by a costumed cast of thousands (many of whom were draftees for the Ethiopian campaign).[13] And Carmine Gallone, the film's director, was reported to have confided to some of his closest friends. "If the Duce doesn't like

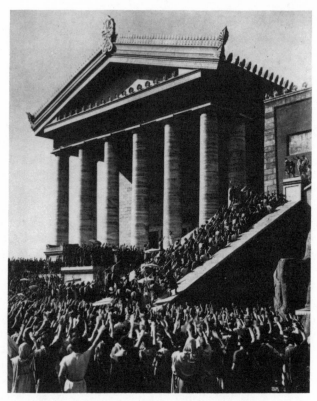

An epic vision conveyed through set design and a cast of thousands in *Scipione L'Africano* (d. Gallone, 1937)

the film I'll shoot myself."[14] Mussolini, however, was said to have been bored with the movie, and Gallone decided not to shoot himself.

It is now difficult to verify the extent of *Scipione*'s public popularity, since much of the information about its box-office grosses was suppressed. The film's protracted and florid soliloquies contribute to its often tedious pace. Yet, despite much unfavorable aesthetic criticism about the film, critics and children alike seem to have recognized its cultural importance. In a highly publicized special issue in August 1939, *Bianco e nero* published interviews with elementary-age school children about the film. One young student, Marrapese Franco, explained that

> The film illustrates the valor with which the ancient Romans fought and the courage that they exhibited. Now our Duce has reeducated the Italian people about the love of country and about the spirit of sacrifice, about order and discipline, restoring to Italy a new international prestige and reviving the Roman Empire.[15]

More mature and presumably more discerning film critics of the time, while acknowledging its aesthetic defects, lauded its value to the Italian people:

> *Scipione l'Africano*, despite its technical and artistic flaws, has fulfilled its aims. Why? The children say it best: for the strength of its subject, for its sense of epic spectacle, for its accuracy in depicting a historical period which has so much to do with our own.[16]

Or as Filippo Sacchi explains in his review of the film for the Venice festival: "He [Gallone] has really attempted to break away from the foreign and modern formula of the historical film; he tries instead to return to antiquity, to return, so to speak, to our own indigenous, popular models that constitute our prestige and our strength."[17] As Sacchi observes here, historical films about the Roman Empire had been numerous in Italy since the early sound films, but *Scipione* was produced for a much more movie-oriented Italian public—audiences who were much more aware of their cultural identity and of the political obligations of this identity.

Because *Scipione* is a reinterpretation of many of the same historical characters and events that are the subject of *Cabiria*, a film made over twenty years earlier, it offers an excellent means for discussing the "historicity of historical discourse" and for considering the significant points of convergence and divergence between two articulations of a modern Italian myth. Whereas *Cabiria* concentrates on the more theatrical and interpersonal conflicts that influenced the battles between the Romans and Carthaginians, *Scipione* devotes considerable attention and considerable monetary resources to the battle scenes themselves. This shift in inflection is generally part of *Scipione*'s concern over *opening* the action onto a more public stage and out of the closed and confined dramatic spaces of nineteenth-century theater. Also in this regard, *Scipione* is not obliged to dwell (as *Cabiria* does) upon the special bond between the muscular man of the people, Maciste, and his more intellectual patrician master; in *Scipione l'Africano*, Scipione simply embodies both of their heroic attributes. Even from the opening scene, Scipione demonstrates an ability to mediate the private political affairs of the Roman Senate and the sentiment of the throngs outside.

Also, *Cabiria* is set almost entirely in exotic Carthage, whereas *Scipione* is more preoccupied with contrasting Rome and Carthage. The architectonics of Roman sets are deeply rooted in "rationalist" building styles and practices of spatial modeling that emphasize monumental scale and reflect the levels of hierarchy of social power. The costumes of the Romans also appear to be informed by a contemporary aesthetic vision of what this Classical period meant for Italy. As Vittorio Novarese, costume designer for *Scipione*, has explained. "We tried to get as close as possible to an absolute historical reality, that is to say toward a style of the epoch and a style of the regime, since it was basically the regime's film."[18] Another way of putting this is to say that the costumes and set designs for Rome, in this sense, are constructed according to cultural codes or a myth that also informed the orientation of Fascism's political theater. These Roman sets and costumes stand in marked contrast with those of *Scipione*'s Carthage, where the seat of government appears dark and primitive and still indulges in the art-nouveau stylizations of *Cabiria*'s Carthage.

Like many of the earlier historical spectacles set during antiquity, *Scipione* conjures for Italian audiences a divine origin, a *principio*, in which the "primary" conflicts in Italian culture occurred. For the modern political apparatus, images of the Roman Empire evoke a primary, unified (though here hierarchic) state— a time before Italy's subsequent centuries of subjugation to foreign countries. Myths of ancient Rome deny Italy's more immediate past. They give the sense of a present without depth, of only a sacred origin. Films about the Roman Empire are thus able to transport their audiences to an embryonic stage of Chaos or crisis, before History, where the Cosmos, as it were, can be reexplained, where all that is *essential* to modern Italian society can be highlighted (what anthropologists such as Mircea Eliade would describe as rites of purification). The political ramifications of these rituals are obvious. For a government to inspire a sense of state, to overcome regionalism, to establish a regime or an organic totality, myths of this kind were invaluable.

Gian-Piero Brunetta notes that there are few overt connections between the hero of the film, Scipione, and Mussolini.[19] Nevertheless, it is difficult to ignore the similarity between this movie's version of Scipione and the image that Mussolini held in the minds of the Italian public; nor should one forget the publicity (press photos, etc.) which Mussolini received when he visited the movie's set and was hailed by its cast as if he were Scipione incarnate. As one of the children interviewed for *Bianco e nero* attests:

> When you see the battlefield at Zama and a soldier says, "Troops, we have conquered Canne!" I thought about our Duce who said, "Let's conquer Adua!" And a few months later he said, "We've conquered Adua!" When Scipione talked to his soldiers before the battle, I remembered the Duce. In the movie house we always applauded Scipione and his men. I want to see the film again.[20]

Perhaps the feature that distinguishes Scipione from many of his counterparts in silent movies and that aligns him with a more petit-bourgeois ideology is his dual role as a family man and as a statesman/warrior. Generally, the Classical protagonists of silent historical films act on their sexual desires; seldom are they motivated by a slightly sentimental sense of obligation to their families, as is Scipione. From the very beginning of *Scipione l'Africano*, the hero's political responsibilities appear inextricable from his role as loving father. The crisis which threatens to divide the nation also obliquely threatens the safety of his family, and he is compelled to defend both. Ultimately, in fact, Scipione's power to resolve political conflict seems to emanate from his more private role as loving father.

The film begins as Scipione urges the Roman Consul to wage war on Africa rather than to serve its invaders. Scipione's address at the Forum actually amplifies the emotional nature of the crisis here. The political debate which divides the Roman Forum in the film's opening scene represents an *essential* conflict in

Italian culture—one which occurred *da principio*. This conflict sets the stage for all subsequent dramatic action in the film; and, by implication, it imparts a purpose to Italian history and creates a precedent for modern social action, national politics, and imperialistic impulses. The film's audience is given an immediate stake in the film's action on two levels. First, through long shots and slow pans over myriad extras standing outside the Forum, Gallone establishes an image of public concern about this conflict. These establishing shots give way to more private scenes of characters in the crowd who speculate in familiar idioms about the Senate's course of action. In fact, the crowd outside appears much less worried than the Senators inside; they brag about Scipione's merits and their own capability of quashing Hannibal's forces if given an opportunity. Then, after the audience is made privy to the sentiments of the masses, they are taken inside the Forum to witness the sacred sanctum of the political process. (Because Italian audiences never actually observed the proceedings of their own government, except perhaps through LUCE newsreels, images of the Roman Forum could not but have affirmed, through accessible models, their way of thinking about political figures, policy, and Fascism.) Among members of the Senate, some of the same debates continue, but are amplified here because of the more intimate setting and because of Scipione's presence. In this political arena, the nuances of the conflict disappear; in fact, there are few who arduously disagree with Scipione's logic or doubt his abilities. But, to settle the conflict, Scipione carries his proposal outside, to the people. Here he delivers a lengthy oration that inspires the crowd to applaud loudly his decision to fight.

After this initial display of Scipione's public popularity, the narrative turns to a family scene, in which Scipione's image as a provider is accentuated. At this level, the film's audience develops a closer familiarity with the protagonist; he seems to be an Everyman, with children who dress in his uniform and a wife who kisses him goodbye and salutes him as he rides off to battle. Significantly, Scipione's family does not live in the city but in a rural villa and is thus tied to a rural tradition. This intimate bond created between Scipione and the film's audience, as they observe his "private" life, is important because it confers to him a power as heroic mediator and as agent of narrative resolution. This bond establishes Scipione as the audience's ideological perogative; he now seems to be acting on the audience's behalf.

Having thus far delineated Scipione as a figure able to manage political and ideological conflict, the film's narrative proceeds to introduce the domain that he protects and the sinister force which has already invaded it and which, by its very presence, has threatened its virtuous potential. The Carthaginians are presented as a hideous band of barbarians. They appear to be mercenaries, interested only in money and disgruntled because they have not received their just wages. They are loosely organized, united only in their mutual greed and in their fear of the wrath of Hannibal—a bearded, slovenly figure with one eye. The degenerate nature of this group of dissidents is underscored as the action breaks to a legion of Roman civilians who sing as they march off to join Scipione's campaign.

The Roman men's departure from their community, leaving the women and children unprotected, renders it an emblem of innocence and passivity. In sharp contrast to the Carthaginian invaders, this community is steeped in family and rural values; in the film's diegetic world, the fertility of the land seems to account for the community's harmony. The sexual connotations of the rural empire should not be discounted either, since innocence, women, fertile fields, etc. form an easily identifiable cluster of signification. The men's departure sets the stage for the community's subsequent *violation* by the barbarians. Furthermore, the Carthaginians' highly materialistic code calls attention to the function of the women, fields, etc. as indexical signs of the men's property and of their bourgeois values. To convey these levels of connotation simultaneously, the Carthaginian attack on the unsuspecting village is presented through quick editing of Carthaginians roughing up an old man, beating and raping women, pillaging a storehouse, terrifying children who were playing in a fountain, then defiling the fountain by bathing in it themselves. After the Carthaginian attack, many of these themes are played out through a romantic triangle that develops when Velia, the fiancée of one of the young Roman men (Arunte), is abducted by Hannibal to become his concubine. This triangle provides a subplot in the film, as Arunte joins Scipione to rescue Velia; the individual goals of the leader and his disciple merge and thus form a mythical Cause.

The second part of the film concerns Scipione's departure for Carthage and the Carthaginians' fearful reaction to the news of his imminent arrival. Much of the action, settings, themes, etc. here are reminiscent of those in silent historical spectacles. Rome's enemy is presented as a decadent and baroque realm of adulterous affairs and political conspiracy. Much of the intrigue in Carthage involves Sofonisba, the daughter of the Carthaginian general and wife of the Numidian king who is an ally of Carthage. Gallone's Sofonisba greatly resembles her *divistic* counterpart in Pastrone's *Cabiria*. She is a ruthless vamp and a woman of mystery—introduced lying seductively on an ornate couch, with only her eyes illuminated (a common ploy in silent films). She becomes embroiled in a passionate affair with Massinissa, former king of the Numidians and an ally of Rome. (It is significant that Massinissa is portrayed by Fosco Giachetti, who had already played in *Lo squadrone bianco*, and would continue to play strong military heroes.) Here Gallone displaces the political rivalry between Rome and Carthage to a highly sexual plane where the temptress is caught between an ally of Rome and an ally of Carthage. Through Sofonisba's sexual desire for Massinissa, the film affirms Rome's naturally virile allure; in fact, Siface, her father, is slightly effeminate. Sofonisba and Massinissa's romantic relationship also foregrounds the sexual level of connotation in the imperialistic myths of woman as a country to be protected or captured, especially since here Sofonisba appears dressed in a leopard skin, and the Romans in metallic tunics. Through Sofonisba and the luridness of Carthage, Gallone also manages to transform his drama into an ideological conflict between the rural/petit-bourgeois values of the Roman community, on whose behalf Scipione is fighting, and urban culture/decadentism. This conflict culminates when Sofonisba dreams of the glaring face of Scipione, a battlefield on fire, and herself chained and burning before a crowd in front of the Forum. Finally, she attempts to seduce Massinissa to seek his protection from the invading Scipione. (In this scene, she is adorned in a dress with a snake design which reveals much of her legs—a form of sexual titillation which also does much to strengthen the imperialistic myth of a foreign country as a desirable woman.) But, when Massinissa rebuffs her advances, she poisons herself, leaving behind for the encroaching Romans only her legacy of a sacred ideal. Scipione arrives in Carthage, where he immediately decrees that Sofonisba's body lie in state with Carthaginian heroes. Her funeral is lavish, attended by the Roman legions, who salute her bier.

In the third and final segment, Hannibal arrives at Carthage, and the two forces prepare for the final conflict on the plains of Zama. The battle scene itself is quite lengthy and replete with graphically violent images. Initially, Hannibal's forces seem destined to win because the Roman infantrymen fear their elephants. In order to quell his troops' fears about the elephants, Scipione launches a spear that penetrates one in the eye (although in a subsequent scene a Roman soldier demonstrates his "sensitivity" by preventing another soldier from killing a baby elephant). Not only are the Romans victorious, but Arunte (who is now fighting alongside Scipione) rescues from Hannibal his fiancée, the film's emblem of virtue and innocence. Her release from bondage prompts the film's audience to recognize both a *pure* Italian state, i.e., one free of upper-crust decadence, and Scipione's and Italy's "obligations" as vindicators.

Scipione l'Africano offers its audience a romantic vision of history in that its narrative involves a kind of odyssey and is circular. After the battle of Zama, the Romans return home—this time, however, in only a single ship. In the film's epilogue, Scipione returns to his villa, where he is transformed again to a family man, surrounded by his wife and children and dressed in more leisurely, less restrictive attire. The narrative logic and its structural circularity suggest that this is his true domain and that the threat which he has just expelled has denied him this role. His conquest and return invest the Empire with a new vitality, and in the final scene Scipione stands with a shaft of wheat (a symbol of fertility), exclaiming, "Good grain; and tomorrow, with the help of the gods, the seed will begin." This ending can be characterized by what American literary critic and cultural historian Richard Slotkin describes as "regeneration through violence." The meaning of the wheat shaft is contingent on the Roman standard (here a rather phallic image), which mysteriously rises erect above a battlefield strewn with bodies at the beginning of the film (during the opening credits) and at the conclusion of the battle of Zama. One is a sign of life and peace and the other of death and violence. But the association of the national standard with a natural image grants to the nation represented by this standard the authority of Nature itself.

Condottieri and the Myth of Chivalry

Perhaps the most celebrated Italian historical film during the 1930s was Austrian director Luigi Trenker's *Condottieri*. Made the same year as *Scipione l'Africano*, Trenker's film received an overwhelmingly favorable public response,

Protecting heroic ideals in *Condottieri* (d. Trenker, 1937)

though some critics condemn its weak narrative unity. *Condottieri* is set in Italy during the Renaissance; however, its iconography, its mountains, lakes, shepherds, etc., offers a more Nordic vision of Italy. This vision can be attributed in part to Trenker's own background as well as to the fact that the film was conceived as an Italian–German co-production; but in many instances the cool, airy heights of this setting serve as a metaphoric landscape for exaggerating the hero's own lofty ideals and aura. Like *Scipione*, *Condottieri* was produced with what then seemed an extravagant budget (9.4 million lira), and it received the prize for "Best Cinematographic Direction" at the Venice Arts Festival in 1937.

As I noted earlier, a significant portion of historical and costume films during the 1930s are set in the Renaissance. Whereas the Renaissance lacks the myths of national unity usually evoked by the Roman Empire, it provides here an ideal setting for intercultural conflict and essentialist themes. Perhaps some of the unattractiveness of 1930s historical films which dealt with ancient periods can be attributed to their association in the minds of their audiences with earlier silent-film styles and to their decadent themes and erotic settings. A perfect example of this attitude would be Gallone's portrayal of Carthage in *Scipione l'Africano*. Even if the Renaissance lacked the kinds of clear models of national unity that were associated with the Classical period, it did offer images of extreme wealth and power and of an intellectual splendor and artistic supremacy in Italian culture. And unlike films that were set during the nineteenth and twentieth centuries, movies about the Renaissance enabled directors to avoid political polemics; its remoteness in time allowed filmmakers greater liberty in dramatizing contemporary conflicts and tensions.

Both Gili and Brunetta see *Condottieri* as an allegory of the Fascist revolution. For Gili, the film's tragic hero, Giovanni de'Medici (played by Trenker), is a more accurate portrayal of Mussolini than is Scipione.[21] Brunetta seems to agree and goes on to explain that Giovanni's encounter and reconciliation with the Pope near the film's end conjures Mussolini's reparation with the Church in 1929.[22] Most of their observations are convincing and reveal something about Trenker's own ideological orientation and about the political relevance of the film's hero, but little about the hero's production and reception—a subject complicated somewhat by the fact that Trenker wrote, directed, and starred in the film.

Like *Scipione*, *Condottieri* concerns a mythical hero's struggle to expel alien forces whose presence prevents Italians from recognizing their own political and cultural solidarity and the popular basis for their sovereignty. To amplify these concerns, the film frames its action with an initial explanation of its central themes: "This film is a "free" evocation of the time and the spirit of the Italian Condottieri who against the fiery background of the Renaissance guided *for the first time* the civil forces of the People who rose up against mercenary troops and brought half-circle the unity of the Italian nation" (italics mine). The inscription's reference to "the first time" reminds the audience of the sacred significance of these events and points to their contemporary role as foundation, or primal scene, for the realization of "popular" identity and action. This realization is, in turn, made emblematic through a statue of the film's hero, Giovanni de'Medici, in battle dress and atop a horse. In the film, Giovanni returns from years of exile with his mother, Caterina Sforza, to avenge his dead father and to claim his birthright, which has been usurped by the pompous, dandyish Malatesta.

Giovanni, like most classic heroes, is characterized as a kind of changeling, one of royal birth who is raised in more humble and natural surroundings. (In this regard, Giovanni resembles the later hero of *La corona di ferro*, Arminio, who lives in harmony with the beasts of the forest.) The first shots of Giovanni on his return from exile evoke the initial photograph of the statue; here the film enhances his solitary grandeur by filming him from below his horse, his silhouette framed by the clouds in the sky. The film also works quickly to establish the centrality of his perspective, using reverse-shot and point-of-view editing as he follows a falcon that seems to guide him and as he gazes from a mountain plateau over a breathtaking panorama.

After joining the mercenaries of Malatesta, Giovanni convinces his colleagues of his abilities through displays of swordsmanship and his revelation to them of his ancestral medallion. Here too, the consort of Malatesta, Tullia delle Grazie, admires his virility and prowess. His convictions about unity and liberty persuade the mercenaries to abandon their purposeless plundering and to follow him as leader of the *bande nere* (a name that alludes none too subtley to Fascist *squadrismo*). From this point, Giovanni and his men are continually aligned with "the people" and at odds with the "false" rulers. Giovanni romances a blonde shepherd girl, Maria, whose virginal qualities are exaggerated not only through her Nordic complexion and modest demeanor but through the mountainous environment where she lives and through her family's traditional customs. In the town, after being imprisoned and tortured for refusing to swear allegiance to the Duke of Argentiere, Giovanni is rescued by his men, who have disguised themselves as common men. And, when Giovanni and his men escape, they find refuge with the simple rustics in the mountains. Finally, after defeating (but sparing) Malatesta in a duel, Giovanni rallies his men and exhorts the town's citizens to march on Rome.

The last part of the film deals with Giovanni's canonization as national–popular hero. His march on Rome is conveyed through a montage of statues of great warriors. On their dramatic arrival, where he and his men break down and rush past an enormous door, Giovanni stands in awe of the Pope—the first figure he recognizes as greater than himself. At the same moment, however, the Pope (through his oracular strength of spirit) perceives in Giovanni a greatness; he pardons and blesses Giovanni, and, as he does so, is illuminated by an etherial light. In the following scene, Giovanni marries Maria Salvati amidst angelic music and a series of dissolving tableaus (a field of wheat, a statue of an angel against the sky, and another statue of a heroic warrior on horseback).

The finale of *Condottieri*, like that of *Scipione*, is an extravagant battle scene wherein Giovanni's leadership and courage inspire the *bande nere* to defeat Malatesta's forces. In this battle, however, Giovanni is mortally wounded. At the moment of his death, his body seems to transubstantiate (through a lap dissolve) into the "real" heroic statue of Giovanni de'Medici, and on his sarcophagus the inscription "Giovanni d'Italia" is highlighted by a celestial light. In this way, the movie fiction becomes an *authentic legend*, which, through Giovanni's tragic death (or "crucifixion"), charges his admirers with a sense of purpose and a commitment to social action and provides an emotional bond between the present and the past.

Although the central action in *Condottieri* is often motivated by romantic relationships, these affairs are not as central to the narrative as they are in other films about the Renaissance, such as Blasetti's extremely popular *Ettore Fieramosca* (1938), which revives the myths of courtly love. In *Condottieri*, Giovanni is not torn between his love for two women; Tullia delle Grazie, a courtesan, is simply another of his admirers. His eventual preference for the more pure ideal of woman occurs as he realizes where his political allegiances lie. Italy must be identified in his and his followers' minds with an ideal, something to be protected; and, in order to realize this ideal, he must reject the image of Italy as courtesan—one who, while alluring as a result of her outward trappings, has been defiled by foreigners. In psychoanalytic terms, Giovanni's honor for Maria sublimates his desire for his mother, Caterina Sforza, who by implication personifies an older, united Italy—his Origin.

It is interesting that Trenker himself ignores the romantic impetus for social action: "I leave to others the telling of cute little love stories, with which they can divert public attention from the only truth on this earth: that of having the courage to put oneself in danger for the good of the world, even at the risk of losing one's life. Live dangerously!"[23] Presumably, what Trenker sees as the indisputable "veracity" in his film is actually its failure to distinguish Nature and Culture or the actual historical personages from modern idealizations of them. According to Trenker's emotional but reductive rationale, "love stories" do not address the heroic ideal or Truth of the nation; romantic *trappings* obscure the political meaning of a film.

1860 and the Italian Risorgimento

Most historical and costume films made in Italy during the 1930s and early 1940s concerned figures and events during the nineteenth century. Of these films, approximately fifteen were about Italy's Risorgimento. The Risorgimento offered Italian filmmakers a rhetorical field upon which modern audiences could witness images of their own unification:

> If people believe with such deep conviction that a moral world is synonymous with the ideals of the Risorgimento, if each person feels any of its essential moments as if he himself were a protagonist, then let's help the people better to understand their history, their Risorgimento, by reconsidering it in a modern way, in its entirety, so that each one feels as if he were a child of that period who exists as a result of that War and that Revolution.[24]

Among films about this period, Blasetti's *1860* (1934) is perhaps the most celebrated. Like *Scipione l'Africano* and *Condottieri*, *1860* deals with common essentialist themes: foreigners as the embodiment of Evil and a preoccupation with rural models and the glories of "Italian" traditions. Also as in the other two historical films, a romantic affair accentuates the emotional nature of social action and its participants' political ideals. Unlike the heroes of historical films I have already discussed, the hero of *1860* is much less a superman than he is a populist figure; and as in *Sole*, Blasetti again uses a number of untrained and little-known actors and actresses to impart an authenticity to his representations of these events.[25] Through this Everyman, Blasetti seems intent on providing modern Italian popular culture with a stake in Italy's history and with an identity in the current political state.

The movie recounts the events leading up to Garibaldi's liberation of Sicily through the plight of a young, provincial Sicilian couple, Gesuzza and Carmeliddu (Carmelo). Very much in the spirit of *Strapaese*, Blasetti's Sicilians speak in dialect—a strategy that distinguishes them from the foreigners who rule Sicily but that also calls attention to the regional and fragmented nature of Italy *before* the Risorgimento. The film's opening titles set the stage, both in a spatiotemporal sense as well as in terms of the value system which the film intends to affirm: "Sicily was still ruled by Bourbons who employed, much to the growing hatred of the *people*, regiments of foreign mercenaries. . . . " As in

Carmeliddu (Giuseppe Gulino) on the battlefield at Calatafimi in *1860* (d. Blasetti, 1934)

Scipione, rural Italy—Sicily—is presented as a space of innocence the virtue and potential of which are threatened by mercenaries and foreigners. In keeping with the innocent nature of this domain, Blasetti's Sicilians seem impotent in the presence of the Bourbon armies; and their sheepskin garments are symbolic signs of this passivity and of their bond with Nature.

During the initial scenes, Gesuzza and Carmelo, who have only been married for ten days, are separated when Carmelo is sent by Gesuzza's father to Genoa to implore military assistance from Garibaldi. In a dramatic escape scene, Carmelo abandons his wife and community just as the Bourbons and Austrian mercenaries arrive to capture and later torture them. With his wife and friends in bondage, Carmelo's mission becomes all the more urgent. Most of the rest of the film becomes (as in *Scipione* or *Condottieri*) an odyssey, an almost sacred quest. Through Carmelo's exhausting trek from Sicily to Genoa, he and the audience experience different regional, political, and class views on the most appropriate action for handling Italy's social crisis. In this sense, Carmelo's journey becomes a grueling rite of passage, a learning and maturing process.

After traversing southern Italy's barren wilderness and then drifting alone in a small boat without food or water, Carmelo is rescued by a Bourbon sailing vessel. Not realizing his identity, the Bourbons transport him to Naples, or Cittavecchia; in this politically contested realm (Bourbon or Italian?), Carmelo moves among bourgeois characters who discuss in dialect the merits and faults of Garibaldi's activity. As he travels north, these bourgeois characters appear to him and the audience as a willy-nilly group who lack political convictions. They seem given instead to incessant speculation and rumors about Italy's future and about other political figures such as Mazzini, Gioberti, and Victor Emmanuel. The decadent nature of these characters is heightened through the film's constant cuts back to the suffering community in Sicily. Although Blasetti presents these bourgeois characters in a rather unflattering manner, they do allow the young Sicilian to encounter an array of perspectives on social action and to raise his political consciousness—something which would not have happened in Sicily. Then again, even though he learns about the ramifications of Garibaldi's activities and realizes that Sicily's struggle is part of a larger "national" conflict, the film suggests that Garibaldi is fighting less for the bourgeoisie than for the young, poor, innocent, and less cosmopolitan people whom Carmelo represents.

Back in Sicily, the Austrians continue to torture Gesuzza and the small village. They mercilessly begin to execute the townspeople in an attempt to obtain information about dissidents or about Garibaldi. At one point, they attempt to convince Gesuzza that Carmelo has been arrested; but, demonstrating that loyalty to her cause is more important than her husband's life, she refuses to provide them with information.

In Genoa, Carmelo learns that Garibaldi's forces have been delayed but that they will soon travel to Sicily. Here, he observes the young soldiers of Garibaldi and realizes that they are much like him, with families and friends who wish them goodbye. Carmelo's and the Sicilian's understanding of their political obligation occurs when Garibaldi sends a public notice: "Considering that in wartime it is necessary for the civil and military powers to be consolidated in the hands of one man, I assume, in the name of Vittorio Emanuele, King of Italy, control of Sicily."[26] When the news reaches Sicily of Garibaldi's imminent arrival, the Austrians hastily abandon the town to prepare for the final conflict.

As in *Scipione l'Africano* and *Condottieri*, this final battle scene (the Battle of Calatafimi) is rather long and spectacular. Carmelo returns in uniform as a Garibaldino. When the legion arrives outside Carmelo's community and he attempts to leave to see his wife, a colonel stops him, explaining that his duty lies with his comrades-in-arms and with the revolution; Garibaldi, he informs Carmelo, lost his own wife while protecting his country. Carmelo is so inspired by this story that, when he finally meets his wife, who has searched frantically for him among the soldiers, he recapitulates the colonel's sermon and explains that his duty now is with Garibaldi. To increase the mystique of Garibaldi's cinematic presence, Blasetti initially films him only in long shots—always as though he were seen from afar by Carmelo or the other soldiers. In more intimate scenes, Carmelo listens as the other soldiers trade legends about Garibaldi's superhuman exploits, of battles he won with only a handful of men. Carmelo becomes so intoxicated by this rhetoric that when he first sees the Italian flag, he can only stare in mute wonder. During the battle, as Garibaldi's forces begin to suffer casualties, Garibaldi himself enters the ranks to instill courage in his men. In a brilliant visual strategy, Blasetti's camera slowly pans the faces of rows of beleaguered soldiers, as though the audience were observing them through Garibaldi's eyes. This device serves to heighten the audience's wonder about this charismatic figure; they never actually see him, only the admiration which he inspires in his men.

As a result of Garibaldi's presence, the soldiers defeat the Bourbons, but, in the process of ridding Sicily of this alien force, Gesuzza's father is slain. His death imparts to the battle, as does Giovanni's in *Condottieri*, a transcendent significance. Carmelo and Gesuzza embrace on the battlefield; reunited, they can now go on to begin a family, while becoming a part of a larger political and national Family. Carmelo's rite of passage, whereby he supplants the father's role in Gesuzza's life, i.e., as he becomes a Man, occurs through his increasing recognition of his responsibilities as an *Italian* citizen. And for the film's modern audience, *his* experience becomes a means of realizing their own obligations and unity, as the interest in this national crisis is made in the film to appear to spread from the south (the locus of Nature and the economically impoverished) to the north (comprised of more educated Italians). And, because the characters in each of these regions speak in dialect, the film is better able to facilitate this realization of unity in diversity.

Napoli d'altri tempi: The Birth of a National–Popular Anthem

The Italian historical film emerged out of a vital nineteenth-century tradition of historical novels, painting, and opera. Although the Romantic preoccupation with origins and the heroism and revolutionary themes of nineteenth-century cultural production may have found a "popular" *style* in melodrama, nineteenth-century Italy lacked a medium and a public literacy that would have placed these subjects well within its social consciousness. Historical filmmaking, as a national–popular project, had to discover ways of translating both these themes and the grandiose register of nineteenth-century cultural expression into a language accessible to a much broader audience. There were, for that matter, Italian historical films based upon nineteenth-century historical novels, e.g., Blasetti's adaptation of Massimo d'Azeglio's *Ettore Fieramosca* and Mario Bonnard's interpretation of Tommaso Grossi's *Marco Visconti*. Inevitably, the process of interpreting and deciphering history occurred through existing cultural artifacts; and, in some instances, historical films depended upon the residual power and mystique of these artifacts to authenticate their historical realities. Vittorio Novarese, costume designer for Blasetti's *1860*, has verified that his costumes were inspired by or based upon artistic representations from the nineteenth century.[27] And Angela Dalle Vacche, building upon other evidence, has proposed that some of the pictorial stylizations in *1860* are rooted in Abba's descriptions and the Macchiauoli paintings of the Sicilian countryside.[28]

In *Napoli d'altri tempi* (*Naples of Other Times*, 1938), one of three Palermi films set in Naples, the maturation of the film's hero–bard and his composition of popular music are made to appear part of Italian society's awakening to a new post-Risorgimento era. In this way, familiar Neapolitan musical scores are depicted as anthems of social change for an emerging national–popular culture. Like Blasetti, Palermi turns to southern Italian culture as a mythical *source* (historically and geographically) for popular models. An early advertisement for the film makes much the same point: "All the songs of Naples, from their emergence to their triumph in the world, by way of the fantastic life of a 'popular' composer."[29] While *Napoli d'altri tempi* again incorporates historical personages, it also creates a fictional performer of familiar songs and a fictional composer for songs that are supposed to be from that period but that were actually scored for the film itself.

The task of coordinating previously composed songs with newly composed ones fell to the prolific musical director of Italian films, Alessandro Cicognini. For later films, Camerini's *Una romantica avventura* (*A Romantic Adventure*, 1940) and Palermi's adaptation of Verga's *Cavalleria rusticana* (1939), Cicognini also was asked to rework classical scores to fit the dramatic action and to help establish a historical reality. For *Una romantica avventura*, Camerini asked him to re-arrange scores by Tschaikovsky and Verdi, and for *Cavalleria rusticana* Cicognini used his own adaptations of Sicilian folk songs rather than Mascagni's operatic score. In *Napoli d'altri tempi*, Cicognini's own compositions are coordinated with his adaptations of scores by Salvator Rosa, Tosti, Di Capua, and Denza; throughout the film, these latter scores serve as a scale against which the value of the new compositions by the narrative's musician hero are tested and legitimized.

The film's narrative is framed by a highly coded photograph of Naples (the harbor with Vesuvius in the distance) and a title that explains the essence of this image: "The Neapolitan song is as ancient as the sea, the sky, the spirit of Naples itself." To dramatize Naples's generative "spirit," its *song*, this photograph and title are followed by a scene of peasant women in folkloristic costumes returning with baskets of flowers, singing a folk song as they walk. This scene of the women with flowers singing (an almost timeless representation) and of the place of folk song in a work routine is then juxtaposed with another scene wherein well-dressed, bourgeois pedestrians stroll along the *lungomare*. This second image dates the film to around the turn of the century. It also establishes what will become (or rather, historically, what *is* becoming) an important connection between folk culture and the Liberal–bourgeois culture of the Belle Epoque, and an equally significant split between the cooperative labor of these women and the fashionable exhibitionism of a more leisurely class on parade. Again, the film ascribes to Naples's music a power to maintain cultural continuity and identity; in another title it suggests that "it is the end of the 19th century that, in inaugurating the first cable car up Vesuvius [here a symbol of social and technological change], the first 'official' song of Naples is born." This process of institutionalizing the city's culture, its anthem, is enacted through a musical number that (as in the beginning of *Love Me Tonight*) seems to animate the entire city.

The number begins inside the "Casa Editrice Musicale di Napoli," where onlookers anxiously await the completion of the score. As the music emanates from its doors and windows, the crowd outside begins to sing along. They in turn inspire other pedestrians, whose refrain is picked up by passengers on the cable car and then by those on a bridge over its tracks—a sequence that charges the cable car's path up the ancient volcano (as symbol) with a current of emotional energy.

On board the maiden voyage of this trolley is the film's exuberant hero, Mario Perla (played by Vittorio De Sica). His centralized perspective, as a participant in this impassioned festivity, helps channel the reverberations of this seminal event and facilitates greater empathy or nostalgia among 1930s audiences for a time that lies at the margins of their collective memory. Mario's presence at this historic celebration also helps register his role as legendary hero and cultural bard; and, as the narrative unfolds, his experiences enlarge the meaning of these first scenes. In fact, after the initial establishing sequences, another title locates the film's remaining actions "some years later," as Mario "has almost become a man," about to enter the twentieth century. That Mario helps initiate and stands at the threshold of a "new age," however, makes him the focus of the tensions and conflicts that ensue as a result of these changes. The fact that his petit-bourgeois status leaves him outside both a folk tradition and the "high culture" only exacerbates these conflicts even more.

Unlike early Hollywood musicals, this film follows Mario's early success and then his gradual disillusionment with upper-crust culture and his fame. After working briefly as a maintenance man, he lands a job as clerk and begins to compose his own scores. At this point, his interest in music seems to result as much from his desire to emulate the masters of Neapolitan music as from an inclination to cultivate a latent and spontaneous musical ability that comes from having grown up in Naples. His musical style itself (the songs composed for the film by Cicognini) is rooted in the folk traditions and working-class culture of Naples but quickly becomes entertainment for Naples's upper-bourgeois society. Therefore, Mario's problems with his music begin to concern his difficulties in discovering the *proper* audience and stage for musical performance.

Mario is initially abetted by an elderly woman, Maddalena (played by Emma Gramatica), who, unbeknownst to him, is his own mother's sister and who has been searching for him since he disappeared after his mother's death. Maddalena first finds hims arguing with a friend, Ninetta (played by Maria Denis), over his newest composition, "Napoli mia" ("My Naples"). But, rather than reveal her identity, she offers to procure a piano for him so that he can compose at home. Soon thereafter, she takes employment as a maid at the house of a wealthy family whose daughter, Maria (Elsa Cegani), is interested in music, and, through her connections here, she introduces Mario to the family's social circle for his first recital. Actually, the family's invitation is prompted by Maria, who has overheard Maddalena singing Mario's song as she works. In trying to impress this affluent and formal group, however, Mario performs songs to which he feels they are more accustomed, such as "O solo mio"; only when he breaks into one of his own compositions—a variation on working-class music—do they become more animated and appear more appreciative.

His notoriety from this drawing-room gathering leads him to an engagement at an open-air pavilion, where his scores are performed with those of the period's masters (or composers whose music a 1930s film audience would recognize as "classics" of that period). Here again, Mario Perla's story becomes interwoven into an Italian cultural history. His romance with high culture and its operatic musical styles overlaps with his budding affection for Maria—especially when she attends the outdoor concert, where Russo and Di Capua's "Maria, Mari" is performed. (Here the fictionalized Maria appears to be the referent of the song's lyrics.) Although the film does not openly ridicule their romance, it does dwell upon the different sensibilities and incompatibilities of leisure and working classes. What makes Mario's desire for Maria and her world appear misdirected is his increasing neglect of his *true* benefactress, Maddalena, and his failure to appreciate Ninetta's unstated and "arbitrary" love for him. At one point, the traditional circle-dancing of Mario's working-class friends, attended by Maddalena (who by now clearly personifies the nurturing force of Naples itself), dissolves into an image of elegantly-attired couples at Maria's house waltzing in a circle. In another scene at an exclusive apparel shop where Maria and her mother are shopping, women gossip about her affair with someone beneath her station. This scene is immediately followed by a scene in the wealthy family's laundry room, where Maddalena complains that cleaning their clothes never stops. Mario's romance with Maria and her lifestyle/musicstyle is primarily complicated by his inability to relinquish his working-class roots and friendship with the silently devoted Ninetta, herself a petit-bourgeois girl, with whom he has always enjoyed a less formal, more spontaneous rapport and to whom he confides his distress over the scandal that his affair has kindled. His anxieties over his futile attempts to fit in eventually prevent him from practicing and composing music. Only when Maddalena reveals her relationship to him and he recognizes the inevitability of her wisdom (as a maternal principle) to redirect his attention to his music does he break off his affair with Maria. A last rendezvous with Maria at the beach, where her fiancé unexpectedly arrives and rudely thrusts some money as compensation into Mario's hand, only strengthens his resolve and increases his disillusionment with Maria's circle; he tosses the money into the sea and begins composing songs for his true "donna angelicata," Ninetta.

His diligence leads him to complete the song about which he argued at the beginning of the film: "Napoli mia." Here again, music serves as a means of reconciling differences and celebrating the continuity and creative power of Naples. The song is sung for Ninetta, but its lyrics (" . . . *la mamma non voglio lasciar*"—the mother I never leave) conflates Naples, the subject of the song's title, and the wisdom and nurturing energy of Maddalena. The celebratory rhythm of the personalized ballad gives way to a public Neapolitan festival which, like the film's opening festivities, unites the two lovers (Mario and Ninetta) and the audience in an unmediated effusion of Naples's "open" and popular spirit. The conclusion also helps pluralize the personalized subject of the song; My Naples becomes Our Naples. Mario's composition of "Napoli mia" and the characters' immersion into Naples's generative and carnivalesque essence suggest that Mario has finally discovered an audience for his music—compositions inscribed with the conflicts and tensions he has experienced as one caught between two cultural traditions. But the audience that he "discovers" is the film's audience, a future audience—an audience for whom the real composer of "Napoli mia," Cicognini, has adapted period musical styles. There is little in *Napoli d'altri tempi* that calls attention to the *authorial* hand or voice of its musical scores; as an expression of an emerging popular form, music in early sound films may easily seem to lack an author or (in this case) to be scored by a fictional figure in the audience's cultural experience. As the original bard of modern Italian popular culture, Mario (and his music) become exemplary of a struggle for recognition and for a stage from which to be heard. Mario's song, "Napoli mia," enables him to realize that Naples is a fertile ground for *anyone* willing and able to see in it these creative possibilities. His Naples (and the film's Naples) is a public, largely outdoor place; the conclusion especially makes this point emphatically. In fact, the film, as a result of its extensive outdoor shooting, has repeatedly revealed the problems of Mario's fascination for the drawing room (with all of its connotative baggage from nineteenth-century theater) and his "natural" place—as movie hero in 1938—*outside* it.

Because music is everywhere in Naples, even Mario's early work maintaining the exteriors of buildings enables him to listen secretly to a master such as Tosti practicing one of his newest compositions. In this scene, the sentimental effects of Tosti's music on Mario are externalized through superimposed nocturnal images of Naples: the harbor, boats along the shore, lovers, the moon, and always the sea. Scenes or images such as these mystify, however, the regenerative interaction of Naples, its music, and its performers' and their audiences' aspirations and nostalgia. In a succeeding bridging sequence, this point can be demonstrated even more graphically. Here, the film plays to the nostalgia of its own audience when two elderly characters (Maddalena and a man), who are attending an outdoor military parade of soldiers departing for Africa, fondly recall their own experiences amidst the Italian revolution. The characters' nostalgia for the revolution (stimulated by military anthems at the parade) is readily recognizable to movie audiences of a later "revolution," an audience who themselves were witnessing once again the departure of troops for Africa amidst military parades and national anthems.

The Authority of Historical Films

I have included *Napoli d'altri tempi* in this chapter because it is a historical film whose central dramatic conflict is not posed as a military or physical contest; yet, even in the abovementioned scene, references to foreign campaigns and revolution frame the actions and outlooks of the central characters. Other historical films of the 1930s whose reconstruction of modern Italy's immutable founda-

A youthful Umberto Solaro, played by Amedeo Nazzari, learns the meaning of chivalry in *Cavalleria* (d. Alessandrini, 1936)

tions is set after the turn of the century also use war as a way of enlarging the ideological significance of and the national stakes involved in its dramatic conflict (in part because the aesthetics of melodrama itself have come to rely heavily upon apocalyptic turmoil or crisis as a condition for its moral struggle). Both in Alessandrini's *Cavalleria* (*Chivalry*, 1936) and in Brignone's *Passaporto rosso* (*Red Passport*, 1935), the outbreak of World War I appears as a final testing ground for their characters' beliefs and conviction.

Cavalleria concerns the esteemed career of a cavalry officer who reforms and modernizes the traditional methods of a military training school. Here, World War I mediates a contemporary audience's understanding of the "Belle Epoque" and a chivalric code. The last shot in the movie particularly works to establish this historical perspective by filming, *through* a barbed-wire barrier along the trenches, a cavalry unit's march into the horizon. On the one hand, the film commemorates its hero's innovative spirit, but it also relies upon the mystique of a more "chivalrous" and extravagant age as a mythical matrix from which this phoenix (his name is Solari) rises.[30]

Passaporto rosso presents the Italians who emigrated just before the turn of the century as both victims of their encounters abroad (rather than economic conditions in Italy that prompted their exodus) and as resourceful entrepreneurs who built fortunes despite their persecution. At the outbreak of World War I, a father must convince his son, who has never known Italy and who has been reared in comfortable surroundings, of his obligations to his motherland in its time of need. The son's conversion and his eventual death on the battlefield demonstrate the *sacrifices* made by those who, despite their fortune abroad, still feel compelled by their deep bond with their country and their heritage. Both *Passaporto rosso* and *Cavalleria* draw explicit connections between events just before World War I and conditions in contemporary Italy. *Cavalleria* begins with a contemporary military equestrian exhibition and, after an intertitle that resets the action in 1901, cuts to an image of a group of women in period costume admiring Solari and his horse. In *Passaporto rosso*, the movie quickly cuts, in the finale, from the death of the fallen son of Italy to 1922, wherein Mussolini appears in brief documentary footage, pinning a medal and planting a kiss on the mother or wife of an unknown soldier.

Again, both films draw upon the crises of the past and the baroque fashions and costumes of the Belle Epoque to enhance and accentuate values that may have become obfuscated in the present. As in the other historical films, the past's reality is conveyed more through outdoor shooting than ever before—a strategy that enlarges the scope of personal or domestic conflict and blurs distinctions between what is public and what is private. But, by creating these kinds of direct bridges with the present, these two films more explicitly than the other historical films, promise to uncover a past that has been forgotten over the decades that they chart. In *Passaporto rosso*, the young son, like the film's audience, must *learn* about his bond, and his education is in part the way the audience is put in touch with a national ideology.

This same strategy is used most conspicuously in Giovacchino Forzano's *Camicia nera* (*Black Shirt*, 1933), one of the few Italian films produced during the 1930s with overt references to Fascism and one of the Italian feature films from this period most frequently cited (along with Palermi's *Vecchia guardia*) as Fascist propaganda. Like *Cavalleria* and *Passaporto rosso*, *Camicia nera* is a historical film whose action transpires over the decades just before and after World War I. And, as in *Passaporto rosso*, a child's education about a national–popular legacy becomes a means of masking the film's didacticism; here, the audience's realization of *their* cultural and political history is mediated through the centralized perspective of a child who "grows up" to understand what it means to be Fascist. However, what is particularly powerful about *Camicia nera*'s politicized rhetoric and its use of the child is its presumptions about the growing literacy of popular cinema by an Italian public; what the audience learns through this film history of Italy's national–popular culture was never more contingent upon their familiarity with popular film styles and models—especially since the film's historical reality and authority occurs through an intricate synthesis of Italian documentary and Italian narrative film strategies (particularly the conventions of family melodrama).

In some ways, *Camicia nera* reworks the narrative of one of Fascist Italy's first feature historical films, *Il grido dell'aquila*, by reenacting the experience of World War I veterans through the interpersonal and familial relationships of its central characters. It follows the experiences of a father whose war-inflicted amnesia and eventual postwar recovery bring his family closer together. When he returns to Italy, he finds his home town destabilized by angry mobs of Socialists. As in *Il grido dell'aquila* and *Vecchia guardia*, he is rescued from a riot by a band of Black Shirts, and by the conclusion he and his family appear to lead more productive lives because of Fascist reforms of the early 1920s. (While both *Il grido dell'aquila* and *Vecchia guardia* conclude with the Fascists' March on Rome, this film includes a brief exposition about reforms after the march.)

Camicia nera also relies upon strategies adopted by Blasetti in *Sole*. The central family in *Camicia nera* are peasants whose rural lifestyle is challenged by social unrest. Like the peasants in *Sole*, the family dwell in the coastal Pontine marsh-lands that were drained and cultivated by the regime's programs, and the conclusion of both films symbolizes the rich future of these peasants and their home-land through images of agricultural reform. *Camicia nera* also uses untrained actors who speak in dialect, but it conceptualizes this ploy so that their "improvisations" are tied to a historical realism: "exact characters—peasants from the marshland and men born of the people—from every region in Italy."

This attempt to authenticate historical representation is most obvious in *Camicia nera*'s repeated use of documentary footage. Once again, however, the authority of the film's historical discourse depends upon Italian audiences' familiarity with LUCE newsreels and with documentaries (the latter of which, unlike the newsreels, frequently treated historical subjects—see chapter 7). Admittedly, *Camicia nera* is a production whose budget may have prohibited the staging of battle scenes, etc.; but, in a film culture in which newsreels and documentaries were, by law, screened with every feature film, this confluence of cinematic modes in one film only helped blur distinctions between narrative and expository film. By intercutting the family's story with documentary footage, *Camicia nera* heightens correspondences between personal and public experience, between a family who are paradigmatic of all Italians and a Nation that acts as a family. In some instances, a family member's narration is presented visually through documentary footage. When the grandfather relates to his grandson (the child who plays a central role) news about recent battles along the front, his words give way to newsreel footage that is itself intercut with staged scenes. And, immediately thereafter, when another peasant arrives with news of the boy's father's valor in combat, messages of the character reading the news are conveyed through more documentary footage. That *Camicia nera* lacks spoken dialogue and uses only intertitles may explain this strategy for some, but it is just as necessary to recognize how documentary, in instances such as this, authenticates the peasant's story and implies that the peasant is speaking for many, not just the boy. The boy's presence is important because, even though he is unable to read and seems unable to assimilate fully (or to visualize as the film's audience does) the adults' messages, he (like the audience) is gradually developing a sense of what is at stake in the family's moment of crisis. In this regard, the mythical significance of the documentary footage results from the film's narrative frame; and, in this particular scene, its reality appears to subsume the perspective of the child and the adult. The narrative increasingly gives continuity to world events—a continuity necessary for a public realization of collective destiny and Being.

The father's amnesia, which results from his war wound, is a crucial narrative strategy in this respect because it dramatizes, through a symbolic Everyman, the traumatic process of forgetting and self-realization (a kind of rebirth) that becomes increasingly tied to the regeneration of Italy by Fascism. Like the boy, the father must learn (or rather relearn) who he is and what his place is in a world changed by cataclysmic social conflict. In fact, the father's recovery in a German hospital is intercut with his family's (and, through documentary footage, Italy's) struggle to come to terms with changing social and economic realities (industrialization and modernization) and of the ruptures engendered by the war. The missing father's road to recovery is also interwoven with the grandfather and grandson's long journey to find him; and the jubilant reunion of the three characters occurs just after the father and son have separately experienced epiphanies—one wherein the father regains his faculties (his "sanity") and another wherein the boy re-envisions a mystical image of a flame (here an affirmation of his "illuminated" condition). In both cases, Mussolini's dictums serve as catalysts for their self-realization. The father, for instance, is rehabilitated by a benign German doctor whose psychotherapy involves jolting the father's memory first with Italian music played over a phonograph (lyrics that induce the father to leap to his feet and kiss a map of Italy) and later by projecting the words of Mussolini onto a movie screen (stimulus to which the father responds with tearful outbursts of "Italia, Italia"). The boy's vision of the flame returns the boy and audience to an early scene (or moment in history) when, lighting an oil lamp in the family's humble home, he first hears the *name* Mussolini (*"la verità"*) read from a newspaper. Significantly, the epiphanies of the father and son are redoubled toward the end of the movie when Mussolini's words are projected on the movie screen and are superimposed over the flame from a simple lamp. This final tableau is charged with meaning by the experiences of the film's central characters, and it serves to illuminate and unify their story—the audience's history.

The "truth" of the Duce's message, however, depends greatly upon documentary footage of the Fascist March on Rome, which has immediately preceded his remarks, and upon the audience's willingness and capability to recognize the connection between the Duce's message and this documentary reality (as reference for his message). Structurally, the veracity of the Duce and his message is tautological or self-fulfilling; he comments upon a cinematic account of history. But, considering the audience's role in this process, one is better able to observe how the authenticity of his messages is contingent upon the degree of audience familiarity with and expectations about narrative and documentary styles, especially since the spirit of Fascism (and here its origins) is continually redocumented in the first ten years of Fascism through a growing array of cinematic techniques.

The conclusion of *Camicia nera* focuses on events following the March on Rome, here presented as narrative redress to the crisis that led up to the march.

After charting years of economic restabilization under Fascism through almost ten minutes of documentary footage, *Camicia nera* returns to the central family's community. On what was once a wasteland, this family and others like it have, with the help of the state, erected a new community whose nontraditional, multilevel buildings attest to a revitalized land and society and to a vision of productivity. The potency and potential of this community are demonstrated by the now mature boy in the film's final scene. As one who has outgrown the tiny flags he waved as a child, but whose youthful enthusiasm is now channeled by his awareness of a social responsibility, he proudly raises an enormous Italian flag over the tallest bell-tower in the new town.

History in *Camicia nera* is, then, both diachronic (or linear) and mythic (or circular). The child's "maturation" is presented as a gradual realization or fulfillment of a mythic vision of "the truth" experienced at an early age (the film's beginning); the father's amnesia brings the father to a similar discovery of a prior self and one that is rejuvenated. Here, too, the codes of nineteenth-century European melodrama, with its Romantic representations of the child as Innocent, its "misprision" and recognition of Virtue, are embedded in social/political history that has been "documented" over the years on film. Ten years after the March on Rome, *Camicia nera* demonstrated the potential of cinema for constructing a national–popular history, but moreover it attests to a need for a mode of historical discourse that is self-authenticating. One of the problems that the film touches upon is the potential unreliability of the written or spoken word, dramatized by the flurry of Socialist leaflets (propaganda) at the beginning of the film. The cinematic image, which, unlike written discourse, serves as a manufactured field of historical reference and actuality, is neither true nor false; and in this film little is done to underscore the *contingencies* of the perspectives on world and national events offered by the documentary footage. Of all the films discussed in this chapter, *Camicia nera* most clearly stands as an example of political propaganda; it responds to new economic instabilities of 1932 by highlighting the prior triumphs and endurance of the nation under Fascism. The members of the audience are invited to learn about their place in a changing social environment through the examples of the father and son, whose own awakenings are embedded within representations of more far-reaching social crises and national concerns. What is lost in describing *Camicia nera* merely as a work of propaganda, however, is a sense of its internal "density" (its complex framing of silent film techniques with those of sound film, of documentary with narrative film techniques, and vice versa) and of its complex interrelationship with other historical films. In fact, *Camicia nera* (more than the other historical films discussed here) draws upon the ubiquitous status of documentary films and newsreels as well as on an Italian tradition of historical films to achieve its resonance. In this regard, national–popular identity is impossible without Italy's emerging field of cinematic models, and the meanings of its popular histories are inextricable from a public literacy of this cultural form.

The pressures of modernization and Italian bourgeois society's lack of faith in traditional religious and political institutions and an increasingly broad public reliance upon easily reproducible forms of communication and entertainment encouraged a desire among movie audiences for a new cultural identity. To legitimize this identity, images were necessary which spoke with a certain authority. The authoritative tone of historical films produced in Italy during the 1930s cannot be easily dissociated from their failure to underscore the distinction between the thing expressed and the images used to express them. Roland Barthes explains that most historical discourse is paradoxical: "the 'fact' can only exist linguistically as a term in a discourse, yet we behave as if it were a simple reproduction of something on another plane of existence altogether, some extra-structural reality."[31] According to Barthes, most historical discourse *asserts* rather than *signifies*; the descriptive element in historical discourse, he contends, actually imparts to it an authoritative (or "authoritarian") nature. This process is especially compounded when visual images are involved, since images themselves *seem* to lack any rhetorical code (certainly not a linguistic one), or when a film's narrative is highly formulaic and thus seems to conceal its cultural codification. For Barthes, the *authority* of a popular form results from its apparent lack of an *author*.

In Italian historical films during this period, other strategies contributed to the transcendent or sacred authority of the events depicted. For instance, the five films that I have examined most closely in this chapter adopt narratives which are both diachronic and circular. Four involve a protagonist's quest, literally presented as a journey from and then to his homeland. However, these films' directors explicitly identify the places where their protagonists visit; and their journeys unfold in a diachronic fashion, punctuated by a final dramatic conflict. This confusion of a circular narrative time with an "actual" historical time once again produces an authoritative tone—one which does not overtly encourage an audience to question the nature of the film's reality, i.e., to see it as myth or tautology.

Similarly, the centrality of the protagonists in these films helps impart a continuity to each film's narrative. In this sense, the film becomes their history, and History their story. Their authority for their audiences results from the hero's ability to manage crisis and to espouse an exemplary wisdom or vision. But more significant here is that their commonsensical or visionary attributes help *naturalize* the hero and his story/history for a historically specific audience; audience admiration is, then, predicated upon the hero's ability to articulate more clearly than the film's other characters the most meaningful and direct course of action and, in so doing, to make history coterminous with an everlasting Present. Both Scipione and Giovanni de'Medici are charismatic figures, superheroes who seem to be fighting on behalf of the film's audience. Luigi Trenker in fact reveals that

> It is only right to portray a knight as a fearless man, one who puts his own life in danger for the honor and liberty of the people, one who with an absolutely altruistic spirit fights for a high ideal. . . . The spectators go to the cinema excited by one and only one desire, and this is basically the great secret of all dramatic

arts, the desire to identify with the character on the screen, the desire to watch and imitate him.[32]

Although Carmelo in *1860* and the father in *Camicia nera* do not necessarily embody the same superhuman qualities that one finds in Scipione or Giovanni, they do provide popular audiences with a means of learning about their culture; and Carmelo's wonder at the presence of Garibaldi or the boy's mythic vision of Mussolini's words only serve to create an emotional bond between superheroes and their disciples. Identification with these Everymen helps create for the audience a common bond of experience, upon which a sense of culture and an exchange of values are based.

Through audience identification with the experience of a central character, the events portrayed may well appear to be facts; and their putative nature imparts to the exemplary social action an ideological legitimacy. Audiences are indeed invited to read these envents and characters as historical facts rather than as the result of the film's rhetorical framing. For this reason, *Spectator* magazine describes *Scipione l'Africano* as a film which demonstrated "an acute sense of actual history and an awareness of the infinite possbilities of the cinema."[33] The realistic accuracy of Italian historical films was also affirmed by Blasetti, who proposed in 1939 that: "An historical film can re-create moments perfectly analogous to those that we live, or rather those with which we can readily identify; they can convey warnings, they can excite, they can induce realizations that serve to maintain or to reinforce today's popular consciousness."[34] As Blasetti notes here, the historical film was one of the most powerful means of cementing popular culture. Through the authority of historical film's realism and mass audience recognition, history seemed to write itself, i.e., to lack any author other than the popular culture itself.

The problem in using the notion of the "closed" and authoritarian text (as described by Barthes or Eco) is that one is apt to marginalize the dialogic processes of historical discourse and, in this sense, to overlook the felt need (particularly by audiences living with these conditions) for this kind of authority to register in a national–popular voice. The films not only emplot and describe historical/mythical conflict but they are also sites for a struggle over History. Therefore, their style can be seen as responding to a need to imagine and to legitimate (because of modernization) a national–popular history—one that is no longer conveyed through traditional novelistic and theatrical codes of Liberal–bourgeois cultural production. And for a socioeconomic class which lacked a clear history, these films become a means of distilling their values. That the government actively promoted many of these historical films as the purest expressions of Fascist ideals confirms less the propagandistic nature of historical films than it does the government's need to participate in this struggle over articulating and ensuring the most self-serving inflections in national–popular histories. And, though most audiences may have found it reassuring to be part of a history or lineage of heroes (figures capable of *direct* action), they may just as well have been inspired by the film's spirit of revolt to purge those aspects of their national past that might seem to threaten the present and future realization of popular ideals.

Thus, while the historical films and their heroes may have offered models of social action, this action was not intrinsically clear-cut. According to 1930s film critic Francesco Ercole:

> Men of action, therefore, not thinkers or artists are easily able to assume central roles in historical films and one can simply say, Men, whose traditional function has been to lead, to come, to incite the masses to action; and really they are no less prophets of a new world than they are disciples of revolution.[35]

The type of social action most common in these Italian historical films involves defending and often asserting cultural traditions (generally represented through rural images) which seem threatened by the influx of alien values. It is not, therefore, surprising that many of these films concerned international or inter-cultural conflict and imperialistic myths (a subject I examine in the next chapter). During a period when Italy's film industry was seen by Italians as a means of disseminating—both at home and abroad—the great myths of Italian culture, the essentialist impulse in these films could not but involve images of violent conflict. It is just as necessary to recognize, however, that these films did not propose a return to the past; in all five of the movies I have considered closely here, the final conflict signals the beginning of a new, "modern" order. The films' audiences witness the demise of the old, decadent culture and the birth of one (often outside, in a public or bucolic realm) to which they belong in the present. And it is the visionary attributes of the film's hero that are instrumental in forging or clarifying this new order.

6 Italian Colonial Films and the Myth of the *Impero*

"Tripoli bel suol d'amore"
("Tripoli beautiful land of love")

—Title of a popular Italian song
during the late 1930s

By 1936, the majority of Italian theaters had been equipped with sound; and, though popular Italian audiences could now view the most contemporary American films, they had not lost their appetite for the individual heroism that they had enjoyed until that time in America's silent films. Nineteen thirty-six was also the year of the Fascist initiative to "mobilize" the Italian film industry; the cinema was to be, as Mussolini decreed, "*l'arma più forte*."[1] The LUCE Institute commissioned Luigi Freddi to resurrect the industry from the ashes of the destroyed Cines studios, and one year later the industry received new life with the completion of Cinecittà. On the political front, the government had begun military campaigns in Africa. As Francesco Bolzoni notes in *Il progetto imperiale*, his examination of the film industry and its impact on Italian culture in 1936:

> The phenomenon of the volunteers in Africa can be explained as a gesture by generous young men (university students who went to war in order to merit the fascist name or in order to liberate the blacks from their chains); or as a campaign ploy by party "functionaries" (Starace, Farinacci, for example) who wanted to maintain a good image for those already drafted; or as a necessity (the peasants who turned to Africa to see whether it was possible to obtain something: some status or some land to cultivate).[2]

By 1939–40, these political and cultural initiatives had escalated into all-out war. Besides its military activities abroad, Italy had banned (through the Alfieri law) domestic distribution of foreign films and had (through various film critics) stated its intent to export Italian culture and to "conquer" foreign film markets.[3] Essentialist pride and intercultural dependency had finally brought Italy into conflict with other nations; it was a time that Luigi Freddi described as the "*tempo militare*."[4]

Because the Italian film industry had become a force in generating a national popular culture, its movies (in an attempt to give presence to the spirit of the period) were frequently given to images and myths of heroic social action and conquest. While film director Augusto Genina argued that the Italian people lacked a *"coscienza imperiale,"* such films were extremely popular. Many of the Italian historical spectacles during the 1930s, e.g., *Scipione l'Africano*, *Condottieri*, etc., involved stories of almost sacred quests and violent conflicts between foreign forces and those which were dedicated to protect an Italian ideal. Besides these historical spectacles and costume films, there were, as well, a number of films which dealt with similar themes but which were set in present-day Africa—movies which were often referred to by Italian critics as colonial films.[5] It is difficult to decide, in light of the popularity of these films, whether Genina was mistaken about the absence of the colonial mentality in Italy or whether, in an effort to stimulate Italy's film industry and to reclaim Italian audiences, Italian filmmakers simply adapted a popular foreign genre. (Not only had American adventure films and Westerns during the 1920s and 1930s been popular in Italy, but Italian audiences were also familiar with British and French colonial films.) The Italian film industry became both a generative source of colonial ideology and a social organization whose direction was shaped in part by the increasingly imperialistic policy of the regime (as a means of exporting Italian culture, particularly to America and Africa). In 1933, for instance, an Italian journalist, Marco Ramperti, described the "natural Italian-ness" of film star Elsa Merlini (as opposed to American actresses) for African audiences.[6] Despite, however, the colonial films' potential for promoting a colonial or imperialistic ideology, they also came to express some of the contradictory impulses and the inconsistencies that impelled this ideology.

Impero and Imperialism

In one sense, Italian films about Africa abetted the Fascist government's attempt to establish an Italian *impero*. The opening titles of Camerini's *Il grande appello*, for example, explain that the film was made entirely on location in the *"territorio dell'Impero."* First, colonization was presented as the romantic or epic endeavor of charismatic warriors and dedicated settlers. Second, like the song cited at the beginning of this chapter, colonial films contextualized the foreign or strange attributes of these lands, making them accessible to Italian audiences through easily identifiable narrative formulas and images. Although one can easily cite the imperialistic impulses in films of other modernizing countries during the 1920s and 1930s, the term *impero* acquires a rather special significance in Italy, where images of statehood, nationalism, and foreign dominion were often couched in a rhetoric about the Roman Empire. For proponents of Fascism, Italy's imperialistic nature was grounded in its traditions; it was, in other words, less political than "spiritual":

> The Empire exists as an image of the nation on a spiritual plane, as the activation of a single consciousness and an imperial will; it conveys a sense of tradition and the spirit of a people who have expressed it directly from their heart when historical events have demanded their most profound commitment in the form of Fascism.[7]

Using the same rationale, others even attempted to distinguish *impero* from "imperialism": "In this sense, fascism is imperial and not 'imperialistic'—what a difference between the two terms! The one is egoistic desire to extend one's political dominion, the other a desire for moral supremacy."[8] *Scipione l'Africano* was emblematic of the kind of grandiose (and costly) spectacle through which modern Italy could affirm its own sacred status as a spiritual empire. While most films can indeed be understood as a collective endeavor, *Scipione* was publicized as a *"progetto imperiale"* because it involved a cast of thousands; its outdoor sets were visited by the Duce, who through press photos and newspaper articles appeared surrounded by images and mythic signs of the Roman Empire.

As is evident in *Scipione*, *Condottieri*, or *1860*, tales of combat with foreigners provided their audiences with images of a united people. The conquests of the Romans over the Carthaginians, or the *Bande nere* over the Duke of Argentiere and his mercenaries, or of the Garibaldini over the Bourbons and Austrian mercenaries are never really presented as unprovoked conflict. These forces fight to defend an "Italian" ideal—one which is otherwise defenseless, innocent, and therefore Virtuous. Armed combat does not seem imperialistic, in the sense of *extending* one's dominion; instead it is a means of stabilizing or restoring harmony to the *impero* or spiritual community. Conflict is "motivated" by an imperative, which may be political but which is also deeply bound up with cultural and ideological transformation. It is the ideological imperative, one grounded in Nature and the *impero*, which makes the conflict seem necessary. The action in these films provides models for the *"progetto imperiale."* The death of Giovanni de'Medici in *Condottieri* established a pedigree for social and political action in the present. And, as in *1860* (or several other films, e.g., *Luciano Serra pilota* and *Cavalleria*), the imperative is dramatized through the death of a father figure, who bestows on his son a legacy with which to live.

I bring up these historical films to call attention to the mythological roots of the colonial films, since both obliquely invoke the images of *impero* and of defending it from foreigners, and to the narrative strategies which they share. There are of course some historical films, most of which are set in the Belle Epoque (e.g., *Napoli d'altri tempi*) and in the seventeenth and eighteenth centuries, which do not express imperialistic themes or involve civil conflict. Likewise, there are a few Italian films about Africa whose stories do not concern military action. But what *generally* distinguishes Italian historical or costume spectacles and the colonial films from other Italian films during the 1930s are: (a) their codes of violence, (b) their "resolution" of conflict through combat, and (c) their radical displacement of ideological contestation to another period (as in the case of historical films) or to another place (as in the colonial films).

The first two are bound up with the myth of the *impero*, i.e., the "spirituality" and sense of shared experience which united peoples of different regions and socioeconomic statuses to create a new order. The new order, a public as well as a private ideal, is nurtured by rituals of purification whereby foreign elements are exorcised. These rituals involve a violent conflict whose victory, due to its violent nature, is unequivocal. The uncompromising victory, in turn, provides the new order with the semblance of legitimacy and authority. This authority does not come from a particular legislating body but from the culture itself, which, through films about armed combat with foreigners, *proves* itself capable of managing tensions as well as of exploring the inconsistencies among different social, political, economic, and regional factions. Although one cannot deny that Italian colonial films concerned "imperialistic" themes, the meaning of armed combat in these films is not solely political. The authority of these films lies in the audiences themselves, in their attraction to such images of conquest and individual heroism.

The displacement which occurs in Italian colonial films is obliquely bound to the myth of the *Impero*. Because the violence and armed combat do not take place in Italy but in Africa—a colony and thus a frontier or marginal zone— the danger of violent conflict appears removed from Italian society. On the other hand, only in this frontier space can the principles of Italian society be exhibited in an unequivocal fashion, through a sort of Us-versus-Them drama. Unlike the historical films examined in the last chapter, however, colonial films are not concerned with *expelling* the agents of alien values. Rather, because the action occurs outside "traditional" Italy (or at its contested fringes), ideological conflict is seldom between Italians and non-Italians but between Italians with different values. The marginalized setting—the armed combat, political instability, etc.— becomes an arena for dramatizing these conflicts.

Narrative displacement also entails dramatic artifice and a stronger reliance on costume and visual spectacle than one usually finds in films about modern Italy *per se*. It is difficult in the case of the colonial films, however, to ignore their function (both political and cultural) as "documentation" of Italians' activity abroad.[9] Of course, this documentation was generally recognized as the project of the LUCE Institute and of the Ministry of Propaganda. As S. E. Alfieri, the head of the Ministry of Propaganda, reports in 1936: "the LUCE institute had been able to reinforce and to perfect by way of a diverse program of work . . . to offer the public an immediate visual chronicle of the marvelous deeds by our soldiers and our workers in North Africa."[10] At an immediate level, it is difficult to dissociate newsreels about Africa from colonial feature-length films. It is not unlikely that, during the same evening, a movie audience would watch LUCE newsreels about Italian military activity and social projects in Africa as well as feature-length films set in Africa. The irony of Alfieri's statement with respect to the "nondocumentary," full-length motion pictures about Africa is that these filmmakers actually provide their audiences with greater emotional stakes in the African campaign than do the newsreels, which, while not without a narrative quality, lack the dramatic conflict and characterizations necessary to heighten the suggestiveness of comparable action or a visual style which brings the audience *into* the action. The "immediacy" of experience and chronicling which Alfieri sees in newsreels is just as much a part of the colonial feature films—in which a narrative continuity and easy audience recognitions of central characters and other images provided Italian spectators a diegetic world with which they could readily identify. The demonstrative nature of these colonial films is affirmed in an anonymous review of *Il grand appello* (one of the films that I examine in this chapter); its author remarks that the film belongs "to an artistic genre where make-up and artifice are not possible," and that its cinematography lacks "affectation, complacence, or aestheticism" but is instead "*humble* in the presence of the genuine humanity of its scenes."[11] Many of the colonial films, e.g., *Lo squadrone bianco*, were actually filmed in colonial Africa with native casts, and their filming was often characterized by film critics as part of the "epic" nature of Italy's activities there.[12] It is clear that, while Italy's colonial films were intended to appeal to audiences' needs for hyperbolic representations, e.g., heroic action and epic conquest, they also offered the *authority* or realism of documentary. As Blasetti explains in an interview with four of Italy's leading directors of colonial films, "the emigration of colonists to Libya is a human and social fact of such great importance that it can be exalted only through a cinematic work."[13] Another way of putting this is to say that the mobility of the movie camera and advances in filmmaking technology by the late 1930s brought Africa to Italy and placed it at the center of national–popular realities. The heroic and documentary nature of colonial film styles are also significant historically, since, by the early 1940s, the realism of war films (both LUCE documentaries and feature-length colonial films) gives way to films such as Rossellini's *La nave bianca* (1941) and De Robertis's *Uomini sul fondo* (1941). Both these films, made by the younger wave of filmmakers in Italy, are frequently aligned by later film historians with Neorealism.

Il grande appello: Oedipus in the Desert

Two of the most celebrated Italian colonial films, *Lo squadrone bianco* (*The White Squadron*), directed by Augusta Genina, and *Il grande appello* (*A Call to Arms*), directed by Mario Camerini, were made in 1936—the year of the "mobilization" of the Italian cinema. It is not surprising that Genina, who during the late 1930s and early 1940s became Italy's "war bard," was commissioned to direct a film set in colonial Africa. However, *Il grande appello* seems somewhat of an anomaly in Camerini's filmography (with the exception of his last silent film in 1927, *Kiff Tebbi*, which was filmed on location in Tripoli). Years later, Camerini himself describes *Il grande appello* as one of the biggest mistakes in his career, but it is difficult to decide whether he dislikes the film's construction or what he perceives as its pro-Fascist overtones.

As is the case with most colonial films, *Il grande appello* is more about Italy than about Africa; in fact, the film was originally intended to be titled *Italia!*

Italy appears as an ideal which is protected by her male guardians; the narrative concerns a father and son's realization of their duty as custodians of this ideal. The movie begins as the mother/faithful lover of these two men lies fatally ill; in her last days, she summons a sailor to relay news about the nature of her condition and to urge the man who has fathered her child to make amends with their son, whom he has abandoned many years before and whom he has never really known. Although her role is minimal, it serves as an important frame for the subsequent dramatic conflict between the father and son. In their minds, her suffering, affliction, and eventual death become emblematic both of a cultural malaise which must be cured and of a legacy, an ideal—made pure by her absence—which must be protected.

News of the mother's illness necessitates a confrontation between father and son, who have adopted highly dissimilar lifestyles. The father (Camillo Pilotto) lives in Djibuti, where he owns a second-class tavern–hotel—an establishment which resembles more The Green Parrot than Rick's Café American in Michael Curtiz's *Casablanca*. As an emblem of the darker nature of "liminality" or cultural instability, this hotel is the sanctuary for unscrupulous businessmen, international arms trafficking, mercenaries, prostitutes—all forms of licentious activity associated with profiteering. The father seems to preside over this deca- dent underworld. He is not, however, an entirely dispicable character, but more a king among thieves—a more portly, less suave version of Pepe le Moko in John Cromwell's *Algiers* (1938). As manager of the hotel, he appears as an opportunist who lacks political conviction or patriotism. Whereas he enjoys listening on the radio to news about Italian victories in Africa, he is also in- volved in supplying arms to Abyssinian troops in their fight against the Italians. It is apparent that the wife's illness and suffering are due in part to her having been abandoned by her husband and to the antipathy she feels for his affairs abroad. News of her impending death, however, motivates him to seek out his son, whom he has never really known.

In contrast to the father, the son is highly dedicated to political and social ideals. He works as a radio operator with a company of Italian laborers in the African wilderness. Their camp appears to be a harmonious community of family men—workers who are dedicated to forging a better life in Africa in order to support their families in Italy. Through images of this desolate wilder- ness and the courageous men who labor there, the modernity and comforts of life back home are highlighted; the audience cannot help but recognize the value of technological conveniences which they might otherwise take for granted— travel, communication systems, etc. One of the most important rituals in the camp is the arrival of mail from home. To establish a closer bond between the audience and these workers, the film introduces the camp through one such mail-call session. In this scene, one worker receives a photograph of his newborn son. However, immediately after his colleagues celebrate news of the worker's fatherhood, Enrico (the young radio operator) receives news of his mother's imminent death. The scene brings these roles into an ironic juxtaposition by focusing on the young man's loss of his own father. Unlike his father, Enrico belongs to an egalitarian order, men who construct roads and who provide agricultural technology for the less civilized Africans rather than trafficking in weapons and other emblems of destruction. One of the clearest examples of this contrast between the father's and son's worlds occurs in a subsequent scene in which nurses with the Italian camp offer medical assistance to Africans wounded by the father's guns.

When the father arrives at the camp to rediscover his son, he is not immediately inspired by their work ethic. He does bring with him frivolity and the spirit of leisure time—the very essence of hotel living—which briefly revitalize the workers, who join him at night in song and drink. The son, however, demurs when his father advises him to relinquish his service to his country and to become his own master by making money in whatever way he can. The father's presence ultimately seems to precipitate misfortune in the camp. The next day the outpost is attacked by Abyssinians who inflict heavy casualties with weapons supplied, ironically, by the father. During the confusion, the son, making a valiant effort to summon military assistance for the defenseless workers, is wounded. (Because the workers are unarmed, they appear passive and innocent—the very epitome of Virtue.) Later, during a mass funeral for the slain workers, the father begins to soften as the names of the dead are read one by one. Again, the film elicits concern for this group by constructing dramatic situations which encourage intimacy or casual familiarity with them, i.e., that they have names, families, values much like those of the film's audience. After the funeral, the men return (to the accompaniment of a rather grandiose musical score) to their work, charged by the injustice of the death of their companions. Here, the father is moved to tears by their courage and resolve.

The father's epiphany sets the tone in the second part of the film for military reprisals launched by the Italian forces against the Abyssinians. When the father returns to his former domain, he begins to rebuke his partners in crime, a rather unsavory Spanish couple who are close to the monacled mastermind of the arms-trafficking in Djibuti. The father becomes more incensed when the Abyssinian attackers celebrate their victory in his bar. During this section of the film, the narrative cuts from scenes of the father's efforts in Djibuti to thwart his former accomplices to scenes of Italian military forces punishing Abyssinian ground troops with their airplanes, cannons, tanks, etc.—displays of their more modern technology. Although the father and son have not reconciled their differences, these scenes establish their spiritual affinity.

In the film's conclusion, the father, through his underground network, learns of an Abyssinian sneak attack. He disguises himself in order to infiltrate the African legions; here his liminal nature, as man of many faces, enables him to accomplish what the regular Italian military presumably could not. In the final scenes, the father single-handedly slays the Spanish agent, who is now leading the Abyssinians. Then, after throwing a few more grenades at an undisclosed target, his previous disloyalty is vindicated by the bullets of the African troops. His momentary heroics have meanwhile alerted the Italian forces to the presence of the enemy and provided them with enough time to mount a successful attack, whereupon they deliver the decisive blow of their campaign. As the father lies dying, he is discovered by advancing Italian tanks, whose operators vainly attempt to revive him; and, in a final moment of recognition, he gazes in wonder at Italian aircraft flying overhead and breathes out his final words: "Italia! Italia!"

For the father, rediscovering his son enables him to realize his duty to his motherland. And, in the father's eventual conversion, the son learns a lesson; he acquires an inspirational model for continuing his work in Africa. The initial differences between the two, and their ultimate reconciliation through a rite of purification, enable the film's audience to witness Italians' abilities to manage differences and to work together. In the film's epilogue, the son receives news of his father's gallantry. Now without father or mother, he becomes emblematic of the new order in Italy—one inspired by hagiographic tales of heroism in combat. These models will presumably be carried with him as he helps forge "new roads" for the empire. Significantly, he himself is not an actual laborer, only a radio operator—an *observer* who participates vicariously in their project. His role provides the film's popular audience with an indispensable perspective in that they too are able to take with them, outside the theater lobby, a sense of purpose in their own labors.

What the film makes problematic about this process of recognition are the ambiguous roles of the father and the son. The father's *deviance*, social irresponsibility, and inability to commit himself to a national cause (at one point he smashes a record of a Fascist anthem, "Giovanezza"), are inextricable from his heroic potential for recognizing and circumventing catastrophe. On the other hand, his son, an idealization of Fascist youth, is so far entrenched in the activities of the colonists that he is ill-equipped to recognize or to act upon the agents that threaten their imperialistic project. These ambiguous representations emanate from the contradictory nature of the film's colonialist ideology and account for the often varied responses of audiences to the film. The film was not very financially successful in Italy, but there were a number of critics who praised its valorization of a Fascist spirit.[14] Years later, Camerini voiced his own perplexity and ambivalence over the film's glorification of Fascist foreign policy and its frank exultation of an expatriate.[15]

Lo squadrone bianco and the Retribution of Desert Life

Lo squadrone bianco received the Mussolini Prize for the Best Italian Film in 1936 at the Venice Arts Festival and is seen by many as the clearest example of Italian colonial films. However, it is based on a story by French writer Joseph Peyre and in many respects resembles tales and films about the French Foreign Legion. The advance publicity about the film often characterized its film crew as "soldiers" who ceremoniously raised the Italian flag above their African camp every morning.[16]

In *Lo squadrone bianco*, the connection between Italian society and the dramatic action in Africa is even more clearly established than in *Il grande appello*. Although both films operate through a frame story set in Italy which precipitates the succeeding action in Africa, more time is devoted to the frame story in *Lo squadrone bianco*, and throughout the film there is continual cross-cutting to Italy to maintain this connection. Although *Squadrone* does not deal with a father and son who are genealogically related, the rapport between the film's young Lieutenant Mario Ludovici (Antonio Centa) and the older, hardened Captain Santelia (Fosco Giachetti) is certainly analogous.

The film's frame story establishes the young lieutenant's lack of direction and an image of Italy as an urban, somewhat decadent realm. Unlike the maternal image of Italy in *Il grande appello*, Genina's Italy first seems given to endless high-society parties and the kind of passionate, *ménage-à-trois* pathos typical of upper-bourgeois theater and novels. The film's opening scene takes place in a sumptuous ballroom where elegantly attired characters dine and dance to waltzes. To contrast the gaiety of this affair, the action cuts to Ludovici's sports car recklessly speeding toward the party. The urgency of his driving becomes apparent through frequent intercutting to the festivities, where his beloved flirts with other male guests. When he arrives late and telephones her apartment (close-ups here of her white telephone), she chides him for his tardiness and appears entirely disinterested and bored. Incensed with her response, he ventures to her apartment, where, without ringing, he explodes angrily into her room. Although he pleads his love for her, she continues to act unconcerned; it is made clear to the audience (but not to Ludovici) that her posturing is all a game to seduce him, that she *really* wants to be taken. After testing his desire and his patience, she locks herself in her room; but, when she decides to see him, he has already left . . . for the deserts of Africa.

As in *Il grande appello*, the frame story portrays Italy as a woman; here however, the image of Woman is more that of a spoiled child, a temptress, someone without convictions. Ludovici flees this female-dominated, unstable, and lavish realm of the *bel mondo* for the austerity of the African deserts, where he hopes to gratify his desire for a fuller, more transcendent life—rather than one motivated by more base erotic desires. In Africa, however, he does not immediately relinquish his upper-crust ways; his experience in Africa becomes a rite of passage through which he must *forget* his beloved and all those things which constitute his former self and which prevent him from seeing the virtues of collective action. The transition from civilian to soldier is therefore gradual. The film's editing makes it seem as though Ludovici wakes up, the morning after his lover's squabble, at an outpost in Libya. Here he finds many of the genteel trappings of upper-crust life: fresh uniforms, black servants who dress him and deliver his coffee, and an almost formal cordiality among the officers. Among these officers, however, is Captain Santelia, a high-minded and rigorous military man who intuits that Ludovici has come to Libya for personal motives, "without vocation"; he does not observe in Ludovici the temperament of a soldier. The captain goes so far as to tell him that he is filling the shoes of a great hero "who gave his life for the passion for this land." The young Ludovici,

Capt. Santelia (Fosco Giachetti) and Lt. Ludovici (Antonio Centa) realize a transcendent bond in the desert in *Lo squadrone bianco* (d. Genina, 1936)—The Museum of Modern Art/Film Stills Archives

distraught over his superior's lack of confidence in him, thus devotes himself to cultivating an image that the captain might find appealing.

The second part of the film concerns the captain's and lieutenant's expedition into the desert to locate African rebels. The lieutenant's trials in the desert, his suffering is an almost biblical penitence for his former narcissism as well as a testament to his romantic unfulfillment and his desire for acceptance by the captain. Still, his conversion is not instantaneous; at first he is distracted, thinking about his past and his lover in Italy. The harsh images of the expedition's solitary existence in the desert are counterpoised through intermittent crosscutting with the more civil and secure confines of the fort or with the extremely sumptuous parlors where his lover, Cristina, lives. (She begins to fill his absence with her desire; she passes evenings at the opera, at society parties, and at other upper-bourgeois rituals—bored and wondering about him.) Apparently as a result of his vacillating and unstable character here, i.e., because he has yet to abdicate completely his social moorings, the young lieutenant seems destined to succumb to the forces of Nature. In a raging duststorm, he becomes delirious and soon loses consciousness, but not before gaining the admiration of the rigorous captain, who is impressed by the young man's desire to prove himself.

Thus, in the film's climax, the captain returns alone to rescue Ludovici, at which time he acknowledges the lieutenant's capability to be a leader of men (or rather of Africans). As a result of his captain's acceptance, Ludovici buries his cigarette case. The case, which he had used frequently at the beginning of the film, is a symbolic sign here of his former self and of his bond with upper-bourgeois culture and the old social order—something he must relinquish to project an image which is attractive to the captain and to those in the audience who admire his code of discipline and self-sacrifice.

The third part of the film concerns the expedition's final conflict with the rebels. The final battle is a stage upon which Ludovici, due to the emotionalism of the crisis, implements all that he has learned from the captain's example, and through the crisis he recognizes the value of both collective action and individual initiative. When some African scouts in their party are ambushed, the captain attempts to launch a rescue. However, in the ensuing combat, his forces encounter fierce resistance and he himself is mortally wounded. Charged by his mentor's death, Ludovici regroups the forces and leads a decisive counterattack, thus assuming the captain's role. After the battle, his troops bury Santelia; his grave marked by a solitary cross in the desert, the captain becomes a part of the sacred lineage of heroes who, like the one he had described to Ludovici, "gives his life for his passion for the land."

In the film's epilogue, Ludovici's return to the fort (as a kind of Italian Lawrence of Arabia) is accompanied by a slow, deliberate, but triumphant musical score; his solemn countenance signals his sense of loss and his new sense of determination and conviction. He bears with him a letter wherein the captain has expressed his last wishes to die in "his" land. By entrusting the lieutenant with his last testament, the captain invests in him and in the audience which admires him his own authority and spiritual bond with Africa. Arriving at the fort, Ludovici and company are greeted by the colonel and a group of Italian tourists, the cosmopolitan set, who are traveling through colonial Africa. Although the film's audience may share these tourists' admiration over Ludovici's presence, they (unlike the tourists) have also vicariously experienced Ludovici's catharsis and have themselves learned that transcendence lies in perserverance, hard work, and collective action rather than in an eternal *bel mondo*. Among this group of civilians is Cristina, Ludovici's lover, whose first vision of him (through low-angle, point-of-view filming) is as a splendid warrior/hero riding atop a camel. Enraptured by this image, Cristina professes her renewed love for him: "How you've changed," she exclaims. His only reply is that Mario Ludovici no longer exists. Firmly explaining to her that his duty is in Africa with his male comrades, he escorts her to the tour bus, which transports her, teary-eyed, back toward Italy. To return with her would be to demonstrate his reacceptance of those sexual and materialistic desires that he has rejected.

As in *Il grande appello*, the death of a father-figure inspires the son to forge a new order—one purged of the egocentricity and materialistic dross which prohibited collective action; here, however, the captain is, from the outset, a role model and one who is more in tune with the spirit of the *impero* than is the father in *Il grande appello*. Ludovici's rite of passage in Africa enables the film's audience to witness conflicts at the base of Italian society, but it also allows them to see these problems managed. Ludovici's rejection of an upper-bourgeois lifestyle and his decision to remain in Africa point out, in unequivocal terms, the values necessary for Italians to realize a sense of community—but one defended and upheld by custodians such as Ludovici, whose conviction prevents them from re-entering this community.

Sotto la croce del sud: Taming Mysterious Territories and Dangerous Women

In *Lo squadrone bianco*, Ludovici's ambivalence about Cristina (i.e., his desire and his inability to act upon that desire) is displaced through his experience in the desert. In terms of the film's colonialist ideology, Africa's desolation magnifies the emotional torment generated by his lack of and his desire for a woman (his antagonist in the film's first scene). In the end, Ludovici's rejection of Cristina occurs largely because of his commitment to the African cause and because he has realized his potential there for self-assertion. It is not simply that he decides in the end to remain in the company of men, but that Africa has become for him a place comprised of qualities he initially sees in Cristina. In the end, Ludovici realizes what the audience has known all along—that Africa, like Cristina, *really* wants to be taken.

In no other Italian colonial film from the 1930s are sexual conflicts so tied to colonialist ideology than in Guido Brignone's *Sotto la croce del sud* (*Under the Southern Cross*, 1938). Brignone's tale of colonial Africa differs from most others in Italy at this time in its total absence of military images. It does resolve conflict through violence but seems inspired more by American adventure movies and serials set in Africa—the Tarzan series, et al.—than by war movies. (Its ending is, in fact, almost identical with the conclusion of *Tarzan Escapes*, 1936.) In general, it does concentrate on male concerns—a feature it shares with most Italian colonial films. However, it does not subordinate sexual conflict to the same extent as the others. In this film, sexual conflict, displaced to a more "primitive" realm, is amplified and is thus more conspicuously responsible for the film's violent conflict. *Sotto la croce del sud* is not without topical themes which address Italy's political involvement in Africa—here, as in other films, the plight of Italian workers in the jungle. It is still necessary to recognize, however, that political messages are mediated by the film's highly emotional presentation of moral and ideological conflict and contradiction; and Italian Africa is, more than ever, presented through a host of popular stereotypes and myths—especially evident in the film's title, which refers to a popular commercial tune played repeatedly through the movie by the leading lady. The film's director, Brignone, states in an interview in 1940 that "in Africa it's always necessary to remember that one is white, and, moreover, that one is Italian and Fascist."[17] In light of Brignone's statement, it is not surprising that *Sotto la croce del sud* plays upon stereotypes about Africa in order to clarify models for being White, Italian, and Fascist.

The film's dramatic action occurs entirely on a rather large African plantation which has been bought after the First World War by an unscrupulous speculator who uses it as a base for his clandestine gold-mining operations. By establishing a precise historical setting for its action, the film enables Italian popular audiences to recognize the epic nature of its events and characters. Not only is Africa presented here as a frontier wilderness (a jungle rather than the desert regions), but the plantation, as an outpost of civilization, appears to have been neglected and is no longer productive (in a ruralist sense). Its present proprietor is not a Gardener, but a cruel and greedy speculator who has corrupted the native inhabitants—his laborers—by paying them with whisky. The proprietor seems to have subverted the area's purpose, which is to maintain an orderly and productive field whose fruits are of a more spiritual nature. The plantation and its proprietor's activities do impart to the film's primary action a subtext of socioeconomic signification; as in Camerini's *Grandi magazzini*, dramatic space appears as work space (though the characters pass more time away from work, in more romantic situations). The plantation is a domain of stark socioeconomic contrasts between the masters of the estate and their African slaves, almost a feudal system through which Italian popular culture is forging its new roads.

In a broader sense, socioeconomic conflict is displaced to the Italian *frontier*, to a marginal realm where the passions of these conflicts can be exaggerated and experienced more intensely by Italian audiences. Because many of these passions are sexual or romantic, Africa appears as a temptress, alluring yet taboo and out of reach—a vamp who stirs desires and jealousy among the film's male characters. These seductive qualities are personified by the film's only female lead, a mulatto named Mailù:[18] her racial ambiguity, make-up (plucked eyebrows that make her eyes appear sinister), and vaguely African garb (floral gowns and oversized metallic earrings and jewelry) are all very much part of her allure and treachery for the Italian workers. As the plantation owner's lover, she embodies the contradictions of the film's class representations; she is at once a slave and concubine and a lady of unlimited leisure and mysterious powers. In the opening scene, she appears enveloped by iconic signs that popular audiences would readily associate with Garboesque, upper-bourgeois decadence—cigarettes, phonograph records, and fashionably revealing apparel. Like her counterparts in silent films, she is sultry and bored—here listening restlessly to a recording of a romantic crooner singing "Sotto la croce del sud" while she gazes at the stars in the African sky; her sense of isolation/bondage is underscored by her visibly deep empathy for the lyrics of the record: "that deep nostalgia for you"—as in someone or something far away. Mailù's malevolence is most evident in her rather ambiguous union with the owner of the plantation, Simone. However, she resents his egoism and obsession with his gold, which he counts every night rather than romancing her.

Simone's cruelty to the African servants, whom he beats and whips, is an extension of his sadomasochistic relationship with Mailù. The sexual relationship simply highlights the tensions between these social and cultural groups and their sadism and masochism increase the audience's distaste for the more general master–slave relationship between Whites and Blacks on the plantation. Having established the corruption of this society, the film introduces characters whose values appear much more egalitarian. The morning after the establishing scene with Mailù and Simone, a company of Italian workers arrive at the plantation, their trucks (emblematic of their mechanized and "civilized" society) bouncing noisily through the wilderness. The film foregrounds two of the leaders of the company: Marco (Camillo Pilotto, who plays the father in *Il grande appello*) and Paolo (Antonio Centa, who plays Ludovici in *Lo squadrone bianco*). Marco's and Paolo's relationship belongs to the father–son paradigm that one finds in other colonial films. Marco, who once owned the plantation, laments its present condition; standing on a ridge, he remarks to Paolo about the vast potential of the land for mining, and he explains his intent to "cultivate" the land using African labor and Italian ingenuity: "in seven months, *un impero.*" It quickly becomes apparent that Marco and Paolo's redemption of the land will also involve the "liberation" of its *people*, and in this sense the film reworks the ruralist codes discussed in chapter 4. Unlike Simone, Marco is a benevolent patriarch—one who recalls Africa's Golden Age, before the war, and the problems that it evokes. The younger Paolo is his initiate, one who embodies the innocence but technological know-how of modern Italian culture. Together, these two figures lead the company of Italian workers, whose sense of family and conservative morality is tested in the less civilized African surroundings. The camp which they establish on the plantation is a microcosm of class cooperation, though many of the trappings and priorities of petit-bourgeois and proletariat society are also clearly evident there. Each worker occupies his own hut, and there are a bar and a supply store as well.

The first part of the film concerns the allure of Paolo and his lifestyle for Mailù, and vice versa. The evening after the company of workers arrives, Mailù again sits gazing at the stars while listening to "Sotto la croce del sud." This night however, she plays the record in order to overpower an anthem about Africa sung by the Italian workers. While most the men scoff at the romantic nature of her song, Paolo is enticed away from his male comrades by its lyrics ("We're *captivated* this evening under the southern cross") and introduces himself to her. "Are there any 'wild beasts' here?" he asks her; she catches his pun, scrutinizes him, and replies, "Sometimes." Like wild and ferocious beasts, Mailù and Simone appear as dangerous quarry for hunters/tamers such as Marco and Paolo. In this scene, the mythic *primitiveness* of the African landscape and its inhabitants frames the couple's arousal, and the sound of Africans chanting, which accompanies their encounter, makes manifest their yet unexpressed sexual desires and attraction. On the other hand, the film's mythic representation of Africa is mediated by the intimate attraction and tensions between these two characters—by Mailù's recognition of Paolo's potency and her *need* (as a result of Simone's neglect) for his attention; by Paolo's ambivalence about Mailù's "untamed" sexuality.

The scene involving the steamy encounter between Paolo and Mailù is immediately followed by a close-up montage of huge trees being felled by Italian and
African workers. This relational editing again ties the meanings of Paolo and
Mailù's affair to the Italian colonial project in Africa, particularly since the
Italian workers' *wives* will arrive after the men have rehabilitated the environment. Mailù appears in this sequence walking through a field of flowers—the
object of an Italian foreman's gaze (what he is working for as well as what
distracts him from his work); and the brief sequence is succeeded by another
wherein close-up shots of men's boots on hoes and shovels that are breaking up
the earth are juxtaposed with long shots of symmetrical rows of crops and
irrigation canals—the new *order* of this fertile landscape. As the land is *cultivated*, however, Mailù's place in this new society becomes increasingly problematic. Amidst exotic and highly evocative foliage (Mailù surrounded by flowers
and Paolo framed by tall cacti), the couple discuss her "free-spirited" nature.
Reflecting upon the diligence of the Italian men, Mailù voices her admiration
for their commitment to marriage and family values; Paolo, however, observes
that the men are not sure whether to rejoice or cry over the arrival of their wives.
As one of the Italian workers later explains in a sardonic fashion: "I used four
wars in Africa as excuses to get away from my wife."

The arrival of the workers' wives transforms the outpost even more into a
miniature Italian community. The arrival of these women is significant because
on the one hand they offer models to which Mailù is attracted. Mailù begins to
desire their middle-class stability, which she recognizes in Paolo; but she seems
eternally bound to Italian myths of hedonism and Africa, to her *race*. Nestled
amidst rushes by the side of a pond, Mailù explains to Paolo that she feels
renewed, and the couple's dialogue again mixes references to her and to Africa:

MAILÙ: So many things have changed these days.
PAOLO: It's the result of hard work.
MAILÙ: But even life has changed . . . I feel renewed.

On the other hand, most of the men in the camp view Mailù as the personifica-
tion of a feminine chaos which threatens to undo their male order. When the
workers' wives arrive, Marco and Simone (the two contesting patriarchs) fear
the distractions they will create among their laborers. As in most colonial films,
Africa is a stage for male camaraderie, and the presence of women often precipitates discord.

The romance between Mailù and Paolo culminates on the day of an African
fertility ritual (primarily scenes of young African men and women facing one
another in straight lines while moving rhythmically and leaning into one another to kiss). The ritual unleashes sexual passions and, in a mysterious manner,
seems to hasten the camp's subsequent unrest and violence. The ritual itself is
filmed in a rather unstylized, expository style, like newsreel footage of tribal
ceremonies and dance featuring bare-breasted African girls, etc. But this footage
is intercut with separate scenes, in low-key lighting, of Paolo and Mailù, whose
impassioned state is starkly revealed through their almost demonic expressions.

The action then breaks to scenes of the Italian families in their huts; they attempt to assimilate and decipher this foreign spectacle:

WIFE: Do the women dance as well?
HUSBAND: Yes, the most beautiful virgins.

For these settlers, the ritual appears similar to Italian courtship rituals in which "the men conquer the women with flowers and gifts" (as another worker explains to his wife). Besides drawing this kind of analogy, however, the Italian families also see the festivities as gratuitous eroticism in the presence of which they are both titillated and embarrassed. In a rather ironic juxtaposition, the action breaks here to Mailù, who reclines seductively in a lounge chair before Paolo. Aroused by the spirit of the fertility ritual, Paolo and Mailù embrace and make love. Because they become more active participants in the ritual and are thus charged with its power, their tryst seems to give rise to the rest of the film's action.

The romantic affair between Paolo and Mailù, set against images of the African ritual, sparks the mood for dramatic conflict by provoking discord on the plantation. During the initial stages of their romance, Paolo and Maliù are spied upon by the sinister Simone. When he confronts Mailù about her affection, she lies to protect Paolo. Unfortunately, Paolo overhears their conversation, believes that she cannot be trusted, and, delirious, decides to return to Italy. News of Paolo's departure affects the entire camp. That evening at the bar, the Italian workers become disgruntled; they fault Mailù, claiming that her tastes are too expensive and exotic for Paolo. As they become more intoxicated on liquor and their own banter, one insists that Mailù, who is working behind the bar, play "Sotto la croce del sud." Immediately, another worker, also jealous over the girl, rebukes him, and a fight ensues.

The "resolution" to this discord is the recognition by the workers that Simone is the *real* agent of corruption on the plantation. In his final display of greed, Simone attempts to rob the camp payroll. To create a diversion, he sets fire to the plantation's warehouse. The fire blazes as the men fight in the bar—a testament to their rampant hostilities. But the fire also inspires in these workers a sense of duty; they immediately cease fighting and rally to extinguish the flames. Some of the men are injured in the confusion, and old Marco runs to the proprietor's home to retrieve a first-aid kit. Here he discovers Simone, who easily disarms the old man and flees. Amidst the emotionalism of the moment, Paolo awakens from his indifference and is spurred to pursue the villain. In a dramatic conclusion, Paolo and a group of Africans locate Simone's stalled truck. Trailing Simone through the jungle as if he were a wild beast, Paolo unleashes the Africans, who are eager to avenge their previous injuries from Simone's whip. They track him to a quicksand pit, where he drowns ignominiously (a fate he shares with the villain of MGM's *Tarzan Escapes,* 1936). Nature prevails in the end; death by quicksand here is a symbolic sign of harmony restored in this culturally contested space. Nature manages what neither Africans nor Italians can do separately, and the earth's swallowing the villain gives a mysterious and dramatic presence to the power of their combined efforts.

In the film's epilogue, Paolo decides to remain with Marco and the workers to restore the neglected plantation and to educate the Africans. In a scene reminiscent of *Lo squadrone bianco*, Mailù leaves Paolo to his new life: "I must leave these fine people in peace." (Ironically, by returning to Italy, she too obtains what she had earlier desired: middle-class stability.) Thus having purged the land of sadistic and greedy speculators, materialists, and erotic women, Marco and Paolo can now realize their initial purpose: "conventional" work values. As Mailù's car departs the camp, Marco turns to Paolo and, in the film's last line, bellows: "Let's go to work." The two men move out of the film's frame to leave the audience with a view of a clear and infinite sky—a shot that conjures the film's title sequence wherein the opening credits are viewed against a series of photographs of sunsets or sunrises. Certainly, this final tableau does much to affirm that the chiaroscuro mysteries of Africa have given way to a transcendent realization (the Light) of progress.

The African fertility ritual can be understood as a narrative device, a pretext, for the suspension of work throughout the film. The mood of the ritual suffuses the film; it allows for images of play and of amorous affairs and for heightened dramatic conflict. Once the ritual activity, the play, and the drama are over, there is indeed nothing left to do but to return to work. However, this hiatus has made the work ethic appear more attractive, more necessary. The fertility ritual is a way of initiating the new egalitarian order—a *"communitas"* which *seems* devoid of the sadomasochistic relationship between Italian organizers and workers (African and Italian) which had previously existed. Earlier, Marco even lectures the receptive and appreciative African workers, amassed in large numbers, about the merits of productivity in unification and of an equitable distribution of labor. As in most colonial films, the new order is achieved through violence; paradoxically, the sadomasochism which appears as part of the old order both produces the violence and is purged through violence. In *Sotto la croce del sud*, Nature itself is the perpetrator of the final conflict. Though the Italian workers in Africa desire to punish and physically exorcise the agent of Evil in order to prepare a sacred space for their community, they ultimately seem unequipped to effect a solution. Instead, Nature itself, the *righteousness* of their purpose, works as an indomitable force to vindicate their new order.

Charting the Wilderness: Africa as Cinematic Frontier

Sotto la croce del sud is an appropriate movie with which to conclude this discussion of Italian colonial films because it most clearly demonstrates how Italian popular cinema attempted to *naturalize* Africa and how African culture begins to inform Italian popular culture. The costumes of Paolo and Mailù (his safari outfits and her art-deco reformulations of Eastern/African costume) or the film's title song both reveal how other public *discourses* (i.e., music and fashion) converge in the audience's understanding of the film's colonialist ideology. Even more significant in this regard, however, is the centrality of African ritual in the film. As in the works of Conrad, Africa offered modernizing European cultures vivid metaphors for articulating the sacredness and mystery which they felt lacking in their urban, bourgeois centers. In Italian colonial films, Africa appears as a domain of primitiveness, where the most profound values in modern Italian culture can be tested and *proven*. At times, these confrontations between Nature and culture, between primitive savagery and civilization, appear comic; the colonel's inability to understand African music and its lack of "poetry," in *Lo squadrone bianco*, is one such example. In many respects, however, Africa's primitiveness is bound up with the nature and function of cinematic spectacle, itself a type of popular ritual wherein society's rules are briefly suspended and reconstrued.

It is evident that Italian colonial films capitalized on the *marginality*, or cultural ambiguity, of colonial Africa to present tales of ideological conflict. As a geographical and cultural frontier, colonial Africa was (for Italian movie audiences) emblematic of "contested space," a realm where the rules seemed to be renegotiated at every turn. In *Il grande appello*, Africa appears as a melting pot of different cultures; attempts are made to allow characters from different regions to speak in dialect or with an accent. In all three of the films examined here, the untamed African landscape appears to accentuate the lack of a solid moral, ideological, and political base. In *Sotto la croce del sud*, the carnival spirit of the tribal ceremonies disrupts work and progress throughout the movie. And, in *Lo squadrone bianco*, the young lieutenant's delirium in the desert prevents him from quickly activating his "natural" abilities as a soldier.

On the other hand, the very instability of the setting compels the characters to reexperience the great myths of their own cultures. The melting pot where the father lives, in *Il grande appello*, confers to him an ambiguous identity; he seems to be a man without a country. But his ambiguous identity enables him to accomplish what the Italian forces cannot do: infiltrate the underworld. His heroic actions in turn inspire his son to forge a new order—one which is presumably more stable. The untamed landscapes and open spaces in the colonial films may give presence to more profound moral and ideological instability than one finds in *boudoir* dramas, but they force the characters to be more resourceful and to draw from within themselves a stronger sense of their convictions. Their emergence from the wilderness often promises a revitalization of the more *closed* and civilized environment to which they belong. The African deserts and jungles also offer them a means of heightening, experiencing, and releasing the rage induced by the claustrophobia of modern, urban routines. Ludovici's delirium enables him to "forget" his former narcissism and materialism and to realize more spiritual values. And the fertility ritual in *Sotto la croce del sud* foreshadows the new order in Africa—one in which the master–slave relationship is sublimated.

Through their identification with the plight of certain characters and through their familiarity with narrative formulas and "realist" film styles, Italian audiences could also *recall* ideology. Violent conflict is inherent in contested, frontier zones; but images and tales of violent conflict enable audiences to experience, often in unequivocal terms, the survival of otherwise transparent value systems—ones through which they live and act each day. The three films which I have discussed here all concern the attempt of Italians to construct the "highways," to clear a space, for the values of their popular culture. Yet the wilderness that they "civilize" is an entirely necessary image in an age of modernization; its presence imparts an epic and heroic quality to their efforts and ultimately, as in *Sotto la croce del sud*, serves to vindicate their actions. Nature seems to purify itself, leaving only those who possess "natural" authority.

The feature-length, commercial films discussed in this chapter were certainly not the first viewing of Africa by most Italians. Some Hollywood films set in Africa (Tarzan movies, travel/adventure films by Schoedsack and Cooper, etc.) were familiar to the Italian public before 1936, and for this reason the conflicts *in* Italian colonial films were generated by industrial and political attempts to reclaim or verify an Italian presence there through filmmaking. Also, a number of ethnographic documentaries on Africa by Italian filmmakers had been produced during the late 1920s and early 1930s. It is clear, however, that, by the late 1930s, Italian filmmaking had emerged as an "instrument" that could enable Italians to chart a changing public sense of cultural and political space. The cinema had come to offer indispensable and accessible frameworks for interpreting, and techniques for imagining, Italy's "new" frontier. And without new methods for filming outdoors, on location, these realities (or images) would have been impossible.

That these procedures for charting the Italian frontier were bound to government initiatives cannot be easily overlooked, especially since Italy's colonization of Africa had moved Mussolini to call for the formation of a special film unit, to be coordinated by LUCE, that would work in the newly named AOI (Africa Orientale Italiana). But to see the feature-length colonial films (and even the documentaries made through this special unit) as political propaganda would be to oversimplify how and why Africa could have been imagined as a model *of* (not simply *for*) national popular experience. Here it would be necessary to consider the rich cinematic experimentation that occurred among Italian filmmakers working in these conditions and how these conditions encouraged filmmaking styles that mediated audiences' understandings of changing national identity. Working outside studios, feature filmmakers came to face many of the same demands as documentary filmmakers. The use of aircraft for filming is one example of a technique largely engendered by the increased dependence in Africa on planes for a variety of purposes and one highly suited to capturing the epic scope of the Italian frontier as mythic landscape. But, beside facing similar conditions, documentary and feature filmmakers in Africa often co-opted resources and participated in one anothers' productions; a number of Italian feature-film directors were commissioned to make LUCE documentaries in AOI. It is inevitable that, because of this increased cooperation of film projects, colonial films (more than any other Italian film genre) came to be an admixture of documentary realism and narrativistic styles. While feature-length colonial films did use established stars for their central characters, they also enlisted Italian soldiers or settlers and untrained Africans. Furthermore, feature-length colonial films often incorporated documentary footage into their narratives, and, in Corrado D'Errico's *Il cammino degli eroi* (*The Path of Heroes*, discussed in the next chapter), Italian colonization is documented through narrative strategies. This kind of blurring of documentary and narrative styles in colonial films may be seen as both necessary for or a consequence of efforts to *capture* an "intrinsically" heroic register of events on the frontier and (in a much broader sense) of social and cultural reorientation. As an anonymous writer for *Lo Schermo* noted in 1936: "No one can deny that the birth of an *impero* might itself be a fact of such emotional force that it is able to become artistic material."[19]

Understanding the potential of cinema for charting or mapping the "national–popular" in Fascist Italy is contingent upon realizing how documentary and narrative modes interacted and how this interaction facilitated a historically unprecedented formulation of national identity. The following chapter considers some of the ways documentary films and newsreels participated in producing this identity; but these films were and should still be read through the cinematic *mythoi* and discourses already examined. The impulse or need to *document* the *epic* register of the national popular experience and the availability of techniques or a "language" capable of achieving this end hastened an increased interdependency of narrative and documentary film styles. As much as "the birth of an *impero*" may have been said to inspire a new style of public discourse ("a new art"), this birth was also the culmination of film styles that had been emerging for decades. Furthermore, it is this practice of integrating documentary and narrative styles that begins to reemerge after the war and the passing of the *impero* as another cinematic aesthetic, Neorealism.

7 LUCE/Cinema/shadows

LUCE/Cinema/shadows

Perchè l'Italia Fascista diffonda nel mondo
più rapida la luce della civiltà di Roma.
("Because Fascist Italy spreads in an
increasingly faster world the light [LUCE] of
Roman civilization.")

—an inscription on a publicity poster for the
inauguration of Cinecittà

We were all oriented toward neorealism; like
Camerini, we were for a truthfulness, not
neorealism of content, of ideology, but in a
formalistic sense, we all were given to an
absolute truthfulness. We were against
everything false.

—Ivo Perilli, director

The Centralization of Italian Cinema

These two brief passages are emblematic of the contradictions of a realist aesthetic of popular forms when it is grounded in historical analysis, and it is to some of these contradictions that I direct attention in this chapter. The last three chapters have repeatedly focused attention to a documentary style or impulse in commercial, feature-length films. In *Treno popolare, Camicia nera*, and many of the colonial films, the *verist* touch is crucial in distancing them from the spectacle of other commercial films (particularly American ones) and in helping legitimize their own characters' actions, situations, and messages. While on-location shooting, technical innovations, and set designs for Camerini's *Gli uomini, che mascalzoni!* may have contributed to a realism uncharacteristic of his other films or of ones discussed in the earlier chapters, this film in no way offers an illusion of documentation. The documentary style can in part be attributed to the prerogatives of the cultural, textual, and spatial ethos of directors making and audiences watching films about the provinces, contemporary history, or life on the fringes of the *impero*. One cannot, however, easily ignore the many ways in which this documentary impulse was part of a larger production project grounded in and supported by an ever growing number of filmmakers working through the LUCE institute in Rome. While no commercial films were produced through para-state agencies in the first decade of Fascism, commercial filmmakers found it increasingly difficult by the mid–1930s to avoid contact with a swelling government bureaucracy.

In the preceding chapters, I have tried to avoid privileging (as many have) governmental efforts to control cultural production. It is nonetheless necessary not to lose sight of ways that both political reform and chaos were very much bound up with the emergence of cinema as a national cultural form. And, conversely, it is important not to ignore how cinema contributed to disseminating (both in and outside Italy) and to exploring ways of representing a national identity and popular ideology. Movie distribution, in all its forms, constituted much of the economic base for a national–popular culture. First, however, this base (as I indicate in chapter 2) was increasingly a site of struggle between Italian and foreign distributors. And second, while in many instances both politicians and those more directly involved in filmmaking may have shared an interest in stabilizing the economic base of cinematic production through an increasingly centralized industrial organization that was supported by both private and state resources, there was never an easy mesh between cinematic production and the growing bureaucracy intended to organize or even to direct cinematic production. It is, of course, for this reason that I have tried to avoid reducing the models that I have hitherto discussed to *functions* in a coherent "Fascist style," and why I have described these films as having offered models *of* rather than *for* a popular experience. While this chapter examines less commercialized, state-controlled film production, its aim (like that of the preceding chapters) is not to demonstrate how Fascism imposed a "false culture" through its control of cinematic production, but to underscore instead ways that the emergence of cultural forms and changes in material conditions, which these forms addressed and exploited, contributed to both political crisis and the emergence of new rhetorical strategies/technologies (i.e., a new dramaturgy) for representing, examining, and ritualistically exorcising this crisis.

To better understand the cultural politics of centralizing filmmaking in Italy, it is first necessary to consider some of the earliest efforts by the government and the private sector to organize cultural production. The 1920s were a period during which Fascism became a powerful force in Italy, and much of its public meanings were conveyed nationally/regionally through its growing connections with popular entertainment and through its efforts to coordinate cultural activities in general. Already artists such as Marinetti and the Futurists, Bontempelli and the "900" circle, etc., had attempted in the years following World War I to form artists' groups or "movements" whose aesthetics were politicized and proclaimed in manifestos and mass media and which at least attempted to create forms more accessible to workers and a broader national audience. Their projects, especially in the case of the Futurists, were less independent and demonstrated more of a social consciousness than those of their nineteenth-century predecessors. Although these artists were frequently too militant or too Modernist to find in Fascism an entirely favorable political ideology (or for Fascist leaders to be convinced about their usefulness), both groups did share this "anti-Liberal" attitude. It seems, therefore, that as much as the government may have orchestrated an organization of cultural production, the political activity of many Italian artists immediately before and after World War I obliquely contributed to an environment of artistic activity congruent with Fascist policy. The regime attempted to institutionalize some of their objectives; and, through the rhetoric of these artists, early Fascist policy was made to seem modern and unprecedented.

The first "anti-Liberal" measures affecting film production more directly occurred after 1925; most of these measures (during 1926–28) attempted to redefine the activity of artists and entertainers by de-emphasizing their "independent" status and to bring them into a newly organized national confederation, the National Confederation of Fascist Syndicates (Confederazione nazionale dei sindicati fascisti), which had been organized by the state. In 1928, those involved in filmmaking became part of six "independent" professional unions that were coordinated, but not run or directed, by the state. And by early 1931, the artistic and professional unions were reorganized into the emerging corporativist "system" of the regime. Within this confederation, those who worked in the performing arts (opera, theater, musical performance, variety shows, cinema, sports, and band) were organized into six unions. During the 1930s, cultural production increasingly fell under the auspices of the Ministry of Popular Culture and increasingly became part of a complex bureaucratic network.

The virtual collapse of the Italian film industry during the 1920s can be attributed in part to the inability of private producers to support domestic films that were competitive with foreign ones. Before and immediately after World War I, the Italian film industry was comprised of regional film companies and private film distributors. The same year as Mussolini's March on Rome, these regional and private companies attempted to consolidate, as a result of the imminent crisis in domestic film production, into the Italian Cinematographic Union (Unione cinematografica italiana). But by 1923, the failure of their collective efforts demonstrated that private industry could not support the changing national/international infrastructure, and, by 1927, UCI had been disbanded altogether. By the very late 1920s, however, centralization of Italian filmmaking occurred less due to government intervention than to the efforts of movie entrepreneur and distributor Stefano Pittaluga, whose Società Anonima Stefano Pittaluga included the production company Cines, a national distribution network for (among others) Universal films, a network of movie theaters (primarily first-run) in a variety of cities, and Italy's most sophisticated studio in Rome.[1] Many involved in Italian filmmaking during the late 1920s and the 1930s still describe him as a primary force in reorganizing and reenergizing Italian film production in those years. Most significant here is the fact that Pittaluga's enterprises were subsidized during the late 1920s by three of Italy's largest banks. But, as a result of the economic depression of 1929–30, his financial resources were significantly eroded; and, in 1931, when the government intervened to assist faltering banks by establishing a para-state agency to guarantee loans to private industry, his production company (by then Italy's largest and most successful) became subsidized by both government and private resources. Upon Pittaluga's death in 1931, the company passed to the banks, who sold the studio and production facilities to industrialist Carlo Roncoroni.[2] Pittaluga's distribution network, however, began to be managed by the LUCE Institute through a para-state agency, the Ente Nazionale Industrie Cinematografiche (ENIC). (ENIC, however, did not function as a production company as much as it coordinated existing conduits for subsidizing film production.)[3] Roncoroni continued as owner of Italy's central studio facilities—first Cines, until it burned in 1936, and immediately thereafter the Cinecittà studios. Not until after Roncoroni's death in 1938, did Cinecittà and its production facilities pass to the government. The government, then, cannot be seen as the sole impetus for the centralization that began to occur in the Italian film industry during the 1920s and 1930s. In many instances, the government's increased involvement in distribution and production obliged it to work through an infrastructure that had already begun to centralize. Although the late 1920s and the 1930s were a period when the Italian government did attempt to incorporate and coordinate a previously private industry, the government continually found itself disposed to support private backing for feature-length films. This rapport between government and the private producers/financiers can be attributed in part to a general ambivalence about the social/political role of making and viewing films. While the government acted in ways that tended to institutionalize filmmaking and viewing, the cinema was still generally perceived only as escapism and entertainment. And it is partially for this reason that newsreels and documentaries fell more easily under state control.

This segregation of filmmaking can clearly be seen in the evolution of LUCE itself—the political and bureaucratic hub of state-sponsored film production. The institute was certainly an early force in centralizing Italian film production and was the most ostensible result of political involvement in Italian filmmaking at a number of levels. In the early 1920s, most documentary films were produced privately. But from its inception, the newly formed Ministry of Propaganda discouraged the production of these films by small private producers and quickly moved to mediate efforts by such groups as the "Ente nazionle per la cinematografia istrutive e educative" and the "Sindicato di istruzione cinematografica." LUCE was formed in 1924 to direct financing of this latter national syndicate, which produced "popular educational" films; and, in 1925, Mussolini authorized formal recognition of LUCE, thus placing the national syndicate under government control. But, while here the government was co-opting a private (though nationally organized) venture that had produced documentaries and films promoting Italian industry, tourism, and culture, it more rapidly assimilated this type of movie production than it ever did the feature-length films. By 1929, LUCE became the regime's technical service for audio-visual production and a center for promoting Italian popular-cultural activities—particularly through its production of a variety of "educational" films, through the growing number of movie theaters in its affiliated (partially private) distribution network, and through its expanding program of *"cine mobili"* or traveling cinema shows. By the mid-1930s, LUCE had become a source of educational films distributed to all levels of schools across the country; and, after Luigi Freddi was appointed the General Director of Cinematography in 1935, he established the Centro Sperimentale in Rome as an educational center for film studies.

Freddi was in many ways responsible for encouraging LUCE's role in mediating government and private production, promotion, and distribution of films in Italy. As Jean Gili has noted, Freddi's idea of government control had more to do with its "moralization" than its politicization of films. And while he called, in one of his first reports as Director, for government control after the examples of Russia and Germany, his primary concern was to satisfy public interests. Here again, the impulse to institutionalize and to centralize filmmaking was informed and mitigated by an ambivalence—an ambivalence which discouraged government production of feature-length and overtly propagandistic films.

Documenting a National Spirit

Centralization facilitated the dissemination of a national identity in a language (mode) accessible to a broad public. Certainly, this identity served those attempting to implement a political agenda and a national policy that were congruent with changing popular ideals. As I have attempted to explain in the last section, however, centralization was an ongoing process of negotiation and struggle over access to these facilities. Highly materialist and economistic approaches to documentaries and newsreels produced through LUCE or through increasingly centralized production facilities and distribution networks cannot really explore the rhetorical texture and the interpretive frames constructed through these kinds of films. As I have explained in the last section, the changing base for film production tended to encourage a segregation of feature-films and documentaries or newsreels. Still, it is important to recognize that generally both types of movies were part of an audience's viewing experience. And here too it is important to realize that both types of films were forms of cultural modeling practiced through a medium that was changing audiences' sense of realism and spectacle.

Walter Benjamin addressed many of these concerns in his evocative essay "The Work of Art in the Age of Mechanical Reproduction" (1935), in which he notes that cinema, as a new technology for popular (political) discourse, had precluded the "auratic" quality of traditional cultures. Movies, according to Benjamin, gratify a modern Western desire to bring events and people closer, "both spatially and humanly," and thus to produce a more democratic society. However, unlike traditional arts, grounded in religious and ceremonial rituals, the "authenticity" of a film's meanings (in a modern context) is politicized. One of Benjamin's conclusions is that most films, due to their capitalistic nature, do not call attention to their own politicization (or to the processes of their production) and fail to offer any real avenues for social change.

More contemporary social theorists have amplified and developed some of these same points about the role of mass media in disseminating and legitimating social and political realities in modern societies. Alvin Gouldner, whose treatment of "the communications revolution" and bourgeois ideology argues that because modern media (he primarily discusses the press) generally abstract discourses (speaker and speech) from their intent/occasion, suggests that social reality and ideology are based upon events that are continually depersonalized and decontextualized. Furthermore, Gouldner's explanation of ideology in post-traditional societies (an explanation to which I could not possibly do justice here) generally vacillates between the same two conclusions about contemporary media and "the public" found in Benjamin's essay. For Gouldner, public realities are self-evident because they are conveyed through "impersonalized" sources and experienced as decontextualized events, yet the public is always obliged to construct its realities and its ideologies out of discourses that are constantly in competition with one another. For both Benjamin and Gouldner, the limits of this diversity and competition are bound up with the hierarchy or structure of the society; it is Benjamin, however, who, while acknowledging the progressive qualities of cinema as a new social force, more frequently offers cynical views about popular realisms and about the public's ability to understand the meanings of motion pictures as something other than self-evident. What scholars such as Benjamin and (later) Gouldner point to is a fundamental problematic in modern Western cultures over political and social realisms. The contributions of structuralists and semioticians have directed attention to the *processes* for producing realities; and their methods remind us, as Bertolt Brecht argued in the 1930s,[4] that realisms are not intrinsic but are provisional and multi-discursive—part of a complex nexus of changing social and cultural conventions. Because, moreover, a *public* and its ideologies are constituted through their modes of discourse (their communicative techniques), their social and political realities have a great deal to do with their competency or literacy of these processes and with their *access* to these technologies. Political systems, likewise, are obliged continually to demonstrate and justify a need for their authority, and they are obliged to do so through changing and competing popular modes of discourse the viabilities of which are again contingent upon public literacy and access in relation to these forms.

The title of this subsection, "Documenting a National Spirit," is an attempt to underscore ways that the "documentary" realism of movies viewed in Italy during the 1920s and 1930s is very much a part of the historical processes of (the emergence of) Italian popular film culture. Likewise, by examining the documentaries and newsreels produced through LUCE in the context of Italy's emerging popular film culture, one is obliged to consider their realism amidst a field of competing cultural models. Historically, the realism of the LUCE documentaries can be attributed partly to their *public* accessibility—especially when they are compared to forms of knowledge (literature and theater) previously accessible only to those more educated or literate and of a higher social status. Because television offers us today easier access to a "flow" of new events in our own homes, we may easily lose sight of just how much documentaries and newsreels were antitraditional (and in Italy, anti-Liberal) forms. And, during a period when the commercial film industry was in a shambles, these documentaries offered important models of national identity—one of the reasons Lando Ferretti describes them as a matrix for writing a "new national *storia*." In the context of emerging cultural forms and of political chaos and reform, documentaries became a way of *verifying* what was "essential" but ineffable to Italian popular culture (and ineffable precisely because of the decay of Liberal traditions and the emergence of a populist spirit). This is, of course, the historical necessity of documentary images in enabling a national identity; their messages constantly referred to a meta-community that could be authenticated only on film (rather than in print or verbally on the radio). Because of the increasing ubiquity of movies, however, documentaries repeatedly verified a national spirit through popular myth. Their vision of meta-community could only be conveyed through codified images that, even in didactic films such as documentaries, had a broad identification value and appeal, and a consensual quality.

As Corrado D'Errico, film director and editor of LUCE's short-lived journal about its own newsreels, proposed in 1936:

> In order to be a success, the documentary must place itself outside history and reflect the mood of the century. . . . It is through documentary that cinema realizes its true function as recorder of history and its tremendous responsiblity, particularly in an age such as ours when the poetic ideals of life are brought to the highest expression.[5]

Documentaries and newsreels offered ways of distilling and magnifying events so that audiences could *re-read* a national landscape that appeared both natural and ideological. And, as much as the documentaries may have facilitated making an ideology appear natural and eternal (as D'Errico's comments suggest), they were frequently given to making Italian popular culture appear historic. (As I will explain later in this section, documentaries were produced to celebrate each year of events in Fascist Italy: titles for Anno V [1927], Anno VI [1928], Anno VII [1929], etc.) The documentaries produced in Italy during the 1920s and 1930s were indeed political, coordinated and supervised as they were by state agencies (much more than were feature films). But the political realities proposed by documentaries were conveyed through a language that tapped into the myths and symbology of its popular audiences; and documentaries more frequently than newsreels examined the customs of workers and peasants.[6] Therefore, that these documentaries (as public texts) frequently presented Italy as a popular space cannot be explained merely in political terms but also with a high regard for the historicity of the modes of discourse and exposition, for the "codes of realism" that were themselves being renegotiated (partly because of the filmic techniques that addressed national–popular consciousness), and finally for the textual complexity and density of their messages (which are too often viewed by social and political scientists as uncomplicated). Evaluating and discussing their meanings and influences, in this sense, becomes a highly interdisciplinary critical enterprise.

Some of the earliest documentaries produced through LUCE around 1925–26 are clearly given to celebrating the mythical qualities of a national landscape. Three widely circulated documentaries during this period presented Italian agricultural reform. *La battaglia del grano* (*The Battle for Grain*) showed attempts by the government to modernize and to increase domestic grain production. *La foresta fonte di ricchezza* (*The Forest—Fountain of Riches*) encouraged conservation of Italian forests. And *Vita nova* (*The New Life*) exhibited efforts to modernize and, at the same time, to coordinate work activities among Italian provinces. While charting social change and reform (a subject common in Italian documentaries from the 1920s), these documentaries presented a complex dependence between tradition and modernity, between natural resources and cultural enrichment (realized as social productivity), between provincial customs and a national experience, between the activities of workers and of the state, and, finally, between cinema's visual realism and abstract, unspoken ideals (especially since these were silent films). In a period of radical social and political change, these early documentaries pointed to a need to preserve as well as to reform and modernize; but, because they were directed at a national audience (from significantly different regions and subcultures) through a mythic or "meta-" language, both the preservation and the modernization they depicted may have appeared much more modest than may have been proposed through more directly political oratory or forms of "local" address. The images of the characters, i.e., the workers and peasants, in these early documentaries were (as Argentieri and others have noted) highly rounded and stereotypical, though never *personalized* as in feature films. The casts of these filmed documentaries were "non-actors," but, because the events and people that became the subjects of these films were chosen for their exemplary and highly connotative value, even their apparel became a kind of costume. (As I explain later in this chapter, Mussolini became the most interesting and problematic case in point.) And, in documentaries on cultural and sporting events, *performers* and ritualized *performance* were the films' subjects. There were also reports that some of these early silent documentaries about agricultural reform and provincial customs were accompanied by *live*, rustic, or folkloristic music and choruses.[7]

The documentaries produced by LUCE or semiprivately (through the Cines studios in the early 1930s) were generally *educational*; but, as filmed texts, they were an educational form that was unprecedented. Movie distribution networks and policy facilitated the national dissemination of a somewhat standardized explanation of a subject. Moreover, the form itself tended to be illustrative rather than openly literary. While these documentaries were didactic and addressed a variety of subjects, they (like the feature films) always conveyed their messages through modeling procedures that were widely accessible. The rhetoric, the "logic" of cause and effect and of the expository sequence (i.e., what facilitates coherence for a popular audience) in these documentary films, relied upon and contributed to the expository strategies that were made possible by changing technology and that were made necessary by public literacy of these codes. Silent documentaries were made to cohere and were inflected in part by inter-titles, and in later sound documentaries a narrator's commentary served much the same purpose. (The first sound documentary, *La traversata dell'Atlantico*, was a LUCE special produced in 1930 about Italo Balbo's solo flight across the Atlantic.) Many of the documentaries produced through the early 1930s continued to use inter-titles instead of oral narration, and, even in the later sound documentaries, oral narration was generally minimal. Oral commentary in both documentaries and newsreels served as an important framing device to highlight or "headline" a subject and to bridge subjects, but the form continued to be given to illustration through images and music (although music in many cases served only to punctuate a moment or to introduce a scene/subject). Moreover, beyond the technical and economic deterrents to greater commentary, the voice-over narration could be said to have weakened the authenticity of the reality created visually; as Sol Worth has noted, one may question the *veracity* of an oral statement or one may question the *reality* of an image, but not vice versa.

Besides these expository techniques, film documentaries, as ritual/political documentation of a national spirit, and as expositions directed at popular audiences, continually participated in (tested and promoted) widespread assumptions by encoders and decoders about "an order of things." It is in this sense that documentaries inevitably shared some of the same features as feature-length narrative films. There are the obvious examples of this similarity in the "direct cinema" of *Treno popolare* or in *Camicia nera*, a narrative film incorporating documentary and newsreel footage to produce a form that draws upon the "authenticity" of cinematic diegesis to establish historical fact. But, more importantly, documentary films engage an audience's narrativity or rather an audience's sense of what narration (and here I would include *exposition*) should or could be. One of the more striking examples of this was Alfieri's (Minister of Propaganda) and Mussolini's frequent dissatisfaction with documentaries about Italy's North African campaign, which they felt were not exciting or dramatic enough.[8] Because, then, documentary production and consumption occurred amidst a field of other cinematic models, documentaries contributed to the very form of some feature films while they themselves were created and viewed through mythic models emerging through more narrative forms. In discussing Italy's film documentaries, one therefore finds striking connections with the other models which I have explored in previous chapters.

As I have already mentioned in this section, many of the documentaries made during the early and mid–1920s were attempts to trace the lineage or origins of Fascism. Seen amidst a tradition of Italian historical cinema, these film chronicles were also given to narrating history and documenting myth. By the late 1920s, after early efforts such as *Il grido dell'aquila* (1923), *A noi* (1923), *Giovinezza, giovinezza, primavera di bellezza* (1923), and *Le tappe della gloria e dell'ardire italici* (1923) by private producers to make films celebrating the March on Rome, documentaries were released annually that encapsulated the year's major events under Fascism: *Anno V* (1927), *Anno VI* (1928), *Anno VII* (1929), *Anno VIII* (1930), and *Anno IX* (1931). These films ordered the year's events generally by editing and reordering newsreel footage from that year. Other historical documentaries from these years include a series of LUCE films released between 1926 and 1933 on antiquity and traces of a distant past (monuments, etc.): *L'arte egizia* (*Egyption Art*), *Fontane di Roma* (*Roman Fountains*), *Foro romano e Palatino* (*Roman Forum and Palatine*), *Pompei negli scavi vecchi e nuovi* (*Pompeii through Old and Recent Excavation*), *Lavoro di restauro al Pantheon* (*Work to Restore the Pantheon*), and more.[9] By the tenth anniversary of Fascism, along with a revivalistic epic such as *Camicia nera* or *Vecchia guardia*, LUCE began to sponsor films chronicling what had become a Fascist legacy. *Primi anni del fascismo*, for instance, is a silent documentary that frames what is basically a heroic profile of Mussolini's early accomplishments and the Italian *impero* by stating that the film itself "reaffirms, before everyone and everything, the intangibility of borders ordained by God and established with the blood of Italy's bravest sons." After this introductory statement, the film cuts to a shot of the Austrian–Italian border, where a monument is inscribed with a homage to Italians slain in World War I; and, in so doing, the film establishes an implicit connection between filmic inscription and this monument to a national history.

Similar to the historical documentaries were those that, in promoting some of the values of *Strapaese*, directed national attention to and fused the traditional customs and topographical beauties of the Italian provinces. There were, moreover, a series of short documentaries about community pageants or the survival of a traditional celebration, e.g., the Palio at Siena or a medieval tournament at Torino. Other documentaries on rural Italy ranged from some 91 short films on Italian geography[10] to such films as *Pane nostro* (*Our Bread*, 1932), which is a visual ode to bucolic living, with only a musical accompaniment (a feature that obliquely aligns it with Murnau's *City Girl*, released in Italy two years earlier as

Our Daily Bread), and *Primavera sul Garda* (*Springtime on Lake Garda*), made in 1935 by D'Annunzio's son. It is also easy to see that some feature-length, commerical films which were set in a rustic environment shared a number of qualities with these rural documentaries. Both Blasetti's *Terra madre* and, later, Palermi's *Cavalleria rusticana* trade in the folkloric costumes and rituals of provincial Italy, and Blasetti's *Terra madre* shares its title with a rural documentary produced in 1929. Moreover, in the feature films *Palio* and *Treno popolare*, the events involving the films' protagonists are continually intercut with on-location shooting in the provinces. In *Palio*, Blasetti uses footage of the race and festivities in Siena, and, in *Treno popolare*, Matarazzo includes lengthy scenes of the hilltop village outside Rome where much of the dramatic action occurs. The early films by Blasetti, particularly *Sole* and *Terra madre*, also conjure the Italian "agricultural documentaries." While the agricultural films were more overtly didactic and distributed to small towns across Italy (where they frequently became social events as well as educational demonstrations),[11] they too verified for urban audiences a way of life and a reality that had become more difficult to recognize by the 1930s.

On the other hand, there were industrial documentaries charting new production processes and technologies (including films about making glass, beer, rubber, etc.) and exhibiting the products of these modern processes (including films about synthetic fibers, automobiles, the newest train technology, telephones, and, by the mid–1930s, weapons). The aesthetic of *Stracittà* is apparent in Corrado D'Errico's early documentary *Stramilano* (1929), which uncovers Milan's "magic realism" through signs of the city's modernity—its department stores, its factories, its streets filled with automobiles, its night life, cabarets, jazz bands, etc. And *Ritmi di stazione* (1933)[12] is both a light meditation on railway communication and ambience as well as a compendium of the myths about modern travel—captured through vivid images from train stations. But, unlike Walter Ruttmann's *Accaio*, in which sequences in the dark factory do resemble a kind of expressionistic documentary,[13] or Camerini's *Grandi magazzini*, which concocts a world comprised entirely of fashionable *nouveatés*, these documentaries tended only to *celebrate* the new occupations created by industrialization and an expanding urban working class.

Other documentaries inspired by and attempting to gratify a widespread epochalist vision were the rich vein of touristic or travel films and the numerous documentaries about exotic lands. One of the first Italian documentary filmmakers working abroad for LUCE was Mario Craveri; his travels in the late 1920s produced newsreels on Japan, China, and India. Short films made during the 1930s about the culture and geographical splendor of foreign countries included *Vecchia vita nordica* (*Ancient Nordic Life*), *Costumi dell'Olanda* (*Holland's Customs*), *Costumi ungheresi* (*Hungarian Customs*), *Razze miste in Birmania* (*Mixed Races in Birmania*), *Indigeni dell'Isola del Borneo* (*The Inhabitants of Borneo*), and *Vita indiana in città e di villagi* (*Indian Life in Cities and Villages*)—to name just a few. As in the feature-length, commercial films about foreigners, or as in those set in foreign countries, these documentaries tended to translate exotic customs in terms accessible to popular movie audiences. One of the more amusing examples of this occurs in a LUCE newsreel on Lake Tana in northern Africa, wherein a narrator's explanation, that this wondrous and exotic jungle is silent but for the "*natural* sounds" of rivers and animals, is accompanied by a musical score reminiscent of Tarzan movies.[14]

In no other documentaries were the myths about foreign peoples (and about Italy's identity with respect to other cultures) more overtly tapped for political ends than in the increasing number of Italian documentaries during the 1930s about North Africa. During the 1920s, LUCE had begun to trade on the para-geographic and explorational documentary films made possible by the Italian presence in Libya and elsewhere in eastern Africa. Some of these cinematic exposés included a full-length documentary by Guelfo Civinini, *Aetheopia* (1924), and then a series of films between 1928 and 1932 on the expanding Italian domains in North Africa. Like the other documentaries about foreign countries, these films emphasized the exotic qualities of panoramas and customs. During this same period, however, LUCE also became increasingly involved with a number of documentaries more directly about Italian campaigns in this region. After *Aetheopia*, Civinini directed *Soldati d'Africa* (*Soldiers of Africa*); this film was followed by others such as *Il ritorno di Roma* (*The Return of Rome*), *Il nostro esercito coloniale* (*Our Colonial Army*, 1928), and *Figli d'Italia caduti in terra d'Africa* (*Italian Sons Who Fell on African Soil*). It was not until 1935, during a period when Italy had increased its campaigns in North Africa and when the government was offering incentives to Italians to colonize Africa Orientale Italiana, that Mussolini ordered the formation of a special unit at LUCE to make films about this new frontier or "fourth shore." The headquarters for this unit was established at Asmara and was directed early on by Luciano De Feo and later by Corrado D'Errico and Giuseppe Croce.[15] Publicity photos of this unit include shots of cameramen among convoys of soldiers and workers, in makeshift platforms in trees, and frequently behind camera tripods that are flanked by (and intended to establish a connection with) tripods supporting machine guns. The efforts of this unit produced eighteen documentaries, in addition to newsreel footage.[16]

Among their films is D'Errico's medium-length documentary *Il cammino degli eroi* (*The Path of Heroes*)—a film that closely approaches the narrative style of commerical films. Like the traditional documentaries, it relied primarily upon images and music, and less upon inter-titles; but it unfolds in twelve sequences that appear as episodes or chapters leading to an epic finale. Each of these segments highlights a force contributing to the "revitalization" of Africa by Italy; and these forces are presented in stages, beginning with the production by Italian factories of machines and materials necessary for this national project and then highlighting those working in Africa (here the postal and medical services) to achieve this revitalization. (Among this group, in section 9 of the film, is the work of the cinematographers themselves and of others involved in introducing the Africans to movies via mobile cinemas.) Only the eleventh segment is immediately succeeded by the "*pace romana*" and shots of plowed fields.

Il cammino degli eroi was made the same year as Genina's *Lo squadrone bianco* and Camerini's *Il grande appello*, both of which concern Italy's Abyssinian campaign. In these latter films (described in chapter 6), documentary sequences, on-location shooting, and emphasis on landscapes and long sequences of the Africans and the Italian workers or soldiers tie the films' dramatic action and central characters to an expository realism and to the journalistic *evidence* that documentaries and newsreels brought home to Italian cinemas. The predominantly expository techniques of *Il cammino degli eroi* (a lack of central characters or of close-ups) are used to objectify its choric voice and the mythopoeic and epic quality of its episodic narration. The Italian military effort in North Africa also precipitated another relatively new cinematographic technique in Italian film: the aerial shot. And only for the pre–World War II Italian movies shot in Africa were airplanes used to film. Aerial filming in *Il grande appello* contributes to the movie's epic vision of the Italian involvement in Africa and to the spectacular battle sequences in the film's finale. And, in some documentaries about the Italian experience in Africa shot during the late 1930s, aerial photography lends a sense of omnipotence and godlike perspective over the sprawling wilderness and a majesty to the waterfalls below.

Again, it is important to recognize the creativity, experimentation, and emerging techniques of documentary filmmaking to better understand how national–popular realities (or realisms) were mediated through changing expository as well as narrative techniques of the cinema. As I have mentioned elsewhere, documentary filmmaking became an experimental form available to young filmmakers working through the GUF organizations, many of whom went on to produce postwar narrative films. Some of the most stylized documentaries of the 1930s were made at the Cines studios under Emilio Cecchi; the group included Blasetti, Di Coco, Perilli, Barbaro, Poggioli, and Matarazzo. As Brunetta notes, their documentaries frequently share many of the montage strategies and formalism found in the Soviet cinema of the 1920s.[17] "Mussolinia di Sardegna" (Cines documentary #14), for instance, is made as part of a series celebrating the tenth anniversary of Fascism in 1933. Directed by Matarazzo, who also directed *Treno popolare* the same year, this short film constructs a visual and aural flow of relationships around a state-sponsored land reclamation project (named after the Duce) in Sardinia. Both the literal and the figurative (metaphoric and metonymic) *energy* that it charts at a dam site is eloquently presented through this flow of images (the river, high voltage lines, generators, etc.) and their semiotic/semantic connections. In this manner, the film is a celebration of a power, presented here as a conjoining of natural and civic forces (water and dam) that are both the agents and products of a national and political vitality—generated, as such, for the tenth anniversary of Fascism. The documentary begins with a long, high shot and pan over a reservoir; the camera then pans to the dam, over the dam, into the dam, and to close-ups of instruments, voltage coils, etc. After taking the viewer from an initial panorama into the heart of the dam, the film then follows electrical lines *from* the dam; this pan is then juxtaposed with a pan across the currents of the river flowing from the dam. The next shots are filmed *on* the river, presumably from a moving boat, and this perspective is then juxtaposed with images of water cascading down and out of the dam. The last shot fades into the electrical conductors inside the dam, and again the film emphasizes energy and flow by panning across electrical lines out of the dam and over the countryside—here to a field generator and to tractors tilling the soil. The first shots of a solitary farmer soon give way to a more lengthy sequence of an entire community (made possible by this state works project), who are involved both with farming and with the construction of new dams. In the last part of the film, the viewer is returned to the water rushing from the dam, then to close-ups of flowers in a field and to crops in another field, and finally to shots of new buildings in this thriving community and back to the grain and milk that this fertile land has produced to nurture the inhabitants. While the film lacks a clear narrative, its expository sequence of images and music becomes a flow that is bound up with the flow of energies which the film itself is charting.

By the late 1930s and early 1940s, Italian documentaries frequently assumed an almost baroque style in their attempts to address audiences increasingly habituated to the ubiquity of these films. Sandro Pallavicini and Pietro Benedetti's 1940 documentary *Sui pattini a rotelle* (*On Roller Skates*) presents this popular recreation as an exhibition of Italy's "new order," its moblization of youthful spirit through social programs, and its success in competitive arenas. The film's construction also attests to a formal sophistication over its predecessors; it lacks inter-titles altogether, is accompanied throughout by the animated and cordial voice of a narrator (unlike those in newsreels), and continually uses dissolves and fades to lend textual and semantic *density* to its action. The film purports to showcase Italy's roller-skating champions, Eglida Cecchini and Arturo Garagnani, both of whom receive star billing in the opening credits. But they actually appear more as participants in and the culmination of an emerging popular activity. The movie is set entirely at a state-operated, outdoor roller-rink—an arena that is filled in the first scene with youthful skaters. Their youth is immediatly contrasted with the age of a bespectacled older man who looks on, smiling, and who then amuses them with his own awkward attempts on skates. In the midst of this brief sequence, the film cuts to a middle-aged woman in a group of seated spectators who is thumbing through (and waxing nostalgic over) an old photo album of skaters dressed in clothes of the Belle Epoque. Here the camera closes in on the photo so that it fills the screen and "comes to life" with a *pas de deux* between a male and female character in what appears to be the same roller rink. Whereas the initial group skated to contemporary jazz music, this couple skates to a waltz. At the conclusion of their number, the camera pulls in on their skates and then back again to reveal the same skaters now elegantly dressed in white jacket and full white dress. They skate, the narrator states, to a "modern rhythm" and are accompanied by a small chorus of women on skates. Tradition is presented here both as the matrix for this modern, popular recreation and ritual and as a vestige of a traditional (Liberal) society where skating was more of an elitist and pompous diversion. To further demonstrate the changing significance of skating, Cecchini offers a skating lesson (to the audience of and in the film); the other female skaters are good-naturedly less successful at imitating her leaps and pirouettes. Immediately following this exhibition by the women, the film cuts to a close-up of a pistol, and the camera pulls back to reveal a uniformed man conducting a skating race among young men. While the women's skating emphasized grace, the men's emphasizes competition. The last parts of the film concern another roller game, another *pas de deux* by Cecchini and Garagnani, and finally a montage of women dressed in folkloric costumes from Italy and other countries performing traditional dances on skates. As the gates close on skaters performing the Tarentella, the narrator explains that skating is a perfect synthesis of sport and artistic activity.

These last two documentaries demonstrate that the *practice* of documentary was very much part of an emerging theoretical dialogue on documentary filmmaking.[18] As Bernagozzi has noted, the theorization of documentary films proceeded along two lines: one in which documentary was described as a mirror image of the regime's greatness and another that offered philological explanations of realist film. While both of these lines inform even the most formally sophisticated Italian documentaries from the 1930s, the latter clearly lends fuel to the Neorealist aesthetics of the early and mid-1940s.

To say that these documentaries, as propaganda, instilled in their audiences a "false consciousness" is to grossly oversimplify the entire subject of popular realisms and the complex and changing processes of communication or representation through which they are invented, modified, and challenged. Italian documentaries produced during the 1920s and 1930s *facilitated* a democratic (though multifaceted) view of national–popular culture, and these films attempted to emphasize a unity of values through readily accessible models of social and political reform. This does not, however, mean that the experience of viewing documentaries was uniform. While the government did much to institutionalize documentaries, not only through the role of LUCE but through distribution networks and laws requiring newsreels in commercial theaters, the screening situation itself varied significantly from region to region. Agricultural films shown in the country would elicit significantly different readings or understandings when screened for an urban audience. Even the government's lack of control over local screenings of feature-length films, which the documentaries accompanied, makes it necessary to consider the range of ways in which the messages of any documentary may have conjoined with the messages of different feature films showing at different locations.

Current Events as Spectacle

Examining documentaries and newsreels in the context of Italy's emerging popular film culture complicates our understanding of their messages simply as government propaganda. One is faced with the tasks of distinguishing their tone from more narrative, commercial forms and of considering how they were continually compelled to adopt and modify the *language* of these popular forms. Their role as propaganda cannot then be easily dissociated from their limited dramatic appeal and their connection with the conventions of other popular texts, nor can this role be understood outside their complex textuality and the complex processes of their "articulation."

As I have explained in the last section, some documentaries focused on current events; but these films usually condensed and conceptualized longer periods of time than did the newsreels. Newsreels, as Ernesto Laura notes, were frequently put together hurriedly, often within 24 hours after the events filmed.[19] It is this lack of visual stylization that also undoubtedly has deflected attention from the newsreel's *treatment* of its subjects (or the processes for producing "facts") to focus instead on their content. But, while one seldom finds the degree of formal experimentation in the LUCE newsreels that is more common in documentaries, it would be inaccurate to say that the formal codes of the LUCE newsreels were not continually being reworked and, moreover, that these formal changes were not in some ways part of a general rearticulation of cultural or ideological codes.

The first LUCE newsreel was released in June 1927; that same year, LUCE produced another 43 newsreels (and 902 copies of these films).[20] In 1928, production increased to 201 (with 4,410 copies); and, in 1929, the number increased to 197 during the first part of the year alone.[21] By the early part of 1940, the number of newsreels in circulation had climbed to over 1,620. In March of 1940, newsreels began to be catalogued again from number one, and, for the next two years, LUCE was responsible for about 100 newsreels a year.[22] During the late 1920s and the 1930s, there were also some revealing changes in their format and content. The early newsreels from the late 1920s are generally between 150 and 200 meters long and cover around six subjects; this length increased during 1931–35 (with the introduction of sound) to between 310 and 450 meters, covering around seven subjects, and then decreased after 1936 to around 280 to 300 meters, generally covering six or seven subjects. Early newsreels frequently began with foreign subjects and concluded with Italian subjects; this pattern changed during the 1930s, when newsreels generally began and concluded with Italian subjects. In many newsreels of 1939–40, Italian subjects often comprised the majority and occasionally all of the features. The Italian subjects in early newsreels from the late 1920s most often involved events in Rome; but, as the regime began to solidify itself and as the political and cinematic *center* of Italy became more established and versatile, newsreels more frequently concerned events in other Italian locations. And, in 1936 and 1937, features on the North African colonies were very common.

As an elliptical and highly condensed succession of events or subjects framed and bridged by titles, music (after 1931), and voice-over narration (most common during the late 1930s), the newsreels offer an incremental magnification and a mosaic-like realization of current events. Formally, the *cinegiornali* (as cinematic journalism) share some of the conventions of radio broadcasts and the photojournalism of magazines. In their most technically sophisticated form during the late 1930s, newsreels lead the viewer from one feature to the next through a narrator, who by this period is used to accomplish contradictory aims. On the one hand, his unemphatic cadence and tone signal to his audience his objectivity as medium or "choric voice" (somewhat different from the master of ceremonies who frequently appeared in theaters during the days of silent film). On the other hand, he continually emphasizes, by headlining and correlating the different features, the newsreel's central themes and their place in the consciousness of a "national audience."

Examples of the strategies for bracketing and interweaving feature news events in the later Italian newsreels is LUCE #2 (March 1940). The film begins with a feature on Bruno Mussolini's appearance at a boxing match between Italian and European squads at the Circus Maximus. After frequent cross-cutting between medium-shots of the young Mussolini and the entirely male audience, a narrator's voice frames this segment by his description of the Italian spectators' admiration and enthusiasm for boxing. To bridge this feature with the next one, he adds here that, while the enthusiasm in Italy for boxing may be strong, it is not unlike that of the Japanese for their favorite sport. Here the newsreel cuts from a long-shot of the crowd at the Circus Maximus in Italy to a long-shot of a sports field in an open-air stadium in Japan. During views of a procession of Japanese "fighters" in traditional costume, the narrator explains that *this* (a highly ambiguous pronoun) is their "typically national sport." At the conclusion of this segment, the film cuts from shots of combatants attacking one another with wooden clubs to shots of young girls and children *practicing* in a classroom. Maintaining the connotative resonance of this last sequence, the narrator then introduces a feature about Indian troops—first seen dancing (again choreographed movements) in traditional garb to their own folk music. "Meanwhile," he notes, "Indian troops in France *fight* against the cold, to which they are less adapted—with an army that is less suited for war." At this point, a trumpet blast (amplified on the soundtrack) "interrupts their recreation" and they mount their horses to ride to the front. The unit concludes as British cars arrive carrying the Duke of Windsor, who inspects their maneuvers. To introduce segment 4, the film cuts to a shot of a German submarine gliding on the surface of the ocean, while the narrator states that "on the sea, every new day produces new victims and new heroes"; and, during a series of close-ups of the sailors, of their handshaking and jovial demeanor at an awards ceremony, the narrator notes that their faces and gestures reveal their dedication. From these last shots, the film breaks to an aerial shot of Manhattan and a muted jazz score. The narrator bridges segments 4 and 5 by introducing New York as a place "where the war at least for now is but a far-off *echo*" (especially, one may imagine, because of the jazz music). After four segments depicting the fighting spirit of those outside the United States, this unit focuses on the ease of American life (and its "rhythms") through a feature on "shapely" American women in bathing suits enjoying effortless exercises on the latest weight-reducing machines. As the narrator mentions their devotion (how unlike the Nazis' happy "dedication"?) to perfecting their figures, the film cuts to a close-up of a wall

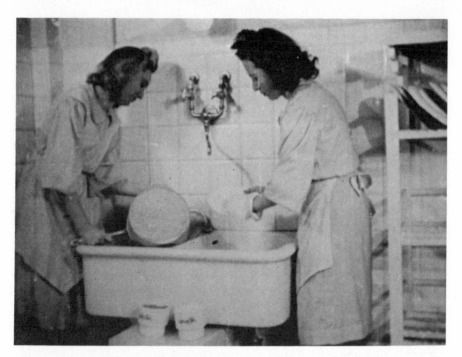

In a later LUCE newsreel, footage about a school for prospective wives in Italy appears just after . . .

. . . footage on the latest fitness fads of American women

clock indicating 8:00 and immediately thereafter a shot of young women in domestic uniforms. "Here instead," the narrator remarks, "young Torinese girls don't have time to worry about their figures." This segment, about a home economics "school for the soon-to-be-married," features the states' work in organizing public instruction of women's roles: "the art of cooking, the art of clean-up, the art of serving with a lithe, courteous manner." When these women retire at this segment's conclusion to sew, to talk, and to listen to the radio (activities not *entirely* unlike those of the American women in segment 5), the narrator adds that they are each waiting to hear from someone. With the final shot of a woman reading a letter from her fiancé, the narrator bridges to the last unit on *men* working in a munitions factory: "Fascism has encouraged citizens to be prepared in every way." This last segment celebrates the technological modernity of Italian factories and the precision and productivity of its men and machines. While much of this segment is in some ways a visual instruction about the processes for making rifles, the last shots are pans across warehouses full of munitions, followed by a cut to a long-shot of soldiers marching (" . . . into the hands of our well-prepared soldiers"). This last reference to soldiers not only offers an important rhetorical frame for the segment itself but also for the entire newsreel, which began with treatments of "fighters."

The increased use of a narrator, the polished aural bridges, and the lack of any kind of visual inter-title between the newsreel's segments all distinguish these later newsreels from their silent counterparts of the late 1920s in both formal/technical and ideological ways. Above all, these techniques enable a much greater sense of expository continuity and thematic contiguity among the newsreel's features; and in so doing they greatly enhance the newsreel's ability to present a world that appears closer and more full of meaning in its synchronization. Viewers of the early silent newsreels were continually taken "outside" the photographic reality of a feature to tableaus and to inter-titles and then on to another news segment; inter-titles encouraged a separation among subject, title, and viewer. The use of inter-titles in earlier newsreels did, however, rely upon a faith in unauthored literary inscription (as compared to the human "presence" of the later newsreels' narrative voice) to establish a *proper* range of interpretations about each feature. Despite attempts to mask its humanity with an arhythmic cadence and tone, the narrator's voice makes his messages more conditional than those conveyed through titles.

Like the documentaries produced in Italy during the 1920s and 1930s, the LUCE newsreels attached values to current events and were inevitably produced and read through social codes of the day as well as through the formal codes I have discussed *vis-à-vis* LUCE #2. For this reason, recent Italian scholars frequently refer to their "ritualistic" role in Italian society during the 1920s and 1930s. Precisely because they were produced by the state and distributed nationally, they were compelled (unlike newspapers, which were primarily regional at that time) to adopt a language accessible to a national audience. But as a form of cinematic journalism (albeit state-controlled journalism), they undoubtedly exerted a cosmopolitanizing influence upon their audiences—especially since they were, at their inception and for many years thereafter, given largely to foreign features and since, unlike documentaries, they seldom dealt with the activities of workers or peasants (unless they were included in treatments of sports events, popular performances, or folkloristic celebration). For years, newsreels offered Italian audiences a view of life outside their provincial or national domains and at the fringes of their rountine experiences. It is for this reason that newsreels became a public spectacle so important for channeling and bridging those events and characters necessary for a public understanding of a national–popular identity. As Gouldner has noted, news enhances public rationality by allowing persons to escape provincializing assumptions and thereby enabling them to *compare* their own conditions with others: "News allows alternatives to be defined as 'realistic' by showing different conditions to exist already, thereby fostering more ready transcendence of the immediate and local."[23] One could say, therefore, that, even though the "outside" references were those filtered through a government agency (which undoubtedly contributed to delimiting the range of alternative references or models), the newsreels did serve as agents or conduits for social as well as cultural change. And it is also likely that their transmission of *news* events created for movie audiences provocative resonances with the feature films which they accompanied.

All of this is not to say that the *discourses* occurring through these newsreels were not also replete with diacritical features given to conjoining the new with the old, the familiar with the exotic. This would be what Barthes describes as the myth-making procedures of popular discourses—of conveying the Other (the "outside" references) in terms that are relatively familiar to the broadest cross-section of a national audience. (An example of this kind of myth-making can be found in LUCE #7, 1940, wherein a feature about the flora of Hawaii is prefaced by the narrator's remark that the narcissus is a ritual flower for Hawaiian women, "who, like Italians, love flowers.") Other examples here would be some of the newsreel features on the United States that I have discussed in chapter 2, although one could just as easily consider any of the large numbers of foreign features in these newsreels. And, while the predominance of American footage in Italian newsreels during the late 1920s (over a hundred features a year by the early 1930s) can be explained as a result of economic dependence by the fledgling LUCE on newsreel footage supplied by the major U.S. distributors, one must also concede the central role of the mythology of America in orientations of Italian popular culture.

The changes in connections reached between LUCE and foreign distributors over the exchange of newsreel footage become an increasingly important force in Italian cultural policy throughout the 1930s—particularly with respect to Germany and America. But the more widespread *understandings* of these national affiliations, and the specific signs of changes in these understandings, can best be examined through the frames of reference and signifying procedures of newsreels themselves.

The first LUCE newsreel in June of 1927, for instance, used four features from MGM newsreels in its six segments.[24] The four MGM segments concerned

Lindbergh's departure from New York, the havoc created by the flooding of the Mississippi River at New Orleans, a British military expedition and the flight of Europeans from Shanghai, and Italian long-distance aviator Francesco De Pinedo in the Azores. The two Italian contributions included King Victor Emmanuel III's review of troops in Rome and his dedication of a monument to fallen soldiers in Rome. Not only are these Italian political ceremonies framed against spectacular or almost apocalyptic occurrences outside Italy, but the commemoration of Italy's dead soldiers is galvanized by its association with the adventures of current international heroes. Moreover, this process of bracketing occurs through the appropriation of discourses intended for an entirely different cultural context. Thus the "outside" events appear more accessible and meaningful to Italian audiences *in* their conjunction with the political ceremonies in Rome; the Italian segments confer to the foreign subjects a mythical significance in the landscape of national–popular affairs. It is also possible to read in this organization of features a contrast between the flux of events "outside" Italy and the order of the ceremonies in Rome. And, by using American footage of an internationally recognized Italian hero (De Pinedo) in a context with Italian footage celebrating domestic heroes, this newsreel enables an important connection to be drawn by Italian audiences between Italy's national and international identity.

In the late 1920s, Italian subjects averaged just under half of the subjects projected in each LUCE newsreel. During the later 1920s and mid-1930s, Italian features comprised between half and two-thirds of each newsreel. By the late 1930s, the stronger ties among Italy, Germany, and Japan became more central to the world view of the Italian newsreels and to the public perception in Italy of its own national identity on an international front. In 1937, Italy and Germany signed a "film treaty"—one which informally included Japan—and "for the first time photoplay relations entered the official realm of international diplomacy."[25] LUCE newsreels more frequently included German and Japanese features, though American subjects are just as common until 1940. Again, unlike the newsreels from the late 1920s, those during this period framed the intermediary sequences with Italian features—a strategy that more assertively established Italy as a matrix for world events and culture. LUCE #1584 (September 1939), for instance, includes six segments. Its first feature involves scenes from Libya, e.g., shots of exotic African animals in cages, followed by interior scenes of Libyan houses. These images of Italian conquests, which are characterized through the cages and houses as domesticated spaces, are succeeded in the second segment by a piece on the New York zoo and the comically ironic similarity between its animals and some of their human spectators. After these first two features is a sequence involving the government's renovation of an Italian castle damaged during World War I. Following a montage and sporadic narration that anthropomorphizes the edifice by highlighting efforts to restore its beauty, the camera moves inside the castle to windows that open magically to reveal an expansive panorama. The final shots of this sequence are close-ups of a cannon and cannonballs and another panorama of the land below—both shots that, by calling attention to enclosed space or territory and that which lies beyond it, resonate with the images of domestication, protection, and freedom found in the previous segments. The fourth feature presents a German boy's group on the Holland border. This segment consists of scenes that exhibit their highly choreographed marching, whistling, and exercising; it concludes with a longer sequence about their collective productivity harvesting crops. After a very brief fifth feature on the visit of Japanese officials to Italy, the newsreel closes with a brief piece about productivity on land-reclamation projects at Mussolinia. The newsreel concludes with the image of a child, who presumably belongs to one of these workers, eating some grapes—the fruit of their harvest and their cooperative industry in revitalizing Italian soil.

By 1940, LUCE newsreels are frequently made up only of segments about events in Italy or in Italian territories such as AOI or Albania. On the one hand, these later newsreels attested to imperialist attitudes among those directing their content and organization, and to an unwillingness to accommodate foreign models. On the other hand, their lack of foreign features signaled Italy's decreasing dependency on foreign distributors to supply the footage necessary ten years earlier for a newly formed LUCE. However, the very lack of "outside" images, which had offered a necessary mythical backdrop and national orientation for Italian events in previous newsreels, undoubtedly weakened the rhetorical efficacy of this later cinematic journalism. In some very important ways, a public recognition of national identity depended upon external references. And, during the years at the onset of World War II, the organization and presentation of information through LUCE newsreels (both through the increased role of the narrator in coordinating subjects and through their gradual exclusion of foreign models) significantly diminished the *spectacle* of current events. As Fellini has remarked:

> I remember them [the newsreels] as being rather tedious, most of all because I was so young and if I went to the cinema I went to see a movie, or a variety show, and so the interruptions of this hovering eagle with this music that seemed to caw, in triumphant and bellicose notes, all in all made for a boring interval—much like today's advertisements that appear between one performance and another. . . . The LUCE newsreels became a little more interesting when there was some kind of beauty pageant or some American starlet who had just arrived in Rome and was being photographed or was waving from the bridge of a departing ocean liner.[26]

Mussolini as *Divo*

Considering the ubiquity of the LUCE newsreels and documentaries during the 1920s and 1930s, it is necessary to recognize that the most widely viewed figure of the Italian cinema for almost twenty years was Benito Mussolini. While other Fascist figures (particularly Achille Starace, secretary of the Fascist party)

A traditional agrarian festival at Forli observed by the visage of Il Duce (shot from a LUCE newsreel)

were celebrated through these films, Mussolini's presence was certainly the most highly charged with meaning. It would not, moreover, be unjustified to suggest that his stardom was more luminous than any other male or female Italian movie actor at that time. However, most traditional social historians writing about Mussolini have generally tended to discuss him apart from his meanings and apart from the unprecedented interaction of communicative processes that clarified and mediated public understandings of him and the "policy" which he represented in the popular consciousness. A question commonly asked by historians is, what would Fascism have been without Mussolini? (To this same question, Mussolini once responded: "The attempt to separate Mussolini from fascism or fascism from Mussolini is the most useless, most grotesque, most ridiculous thing that could ever be imagined.")[27] I would like to build on this query by posing yet another question: What would Mussolini's words have been without his gestures, and what would both word and gesture have been without the techniques made possible through movies? While it is certainly true that Mussolini's discourses were attended by thousands of spectators (who listened, nonetheless, through amplification systems and amidst floodlights), it would be impossible to disengage public understandings of his messages from the interpretive models or frameworks disseminated through "popular" forms such as the cinema. And, although his discourses were transmitted through the press and over the radio, it is film, I would contend, that did most to convey this personality through heroic, larger-than-life images, that enabled greatest public access to him (even live, he was often seen from afar), and that still serves as the most vivid record most people have of him.

Movies, in amplifying the *personal* qualities in Mussolini, can be said to have facilitated the construction of his public *personality* (as a celebrated, "popular" figure). To say this is not to gloss over the processes of encoding and decoding Mussolini's cinematic presence, for he was certainly constructed as much through his own performance and by those making movies as by the audience. As I have already mentioned elsewhere, the power or resonance of performance depends upon a literacy, by those encoding and decoding it, of cultural models and of generic formulas and conventions. My interest here, then, is not so much in explaining the connection between Mussolini the person (as referent) and his public personality (as a signifier) as it is to explore how his public personality (as national–popular myth) was produced through his multiple *personae* (as signs or masks generated through cinematic performances).

While political figures have in the twentieth century come to depend upon the media to transmit their agenda, they do not necessarily desire to be viewed as entertainers. And, as Barthes notes, a politician's set of choices (his agenda) may easily be spirited away through the familiar, ideological *persona* that he has acquired through the mass forms of communication upon which he has come to rely to reach and establish his constituency.[28] An important analogue to this view can be found in Richard Dyer's remarks about the politicization of movie stars; Dyer argues that movie stars do not present their views as political (in a narrow sense), only as aspects of their *personalities*—i.e., what the public observes through a star's movie roles as well as through journalism, fan magazines, etc.[29] Building upon observations by Francesco Alberoni, Dyer goes on to add that, despite their corresponding charismatic appeal, movie stars are not as "institutionalized" as are politicians.

One of the central problematics of Modernist art (later of Pop art) and of much twentieth-century social theory is, as George Lukacs (among others) has noted, this construction of social *personality*.[30] More recent social theorists, such as Richard Sennett, Christopher Lasch, and Herbert Marcuse, have attempted to explain the historical implications surrounding the emergence of societies in which only a few people are "personalities" and in which a sense of what is public and popular becomes a contingent force in the production of "personalities." But, when these scholars describe how the power and appeal of public celebrities are conveyed through mass media, as Sennett does in his rather cynical account of circumstances surrounding "the fall of public man," the public is often depicted as a body hungry for charismatic figures in whom they may lose a sense of themselves as alienated individuals. What this perspective fails to acknowledge is the textual complexity of public celebrities in a given social context and of the historical necessity of stars in displacing contradictory ideological impulses in specific modern societies. As Barthes has noted, politicians are transformed through photography and television into highly charged signs that operate within a nexus of other sign-systems and a society's mythologies. The public personalities, as popular heroes, made possible by the cinema are an expression of a collective need to address and manage the kind of ideological conflicts, contradictions, and instabilities generated by the social transitions which I have already discussed and by frictions between residual and emerging cultural forms. The heroes of movies in a period of transition demonstrate the possibility of destroying traditional social, political, and cultural categories (roles) and of establishing new ones. Those who could change roles and expand their personalities dramatized ideology not as an invariant essence but as multifaceted variation.

The correspondence between a movie star and his roles is crucial to understanding how he operates as popular hero. Both in historical and in phenomenological terms, the movie star differs from famous theatrical actors or from popular literary heroes. A literary hero is like a movie star in that he is generally more recognized in the popular consciousness than is the name of his author and in that, in serial form, he exists outside of any one literary text. In other words, the hero operates within the structure of the plot and in relation to other roles. Gramsci writes that "popular literary heroes, when they are absorbed into the popular consciousness, separate from their literary origins and acquire the authenticity of an historical figure. . . . This is not to say that they become 'historical figures' in a literal sense (even though this too does happen), but that, in order to make their fictional world intelligible, they acquire a kind of fabulated materiality."[31] On the stage or screen, however, the hero has a corporality that is visible and not merely imagined. The gesture of the performer becomes, as Brooks and Barthes have proposed, a hyperbolic and unequivocal expression for clarifying messages that, spoken, may remain ambiguous; films (particularly silent ones) utilize the economy of a gestural language and therefore make possible an immediate intelligibility of direct and heroic action. An important difference between roles played by theatrical actors and movie actors is discussed by Erwin Panovsky, who notes that various actors may over time perform a role in a play but that a movie role is played only once by and is remembered for its star. Movie roles, in this sense, expand their star's personality rather than limiting it. The public personality, as myth, is thus multi-accentual—constituted of all its previous roles; each performance draws upon the collective resonance of this public personality and upon its place in the audience's mythology of movie stars.

To understand the power and resonance of Mussolini's mythical presence in the public consciousness, it is in part important to view his cinematic presence (in LUCE newsreels and documentaries) amidst a field of competing models in Italy's emerging film culture. The term I am using, *divo*, refers in Italian to the Olympian (divine) aura of some theatrical and operatic actors; it was, however, applied to popular movie actors—especially since some of the early stars of Italian films were *divi* and *dive* from the theater. By the late 1920s, and particularly during the 1930s, magazines featuring the "off-screen" lives and studio promotions of movie actors became very common in Italy. Certainly, however, the epic proportions of images on the cinema screen, the enormous casts of the early historical films, close-ups, and the early optical illusions or special effects of the cinema all contributed to making film a medium aptly suited to imparting these other-worldly, grandiose qualities to actors on a movie screen. Outdoor settings enhanced a dramatic landscape that, unlike the traditional theatrical stage, accommodated and encouraged greater displays of physical and acrobatic skills. While one may, therefore, point to the performances of Hollywood actors such as Mix and Fairbanks as satisfying the appetite of bourgeois audiences for charismatic figures (men who could do things that few others in their movies could), the medium itself facilitated the feats of heroic action (even comic ones) that time and again demonstrated their superhuman personalities. In fact, the coming of sound did much to transform the role of movie hero and displays of heroism.

Mussolini's appearances in early Italian newsreels and documentaries (and his public personality in general) conjure a pedigree of acrobats and "strongmen" from 1920s Italian films—the only genre to have weathered the calamities of the Italian film industry during these years and the only genre capable of competing with American films. The mythological names of these strongmen—Ajax, Sansone, and above all, Maciste (often described in his films as "the good giant")—were part of their divistic luminosity in Italian popular culture; however, unlike the theatrical *divi* and *dive* of silent films, these actors generally played populist characters whose strength was contrasted against the decadence and languor of upper-crust figures. They were, essentially, men of action—as is evident in Maciste's prewar role in *Cabiria* or in Sansone's role as a populist figure from an upper-crust background in *Sansone acrobata del Kolossal* (1921). Their roots were not theatrical but in the circus; in fact, *Sansone acrobata* is partly set among a circus troupe. Maciste, the most famous of them (although most of their films became popular throughout Europe), was, after all, an Italian success story; a dock worker, with no formal acting training, he became one of Italy's most celebrated heroes of the 1920s. And, like the heroes of popular literary romances, these strongmen appeared in different films as basically the same personality (*Maciste in Hell*, *Maciste on Vacation*, *Maciste Against Death*, *Maciste in Love*, etc.).

Like these strongmen from the 1920s, Mussolini (whose own pseudonym, Il Duce, was not popularized until the late 1920s) was part of an ongoing *serial* of movie appearances to which were attached such epitaphs as Mussolini–aviator, Mussolini at the thresher, Mussolini–athlete, and so forth. His gestures, while they may have invoked the histrionics of artistic heroes such as D'Annunzio or Marinetti, were more consonant with the acting style of the heroes of silent film. Nor was he presented as an introspective character with a great deal of psychological complexity; and only rarely did the newsreels offer signs of his "private" life—a setting associated more commonly with the traditional, less popular theatrical melodramas. In these films, he was constantly presented in public—an environment he acted upon and of which he was, at the same time, the very

Heroic strongman of early Italian cinema, Bartolomeo Pagano (alias Maciste—here in *Cabiria*), helps establish an indispensable *persona* for subsequent political drama and Il Duce—The Museum of Modern Art/Film Stills Archive

The Duce striking one of his now more familiar poses in a LUCE documentary

center (both literally and figuratively). Unlike these strongmen, Mussolini was able to play more stately roles (as dignitary on ceremonial occasions), but he generally brought to each of these roles the personality established through his other film roles and through other popular media. Part of his appeal as a public personality resulted precisely from his early versatility as *actor*; unlike the more traditional figure of political sovereignty, the King, he was presented through films in a variety of roles.

In order to consider his range of performance (the multiplicity of his personality) and the contradictions that this field of roles encompassed, it may be helpful to review some of the ways his roles perpetuated some of the central *mythoi* which I have charted through previous chapters. One of Mussolini's most common *personae* in the newsreels and documentaries—one most consonant with his title, Il Duce—was that of the warrior. During the late 1920s and the 1930s, Mussolini appears in a variety of military uniforms—an array that seems to have less to do with changes in fashion than with the occasion for his appearance. It is no coincidence either that Mussolini consciously associated himself with other warriors from Italian films of the mid-1930s, visiting the set of *Scipione* and lauding the spirit of Trenker's *Condottieri*. By the late 1930s, as I explain momentarily, this *persona* had become so dominant that he began to lose much of the "dramatic" versatility of the preceding years. The mid- and late 1930s was a period during which Mussolini was frequently presented abroad, particularly at the frontiers of Italy's new domain (AOI and Albania) and with Nazi officials during his visit to Germany in 1938. In conjunction with these features about Mussolini abroad, he was also presented performing different roles in Italy. In newsreels (#161B), he appears at Pomezia planting trees and sowing newly plowed fields to inaugurate a planting season (and, presumably, to guarantee the fertility of this soil), and in "Il Duce trebbia il grano nell'Agro Pontino" ("The Duce Threshes Wheat in the Pontine Fields," 1938) Mussolini appears bare-chested (itself a sign or a *persona*), inspiring his in-film audience of peasant workers with his prodigious display of strength and endurance, and demonstrating the "progress" of efforts to revitalize what was once a marshland. (The narrator all the while explains: "The Duce threshes without even the slightest signs of tiring. . . . It seems that work gives him greater vigor.") It is this documentary that, as a number of Italian film historians have noted, aligns his role here with that of Scipione at the end of *Scipione l'Africano*. Contiguous with these appearances in the country are his roles in urban environments: visiting the Fiat plant in 1923, hosting affairs of state in Rome, as Builder— laying brick or breaking ground for new housing or public works projects (LUCE #1598). (Here again, he appears in some shots framed by Fascist leaders and, in others, amidst workers who seem visibly inspired and animated by his presence.) His emphasis on traditional values (concretized or exemplified through his appearances in the provinces) is then complemented by his "progressive" rhetoric. This future-oriented perspective seems to inform other features wherein Mussolini appears to have mastered new technologies—as an aviator, as a motorcyclist, and as an observer of a new device intended to transform sand into iron (LUCE #8, 1940).

Another *persona* which pervades all of these features, and which is fore-grounded in some others, is that of Mussolini as patriarch. Even at performances or demonstrations, he is not overtly cast as student but more as witness to an event that his very presence charges with a grandiose significance by his public personality (as extremely evocative national–popular myth). There is his public appearance as family man in the LUCE monograph about his daughter's mar-riage to Galeazzo Ciano in 1930. Mussolini appears here without his uniform, surrounded by his wife and children as gratified father and as a regal host entertained by dancers in folkloric costumes. A less public American–Italian co-production about Mussolini, "Vita romana del Duce," follows a "typical" day in his life as a family man: riding on horseback every morning, going to work early with his chauffeur ("a former race car driver who has driven the Duce's car since the March on Rome"), and returning home to his family, where he reads the newspaper. Italian films such as this one are, however, rare and tend, because of their emphasis on Mussolini as an individual, to contradict more directly his more preferred image as a public man. But "Vita romana" does present him in a way accessible to the experience and sensibilities of middle-class and working-class audiences, as someone with a strict routine and surrounded by his family and property. Beyond these films, there are a number of newsreels featuring the Duce, as a kind of patriarch, in attendance at youth programs or schools (as in LUCE #11).

In discussing the Duce as an organizing force through features in documen-taries and newsreels (as a heroic figure seen acting upon different environments yet always at the very center of the environment itself), one may also consider how his presence affected and was affected by contiguous features. In newsreels, his various *personae* are part of a sequence of featured subjects which, due to the expository economy of these films, allow for the messages or themes of features to overlap with one another. LUCE #1610 for instance, frames its intermediate segments with features about Mussolini. In LUCE #1613, the final segment, about the Duce's visit to Pomezia, is much longer than the preceding five units, though the third feature also concerns Mussolini. And, in LUCE #1612, an opening segment about events in Rome commemorating the seventeenth anni-versary of Fascism, wherein Mussolini is filmed chatting with the crowd along a parade route, is followed by a feature about huge flocks of sheep on mountains in Washington, U.S.A., that are "controlled by only one man and three well-trained dogs." This second unit is succeeded by a segment on "the festival of the seed" in Forlì, where an enormous effigy of the Duce in the town's central piazza confers a political and mythic significance to a traditional, local ritual.

Within a piece in which he appears, he frequently functions as the basis for the continuity of the feature. He is often visually framed and centered by other people and structures. And, in a number of newsreels, reverse-shot editing and over-the-shoulder photography offer the audience a perspective (more typical of narrative cinema) corresponding to that of the Duce. Again, however, this latter strategy is not common; in most newsreels and documentaries, he is more a public *object* (filmed through close-ups and medium shots) than an individu-alized *perspective*.

Mussolini's presence in LUCE documentaries also becomes a force in organizing social/political histories. In "Primi anni del Fascismo" ("The First Years of Fascism"), Mussolini is quickly established as a vindicator of a heroic, but tragic, Italian past. The film (silent, with only inter-titles) begins by underscoring the apocalyptic signs of Fascism's coming in Italy: "a reaffirmation, against everything and everyone, of the boundlessness of borders established by God and conquered with the blood of Italy's bravest sons." After a brief shot of a monument on the Austrian border inscribed with a homage to those fallen in World War I, it immediately ties key words in this prologue (both the opening titles and the monument's inscription) to Mussolini's indefatigable bond with current soldiers. In the first sequence, he appears in civilian attire, visiting a hospital for soldiers. Then he reviews bare-chested soldiers at the Scuola Centrale, Campo dell'Oro (the soldiers form human pyramids to greet him), tank exercises, the latest military ships (where again he wears civilian clothes, but with a navy captain's hat), the pilots of amphibious aircraft (one of which he pilots, now in goggles and leather aviator's jacket), and finally native troops in Africa (among whom he appears brandishing a sword and attired in military uniform). Just before the film's conclusion, scenes of the "humble house" where the Duce was born (dramatized with shots of a woman leaving the house with a baby in her arms) are juxtaposed with "private" shots of him reading a newspaper (a man who "keeps abreast of events abroad") in the spacious Palazzo Chigi. Here Mussolini appears again as both agent and product of Fascism's success in Italy. To punctuate this theme, the documentary concludes with a brief scene of Mussolini (now in coat and tie) walking toward the camera, looking directly at the audience, while he sniffs a rose.

In a much later documentary, "Credere, Obbedire, Combattere" ("Believe, Obey, Fight," 1939), a somewhat less versatile Mussolini functions to coordinate the film's celebration of the progress of Fascism at its seventeenth anniversary. The Duce's words in this sound film replace the inter-titles of earlier documentaries and serve as bridges and frames for the various sequences on national reforms, tied in these years to the Italian *impero*. The documentary opens with titles and a blast from trumpets heralding the birth of the *impero*, and Mussolini's first appearance is on a balcony exhorting an unseen crowd (and the movie audience). The Duce looks directly into the camera and is centered within the frame. To dramatize his claims and prophecies about this new stage for Fascist Italy, the film cuts to shots (taken over his shoulder) of his first blows with a sledgehammer to crush a wall in a ceremony marking the commencement of urban renovations. His gestures in this scene are matched to resemble those of T-shirted Italian field-workers in the following shots—ones that develop into a richly orchestrated montage of man and machine clearing and cultivating land. Thus the Duce's inspirational oratory and rhetorical gestures give way to gestures that are both real and dramatic (his breaking a wall); and these actions, in turn, appear to spark (in a synecdochic fashion) those of the "people." This technique (of magnifying a key word and dramatizing it) is repeated throughout the documentary and imparts to the film an almost incantatory rhythm. In the

The early years as Il Duce (shot from LUCE documentary)

next sequence, for instance, the audience is returned to Mussolini on the balcony, where he summarizes more of the accomplishments celebrated by the anniversary. The film cuts here to a before-and-after sequence about land reclamation in the marsh regions. Following a long-shot of wheat shafts waving in the wind and following scenes of peasants singing as they work this field, the film cuts to close-ups of Mussolini assisting their efforts at the thresher. To punctuate this sequence, the film highlights another key word ("to build") from Mussolini's address against a photograph of factories, and then once again dramatizes the word through images and music. While the movie documents reforms across the nation, this reform is structurally and figuratively moored to the personality of Mussolini, whom the audience witnesses performing a variety of social and dramatic roles.

Watching these two documentaries, one silent and one with multiple uses of sound, one is struck by the ways in which transformations of Mussolini's screen presence result from changes in the medium itself. It is difficult to determine whether, as Cardillo suggests, Mussolini's gestures have truly lost their rhetorical efficacy in the late 1930s—overshadowed by the frenzied style of Hitler. On film, Mussolini's oratory is intercut with cameos that are more demonstrative than they are oratorical but that amplify the meanings of his oration. Furthermore, film offered a reality that, in weaving scenes from his past with scenes from the present, helped mask any overt lack of versatility or dramatic energy in any one of his performances. The use of sound does, however, deflect some attention from his gestures—as in "Credere, Obbedire, Combattere." And, in some ways, Mussolini's grandiloquent visual and aural style does seem somewhat anachronistic in a period (the 1930s) increasingly given to more urbane, less effusive male heroes of early sound film. (The newsreels and documentaries were projected, after all, as part of a series of films each day; and, by the late 1930s, sound films were more common across Italy.) As Leo Braudy has noted, "sound admitted the less resounding emotions and paid its tribute to individuality, bringing films a little closer to the life of the audience, even in the most grandiose subject."[32] In sound film, the speaker's words and his motives merged more vividly than in silent film, with its inter-titles.

Mussolini's appearance in newsreels increased gradually during the early 1930s, though he actually appeared in a greater percentage of these films during 1928–29.[33] By the late 1930s, the average number of his appearances had doubled. But, in 1939–40, his appearances dropped by half. In part, the more Mussolini's personality became institutionalized amidst a popular film culture, its possibilities for *political* action diminished. As Richard Sennett explains, "this collective figure goes easily out of focus, in part because of his abstractness, in part because the very modes of perceiving personality destablize the personality perceived."[34] In the later years, Italy's search for a collective identity through popular cinema casts uncertainty about Mussolini's reality and his exact place in the collective interests. His mobility and multi-vocality, which in the earlier years attested on film to the vitality of cultural politics in Italy, gradually became a more immobile category or stereotype in a changing collective imagination. To understand this, however, we must be willing to recognize the increasingly tenuous differences in this period between filmed events and filmic events—a distinction that has become even more skewed in an age of television, in an age when public literacy of film form has become more a part of lived experience.

Conclusions

The Italian films in each of the categories I have examined share an important feature: their presentation of conflict over cultural values. As social rituals, Italian films enabled their audiences to renegotiate or clarify their changing social and cultural environment, to discover meaning in a world increasingly lacking a divine or monarchal authority. They serve as artifacts of ways cultural space *was* interpreted and (for audiences) ways this cultural space *could be* interpreted. (As such, they enable us to better understand what Italian society saw as its range of collective potential and its options for articulating that potential in a public doman.) Audiences could observe characters forge communities in an impersonal urban milieu, amidst a hostile African wilderness or the decadence, transience, and cosmopolitanism of life in the Grand Hotel. The narrative resolution of these films generally promised a "new order"—one often inspired by rural traditions yet capable of facing the challenges of an urban, industrial society. The youth of these films' stars (as agents or objects of conflict and resolution) and a growing cadre of personalities without theatrical experience could not but have contributed to the aura of this new order.

Among these films, the nature of narrative conflict and resolution varies, as do the "spatial models" against which this conflict occurs. Camerini, for instance, tended to favor modernistic urban models to convey traditional themes and to underscore the resiliency of the Italian family. Other films demonstrated the manner whereby traditional values assist those unaccustomed to the perils of urban living; their experiences bring to these traditional values a new significance. Or, as in the case of historical and colonial films, a legacy bequeathed by an older generation inspires the new order to proceed undaunted toward a glorious future. Moreover, in the colonial and some of the historical films, communal conflict and personal struggles assume a rather violent nature. In the phantasmorgoria of the Grand Hotel, characters are temporarily put under a spell; the protagonist searches as if in a labyrinth for a way out or for a new direction. The "new order," then, because it is contingent on these different images and formulas, is variegated and contradictory. Narrative resolution and modeling, which are attempts to manage and direct contradictions and a world in flux, give presence to a public ambivalence about its cultural environment, and they attest to both a need for and the transience of consensus.

Crucial, however, in charting these models and their points of convergence and divergence is a sense of the *search*—the experimentation, adaptation, and conservation—that was just as much a part of cinematic production as it was of

Fascism's contradictory rhetoric about tradition and "new orders." To bracket, for purposes of analysis, tendencies or formulas and conventions of film production runs the risk of glossing over this ongoing search for and testing of a mythic *language*—one most assessible and most deeply suited to a historically specific audience. Therefore, the preceding chapters may serve as a transcription of modeling procedures that were engaged and tested through popular films in Fascist Italy. Examined within a changing matrix of popular models, any one of the films discussed in the preceding chapters should appear richly contradictory and variegated—inscribed with the tensions created by its competition with other models and by the public struggle to imbricate its interpretive frames in a forum of public discourses. For this reason, the films that I have selected never quite seem to encompass one myth. To view these films in terms of the ongoing processes of cultural production, one is hard-pressed to nail down an exact meaning for each film or to measure quantitatively a cumulative meaning or effect. The approach I have undertaken here instead attempts to clarify a range of *potential* meaning and action necessary for public interaction and decision making (whether conscious or unconscious). In this way, these films help illuminate the worries and concerns, the hopes and aspirations of all those involved in producing a popular film culture—but a popular film culture that is not somehow autonomous from political action and discourse. The symbolic formations that I have described were deeply embedded in a political and cultural rhetoric through which the film industry, as agent of that culture, and the government, in its role as policy maker, defined and imagined their own agendas for a national and international public.

In light of the emphasis here on the dynamic processes of encoding and decoding social and political action and considering the "thickness" and diversity of images and formulas which make up the models of social and political action, the question remains as to whether there really was such a thing as an Italian Fascist film. It is admittedly a complex question—one whose answer is contingent partly upon how one defines culture and the popular, and upon how one sees them functioning in a "totalitarian" state (if I may use for a moment a somewhat outmoded, reductive and pejorative term from political science). To respond to this primary question and these related theoretical concerns, it is necessary to reflect again briefly on the relationship between political action and symbolic action in Fascist Italy, relying on some of the popular themes from Italian movies in the 1930s to help clarify this relationship.

Whose Fascism?

One of my primary aims here is to deflate the notion, seemingly held by a number of social and political historians, that the Italian government was largely responsible for creating or masterminding social conformity and political consensus. Due to the lack of unequivocal evidence, few recent social historians agree on the amount of control which Mussolini had over the system; and, as A.

James Gregor notes in his recent discussion of this problem, it remains to be decided whether that control was sufficient to satisfy the requirements of total-itarian power.[1] Social historian Juan Linz even argues persuasively that vital "non-Fascist" forces—the military, the Church, and the organized business community—created within the Fascist system a "limited pluralism." Linz sees Mussolini as having attempted to establish a political policy by exploiting the tensions among the plurality of social forces/groups in an effort to implement his (ofttimes faulty) program. In light of the government's lack of a coherent and consistent policy, and because of the mass media, the novel forms of con-sumption, and (as de Grazia notes) the organization of recreational pastimes that developed concurrently within Fascism, it would be incorrect to assume that government propaganda was solely responsible for achieving and maintain-ing consensus in Italy.

Linz's observations about the limited pluralism of Fascism call attention to the vital function, even in "mass mobilizing" regimes, of what Louis Althusser has described as the "ideological State apparatus." Althusser's theory is based upon a distinction he draws between a Repressive State Apparatus, which extends do-minion uniformly and which belongs entirely to the *public* domain, and the Ideological State Apparatus, whose unity—"presupposing it exists"—is not immediately visible because it is more a part of the private domain, e.g., churches, political parties, trade unions, families, some schools, most newspapers, cultural ventures, etc.[2] For Althusser, the Repressive State Apparatus "functions mas-sively and predominantly *by repression* . . . while functioning secondly by ideol-ogy." The Ideological State Apparatus, on the other hand, "functions massively and predominantly *by ideology*, but it also functions secondarily by repression, even if ultimately, but only ultimately, this is very attenuated and concealed, even symbolic." Althusser's discussion of ideology and its ability to maintain unity and order is important here because it helps elucidate how consensus was managed *outside* the political sphere.

But, while admitting that order can be achieved in the private sector, Al-thusser devalues the conflicts of a pluralistic society by pursuing instead his thesis about a "dominant" ideology and its maintenance of order. Geertz's interpretation of ideology and nationalism seems more suited to explaining the limitations of political policy and to treating the contradictory nature of ideol-ogy, i.e., essentialism and epochalism, in developing nationalistic countries. First, Geertz argues that "the function of ideology is to make an autonomous politics possible by providing the authoritative concepts that render it meaning-ful, the suasive images by means of which it can be sensibly grasped."[3] He proceeds to point out that formal ideologies tend to emerge and take hold in time of intense political instability—"precisely at the point at which a political system begins to free itself from the immediate governance of received tradition, from the direct and detailed guidance of religious or philosophical canons on the one hand and from the unreflective precepts of conventional moralism on the other."[4]

Clearly, Italy's redefinition of its cultural domain, brought on in part by rapid industrialization and by the proliferation of communication and distribution networks, most concerned a wide cross-section of Italian society (though particularly the lower middle and working classes). According to Geertz's rationale, they could no longer discover in general prewar cultural orientations adequate images of the political process or their place in this process; they demanded an autonomous polity—separate and distinct cultural models of political action. By the late 1920s, the Italian cinema was beginning to address these needs. Films which promised a "new order" played upon their audiences' fears and aspirations about social change and reform. And, among these films, some dealt more directly with essentialist pride and others with epochalist hope—the fundamental contradictions of imaging this "new order."

A no less potent (and perhaps more relevant) theorization of the relationship between culture and social action, however, can be found in writings of Gramsci and of those (Hall, Hebdige, Mercer—to name a few) who have applied his work to their own theories of cultural hegemony. What their work brings to this discussion is a sense of the ongoing struggle and negotiation that is always to some degree involved in achieving public consensus or in disseminating a political perspective on the widespread exchange of cultural symbols. In this respect, politics are tied to a variety of competing discourses and to a cultural hegemony that is seen as a continually reconstituted balance and as provisional alliances among various social and cultural forces. By the 1930s, an Italian film public may have had much to do with the formation of hegemonic ideas, but this public was not comprised of any one social class (note in chapter 2 the different values of first- and second-run movie houses), its literacy of cinema codes and signs was not uniform, and regionalism in Italy *still* created significantly diverse viewing situations/readings. Furthermore, while it may be more appropriate today to discuss the dominance of middle-class ideology in popular forms, the emergence of film in Italy during the 1920s occurred along with an urbanization, industrialization, and bureaucratization that were just creating a need for a Voice for that social class.

Political Action in an Illusory Universe

A second point which should be addressed in order to understand the symbolic and rhetorical nature of political action and the cultural politics of symbolic action in Italy during the 1920s and 1930s concerns the historically unprecedented force of mass-produced images (specifically cinematic ones) in the political arena. While Geertz's comments about ideology in developing nationalistic countries do help explain the political nature of cultural expressions in Fascist Italy, they do not necessarily clarify how the ubiquity of images distinguishes modern states. One scholar who develops this notion exhaustively is the French sociologist Jacque Ellul.

For Ellul, the ubiquity of images has created an "illusory universe" in which fact is always mediated by visual and verbal signs. For man in traditional society, he argues, facts transformed into images by some collective mechanism were rare and secondary: "Troubadors brought their fellow men songs on historical themes, merchants brought news from a far-away world; but they did not really concern the listener, who remained aloof from these stories—such things were only distractions, not part of the setting in which he lived."[5] Conversely, modern man may span the globe through images—i.e., he lives in a "uni-verse"—but experiences it only indirectly; the modern universe has been "retranslated and edited." Here Ellul's observation concurs with that of Roland Barthes, who notes that the ubiquity of images actually facilitates the illusion that information is *factual* rather than contrived: "This is without a doubt an important historical paradox: the more technology develops the diffusion of information (and notably of images), the more it provides the means of mastering the constructed meaning under the appearance of the given meaning."[6]

Because all political problems arise in this illusory universe, the political universe itself is not a real universe nor is it a universe of lies—it is only a discursive universe. "Political action," according to Ellul, "must obey a double principle: it must be translated into a flow of images and stereotypes and must not contrast real facts with such images."[7] Ellul, referring to Walter Lippmann's similar observation, proposes that images through which modern man sees the world are value-laden. Thus, any political action "must be conceived with the distorting glasses always worn by public opinion in mind."[8] Again, Ellul's message resembles those of Roland Barthes, who in his essay "Photography and the Electoral Appeal" discloses how photographic images exorcise politics, though they may be used as political tools: "Inasmuch as photography is an ellipse of language and a condensation of an 'ineffable' social whole, it constitutes an anti-intellectual weapon and tends to spirit away "politics" (i.e., a body of problems and solutions) to the advantage of a 'manner of being.' a socio-moral status."[9] Like Ellul, Barthes sees photography in the political arena as a type of *mirror* which offers the public its own likeness, but clarified and exalted as a type.

Not facts but *propaganda*, Ellul explains, transforms individual experience into public opinion and then modifies that public opinion. Significantly, however, he sees propaganda as taking two forms, what he calls vertical and horizontal propaganda (or "political" and "sociological" propaganda). The former is the more traditional definition of propaganda; vertical propaganda imposes meaning and comes from above the Crowd—one which presumably is passive. Horizontal propaganda, on the other hand, occurs *within* the society, among its members; it seems more innocuous and is a more difficult process to understand because it is almost transparent. Yet in many respects it is just as forceful (and, for Ellul, insidious) as vertical propaganda; an advertiser's audience, for instance, appears to Ellul to be just as naïve and passive as those who attend a political rally. Ellul's theories about propaganda are useful here since they expand the traditional definition and acknowledge the ideological base of political rhetoric and action. Propaganda, as *schema* and stereotypes, is seen as a process of structuring and "censoring" (if that is possible) an image's meta-information: "those dispensing information inevitably organize this translation and, as a result, ceaselessly reinforce, develop, make more complex, and shape this universe to images which modern man confuses with reality."[10] According to his conceptualization of horizontal propaganda, images do not *seem* controlled or motivated; instead they appear to lack an author and to emanate from Nature itself. Finally, however, despite his willingness to affirm that propaganda occurs in a covert fashion, Ellul (like Althusser) does not explore the diversity in the body of attitudes which inform political action, nor does he consider the multivocality of those images. Instead, he sees images as homologous products of mass media, and as causes of public opinion rather than as paradoxical structures of feeling and responses to a public ambivalence about the state of things.

Politics in Cinema and Cinema in Politics

It is possible for cinema to assume the function of propaganda if one includes as propaganda the sort of "horizontal" discourses that Ellul has described. Conversely, political action—according to Ellul's rationale—occurs in modern societies only through myths. However, one should also keep in mind that cinema does not operate only at this level, that—as Barthes suggests—the political meaning of an image is inextricable from the image's moral and ideological levels of connotation, and finally that this political level of connotation is negotiable, i.e., not bound to any particular interpretation other than that, for some, it may confirm that things are as they are. The degree to which Italian cinema (or specific films) in Fascist Italy was propagandistic is made problematic if one recognizes the dialogic processes for achieving hegemonic or consensual meanings and balances. Even documentary films, which through LUCE were most tied to the government's political interests, were read amidst competing models and in a variety of contexts and alignments with other films. In some of these contexts, a LUCE production may not have been propagandistic, and, in some contexts, a feature film may have been propagandistic. It also follows that different social groups were able to attach different labels to the same film. And, while a film may be the result of a collective struggle and a creative effort that is in part political, it does not *intrinsically* affirm only one political perspective. This does not mean, on the other hand, that film production during the 1920s and 1930s was beyond governmental restraints; the government had much to do with establishing the economic infrastructure of the industry by the mid-1930s, and it actively promoted some films while censuring others. But the government's involvement in the modification of the industry's infrastructure also contributed to increased film production. And, with regard to feature films, the government's policy consistently demonstrated its ambivalence over whether to institutionalize a cultural form whose place in Italian society was neither entirely central nor peripheral.

It takes a certain type of cinema, a "popular" film style, to operate—in the Ellulian sense—as propaganda; and even then, popular cinema serves other functions besides that of political propaganda. But both Barthes and Ellul see cinema only in its popular and "classical" forms (though Ellul tends to view it as a *mass* art while Barthes views it more as a *popular* art—a distinction which I intend to clarify). The type of cinema that Ellul and Barthes would discuss as propagandistic is one which does not encourage its audiences to consider why they respond to a film's symbolic action as they do, nor to distinguish symbolic action from Nature or political rhetoric from class interests. For both Barthes and Ellul, cinema—or, more precisely, the *realism* which they attribute to popular or mass entertainment—is in many respects "authoritative." Here, either cinematic reality or diegesis is deliberately held up as Nature, or, through a failure to induce the audience to reflect upon its coding and signifying procedures, audiences are allowed to confuse cinematic diegesis with the world of real characters, roles, and events. Barthes, for instance, sees the perspective provided by popular narrative film styles as being neither impassive or detached, as in documentary film, nor radically disjunctive, as in avant-garde or experimental films.[11] For Barthes, popular films do not signify, they assert.

Whether one accepts Barthes's or Ellul's attitude toward popular films, movies in Fascist Italy certainly do exhibit many of those features which these two theorists might associate with an authoritative style. The outdoor shooting in *Gli uomini, che mascalzoni!*, for example, prompts film critic Sacchi to marvel at Camerini's ability to capture "the Lombard spirit" of Milan, those regional, natural, ineffable qualities that a national audience had never recognized in the city. Sacchi fails to discern the ideological nature of outdoor shooting in this film or that outdoor shooting enables Camerini to present the man on the street—characters with whom the film's audience could readily identify. The historical films are yet another example; as we have seen, their directors and critics frequently conflate the circular time of their narratives with an "actual" historical time. Historical films also concern the lives of charismatic figures, e.g., Scipione or Giovanni de'Medici—superheroes who seem to be fighting on behalf of the films' audiences. Or, as in Blasetti's *1860*, an audience's perception of Garibaldi is mediated through the eyes of an Everyman, Carmelo. The colonial films and *Camicia nera* help blur distinctions between narrative and documentary styles by mixing documentary footage with more theatrical and stylized scenes. One could even point to the Italian film industry's attempts to cultivate cinematic "stars," matinee idols such as De Sica or Assia Noris, who brought to their films an ability to bridge the sublime and the ridiculous, high society and popular culture, and to embody the virtues of an entire generation.

What makes strategies such as these seem authoritative to Barthes or Ellul is their power to induce intense audience recognition and identification rather than alienation and reflection. As in more overtly political oratory, popular films enable audiences to learn who is fighting and on which side they belong by imaging potential alliances. But, because the values of a film's central character/hero may appear ambiguous over the course of the narrative, and because the alliances imaged by the narrative and its central characters are symbolic, and thus provisional, they are grounded upon a public literacy of and access to the convention of the discursive medium and are continually being tested against competing or alternative frames of reference generated by the cinema or other media. In this sense, cinema offered an expanding repository of models necessary for imagining and framing reforms.

The emergence of mass cultural forms such as cinema imparted to political states of the 1920s and 1930s (not only in Italy but also in Germany, Spain, Russia, and America) their unprecedented "mass-mobilizing" characteristics. But these forms also became for working and lower middle classes their only access to the institutional political forums. Many social historians who have found in Fascist Italy a paradigm for mass-society theories have generally emphasized only the former concern. This oversight is all too evident in much of the work of historians who, like A. James Gregor, draw from their studies of Italian Fascism evidence that all developing political or social systems increase their "regulative and extractive" capabilities in order to ensure the resources necessary for regular expansion:

> The distinction seems to be between liberal systems that modernized and indus-
> trialized by and large in the nineteenth century when centralization was largely
> dysfunctional because of logistic, communications, and information shortfall,
> and those hegemonic systems that have modernized and industrialized in the
> twentieth century, when logistic, communications, and information and control
> capabilities have made centralization a functional adjunct to the process.[12]

If films in Fascist Italy are "authoritative," one must still decide for whom (for the "people," or for those in power?) and for what purpose. In part, this decision depends on whether one discusses commercial or state-supported entertainment as "mass" art or as "popular" art, i.e., as a means of manipulating audiences and promoting mediocrity in order to perpetuate an economic or political elite or as a means of fostering a sense of cultural identity, reflecting popular desires, and enabling greater audience participation. I would want, however, to take this question further, to raise questions about *how* historical alliances are formed through public definitions or representations of these alliances. The addendum I would therefore make to Gregor's observation is that the emergence of cinema in Italy as a national–popular form (a kind of communications and cultural revolution) accelerated a social and ideological crisis by breaking from nineteenth-century attitudes about language and culture, and by providing discourses and textual production necessary for the realization and maintenance of new social alliances. Public literacy of cinema began to reshape national–political realities and public consciousness about national traditions and the future of the nation by enabling new modes of defining "the popular." To illuminate these processes and shifts brought about through cinematic production, I have tried to call attention to the sites where, in a ritualized fashion, new communicative technology and literacy changed and enriched the public's sense of place by encouraging a language capable of modeling these national reorientations.

While it is tempting to discuss the production of popular meaning in Fascist Italy as a paradigm for understanding modern media culture, it is more important to recognize the historic (and thus political) nature of movie-watching in the 1920s and 1930s. Italian media theorist and semiotician Francesco Casetti has described what he feels is "the fall" of cinema in Italian society. He discusses this collapse in three general ways: (a) the disintegration of cinema as a *body* or industry unto itself, (b) the loss of faith among recent filmmakers and movie audiences in cinema's *universal appeal*, and (c) the demise of cinema's ability to present an unprecedented vision of the world. Casetti's observations call attention to the necessity to avoid making sweeping generalizations (as Barthes and Ellul have done) about the relationship between cinema and other popular or mass arts and between cinema and society.

"*Cultura popolare*" and the Nation

Discussions about the meanings of "the national–popular" in Italy, or the historical procedures for defining it, can be traced to Gramsci's work during this period. Gramsci notes that Italian Fascism emerged amidst a historic split in Italy between the *meanings* of "national" and "popular," between the traditional agents or "directors" (artists, philosophers, statesmen) of an "elitist," institutionalized culture and a "grassroots," rural, and working-class culture. After the turn of the century, the agents of a traditionally national culture began to lack a public; the public forms were those appropriated from the traditional "folk" or (in Italian) "popular" culture and those imported from foreign nations that had already discovered a public for popular forms (e.g., French romances and detective stories). It is this split between and this struggle to align the national and the popular that Gramsci sees as characteristic of cultural production in modern Italy. It is *through* the production of competing cultural forms and of a popular language that, for Gramsci, the meaning of "the national" is recast. But, he argues, because those forms consumed or enjoyed by Italian popular audiences are ones that have been appropriated (either from foreign nations or from traditional folk culture), the popular cannot be seen as homogeneous or univocal or as having but one meaning; it is instead *produced*—based upon provisional alliances and understandings and upon an ongoing struggle to form and to assert these understandings. Again, this formulation of popular culture has a number of pertinent applications to Italian film production during the 1920s and 1930s, since the most widely watched movies in Italy were foreign and since, even though the cinema enabled potential alliances between middle and working classes and between urban and rural audiences, the popular film culture did not dramatize a single class experience. And, as I explained in previous chapters, Italian films mythicized a rural, folk tradition while bringing models of cosmopolitan culture to the provinces and working-class theaters. Cinema's ambiguous place in Italian society (as a form that was neither entirely marginal nor central to other institutions), and the government's ambivalence about its roles, also complicate our understanding of cinema's role as a "culture industry" in producing a national–popular culture.

The struggle that Gramsci saw over articulating or defining a national–popular culture was symbolic in that it was deeply embedded both in the material means for producing national–popular symbols and in that it continually tapped into the great national themes of the day. And, as a symbolic struggle over the symbolic formulations of national audiences, popular culture in Fascist Italy cannot be seen as entirely autonomous or as entirely manipulated. This is to say that there were attempts by the government to organize a national culture, but that an examination of the government's cultural policy, and its intervention in the production of popular forms such as film, discourages one from understanding cultural production as a generative process.

Popular culture was produced in Fascist Italy through a variety of discourses. The government and other social institutions continually *drew upon* a language whose signs referred to a national public; but, all the while, they were compelled to *respond* to a culture that was becoming an increasingly powerful force in social affairs. While "the nation" and "the people" were terms that ran through a variety of social, political, and scientific discourses in Fascist Italy, there were frequently similar uses and shared meanings. Nonetheless, even these similar applications of the terms conveyed the kinds of contradictions that Gramsci attaches to them. Thus, the most common use of "popular culture" in Fascist Italy was in reference to *modern cultural pastimes*.[13] Italian ethnographers, most of whom were positivists, saw their subjects—the folk or "the people"—as the repository and bearers of true national virtues.[14] And the OND's efforts to celebrate vanishing folk traditions and to tie them to a contemporary national identity did much to yoke "the popular" with Fascism. The political model for popular culture and its use in political rhetoric are attempts to synthesize two notions of community—what Ferdinand Tonnies has termed *gemeinschaft* and *gesellschaft*, i.e., a preindustrial community with open and emotional communication and a postindustrial one based on the division of labor and in which individuals engage each other only partially. In a 1936 standardized manual circulated by the Ministry of Education, culture is defined as *"l'attività propriamente creatrice di un popolo nel dominio dello spirito."*[15] "The people" or the nation, according to this explanation of culture, exercise a *creative* power which is both political and spiritual.[16] Through this kind of rhetoric, the regime casts politics in antimaterialist terms while equating art with political reform. On the one hand, the arts, seen as an expression of a *popular* culture, were to have characterized the desires of a certain nation at a specific point in history: "it is absurd to pretend that art occurs entirely outside the times and the moral climate from which it springs, and by which it is nourished, while sustaining these times and this environmental and, above all, spiritual climate."[17] On the other hand, political and social action in popular culture were characterized as a response to public opinion and to the "spiritual" or *essential* needs of "the people." As Mussolini himself proudly claimed, "politics works on the spirit of men"; politics does not censure or act directly on behalf of the arts but on "the extensiveness and the *totality* of the spirit" (italics mine).

To provide a rhetorical base for Italian popular culture, Fascist ideologues and intellectuals frequently contrasted it with the older Liberal order:

While, in the liberal sense, culture is an ornament of the intellect, which the individual desires for his own intimate and egoistic enjoyment—an enjoyment that is intellectual and absent of life—for Fascism "culture" is the most informed and full form with which man manifests his social, spiritual and historical action.[18]

What is particularly significant about this reference to a popular Italian culture is that it attempts to conjure resonances deep within the etymological texture of the term *popolo* while simultaneously directing attention to the basis for differences with the traditional, Liberal codes. In this latter sense, popular culture appears as something new, yet something obfuscated and struggling to be recognized (precisely through new forms such as cinema). One finds much of this same rhetoric in Italian films from the 1930s, wherein the cosmopolitanism of the *bel mondo* is ultimately presented as decadent and entirely lacking a sense of community.

Fascism as Meta-Community through Meta-Communication

I would now like to take these points about the historical and ideological meanings and significance of popular culture and the nation one step further and to recover a topic that I broach in the introduction of this book: the relationships among public literacies, cultural politics, and the Nation. Particularly relevant in this respect are Gramsci's observations about the "grammars" or techniques of national–popular languages.[19] A unified culture, he argues, is based upon a shared sense of a language through collective acquisition of its grammar or techniques; and "grammar" does not exist outside of narration (i.e., of stories and histories): "A grammar is story/history or *documento storico*: it is the photograph of a specific phase of a national (collective) language which has been formed historically [*storicamente*] and is continually developing. . . . "[20] But, while a grammar may be learned, and is thus historical, there are attempts to "normalize" language by standardizing or institutionalizing (through books, educational facilities, etc.) the processes for learning the language's grammar or techniques:

Written *normative grammars* tend to embrace all of a national domain and all its *linguistic volume*, in order to create a unitary national linguistic conformity that on the other hand places more importance on expressive *individuality*, because it creates a skeleton/framework more alive and complete than the national linguistic organism of which every individual is a response and an interpreter/speaker.[21]

Because a "normative grammar" attempts to institutionalize and to direct the procedures for cultural expression and modeling, it is a political act; and, as Gramsci suggests, those who participate in normative grammars may accede to an ahistorical and *totalistic* language model. But cultural dialogue depends as much on "grammatical conformity" as it does on spontaneous articulations or performances that are necessarily "disconnected, discontinuous, limited to local social classes and local regions."[22] In this respect, Gramsci makes much the same point as Lotman when he notes that *every* culture manifests tendencies toward a unifed and noncontradictory meta-language and tendencies for the semiotic mechanism within the culture to multiply and diversify. For both Gramsci and Lotman, multiple and "spontaneous" performances—the act of re-inventing the grammar with every performance—satisfy a culture's need to revitalize its meta-language (the basis for cultural expression) and to prevent the cultural stagna-tion that would occur from a total predominance of the meta-lingual tendency where expression would be unnecessary.

Filmic discourse does not operate through linguistic codes, nor can it be said to have a grammar in the same sense that a written language does. However, understood as a national–popular cultural form, whose formulas and conven-tions were still in the process of emerging from theatrical codes and were actively appropriated from foreign models, Italian films found it necessary to constantly include meta-communicative signifiers. It is, after all, through a text's meta-communication that its audience is reminded about the appropriate or necessary codes and channels for understanding its messages.[23] A popular film's meta-communicative properties also give presence to a *meta-communal* field of experience, i.e., the implied "us" that is necessary for any public discourse or performance. It is in this respect that a local audience's sense of belonging to a larger, unseen community is predicated upon that audience's familiarity with the communicative codes conveyed through a film's meta-communication. Still, because meta-communality, as a *totalization* of public awareness, is imaged/imagined, its meaning (or the meaning of its implied totality) is contingent upon changing forms and a public's ability to read these forms. Meta-communi-cation may seem context-independent (an immutable, self-actualizing standard) because it invokes a shared vision or understanding (not necessarily shared experience) of its public. But, because audiences must be reminded what codes or channels are appropriate and necessary for understandings to occur, neither meta-communication nor the meta-community it implies can be seen as co-herent or autonomous—only as historical and constantly re-invented. Further-more, attempts to standardize and institutionalize meta-community can only occur through a variety of competing performances and models—each one invoking a different framework for interpreting communal values.

I raise these points in hopes that they may help call attention to the ways that Fascism's totalistic vision (or the totalistic visions *of* Fascism) are necessarily produced and reproduced. (Dare I invoke here the symbolic image of the bundled branches through which the Italian term "fascistic" was represented in the rhetoric of its early proponents?) Understanding Fascism is not the only (or the best) way of examining Italian film production from the 1920s and 1930s, just as an examination of Italian film before World War II does not exhaustively explain Fascism as a political ideology. Fascism, however, cannot be understood (as Fellini's *Amarcord* reminds us) outside the popular discourses, the "local performances," that facilitated its practice, interpretation, and dissemination.

Only when one ignores the innovations and what Geertz might call the "thickness" of these discourses is one compelled to dwell upon the normative, metalinguistic characteristics of a national culture and thus to grant to the constructors of totalistic models the privilege they would grant themselves.

Cultural Policy

De Grazia's exploration into the Fascist government's attempt to maintain an *organic* state through the *organization* of leisure time offers many indespensable insights about the organization of mass culture in Italy during the 1920s and 1930s. But it does not clearly reveal the tensions and contradictions in the articulation of this culture—those aspects of popular culture in Fascist Italy which are perhaps best examined through *texts* through which the national–popular culture attempted "to create for itself" a new image. As I have attempted to demonstrate here, this "new order" resulted from a recognition among different social strata and different regional cultures, as a result of modernization and of a need for achieving modern and slightly cosmopolitan images as well as for recuperating traditional, "rural" values.

In many respects, cinema in Fascist Italy gave presence to the struggle or search for this new sense of culture. Because essentialist pride and epochalist hope largely constituted the matrix for Italian nationalism in these years, i.e., for a cultural ideology based on the friction between these two contradictory styles of structuring feelings, it is not coincidental that this ideology was at the root of the crisis in the Italian film industry. The demise of the industry in the 1920s, and the rapid proliferation of American distribution networks in the wake of this collapse, dramatically increased the cultural and political stakes in the crisis. As I have indicated in chapter 2 on American films in Italy, there were those in the Italian film industry who preferred a cinema that dealt with regional issues and that exalted traditional values just as there were others who envisioned a road to recovery patterned after Hollywood's successes. The influx of foreign values through American and other European movies created a need for a policy about cultural production, but this policy often manifested the deep ambivalence of policy makers as much as it attempted to manage their differences.

Having lost its audiences, the Italian film industry was compelled to restructure itself and to evaluate its goals. To do this, however, it needed to rediscover its audiences' tastes, desires, and ways of seeing—of imagining their worlds. In this sense, its project overlapped with its audiences' search for a sense of community. The film industry could not necessarily redirect the public's impulses, only respond to and clarify them; therefore, understandings occurred as the codes of filmmakers began to overlap with the local codes of their audiences.

While a number of social and political historians see Italian Fascism as having organized consent and as a silent supporter of either "escapist" white-telephone films or of "propagandistic" documentaries or spectacle films, it should be apparent that the government was (whether or not one believes its rhetoric) an agent *of* Italy's popular cultural forms. All political bodies must, for that matter, discover their constituency through a common language, and thus the film industry's attempts to identify its audience frequently converged with the government's efforts to do the same.

The influx of foreign cultural forms and the split between the public meanings of national and popular culture necessitated extreme political measures to help centralize cultural production, to call attention to the nation's need for cultural texts that were structured toward the public's need for a common Voice which spoke to the central concerns of the day. To privilege the government's role in orchestrating a public need for a common center is, first of all, to miss the way that culture and politics do in various contexts inform one another. In a country such as Italy, which (beside Pittaluga's short-lived impact) lacked a Jack Warner, a William Fox, or an Adolph Zukor, the government found itself increasingly involved in bolstering an industry that had become deeply obligated to other levels of the Italian economy. But even the policy that grew around its involvement was never coherent and never entirely given to total control over film production. Because Italian cinema (unlike radio or, later, television) had emerged amidst dance-halls and cabarets (i.e., at the periphery of Italian society), there was a felt need by a government dedicated to organizing leisure activities to "legitimize" and institutionalize movie watching. But the cinema's early ties to these less socially acceptable zones prevented bureaucrats from ever feeling entirely comfortable about its connection with other social and political institutions.

This, of course, poses a difficult question on a social plane: to what extent was the film industry's rhetoric political or to what degree was political policy actually cultural policy? Because cultural expressions and political propaganda were so integral, it is difficult to discuss Italian films without acknowledging their potential in political discourses, just as it is impossible to discuss Fascist policy without examining how it was shaped by and through cultural production. What it is necessary to recognize is that early efforts to institute a cultural policy arose concurrently with the growth of Italy's film industry. As is evident in the work of those who have examined early film industries as "culture industries," cinema not only enabled nations such as Italy, America, Germany, and Russia to instill in their people a sense of national community and political unification but, in so doing, brought these nations into violent conflict with each other. It is largely due to these events that nations today which are no longer "modernizing" are compelled to view cultural policy as much an agenda for national cultural productivity as a means of managing intercultural tensions or maintaining a plurality of cultural voices.

The Passing of the Rex

It may now appear to some that the proliferating film distribution networks of the 1920s and 1930s have today flourished into more direct and sophisticated international communication "systems," and, just as important, that Titta's ado-lescent visions of grandeur have aged into a more antiheroic vision given to parody and pastiche—a vision suited less to a large screen than to one that diminuates its images, one enjoyed in the intimacy of one's own home rather than in the dark company of strangers. As Casetti notes, film culture has given way to a video/information culture. And one of the more significant results of these changes in the techniques/technologies of national–popular cultures is that political realities are less "cinematic" and less *epic*. The self-assured "agents of narrative resolution" in Italian and American movies during the 1930s, e.g., Trenker's vindicators of the oppressed, De Sica's comic heroes, and agile, tap-toed American Music Men who performed for captivated young Fellinis, have become miniaturized, more self-reflective and serialized, and frequently fodder for bevies of statisticians, analysts, and commentators whose activity precludes the images of *direct action* envisioned by movie audiences in more demonstrative times.

Some have described this transition as the triumph of early twentieth-century Modernism, while others would point only to the historical failure of Modern-ism, the absence of a future-oriented vision amidst a "postmodern" environ-ment—one where the distinction between the real and the imaginary is lost in a flood of *simulacra* or where the real is endlessly reconstituted from fragmentary models of affects. The critical imprecision of this kind of rhetoric is, in some instances, its assumption of a historical rupture, of its attempt to see the postwar cultural experience (particularly with regard to the emerging social centrality of television and its "flow" qualities) as somehow discontinuous with nineteenth- and twentieth-century public life. Nonetheless, this kind of exposition and the cultural production of this recent period have made way for considerations that are not easily avoided in current discussions of cultural politics and cultural history—particularly as they illuminate the transient and contingent nature of public experience.

In Italy, these discourses give rise to a number of films finding, in the *crisis* of the immediate prewar years, a model of Modern cultural and psychological fragmentation and, hence, of the impossibility of realizing or returning to origins (e.g., *La strategia del ragno* or *Il conformista*). By the 1970s, the Italian cinema also realizes its potential as a *techne* for modeling postmodern national histories (particularly evident in recent films by Fellini, Scola, and to a certain extent Bertolucci), but here histories that cannot find (or rather bring them-selves to find) an *authoritative* voice in cinematic diegesis or to represent a *totalistic* vision of history. Nor do they seek to celebrate consensus over their or others' representations of Italy's past, but instead are committed to underscoring how the production of images and narratives in twentieth-century Italy has served as the *point* of and for consensual formations. Perhaps most significant in this regard is their attempt to deconstruct the epic and heroic pretense of cinema in Italy's cultural history—and here again Fascism offers an ideal locus for such treatments.

I would argue that these impulses signal a growing need to rethink (through a "public" forum) the role of the cinema as national–popular industry and expressive medium. And it is largely for this reason that *Amarcord* serves as my point of departure. As a national–popular history, *Amarcord* is no less insightful or comprehensive a modeling of Fascist Italy than the reams of political and social histories on the subject. Its authority, however, may not be as readily accepted, since it continually questions its own authority, as historical narration, and deconstructs the historical reality of the regime. And, in this sense, it is a testament to the "postmodern" conditions that have compelled a rethinking and recontextualization of Fascism.

I am still, after ten years, taken by Fellini's unabashed portrayal of the town's inhabitants, who rock late into a foggy night on a sea of cellophane in order to glimpse something bigger than all of them—a majestic and luminous cardboard liner, the *Rex*. And, in that my own project is imbricated with *Amarcord*, I see this book as what Foucault might call a counter-history to "monumental histories," i.e., a history devoted more to subjects not usually *highlighted* because they have been overshadowed by the Rexes of Western culture. Particularly relevant here is a sensitivity to the mechanisms and techniques that have enabled production and reproduction of consensual formations upon which the Rexes of this century have always sailed.

Throughout much of this century, national cinemas have come to be particularly important stages for modernization and sites for the politics of emerging national–popular cultures. Furthermore, national cinemas have come to serve as significant (though not always conspicuous) historical links between a nation's previous "literary" culture and its current television/video environment. As Fellini attempts to show in *E la nave va*, the life of movies has become a model of modern cultural history and a complex referential framework or legacy for encoding and decoding history and cultural domain. Filmmaking, from this perspective, has become so embedded in the way we have imagined our past, our present, and occasionally our future that it is difficult to find subjects which fall totally outside its referential field or to exclude completely the role of film culture in mediating social and political realities and possibilities. *E la nave va*, for instance, begins by taking its audience through the early cinematic processes of coding reality and history to Fellini's current attempt to deconstruct moviemaking's role in documenting/narrating modern history—imaged at the end of the movie as a camera dollies away from the film's set to reveal Fellini filming his ship on an artificial sea.

In "recording" the *course*, the navigational routes, of the Rexes of Fascist Italy, I seek here to map the *territorializations* of cultural production and, just as importantly, to acknowledge ways that some mapping (by territorializing certain critical alliances) often tends to mask the contradictory and "nomadic" nature of its subjects and its own charts. In case you may have overlooked or forgotten him, then, I refer you to an early Italian movie projectionist (of dubious character), Serafino Gubbio, who noted that: "We have to fix this life, which has ceased to be life, so that another machine may restore to it the movement here suspended in a series of instantaneous sections."

Appendixes

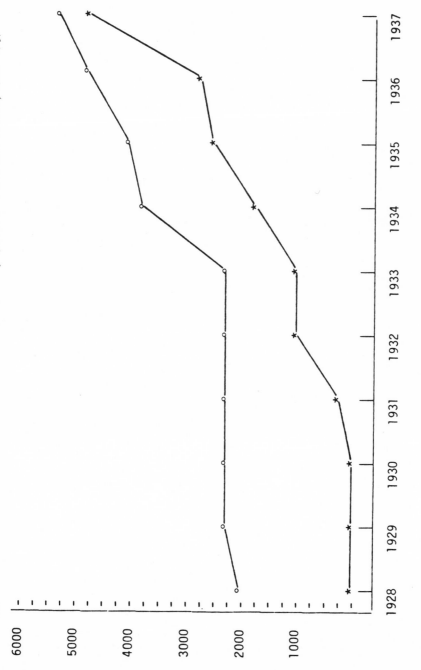

Appendix A: Number of Motion Picture Theaters in Italy (Those Wired for Sound) 1928–1937

° silent
* sound

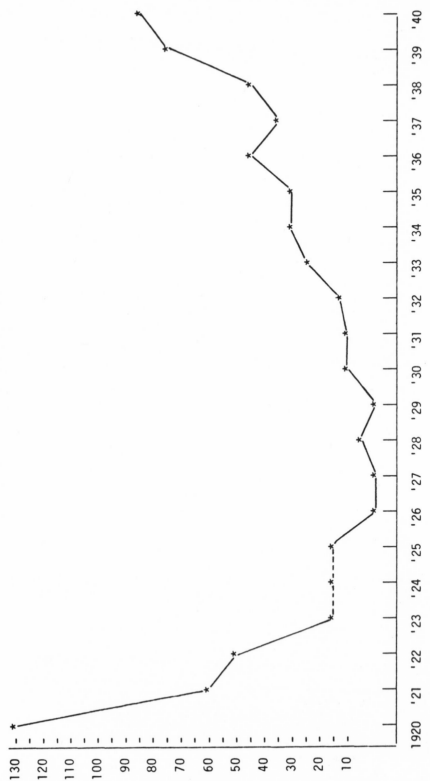

Appendix B: Number of Italian Films Produced between 1920 and 1940 (figures include Italian films made outside Italy)

---- information on these dates either not provided or contradictory

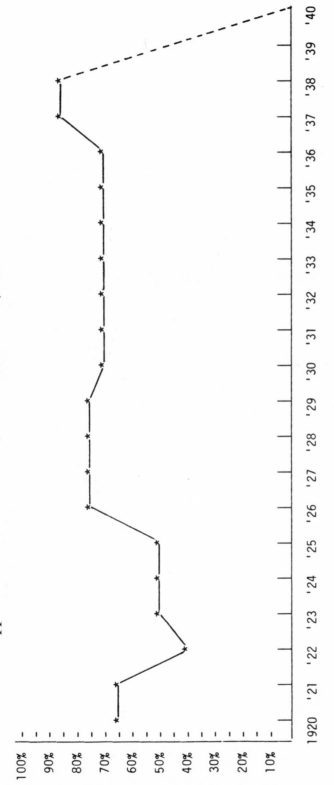

Appendix C: Percent of American Films Shown in Italy between 1920 and 1940

- - - - information on these dates either not provided or contradictory

Appendix D: Number of Theaters in Each Province in 1929 (of this number, roughly two-thirds operated only as motion picture theaters—2,025)

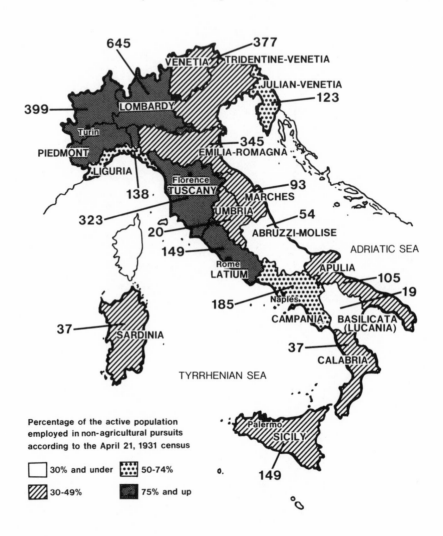

Percentage of the active population
employed in non-agricultural pursuits
according to the April 21, 1931 census

- [ ] 30% and under
- [ ] 30-49%
- [ ] 50-74%
- [ ] 75% and up

Notes

Preface: Grandfather Fascism and *Amarcord*

1. Corrado Augias, "Ho inventato tutto. Anche me: conversazione con Federico Fellini," *Panorama* (January 14, 1980), p. 95.

2. Federico Fellini, "*Amarcord*: The Fascism Within Us (An Interview with Valerio Riva)," in *Federico Fellini: Essays in Criticism*, trans. Peter Bondanella, (New York: Oxford University Press, 1978), p. 25.

3. "L'America, la democrazia per me era Fred Astaire che ballava sulle terrazze con lo sfondo dei gratacieli, o Greta Garbo che ci guardava con quell'aria funebre, da preside. Non c'era la possibilità d'immaginarsi altre cose, che Nenni era in esilio, che Gramsci stava in carcere. Sopra la cattedra c'era la foto di quella specie di mammone con una casseruola in testa, dall'altra parte c'era il re col pennachio di aspri, in mezzo il papa e sopra, piccolo piccolo, il crocefisso. Questa era la realtà sociale, politica, metafisica. Talmente familiare da diventare vaga, irraggiungibile." Augias, p. 95.

4. Nino Rota, the composer for *Amarcord* and many of Fellini's films, began composing musical scores for Italian movies during the 1930s (see *Treno popolare* in chapter 4).

5. Fellini, p. 5.

6. Joan Mellen, "Fascism in the Contemporary Film," *Film Quarterly* (Summer 1971), p. 2.

7. Tullio Kezich, "Hanno fatto pace col nonno fascista," in *Cinema italiano sotto il fascismo*, ed. Riccardo Redi (Venice: Marsilio, 1979).

8. In the beginning of *Roma*, Fellini's narrator discusses the local cinema of his youth as a seminal force in constructing his early and later realities. And in "Amarcord Maciste" (reprinted in *Gli uomini forti*, eds. Alberto Abruzzese, et al., Milan: Mazzotta, 1983), Fellini himself describes the inspiration of the popular movies from his youth on *Amarcord*.

Introduction

1. Lino Miccichè, "Il cadavere nell'armadio," in *Cinema italiano sotto il fascismo*.

2. Francesco Casetti, "Nascita della critica," in *Cinema italiano sotto il fascismo*.

3. Anna Panicali, "L'intelletuale fascista," in *Cinema italiano sotto il fascismo*.

4. Primarily at the Museum of Modern Art in New York and at the Motion Picture Division of the Library of Congress in Washington, D.C.

5. Denis Mack Smith, *Italy: A Modern History* (Ann Arbor: University of Michigan Press, 1959), p. vii.

6. Giampiero Carocci, *Italian Fascism* (Baltimore: Penquin Books, 1975), p. 16.

7. Robert P. Clark, *Development and Instability: Political Change in the Non-Western World* (Hinsdale, Ill.: Dryden, 1974), p. 12.

8. Clifford Geertz, *The Interpretation of Cultures* (New York: Basic Books, 1973), pp. 202–3.

9. Ibid., p. 220.

10. "La Nazione che prima si salverà dall'asprezza delle contingenze attuali, che coin-

volgono tutto il mondo, sarà quella in cui tutti i cittadini, anche quelli cosidetti privati, per primi sapranno pensare ed operare non in funzione soltanto del personale interesse, ma anche e sopratutto dell'interesse della colletività, cioè della Nazione. . . . Fra i pochi elementi che fino a tre anni fa sfuggivano ancora a questa disciplina, sola creatrice di potenza e di forza, era la cinematografia. . . . Perciò la nuova produzione nazionale, pur portando il segno inconfondibile del nostro tempo italiano e fascista, anzi forse appunto per questo, acquista già un valore ed un significato internazionale." Luigi Freddi, "Produzione italiana 1935–XII 1937–XV," *Lo schermo* (June 1937), p. 14.

11. "Se si bada a ciò che costituisce il successo della produzione americana e tedesca (e russa in Russia), si scorge subito che esso deriva dall'essere il cinematografo fondato in quei paesi sopra un sentimento psicologico nazionale, espresso in propria forma cinematografica." Corrado Pavolini, "Dare all'Italia una 'coscienza cinematografica'," *Il Tevere* (1 May 1930).

12. Ibid.

13. For more on the Italian "strongman" films from the 1920s, see *Gli uomini forti*, edited by Alberto Farassino and Tatti Sanguineti (Milan: Mazzotta, 1983).

14. For a discussion of journalistic film columns and of film journals, see *Nuovi materiali*, vol. 75.

15. For more on these productions and the government's promotion of them, see *Il teatro per il popolo* (author unknown) (Milan, 1938).

16. "L'arte cinematografica si trova nelle migliori condizioni possibili per poter dominare il più grande, il più vario, il più completo pubblico, per imporre se stessa come arte centrale di un'epoca." Massimo Bontempelli, "Si gira . . . si gira . . . si gira," *Il Tevere*, 14 August 1926, cited in Gian-Piero Brunetta, *Storia del cinema italiano 1895–1945* (Rome: Riuniti, 1979), p. 260.

17. "Noi affermiamo che, allo stato delle cose, una produzione italiana anche buona (*che è il primo problema*) non sfiorerebbe neppure da lontano il secondo e più importante problema: che è di creare una coscienza cinematografica nazionale." Pavolini.

18. *Bianco e nero*, vol. 3, 1938.

19. John Fiske and John Hartley, *Reading Television* (London and New York: Methuen, 1978), p. 17. My own view on this subject is also based in part upon Pier Paolo Passolini's evocative description of cinema as a kind of "writing/scripting" (or *scrittura*) of reality.

20. Note the distinction which Umberto Eco draws between "encyclopedia" and "dictionary" in *Semiotics and the Philosophy of Language* (Bloomington: Indiana University Press, 1984).

21. Victoria de Grazia in *The Culture of Consent* (Cambridge, 1981), p. 160, attributes only half that number to its urban network for 1937. My source is Guiglielmo Ceroni, "Il cinema del popolo: alla mostra nazionale del Dopolavoro," *Lo schermo*. (July 1938).

22. Ibid.

23. Brunetta, p. 304.

24. The Centro Sperimentale actually grew out of the Scuola Nazionale di Cinematografia, which was begun in 1934.

25. Actually, the first Italian film clubs were initiated in the mid-1920s by Italian intellectuals and artists such as Bontempelli, Comin, Giacomo Debenedetti, et al. By 1929, there were approximately 21 cinema journals in Italy.

26. Brunetta, p. 347.

27. Gaetano Salvemini, *Under the Axe of Fascism*, 1936 (New York: Citadel, 1971), pp. 327–29.

28. "Il cinematografo è una scoperta del popolo. È stato l'inevitabile e potente intuito che la folla anonima, confusa e multiforme possiede, pur senza saperlo, a dare la consacracazione del successo del nascente cinematografo. . . . L'importanza che nella nostra vita moderna può prendere, se non ha già preso, il cinematografo appare sempre più formidabile. Le generazioni d'oggi vengono educate non più con i segni di gesso su una

lavagna ma, si può dire, con la proiezione di film culturali." Raffaello Matarazzo, "Popolarità del cinema," *Il Tevere* (26 August 1929), quoted in *Nuovi materiali*, p. 70, n. 71.

29. "Il cinematografo fa parte ormai della vita culturale di una nazione. I vari periodi letterari saranno espressi anche attraverso i film e i nostri posteri possederanno delle sale cinematografiche che considereranno come le loro biblioteche." Raffaello Matarazzo, "La preparazione dei giovani" (*Il Tevere*), 9 April 1930, quoted in *Nuovi materiali*, p. 70, n. 71.

30. Roland Barthes, "The Photographic Message," in *Image, Music, Text* (New York: Hill and Wang, 1977).

31. Bill Nochols, *Ideology and the Image* (Bloomington: Indiana University Press, 1981), p. 1.

32. Jurij Lotman, "On the Metalanguage of a Typological Description of Culture," *Semiotica* 14/2, pp. 101–2.

33. Stephen Heath, *Questions of Cinema* (Bloomington: Indiana University Press, 1981), pp. 36, 39.

34. Roland Barthes, "Introduction to the Structural Analysis of Narratives," in *Image, Music, Text*, p. 102.

35. See Nicholas Vardac, *From Stage to Screen* (Cambridge, Mass.: Harvard University Press, 1949).

36. See Laura Barbiani and Giuliano Lenzi, "Autori drammatici e soggetti cinematografici," in *Nuovi materiali*, p. 70, n. 71.

37. Ibid.

38. The notable exception to this was Luigi Pirandello. The first Italian sound film, *La canzone dell'amore*, was an adaptation of Pirandello's novella *Il silenzio*, and the story for Ruttmann's *Acciaio* was attributed to Pirandello. In 1936 (the year of Pirandello's death), Righelli directed a version of Pirandello's *Pensaci Giacomino!* and Camerini directed a version of *Ma non è una cosa seria*. In 1939, Baffico directed *Terra di nessuno*, a rewriting of two Pirandello novellas.

39. Brunetta, p. 436.

40. See the discussion of this film in chapter 3.

41. See Dwight McDonald, "A Theory of Mass Culture," 1953, and T. W. Adorno, "Television and the Patterns of Mass Culture," 1954, both reprinted in *Mass Culture: The Popular Arts in America*, Bernard Rosenberg and David Manning White, eds. (New York: The Free Press, 1954).

42. See David Morley, "Text, Readers, Subjects," 1978, in *Culture, Media, Language*, Stuart Hall, et al., eds. (London: Hutchinson, 1981).

43. Teresa de Lauretis, *Alice Doesn't: Feminism, Semiotics, Cinema* (Bloomington: Indiana University Press, 1984), p. 44.

44. Antonio Gramsci, "Introduzione allo studio della filosofia. Che cosa è l'uomo?" *Quaderni del carcere* (Turin: Einaudi, 1975), pp. 1343–46.

45. Stuart Hall, "Encoding/decoding" in *Culture, Media, Language*.

46. Raymond Williams, *The Sociology of Culture* (New York: Schocken, 1982), p. 201.

47. Exceptions to this would be Anton Giulio Bragaglia's *Thais* (1926) and Carlo Ludovico Bragaglia's *O la borsa o la vita* (1933).

48. Geertz, pp. 407–8.

49. Tony Bennett, *Formalism and Marxism* (London and New York: Methuen, 1979), p. 148.

50. David Chaney, *Fictions and Ceremonies: Representations of Popular Experience* (London: Edward Arnold, 1979), p. 26.

51. For a complete listing of Italian movies and credits from 1930 to 1943, see Francesco Savio's *Ma l'amore no* (Milan: Sonzogno, 1975).

52. Claude Levi-Strauss, *Mythologiques I: le cru et le cuit* (Paris: Plon, 1964), p. 20.

53. C. Wright Mills, *Power, Politics, and People: The Collected Essays of C. Wright Mills*, ed. Irving L. Horowitz (New York: Oxford University Press, 1963), pp. 433–34.

1. *Castelli in aria:* The Myth of the Grand Hotel

1. *The Cabinet of Dr. Caligari*, *Waxworks*, and *Variety* are all examples of German Expressionist films which directly concern carnivals.

2. "L'enorme fortuna raggiunta dal cinema americano in pochi anni, non si deve attribuire ad una organizzazione finanziaria iniziale, ma bensì all'affermazione del prodotto, il quale interessò il mondo perchè revelò le passioni, i sentimenti, i caratteri e le abitudini dell'uomo e della donna americani in tutte quelle manifestazioni della loro vita che nessun libro, nessuna commedia, nessun racconto giornalistica, documentò con tanta esattezza." Mario Baffico, *Il cinematografo* (17 May 1933), p. 2.

3. Robert Sklar, *Movie-Made America* (New York: Vintage, 1975) p. 102.

4. Interview with Laura Nucci by Savio in *Cinecittà anni trenta* (Rome: Bulzoni, 1979), p. 861.

5. Gerald Mast, *The Comic Mind* (Indianapolis: Bobbs-Merrill, 1973), p. 203.

6. This film is discussed more fully later in this chapter.

7. Variations on this narrative strategy would include Gennaro Righelli's *La fanciulla dell'altro mondo* (1934), which concerns a pair of penniless young musicians who meet on a liner sailing to Italy. In this movie, the young man, who is a stowaway, makes the girl believe that he is wealthy; this charade in turn precipitates a comedy of mistaken identities. Corrado D'Errico's *Freccia d'oro* (1935) takes place on a luxury train that is traversing an unspecified country (actually more the *bel mondo*); this train closely resembles Goulding's Grand Hotel in its array of social types. A liner or a luxury train are, with respect to the *hôtel de luxe*, merely alternative dramatic stages or metaphors for myths of change and mobility.

8. This is listed as 1938 in Savio's *Ma l'amore no* and as 1939 in Brunetta's *Storia del cinema italiano*.

9. "Questo tipo di commedia [*Ai vostri ordini, signora!*] io non lo starei a difendere perchè era lo sfruttamento che il prodottore dell'epoca cercava di fare con un attore o di una attrice di successo." Mario Mattoli interview in *Bianco e nero* 1 (1977), pp. 38–65.

10. Mattoli's film is, in fact, an adaptation of French author André Birabeau's comedy *Déjeuner du soleil*.

11. Ester De Miro, et al., *Il cinema italiano dal 1930 al 1940* (Genoa: Tilgher, 1974), p. 28.

12. "Con *Gli uomini, che mascalzoni!* De Sica era un attore cinematografico; non solo: diveniva di colpo la *stella* maschile numero uno del nostro cinema. . . . Da allora egli ha avuto il suo personaggio . . . un personaggio italiano e sincero. Un giovanotto sentimentale, dai gusti facili e alla mano, abituato a lavorare di buona lena, e, dopo il lavoro, a trovare spazi familiari e tranquilli. Un gran bravo figliolo. Tutta italiana è la gentilezza timida di quel giovanotto. Candore della strada e di quella vita senza finzioni; l'amore si incontra per caso, genuinamente, senza complicazioni . . . " Gianni Puccini, *Galleria* no. 4, (10 March 1938), p. 172.

13. Ernesto Laura, "A proposito di generi: il film comico," in *Cinema italiano sotto il fascismo*, pp. 117–28.

14. Henri Bergson, "Laughter," in *Comedy* (Garden City: Doubleday, 1956), pp. 171, 187.

15. Luigi Freddi, "Arte per il popolo." *40th anniversario della cinematografia* (1935).

16. "non sarà cinematografia borghese dei divi e delle dive . . . ma cinematografia realistica, nel senso di realtà spirituale . . . cinematografia di popolo e per il popolo in senso umano e non demagogico a seconda della nostra tradizione di arte popolare." Luigi Chiarini, *Cinematografo* (Rome: Cremonese, 1935), p. 40.

17. "Il popolo non va al cinema per divertirsi frivolamente con le gambe delle girls . . . il popolo va al cinema per commuoversi, per apprendere, per penetrare più a fondo nella vita. . . . Il popolo ama i cibi forti e schietti e detesta gli intigoli insipidi e delicati tanto cari agli stomaci dispeptici." Ibid., p. 19.

18. Luigi Chiarini, "Esperienza," *Bianco e nero* 7 (May 1943), p. 15.

19. "Questo genere è un prodotto di decadenza e di crisi che sorge quando tipo di film se non l'illusoria fiducia in una qualche speditezza di eloquio che consenta la confezione rapida di opere che si credono commerciali perchè impiegano senza pudore i più banali mezzi per piacere e si propongono come unico scopo quello di divertire." Umberto Barbaro, *Bianco e nero* 3 (September 1939), p. 9.

20. "Stupisce in Genina la fabbricazione di questa specie di opuscolo CIT che è *Castelli in aria*, del tutto impari alla fama del suo autore, solidamente basata sul *Cirano*, sul *Corsaro*, e sulla indimenticabile *Miss Europa*." Ibid.

2. "Cose dell'altro mondo": American Images in Fascist Italy

1. Augias.

2. Of particular relevance here is Alberto Consiglio's and Giacomo Debenedetti's article "Il senso dell'avventura," *Cinema* 7 (10 October 1936), pp. 263–66.

3. "Gli States sono un mito eccelso: la suprema corona di ogni impresa umana può essere conseguita solo negli States . . . tutti ricchi, tutti evoluti, tutti signori: così pensava i cittadini americani un giovane europeo che si apprestasse ad emigrare negli Stati Uniti." Mario Soldati, *America primo amore*, 1935 (Italy: Mondadori, 1959).

4. Cyril Black, *The Dynamics of Modernization* (New York: Harper and Row, 1966), pp. 131–32.

5. Ibid., pp. 132–33.

6. For more on this, see chapter 7.

7. Brunetta, p. 208.

8. Brunetta offers a more detailed explanation of the collapse of the Italian film industry in these years in his chapter "Ascesa e caduta dell'Unione Cinematografica Italiana."

9. Brunetta, p. 213.

10. See Appendix B on annual Italian film production and Appendix C on the annual percentage of American films in Italy.

11. *Corriere della sera* (6 January 1929), p. 5.

12. Alessandro Blasetti article in *Kines* 15 (28 April 1927).

13. Alessandro Blasetti, "Binocolo sull'abisso. Quel che vuol nascondere lo schermo parlante," *Il Tevere* (5 August 1929).

14. For more on this, see "The Centralization of the Italian Film Industry" in chapter 7 and Jean A. Gili, *Stato fascista* (Rome: Bulzoni, 1981), pp. 126–27.

15. Gili, p. 121.

16. Ibid., p. 37.

17. See *Film Daily* (1936) report on Italy.

18. "Invece, intervenne il Monopolio che portò come conseguenza la esclusione dei film americani e l'acquisto in ragione dieci volte superiore di film francesi, inglese, tedeschi. Si è quindi chiusa la porta in faccia all'industria americana, che produce film giovani, sereni, onesti, ottomisti, divertenti, spesso d'alto valore etico e spessissimo di nobile significato." Luigi Freddi, *Il cinema*, vol. 2 (Rome: l'Arnia, 1949), p. 125.

19. Alfredo Guarini, "Quando Vittorio Mussolini, il 'commandante,' arrivò ad Hollywood," *Film oggi* (March 1946).

20. " . . . con la maggiore freschezza . . . quanto sarebbe periocoloso e dannoso per la rinascente industria cinematografica italiana l'accordarsi all produzione europea, invece di cercar la via e il metodo per eguagliare quella americana . . . Per la nostra cinematografia il seguir la scuola americana . . . può dir molto. . . . Dal punto di vista morale, la nostra giovanezza trova logicamente meno volgare e sensuale una sfilata di cento belle ragazze che no la trita farsa a doppio senso di pura marca francese, piena di sottintesi, di malcelate nudità e di ceribralismi sterili." Vittorio Mussolini, "Emancipazione del cinema italiano," *Cinema* 6 (25 September 1936), pp. 213–15.

21. Lando Ferretti, "Per il film italiano," *Lo schermo* 10 (October 1936), pp. 10–11. Alberto Rossi, "America, Europa e noi," *La gazzetta del popolo* 250 (20 October 1936), p. 3.

"Gli americani in Italia," *Cinema* 8 (25 October 1936), p. 300. G. G. Napolitano, "Cinema italiano? Cinema italiano," *Cinema* 9 (10 November 1936), pp. 337–40.

22. See Baffico.

23. "Dopo l'inaugurazione di Cinecittà con prevedible aumento della nostra produzione per l'avvenire, con lo svilluppo che grazie al ministero della cultura popolare sta prendendo la cinematografia italiana in Italia e all'estero, così come un'intellegente pubblicità largamente e continuamente svolta ha permesso di affermare in America e in tutto il mondo 'il mito' della cinematografia americana." Jacopo Comin, "Lanciare la cinematografia italiana," *Cinema* 23 (10 June 1937). See also Alessandro Blasetti, "Con Cinecittà si è cominciato," *Giornale d'Italia* (18 June 1937), reprinted in *Nuovi materiali*, vol. 71, pp. 137–39.

24. According to Will Hays's Annual Report to the Motion Picture Producers and Distributors of America (March 1937), 24 Italian films were shown in the United States during the 1936 season.

25. "La cinematografia è considerata come un'industria politica ed è sorretta politicamente. . . . È lo spirito americano che si diffonde da quei film, anche noi dobbiamo diffondere lo spirito italiano." Guiglielmo Giannini, *Kines* 15 (28 April 1927). See also Giannini, "Dobbiamo morire?" *Kines* 1 (5 January 1930).

26. See Herbert Schiller, *Communication and Cultural Domination* (New York: International Arts and Sciences Press, 1976).

27. Chin-Chuan Lee, *Media Imperialism Reconsidered* (Beverly Hills: Sage, 1980), pp. 104ff.

28. William Everson, *American Silent Film* (New York: Oxford University Press, 1978), pp. 205–6.

29. Garth Jowett, *Film: The Democratic Art* (Boston: Little, Brown, 1976), p. 186.

30. David Cook, *A History of Narrative Film* (New York: W. W. Norton, 1981), p. 19. See also Jowett, p. 186.

31. See Jane Feuer, "The Self-reflective Musical and the Myth of Entertainment," in *Quarterly Review of Film Studies* 2 (August 1977), pp. 313–26.

32. Thomas Schatz, *Hollywood Genres* (New York: Random House, 1981), p. 85. See also Robert Warshow, "The Gangster as Tragic Hero," *Partisan Review* (February 1948).

33. Schatz, pp. 83–84.

34. Ibid., p. 85.

35. If European characters appeared in *American* settings (as they tended to do more frequently by the 1930s), they were often invested with unsympathetic qualities. Some of the more common Italian stereotypes were the early film gangsters, e.g., Rico "Little Caesar" Bandello and Tony "Scarface" Camonte, or the foppish gigolos of film comedies and musicals, e.g., Carlo in *My Man Godfrey*, Rodolfo in *The Gay Divorcee*, and Adolfo in *Top Hat*.

36. Warren I. Susman, "The Thirties," *The Development of an American Culture*, eds. Stanley Coben and Loren Ratner (Englewood Cliffs, N.J.: Prentice-Hall, 1970), p. 184.

37. Most of this information has been derived from the Milanese newspaper *Il Corriere della Sera* (1928–39).

38. Cited in Adriano Aprà, "La 'rinascita' sulla pagina cinematografica del *Tevere* (1929–1930)," *Nuovi materiali*, vol. 71, p. 60.

39. An example of the popularity of epic spectacle would be *Ben-Hur*, which ran at the Supercinema in Milan for almost a month in 1932, or *The Gaucho*, with Douglas Fairbanks, which was frequently recycled for much of 1928–31.

40. An article which appeared in *Lo schermo* (1937), "Il sonoro e i cinema della periferi," indicates that, in 1936, second- and third-run houses received 80 percent of the grosses of Milanese theaters. This would suggest that they served even more than 80 percent of Milan's audiences that year.

41. "Cinema di tutti, ma in special modo cinema comodo, vicino all casa, ove lo spettacolo si rinnova ogni due giorno e il giornale LUCE è solo in ritardo di qualche

giorni sui cinema maggiori; ove marito e moglie preoccupati di seguire lo svolgersi del film, non si curano del loro vispo bimbetto che fa esercizi ginnici sulla mobile poltrona accanto, disturbando due sposi che, inconsapevoli della tragedia che si vive sullo scher-mo, tessono con dolci parole un idillio. Cinema di periferia, ove fra una parte e l'altra, i bimbi e i grandi maniano caramelle e bruscolini, ove l'un l'altro ce si guarda con occhio sincero perchè si sa che tutti si è spesa una lira, la semplice lira che nella sua modestia ha un invidiabile valore livellatore." Author's initials only, "Il sonoro e i cinema della per-iferi," *Lo schermo* (June 1937).

42. Part of the success of these animated cartoons can be attributed to the popularity by 1933 of Topolino comic books in Italy.

43. Sklar, p. 204.

44. *Il Corriere della Sera*, 14 November 1928.

45. *Il Corriere della Sera*, 6 January 1930.

46. Mario Quargnolo, "La censura cinematografica de Giolitti a Mussolini," *L'Osser-vatore politico letterario* (July 1970), p. 68. I have taken the titles of the Valentino films from the pages of *Il Corriere della Sera*.

47. Arrigo Benedetti, "Il cieco che accompagna il muto," *Cinema* 10 (25 November 1936), p. 370.

48. "Ormai ci si entra spensieratamente nelle sale cinematografiche, quasi direi senza respetto: allora no: il silenzio dello schermo imponeva riguardo: il coro delle didascalie lette ad alto voce dagli spettatori faceva venire in mente addirittura un oratorio; e più misterioso di quelli chiesastici." Ibid.

49. Gili, p. 34.

50. Quargnolo, pp. 68–69.

51. "Immerso nell'atmosfera del copione originiale, il traduttore ha perduto, non sol-tanto il senso della lingua italiana, ma anche quello del costume, della vita nostra. Ha dimenticato che fin dove è possibile, l'ambientamento del film è rimesso a lui." Raffaelo Patuelli, "Il gergo dei film tradotti," *Lo schermo* (July 1936), pp. 28–31.

52. Gili, pp. 38ff.

53. "Il problema della lingua cinematografica, per dir così, perderebbe molto delle sue complicazioni a tutto vantaggio anche della diffusione della cultura, che lo stretto legame tra linguaggio e cultura lo schermo più del libro . . . sa mettere in practica." Ettore Allodoli in *Bianco e nero* (1937), p. 9.

54. See John E. Harley, *World-Wide Influences of the Cinema* (Los Angeles: University of Southern California Press, 1940), pp. 150–52. See also Gili, pp. 46–50.

55. Harley, pp. 150–52.

56. Gili, pp. 47–48.

57. Pagano's films include *Cabiria* (1914), *Il testamento di Maciste* (1919), *Maciste inam-morato* (1919), *Maciste in vacanza* (1920), *Maciste salvato dalle acque* (1920), *Maciste e il nipote d'America* (1924), *Maciste imperatore* (1924), *Maciste contro lo sceicco* (1925), *Maciste all'inferno* (1926), *Il gigante delle Dolomiti* (1926), and *Maciste nella gabbia dei leoni* (1926).

58. According to Umberto Melnati, who plays the supervisor in *Due cuori felici*, the film was a remake of a German film produced at the same time. The script was co-authored by Max Neufield. Savio, *Cinecittà anni trenta*, p. 763.

59. James Hay, "Dancing and Deconstructing the American Dream," *Quarterly Review of Film Studies,* vol. 10, no. 2 (Spring 1985).

60. Savio, *Ma l'amore no*, p. 96.

61. "Si continua ad insistere nel presentare uomini e fatti di scappatoia) . . . Nunzio Malasomma . . . con l'intenzione di mettere in ridicolo, o più leggermente in berlina, l'ambiente carcerario degli Stati Uniti, è riuscito solo a sfiorare il paradosso (detenuti che vanno in libera uscita)." Francesco Callari, *Film* (16 December 1939).

62. Antonio Pietrangeli, "Harlem," *Bianco e nero* (June 1943).

63. Savio, p. 826.

64. Mino Argentieri, *L'occhio del regime* (Florence: Vallechi, 1979), p. 55.

65. Umberto Colombini, *Hollywood, visione che incanta* (Torino: Lattes, 1929). Colombini, *Il mito di Hollywood* (Milan: La prora, 1931). Arnoldo Fraccaroli, *Hollywood, paese d'avventura* (Milan: Treves, 1929). Alberto Rabagliati, *Quattro anni fra le "stelle" (aneddotti e impressioni)* (Milan: Bolla, 1932). Giovanni Vaccaro, *Glorie e miserie di Hollywood* (Milan: Stampiera Commerciale Editoriale, 1937).

66. Alberto Consiglio and Giacomo Debenedetti, "Il senso dell'avventura" *Cinema* 7 (10 October 1937), pp. 263–64.

67. Ettore Margadonna in *Scenario* (February 1932).

68. Alberto Consiglio in *Cine-Convegno* 1 (25 April 1933). Fabrizio Sarazani, "Film internazionale," *Cinegiornale* 14 (15 September 1935).

69. Emilio Cecchi in *Bianco e nero* 3 (March 1939), pp. 120–23.

70. See Claudio Carabba, *Cinema del ventennio nero* (Florence: Vallechi, 1974), pp. 167–70.

71. "Quel senso di vita diversa che i nostri nonni andavano a cercare a Parigi, o al massimo a Londra e a Berlina, oggi s'è rifugiato di là dell'Oceano e non si può trovarlo meno lontano di Nuova York." Emilio Cecchi, "Letteratura americana e cinema," *Cinema* 84 (25 December 1939), p. 374.

3. *Grandi magazzini: Stracittà* and the Department Store as Temple of Consumer Culture

1. Alvin Gouldner, *The Dialectic of Ideology and Technology* (New York and Toronto: Oxford University Press, 1976), p. 87.

2. Black, pp. 30–31. According to Robert P. Clark (chapter 5), however, sociologists such as Black have tended to exaggerate the destabilizing effects of political and social change as a result of their idealistic view about traditional life.

3. Rodolfo Morandi, *Storia della grande industria in Italia* (Bari: Laterza, 1931, reprinted Torino: Einaudi, 1966).

4. Nicos Poulantzas, reprinted in A. James Gregor, *Italian Fascism and Developmental Dictatorship* (Princeton, 1979), p. 315.

5. Monroe Spears, *Dionysus in the City* (New York: Oxford University Press, 1970), pp. 69–71.

6. "Posti sul confini che separa campagna e metropoli, presente e passato, i nostri scrittori, mentre soffrono acutamente la crisis culturale propiziata dall'industria, alzano la bandiera del mito e dell'azione mitopoietica, onde farsi psicologhi del pubblico moderno: vati depositari d'una magia linguistica che dovrebbe ripetere l'antico incantesimo orfico, ammansendo con nouve melodie i 'mostri' metallici delle fabbriche e delle strade moderne, riplasmando il novello caos nel vetusto incanto della forma." Roberto Tessari, *Il mito della macchina* (Milan: Mursia, 1973), p. 11.

7. Ibid., p. 15.

8. See Bontempelli's "522" or his essay on the sailing of the *Rex* in 1936.

9. "L'industria, siccome nelle remote albe l'eroismo, ha apprestato la materia per i futuri miti, per la nuova epopea . . . L'opera delle nostre officine, il ritmo dei nostri motori, l'impeto delle nostre macchine e finalmente lo scontro supremo, il duello risolutivo tra vapore ed elettricità, come già l'estrema battaglia tra Ettore e Achille, tra il Titano fumido e nero, orrendo e rintronante lanciatore di faville, furia d'Averno, balzante fuori con enorme occhi rossi dagli antri delle sue gallerie, e l'Angelo puro e limpido, invicibile, frusciante nell'aria, armato di una spada intangibile e fiammeggiante, dell'eterno fulmine di Zeus, appariranno . . . siccome imprese leggendarie, epilogo di un tempo di straordinario fermento, di caos iniziale. E non dall'uomo, non dalla città, ma dalla macchina forse si intitolerà il nuovo poema." Mario Morasso, *La nuova arma (la macchina)* (Turin, 1905), pp. 126–27.

10. "Il tempio inteso come riunione della colletività in vista di appagare la predomi-

nante aspirazione delle anime fu sostituito dal Grande Magazzino o dalla Città-of-ficina . . . il campo di battaglia nel Grande Magazzino, nella Città-officina, nella Borsa, nel Mercantilismo . . . le virtù eroiche tornarono a risplendere con originale fulgore." Mario Morasso, *L'imperialismo artistico* (Turin, 1903), pp. 214–15.

11. Ruttman had already made a documentary on steel production in Germany and an expressionistic treatment of the City (*Berlin, die Symphonie einer Grosstadt*, 1927).

12. "Il novecento che vede il cielo solcato come il mare, che ha le orecchie piene del rombo del cilindro motore, deve armonizzare i suoi rumori come gli altri secoli ar-monizzarono i loro: e lo jazz-band è il primo effetto della rivoluzione musicale figlia dell'automobile . . . La civiltà del nostro secolo è dunque meccanica, e la meccanica è diventata poesia, oggi. . . . Meccanica è dunque la nostra civiltà, e bisogna vantarsene, non vergognarsene. Meccanica deve essere quindi la nostra arte." Guiglielmo Giannini, "Sul film sonoro," *Kines* 21 (2 June 1929).

13. De Grazia, chapter 5.

14. "riassume e continua il gigantesco sviluppo della civiltà tecnica." B. Spampanata, "Dove arriva lo stato," *Critica fascista* 1 (1932), p. 19.

15. Chiarini, p. 66.

16. According to Umberto Barbaro's review of the 1939 Biennale di Venezia (*Bianco e nero* 3 September 1939, p. 9), *Grandi magazzini* was extremely popular that year in Venice.

17. Other films by Camerini which adopt this narrative strategy include *Gli uomini, che mascalzoni!* (discussed in this chapter) and *Il Signor Max* (discussed in chapter 1).

18. *Safety Last* was itself a popular movie in Italy, continuing to run in Milanese theaters as late as 1930.

19. H. Pasdermadjian, *The Department Store* (London: Newman, 1964), p. 7.

20. Savio, *Cinecittà anni trenta*, p. 218.

21. Directed by Mario Mattoli and starring Dina Galli, Armando Falconi, Roberta Mari, and Paolo Varna.

22. Pasdermadjian, pp. 40–41.

23. Giuseppe Terragni, "La costruzione della Casa del Fascio di Como," *Quadrante* 35 (1936), pp. 5–6, 14–15.

24. *Corriere della sera* (7 October 1928).

25. See Pasdermadjian, p. 43.

26. Richard Sennett, *The Fall of Public Man* (New York: Vintage, 1974), p. 146.

27. Ibid., p. 148.

28. "È un film profondamente nostro, di carattere e di atmosfera . . . Il luogo dell'azio-ne è Milano. È la prima volta che vediamo Milano sullo schermo. Ebbene, chi poteva supporre che fosse tanto fotogenica? . . . [Camerini ha saputo] cogliere con una finezza estrema certe inconfondibili caratteristiche del volto e del movimento di Milano, a dar-cene, senza sforzo, e senza quegli abusi documentari, che qualche volta riducono i film di questo genere a delle raccolte di cartoline di monumenti celebri, il colore tutto lombardo, l'operosa vitalità." Filippo Sacchi, review of the Mostra di Venezia, *Corriere della sera* (12 August 1932).

29. "L'Italia è presentata con *Gli uomini, che mascalzoni!*, senza pretesa ma dimostrando come si può trattare la commedia intimista, garbata, comico-sentimentale, sopra una Milano che non tutti gli ambrosiani sapevano di avere, e per i quali il film è stato una vera scoperta . . . " Manlio Miserocchi, *L'Illustrazione Italiana*, Milan (28 August 1932).

30. Everson, p. 204.

31. See the interview with Goffredo Alessandrini in Savio, *Cinecittà anni trenta*, p. 12.

32. "Nasceva, questo film, mentre era nel punto più acuto quella trasfromazione di un ordine e di un sistema sociale che era stata battezata 'la crisi mondiale del 1929': in tutte le famiglie si sentiva il bisogno di aumentare le entrate del bilancio domestico. E le si-gnorine, chiuso album di mode e deposito il ricamo in fondo un cassetto, studiavano dattilografia, stenografia, computisteria, per entrare nelle banche, negli uffici, nelle aziende." Rosario Assunto, "L'ultime mitologia," *Cinema* (25 November 1940).

33. This film was remade by Camerini in 1943. It starred Alida Valli, Gino Cervi, Antonio Centa, and Jules Berry.

34. *La signora di tutti* won an award for best "technical" achievement in an Italian film for 1934.

35. "Mostriamo come nella famiglia europea l'eguaglianza tra uomo e donna non riposi su una vota formula giuridica, ma sorga da un'equa divisione di compiti . . . il compito virile predominando nella sfera familiare; l'uomo capo della famiglia, nell'azione e nella rete dei rapporti esterni, la donna padrona del focolare, "domina" della sua casa, madre nei confronti dei figlioli, ma anche nei confronti del marito madre prima che moglie." Alberto Consiglio, *Cinema* (25 October 1937).

4. *Terra madre* and the Myth of *Strapaese*

1. For more on Bontempelli's "900" group and its ideological relationship to *Stracittà*, see Luciano Troisio, *Le riviste di Strapaese e Stracittà* (Treviso: Canova, 1975).

2. Curzio Malaparte, "Ragguaglio sullo stato degli intellettuali rispetto al fascismo," in A. Soffici, *Battaglia fra due vittorie* (Florence, 1923), p. xiii.

3. "Strapaese è stato fatto apposta per difendere a spada tratta il carattere rurale e paesano della gente italiana; vale a dire, oltrechè l'espressione più genuina e schietta della razza, l'ambiente, il clima e la mentalità ove son custodite, per istninto e per amore, le più pure tradizioni nostre. Strapaese si è eretto baluardo contro l'invasione delle mode, del pensiero straniero e delle civiltà moderniste, in quanto tali mode, pensiero e civiltà minacciano di reprimere, avvelenare o distruggere le qualità caratteristiche degli italiani, che del travaglio contemporaneo, tendente a creare lo Stato unitario italiano, debbono essere l'indipensabile base e l'elemento essenziale; come sono state, se si pensi, le impareggiabili nutrici del genio, dell'arte e dello spirito?" Mino Maccari, *Il selvaggio* 4 (16 September 1927). Years later, Maccari argues that *Strapaese* was never really a "movement"; see Troisio, p. 33.

4. "Cerchiamo, per quanto è possibile, di separare il primo futurismo—specie di salutare massagio su un corpo intorpidito e fiacco—dal futurismo 'di poi' sempre inteso soltanto come movimento artistico internazionalistico, manierato, convenzionale, democraticizzato, adatto al bolscevismo, ma assolutamente ineompatibile col regime fascista." Ibid.

5. "Noi giovani si dovrebbero avere idee chiare, ormai, ed alla voce *romanzo*—messi in pari con Palazzeschi, fermarsi a Tozzi e a Verga. Con questi contadini e con questi pescatori c'entra aria sana ne'polmoni e ci giova allo spirito." "Vita di Tozzi," *Il Bargello* 7 (31 March 1935).

6. Geertz, p. 252.

7. "Nonstante questi elementi che si appoggiano ad una tradizione culturale e a dei modelli nazionalistici che potranno continuare anche dopo la caduta del fascismo, il ritratto dell'italiano subisce necessariamente delle modifiche: si inizia un processo di nobilitazione delle forme dialettali, sposando in apparenza più la causa 'strapaese' che quella di 'stracittà'. Ma l'Italia minore, contadina e proletaria, l'Italia dialettale, mentre, sul piano della produzione maggiore, si afferma l'Italia stracittadina, col volto e morale uniforme e rassicurante delle classi medio-borghesi." Brunetta, p. 386.

8. Cited in *Il cinema italiano degli anni venti*, p. 86.

9. "Il film si chiama *Sole!*, che è intano un bel titolo luminoso ed italiano: l'ha ideato uno sconosciuto, l'ha diretto uno sconosciuto, l'han recitato degli sconosciuti; ed è una rivalazione." Corrado Pavolini in *Il Tevere*, Rome (17 June 1929).

10. "Dopo una quindicina d'anni, che sono stati una specie di tenebroso ed ignorantissimo Evo Medio della cinematografia italiana, ecco un lavoro degno di noi e del nostro tempo, degno degli Americani, che è tutto dire in questo genere d'arte, degno di andare in giro per il mondo." Alberto Cecchi in *L'Italia Letteraria*, Rome (23 June 1929).

11. Blasetti interview in Savio, *Cinecittà anni trenta*, p. 118.

12. Ibid., p. 109.

13. Ibid., p. 112.

14. *Nerone* is a cinematic adaptation of Petrolini's farcical drama, and *Resurrectio* is the story of a mediocre musical conductor who, on the verge of suicide, experiences a conversion and goes on to live happily ever after.

15. Blasetti interview in Savio, *Cinecittà anni trenta*, p. 115.

16. In his history of Italian cinema, *Vecchio cinema italiano* (Zanetti: Venice, 1940), pp. 217–18, Eugenio F. Palmieri argues that *Sole* is not an imitation: "Siamo di fronte a un italiano italianamente educato . . . È un film di folla—nato dal popolo per popolo." The irony of Palmieri's belief that *Sole* was film "of the people and for the people" is that the film never achieved any financial success.

17. See Blasetti interview in Savio, *Cinecittà anni trenta*, p. 117.

18. Leo Longanesi, "Breve storia del cinema italiano, " *L'Italiano* 17–18 (1933), cited in *Il cinema italiano dal '30 al '40*, p. 45.

19. De Grazia, pp. 180–81.

20. Ibid., p. 180.

21. Dino Falconi in *Il popolo d'Italia* (17 November 1933). Fillipo Sacchi in *Il corriere della sera* (15 November 1933).

22. Spada interview in Savio, *Cinecittà anni trenta*, pp. 1055–56.

23. "Hanno serenemente e allegremente riportato il cinematografia alla sua sede *naturale*, l'aria aperta, tanto più cara ed amabile quando e, come qui, la limpida aria che avvolge i dolci paesaggi d'Italia." Falconi.

5. Historical Films and the Myth of Divine Origins

1. "Love of tradition is no different than love of country [in both senses], nor does this love have limits. In fact, it destroys limits and generates a way of living that has roots in other lives, in a past which is always receding and which is felt, since it is love, to be already living in the future."

2. Jean A. Gili, "Film storico e film in costume," in *Cinema italiano sotto fascismo*, p. 130.

3. Ibid.

4. Examples are Carabba, p. 56, and Philip Cannistraro, *La fabbrica del consenso* (Rome: Laterza, 1975), p. 308.

5. An example is Lucio D'Ambra, "Il film più fascista è il film storico," *Lo schermo* 7 (July 1938), p. 14.

6. Ciano's address is reproduced in its entirety in Carabba, pp. 123–25.

7. "Così la documentazione storica delle nostre vittorie e delle nostra opera di civiltà, rimarrà per noi italiani perenne di orgoglio e di sprone mentre per stranieri rappresenterà un monito alto e severo." Cited in Giuseppe Croce, "In Africa Orientale col reparto fotocinematografico dell'Istituto Nazionel LUCE," *Lo schermo* 6 (June 1936), pp. 13–15.

8. This list includes *Passaporto rosso* (1935) by Guido Brignone, *Scarpe al sole* (1936) by Marco Elter, *Cavalleria* (1936) by Goffredo Alessandrini, *Scipione l'africano* (1937) by Carmine Gallone, *Condottiere* (1937) by Luis Trenker, and *Ettore Fieramosca* (1939) by Alessandro Blasetti. Jacopo Comin, voice *Cinema*, in *Dizionario di politica del Partito Nazionale Fascista* (Rome, 1940). Gili, "Film storico e film in costume," p. 144, notes that the other four films are *Squadrone bianco* by Augusta Genina, *Aldebaran* by Blasetti, *Sentinelle di bronzo* by Romolo Marcellini, and *Luciano Serra pilota* by Alessandrini.

9. In Venice in 1937, *Scipione* won the Coppa Mussolini as the best Italian film; the same year, *Condottieri* won the Coppa della Direzione for its cinematography (reserved for "film a sogetto che abbia meglio interpretato bellezze naturali e artistiche"—"best film treatment of natural and artistic beauty").

10. Roland Barthes, "Myth Today," in *Mythologies* (New York: Hill and Wang), p. 148.

11. Gili, "Film storico e film in costume," p. 134.

12. Interview with Marcello Spada in Savio, *Cinecittà anni trenta*, p. 1059.

13. Review of *Scipione* (author unknown) in *I nostri film* 5 (15 April 1936).

14. Carabba, p. 55.

15. "Il film ci illustra il valore col quale combattevano gli antichi romani ed il coraggio che essi avevano. Ora il nostro Duce ha rieducato il popolo italiano all'amore di Patria e allo spirito di sacrificio, all'ordine e alla disciplina redando all'Italia il nuovo prestigio nel mondo, facendo risorgere l'Impero Romano." *Bianco e nero* (August 1939).

16. "*Scipione l'africano* dunque a parte le sue deficienze tecniche e artistiche, ha raggiunto i suoi scopi. Perchè? Ve lo dichiarano i bambini: per la nobiltà della materia trattata, per il suo carattere spettacolare, per l'aderenze del periodo storico preso a fondamento alla vita del nostro tempo e per l'interpretazione che di questo storia si è fatta." Ibid.

17. "Egli [Gallone] ha perciò voluto 'romperla con la formula forestiera e moderna del . . . film storico, e tornare all'antico, tornare cioè a quei modelli popolari e nostrani che hanno fatto il nostro prestigio e la nostra forza'." Filippo Sacchi, review of the Mostra di Venezia, *Il corriere della sera* (26 August 1937).

18. Interview with Novarese in Savio, *Cinecittà anni trenta*, p. 847.

19. Brunetta, p. 399.

20. "Quando si vede il campo di Zama e un legionario dice: 'Legionari abbiamo vendicato Canne!', ho pensato al nostro Duce che diceva: 'Vendichiamo Adua!' E pochi mesi dopo disse: 'Abbiamo vendicato Adua!' Quando Scipione ha parlato ai soldati prima della battaglia ho pensato al Duce. Nel salone abbiamo applaudito sempre Scipione e i suoi legionari. Vorrei rivedere il film." *Bianco e nero* (August 1939).

21. Gili, "Film storico e film in costume," p. 135.

22. Brunetta, p. 398.

23. "Lascio ad altri la realizzazione di storielle d'amore, con le quali si vorrebbe distogliere il pubblico da una verità unica in questa terra, quella cioè di dover aver coraggio e mettersi a repentaglio per quanto c'è di buono al mondo, a costo anche della vita. Vivere pericolosamente!" Luis Trenker, "Perchè ho fatto *Condottiere*," interview in *L'eco del cinema* (May 1937), pp. 64–65.

24. "Se la folla con tanta riconoscente commozione intende tutto il mondo morale, la fede degli uomini del Risorgimento; se dei suoi momenti essenziali si sente ancora protagonista come lo è ora dei contemporanei; aiutiamo la folla a conoscere meglio la sua storia, il suo Risorgimento, a ripensarlo in un moderno, nel suo intero svolgimento sicchè ciascuno si senta figlio di quell'epoca che è per quella della Guerra e della Rivoluzione." Mario Morandi, "Proposta per un film del Risorgimento italiano," *Lo schermo* (July 1936), pp. 44–46.

25. Interview with Blasetti in Savio, *Cinecittà anni trenta*, p. 125.

26. "Considerando che in tempo di guerra è necessario che i poteri civili e militari siano concentrati nelle mani di un sol uomo, Assumo nel nome di Vittorio Emanuele, Re di Italia, la dittatura di Sicilia."

27. Interview with Novarese in Savio, *Cinecittà anni trenta*, p. 846.

28. Angela Dalle Vacche, "A Philological Approach to the Relation Between Historiography and Style in Blasetti's *1860*" (unpublished manuscript, 1983).

29. Cited in Savio, *Ma l'amore no*, p. 225.

30. Having won over the years the admiration of his teachers, his peers, and his students, he abandons the cavalry school when his favorite horse, which he is riding in an exhibition, stumbles and must be killed. (This event is made to coincide with the marriage of his beloved, for financial reasons, to a wealthy diplomat.) After replacing his horse with an airplane—as much an indexical sign of modernization as it is a symbolic sign of the transcendence of his military fraternity—Solari brings his years of preparation to the skies over war-torn Europe. Although he has lost his girl and his horse, he has not lost touch with his early ideals; and, when he is shot down after a final display of heroism, he is visually resurrected through the image of nine horsemen with bugles, who (in a kind

of theatrical tableau) sound a triumphant dirge in the sky, superimposed against the clouds.

31. Roland Barthes, "Historical Discourse," trans. Peter Wexler, *Social Science Information* 6 (August 1967).

32. "Si è in grado di rappresentare il tipo cavalleresco d'uomo intrepido, che mette a repentaglio la propria vita per l'onore e la libertà del popolo, che con spirito assolutamente altruista lotta per uno scopo elevato . . . Gli spettatori vanno al cinema animati da un solo ed unico interesse, ed è questo in fondo il grande segreto di tutta l'arte rappresentativa, l'interesse di paragonare se stessi col personaggio che agisce sullo schermo, l'interesse di studiare il modo di imitarlo." Trenker.

33. Review of *Scipione* in *Spectator* (June 1936), cited in Carabba, p. 55.

34. "Un film storico può rievocare momenti perfettamente analogici con quelli che viviamo, o comunque che abbiano con essi un riferimento tanto evidente da questi riferimenti, possono scendere moniti, incitamenti, cognizioni che valgano a esercitare e rinforzare la coscienza popolare di oggi." Alessandro Blasetti, "Cinematografo storico e documentario," *Film* 2 (28 January 1939).

35. "Uomini di azione, dunque, non pensatori o artisti possono utilmente essere assunti a figurare centrali di film storici: vale a dire, uomini, la cui funzione storica si sia prevalamente risolta nel condurre, trascinare, spingere, spronare all'azione le masse, e perciò non meno profeti di restaurazione, che apostoli di rivolte." Francesco Ercole, "Film Storici," *Lo schermo* (June 1937).

6. Italian Colonial Films and the Myth of the *Impero*

1. Francesco Bolzoni, "Il grande apello," in *Il progetto imperiale: cinema e cultura nell'Italia del 1936* (La Biennale di Venezia, 1976), pp. 35–36.

2. "Il fenomeno dei volontari in Africa si spiega o come gesto di generosità giovanile (gli universitari che andavano alla guerra per meritarsi il nome di fascisti o, addirittura, per liberare dai ceppi gli schiavi negri); o come una trovato elettorlistica di 'funzionari' di partito (Starace, Farinacci, per esempio) che volevano, così, conservare il loro ascendente sugli iscritti; o come necessità (i contadini che si recavano in Africa per vedere se era possibile recavarvi qualcosa: un posto o della terra da coltivare)." Bolozoni, p. 35.

3. Vezio Orazi, "Cinematografico e il teatro," *Film* 16 (April 1940).

4. Luigi Freddi, "Guerre e guerrieri sullo schermo: intervista con Luigi Freddi," *Lo schermo* (July 1936).

5. These films include *Il grande appello* (1936) by Camerini, *Jungla nera* (1936) by Jean-Paul Paulin, *Lo squadrone bianco* (1936) by Genina, *Sentinelle di bronzo* (1937) by Marcellini, *Sotto la croce del sud* (1938) by Brignone, *Luciano Serra pilota* (1938) by Alessandrini, *Girabub* (1942) by Alessandrini—the only one of these films shot at studios in Cinecittà—and *Passione africana* by Righelli (a film never completed because of the war).

6. Marco Ramperti, "Lo schermo in colonia," *La stampa* (8 August 1933).

7. "L'impero si attua quindi come una proiezione nel campo dello spirito della nazione, come un potenziamento delle singole coscienze e volontà imperiale, esprime tutta la tradizione e la volontà di un popolo che dal suo seno l'ha espresso direttamente quando la fatalità storica lo ha richiamato alla sua più profondo vocazione attraverso il Fascismo." Mario Zagari, "Spiritualità dell'impero," *Libro e moschetto*, 1937, reprinted in *Eià, eià, eià, alalà: la stampa italiana sotto il fascismo* (Milan: Feltrinelli, 1971), pp. 316–17.

8. "In questo senso il fascismo è imperiale, cioè non 'imperialistico', che profonda è la differenza fra i due termini: l'uno è egoistico desiderio di arbitrario predominio politico, l'altro volontà di supremazia morale." Ugo Mursia, "Imperialismi," *Il Bo*, 1936, reprinted in *Eià, eià, eià, alalà*, pp. 296–97.

9. See Ferbo's interest in them for this reason in his "Il film coloniale," *Lo schermo* (October 1937), p. 26.

10. " . . . è così che l'Istituto LUCE ha potuto rafforzarsi e perfezionarsi secondo un multiforme programma di lavoro che va attuando a gradi e che gli ha consentito di offrire al pubblico una immediata cronaca visiva delle meravigliose imprese dei nostri soldati e dei nostri operai nell'Africa Orientale." Cited in Giuseppe Croce, "In Africa Orientale: col reparto fotocinematografico dell'istituto nazionale LUCE," *Lo schermo* (July 1936).

11. "*Il grande appello*: un film straordinario di Mario Camerini," *L'eco del cinema* (November 1936), p. 8.

12. Ibid.

13. Interviews in *Film* 19 (May 1940).

14. Particularly evident in an anonymous review of *Il grande appello* in *Cinema* 8 (25 October 1936).

15. Interview with Camerini in Savio, *Cinecittà anni trenta*, pp. 215–16.

16. "Mentre si gira *Squadrone bianco*," *L'eco del cinema* (June 1936), pp. 14–15.

17. "In Africa bisogna ricordarsi sempre di essere bianchi, e, per di più, di essere italiani e fascisti." Brignone interview in *Film* 19 (May 1940).

18. Mailù is played by Italian film actress Doris Duranti, who appears in other colonial films, e.g., *Girabub* and *Sentinelle di bronzo*.

19. "Il cinema per l'Impero," *Lo schermo* (June 1936).

7. LUCE/Cinema/shadows

1. Cines had moved from Torino, where it was established as Cines–Pittaluga in 1926, to Rome in 1930.

2. In these years, Roncoroni established the Società Anonima Italiana Stabilmenti Cinematografici.

3. ENIC was responsible in the late 1930s for some of the most spectacular films (e.g., *Condottieri* and *Scipione*), but it became very conservative after the meager financial successes of these films.

4. Bertolt Brecht, "The Popular and the Realistic," 1938, reprinted in *Brecht on Theater*, trans. John Willett (New York: Hill and Wang, 1984).

5. "Il documentario, per considerarsi riuscito, deve mettersi fuori della cronaca e rifletere il clima del secolo . . . È col documentario che il cinema si addossa la vera funzione di storico e ne supporta la lusinghiera e tremenda responsiblità, particolarmente in un epoca come la nostra in cui i valori lirici della vita sono portati alla più alta espressione." Corrado D'Errico, "Stile LUCE," *Lo schermo* (July 1936).

6. Argentieri, p. 98.

7. Ibid., p. 27.

8. Ibid., p. 15.

9. For a more complete list, see Argentieri, p. 35.

10. Ibid., p. 29.

11. See Alberto Conti, "L'istituto LUCE e agricoltura," *Lo schermo* (June 1936).

12. Argentieri, p. 109, speculates that D'Errico is also the director of this film.

13. As noted above, Ruttmann had made documentaries in Germany before coming to Italy.

14. LUCE newsreel # 9 (April 1940).

15. See Augusto Ajazzi, "L'arduo lavoro cinematografico sui fronti dell'Africa Orientale," *L'eco del cinema* (February 1936).

16. Croce.

17. Brunetta, p. 351.

18. See D'Errico, "Stile LUCE," on the artistic nature of documentary filmmaking.

19. Interview with Laura in Massimo Cardillo, *Il duce in moviola* (Bari: Dedalo, 1983), pp. 125–27.

20. The first fifty LUCE newsreels are now lost, but catalogues of their contents and those of later newsreels are available at the Archivio LUCE in Rome. Lists of the contents of LUCE newsreels after 1938 (and the newsreels themselves) are available in the

United States at the Motion Picture Division of the Library of Congress in Washington, D.C.

21. Argentieri, p. 25.

22. There is, however, some speculation about the exact number of newsreels produced during these years. Ibid., pp. 160–61.

23. Gouldner, p. 96.

24. Argentieri, p. 24.

25. Harley.

26. "Ho un ricordo di vaga noia, prima di tutto perchè ero un ragazzo e se andavo al cinema ci andavo per vedere il film, o il varietà, e quindi l'interruzione di quest'acquila svolazzante con quella musica che gracchiava, dalle note trionfali e guerresche, dava una sensazione di intervallo noioso come accade adesso per la pubblicità tra uno spettacolo e l'altro . . . I film LUCE diventavano appena un po'più interessanti quando c'era qualche documentazione che riguardava, non so, o l'elezione di una miss o qualche divo americano che era arrivato a Roma, che veniva fotografato . . . o che salutava dal parapetto di una nave in partenza." Interview with Fellini in Cardillo, p. 138.

27. Cited in Gianfranco Arcangeli, *La cattura della ragione* (Nuova spada, 1979), p. 89.

28. Barthes, "Photography and the Electoral Appeal," in *Mythologies*.

29. Richard Dyer, *Stars* (London: BFI, 1979), p. 31.

30. See Lukacs, "The Sociology of Modern Drama," 1914, reprinted in *Theory of the Modern Stage*, ed. Eric Bentley (New York: Penguin, 1983).

31. Antonio Gramsci, *Letteratura e vita nazionale* (Turin: Einaudi, 1950), p. 128.

32. Leo Braudy, *The World in a Frame* (Garden City: Anchor, 1977), p. 190.

33. In 1928–29 he appears in approximately 40 newsreels, in 1930 approximately 27, in 1937 approximately 64, in 1938 approximately 75, and in 1939 approximately 30.

34. Sennett, p. 238.

Conclusions

1. Gregor, p. 321.

2. Louis Althusser, *Lenin and Philosophy* (New York: Monthly Review Press, 1971), pp. 142–44.

3. Geertz, p. 218.

4. Ibid., p. 219.

5. Jacque Ellul, *The Political Illusion* (New York: Knopf, 1967), p. 113.

6. Barthes, *Image, Music, Text*, p. 46.

7. Ellul, p. 128.

8. Ibid.

9. Barthes, *Mythologies*, p. 91.

10. Ellul, p. 117.

11. Barthes, "The Romans in Films, *Mythologies*.

12. Gregor, p. 304.

13. De Grazia, p. 202.

14. Ibid., p. 206.

15. *La cultura fascista*, Partito nazionale fascista ed. 2 (Rome: La libreria dello stato, 1936).

16. Ibid., p. 9.

17. Ibid., p. 14.

18. Ibid.

19. Gramsci, pp. 197ff.

20. Ibid., p. 197.

21. Ibid., p. 199.

22. Ibid., p. 198.

23. See Richard Bauman, *Verbal Art as Performance* (Rowley, Mass.: Newbury House, 1977).

Bibliography

Althusser, Louis. *Lenin and Philosophy and Other Essays*. Translated by Ben Brewster. New York: Monthly Review Press, 1971.

Aprà, Adriano, and Patrizia Pistagnesi, eds. *The Fabulous Thirties: Italian Cinema 1929– 1944*. Milan: Electa International, 1979.

Arcangeli, Gianfranco. *La cattura della ragione: aspetti della propaganda fascista*. Nuova spada, 1979.

Argentieri, Mino. *L'occhio del regime: informazione e propaganda nel cinema del fascismo*. Florence: Vallecchi, 1979.

Bakhtin, Mikhail. *The Dialogic Imagination*. Edited by Michael Holquist. Translated by Caryl Emerson and Michael Holquist. Austin: University of Texas Press, 1981.

———. *Rabelais and His World*. Translated by Hélène Iswolsky. Bloomington: Indiana University Press, 1984.

Barrett, Michèle, et al., eds. *Ideology and Cultural Production*. London: Croom Helm, 1979.

Barthes, Roland. *Camera Lucida*. Translated by Richard Howard. New York: Hill and Wang, 1981.

———. *Image, Music, Text*. Translated by Stephen Heath. New York: Hill and Wang, 1977.

———. *Mythologies*. Translated by Annette Lavers. New York: Hill and Wang, 1972.

Benjamin, Walter. "The Work of Art in the Age of Mechanical Reproduction." *Illuminations*. Translation. New York: Harcourt Brace Jovanovich, 1968.

Bennett, Tony. *Formalism and Marxism*. London and New York: Methuen, 1979.

Bernagozzi, Giampaolo. *Il mito dell'immagine*. Bologna: CLUEB, 1983.

Bernardi, Aldo, and Vittorio Martinelli. *Il cinema degli anni venti*. Rome: Centro Sperimentale di Cinematografia, 1979.

Black, Cyril. *The Dynamics of Modernization*. New York: Harper and Row, 1966.

Bolzoni, Francesco. *Il progetto imperiale: cinema e cultura nell'Italia del 1936*. La Biennale di Venezia, 1976.

Boon, James. *From Symbolism to Structuralism*. New York: Harper and Row, 1972.

Bordoni, Carlo. *Cultura e propaganda nell'Italia fascista*. Messina and Florence: D'Anna, 1974.

Braudy, Leo. *The World in a Frame: What We See in Films*. Garden City: Anchor, 1977.

Brooks, Peter. *The Melodramatic Imagination*. New Haven: Yale University Press, 1976.

Brunetta, Gian-Piero. *Storia del cinema italiano, 1895–1945*. Rome: Riuniti, 1979.

———. *Intellettuali, cinema e propaganda tra le due guerre*. Bologna: Pàtron, 1972.

Burger, Peter. *Theory of the Avant-Garde*. Minneapolis: University of Minnesota Press, 1984.

Canistraro, Philip. *La fabrica del consenso*. Rome: Laterza, 1975.

Carabba, Claudio. *Cinema del ventennio nero*. Florence: Vallecchi, 1974.

Cardillo, Massimo. *Il duce in moviola: politica e divismo nei cinegiornali e documentari "LUCE"*. Bari: Dedalo, 1983.

Carocci, Giampiero. *Italian Fascism*. Translated by Isabel Quigly. Baltimore: Penguin, 1975.

Carr, Edward Hallet. *What is History?* New York: Vintage, 1961.

Chaney, David. *Fictions and Ceremonies: Representations of Popular Experience*. London: Edward Arnold, 1979.

Chiarini, Luigi. *Il cinematografo*. Rome: Cremonese, 1935.

Clark, Robert P. *Development and Instability: Political Change in the Non-Western World*. Hinsdale: Dryden, 1974.

Coben, Stanley, and L. Ratner, eds. *The Development of an American Culture*. Englewood Cliffs, N.J.: Prentice-Hall, 1970.

Cook, David. *A History of Narrative Film*. New York: W. W. Norton, 1981.

De Grazia, Victoria. *The Culture of Consent: Mass Organization of Leisure in Fascist Italy*. Cambridge and New York: Cambridge University Press, 1981.

De Miro, Ester, et al., eds. *Il cinema italiano dal '30 al '40*. Genoa: Tilgher, 1974.

Dyer, Richard. *Stars*. London: BFI, 1979.

Eco, Umberto. *La struttura assente*. Milan: Bompiani, 1968.

———. *The Role of the Reader*. Bloomington: Indiana University Press, 1979.

———. *Semiotics and the Philosophy of Language*. Bloomington: Indiana University Press, 1984.

Eliade, Mircea. *Myth and Reality*. Translated by Willard R. Trask. New York: Harper and Row, 1963.

Ellul, Jacque. *The Political Illusion*. Translated by Konrad Kellen. New York: Knopf, 1967.

Everson, William. *American Silent Film*. New York: Oxford University Press, 1978.

Farassino, Alberto, and Tatti Sanguineti, eds. *Gli uomini forti*. Milan: Mazzotta, 1983.

Federico Fellini: Essays in Criticism. Edited by Peter Bondanella. New York: Oxford University Press, 1978.

Fiske, John, and John Hartley. *Reading Television*. London and New York: Methuen, 1978.

Friere, Paulo. *Pedagogy of the Oppressed*. Translated by Myra Bergman Ramos. New York: Continuum, 1984.

Geertz, Clifford. *The Interpretation of Cultures*. New York: Basic Books, 1973.

Gili, Jean A. *Stato fascista e cinematografia: repressione e promozione*. Rome: Bulzoni, 1981.

Gouldner, Alvin. *The Dialectic of Ideology and Technology*. New York and Toronto: Oxford University Press, 1976.

Gramsci, Antonio. *Letteratura e vita nazionale*. Turin: Einaudi, 1950.

———. *Quaderni del carcere*. Turin: Einaudi, 1975.

Gregor, A. James. *Italian Fascism and Developmental Dictatorship*. Princeton: Princeton University Press, 1979.

Gurevitch, Michael, et al., eds. *Culture, Society and the Media*. London and New York: Methuen, 1982.

Hall, Stuart, et al., eds. *Culture, Media, Language*. London: Hutchinson, 1980.

Harley, John E. *World-Wide Influences of the Cinema*. Los Angeles: University of Southern California Press, 1940.

Heath, Stephen. *Questions of Cinema*. Bloomington: Indiana University Press, 1981.

Hebdige, Dick. *Subculture: The Meaning of Style*. London and New York: Methuen, 1979.

Jameson, Fredric. *The Political Unconscious: Narrative as a Socially Symbolic Act*. Ithaca: Cornell University Press, 1981.

Jauss, Hans Robert. *Toward an Aesthetic of Reception*. Minneapolis: University of Minnesota Press, 1982.
Jowett, Garth. *Film: The Democratic Art*. Boston: Little, Brown, 1976.

Kracauer, Sigfried. *From Caligari to Hitler*. Princeton: Princeton University Press, 1947. Reprint edition 1974.

Lazarus, Arthur. *Department Store Organization*. New York: Dry Good Economist, 1926.
Leach, Edmund. *Culture and Communication*. London: Cambridge University Press, 1976.
Lee, Chin-Chuan. *Media Imperialism Reconsidered*. Beverly Hills: Sage, 1980.
Levi-Strauss, Claude. *Mythologiques I: le cru et le cuit*. Paris: Plon, 1964.

Mack Smith, Denis. *Italy: A Modern History*. Ann Arbor: University of Michigan Press, 1959.
Marx, Karl, and F. Engels. *Selected Works*. Moscow: Foreign Language Publishing House, 1972.
Mast, Gerald. *The Comic Mind*. Indianapolis: Bobbs-Merrill, 1973.
Mcanany, Emile, et al., eds. *Communication and Social Structure*. New York: Praeger, 1981.
Metz, Christian. *Film Language*. London: Oxford University Press, 1974.
Mida, Massimo and Lorenzo Quaglietti. *Dai telefoni bianchi al neorealismo*. Rome and Bari: Laterza, 1980.
Mills, C. Wright. *Power, Politics and People: The Collected Essays of C. Wright Mills*. Edited by Irving L. Horowitz. New York: Oxford University Press, 1963.
Morley, David. *The "Nationwide" Audience*. London: BFI, 1980.

Neale, Steve. *Cinema and Technology: Image, Sound, Colour*. Bloomington: Indiana University Press, 1985.
Nichols, Bill. *Ideology and the Image*. Bloomington: Indiana University Press, 1981.
Nuovi materiali sul cinema italiano. Volumes 71 and 72. Ancona: Carletti and Co., 1978.

Pasdermadjian, H. *The Department Store: Its Origins, Evolution, and Economics*. London: Newman, 1964.
Pepper, Stephen. *The Basis of Criticism in the Arts*. Cambridge: Harvard University Press, 1945.

Rassmussen, David M. *Mythic and Symbolic Language and Philosophical Anthropology*. The Hague: Martinus Nyhoff, 1971.
Redi, Riccardo, ed. *Cinema italiano sotto il fascismo*. Pesaro: Marsilio, 1979.
Renzi, Renzo. *Il fascismo involuntario e altri scritti*. Bologna: Cappelli, 1975.

Savio, Francesco. *Cinecittà anni trenta: parlano 116 protagonisti del secondo cinema italiano*. Rome: Bulzoni, 1979.
———. *Ma l'amore no: realismo, formalismo, propaganda e telefoni bianchi nel cinema italiano di regime (1930–1943)*. Milan: Sonzogno, 1975.
Schatz, Thomas. *Hollywood Film Genres*. New York: Random House, 1981.
Schickel, Richard. *The Disney Version*. New York: Simon and Schuster, 1968.
Schiller, Herbert. *Communication and Cultural Domination*. New York: International Arts and Sciences, 1976.
Sennett, Richard. *The Fall of Public Man*. New York: Vintage, 1974.
Sklar, Robert. *Movie-Made America*. New York: Vintage, 1975.
Spears, Monroe. *Dionysus in the City*. New York: Oxford University Press, 1970.
Soldati, Mario. *America primo amore*. Milan: Mondadori, 1935.

Tannenbaum, Edward R. *The Fascist Experience: The Italian Society and Culture 1922–1945.* New York: Basic Books, 1972.

Tessari, Roberto. *Il mito della macchina.* Milan: U. Mursia, 1973.

Tra una film e l'altra: materiali sul cinema muto italiano 1907–1920. Pesaro: Marsilio, 1980.

Troisio, Luciano ed. *Le riviste di Strapaese e Stracittà.* Treviso: Canova, 1975.

Vardac, Nicholas. *From Stage to Screen: Theatrical Method from Garrick to Griffith.* Cambridge, Mass.: Harvard University Press, 1949.

Vincere, vinceremo: la guerra fascista (1940–43). Rome: Istituto LUCE, 1975.

Volosinov, V. N. *Marxism and the Philosophy of Language.* New York: Seminar Press, 1973.

Williams, Raymond. *The Sociology of Culture.* New York: Schocken, 1982.

———. *Marxism and Literature.* Oxford: Oxford University Press, 1977.

Winner, Iris Portis, and Jean Umiker-Sebeok, eds. *Semiotics of Culture.* The Hague: Mouton, 1979.

Index

Movie Titles

Names